The 1st Amendment in the Classroom Series, Number 1.

READ

The Freedom to

EDITED BY HAIG A. BOSMAJIAN

NEAL-SCHUMAN PUBLISHERS, INC.
NEW YORK   LONDON

**THE FIRST AMENDMENT IN THE CLASSROOM
SERIES**
Edited by Haig A. Bosmajian

The Freedom to Read Books, Films and Plays. The First
Amendment in the Classroom Series, No. 1. Foreword by Ken
Donelson. ISBN 1-55570-001-2.

Freedom of Religion. The First Amendment in the Classroom
Series, No. 2. ISBN 1-55570-002-0.

Freedom of Expression. The First Amendment in the Classroom
Series, No. 3. ISBN 1-55570-003-9.

Academic Freedom. The First Amendment in the Classroom
Series, No. 4. ISBN 1-55570-004-7.

The Freedom to Publish. The First Amendment in the Classroom
Series, No. 5. ISBN 1-55570-005-5.

Published by Neal-Schuman Publishers, Inc.
100 Varick Street
New York, NY 10013

Copyright © 1987 by Neal-Schuman Publishers, Inc.

Library of Congress Cataloging-in-Publication Data

The Freedom to read.

(The First Amendment in the classroom series ; no. 1)
Includes index.
1. Educational law and legislation—United States—
Cases. 2. Text-books—Censorship—United States—Cases.
3. Students—Legal status, laws, etc.—United States—
Cases. I. Bosmajian, Haig A.
KF4118.F57 1986   344.73'071   85-25994
ISBN 0-918212-96-0   347.30471

Contents

Preface

THE *First Amendment in the Classroom Series* responds to the need for teachers, students, parents, and school board members to become more aware of how First Amendment rights apply to the classrooms of a free society. Those cherished rights, if they have any meaning, are directly relevant and essential to our schools. What is especially needed is a wider familiarity with and understanding of the arguments and reasoning used to reach judgments regarding First Amendment issues, so often controversial and divisive, affecting what goes on in the classroom. To be unfamiliar with those arguments is to be unprepared to defend the First Amendment rights of students and teachers. Those arguments will be found in this series devoted to (1) the banning of books, plays, and films; (2) religion and prayer in the classroom; (3) symbolic speech; (4) teaching methods and teachers' classroom behavior; and (5) school publications and underground newspapers. My earlier volume, *Censorship, Libraries, and the Law,* covers cases of school library censorship.

When United States District Judge Hugh Bownes declared unconstitutional a Portsmouth, New Hampshire, Board of Education rule forbidding "distribution of non-school sponsored written materials within the Portsmouth schools and on school grounds for a distance of 200 feet from school entrances," he declared in the order of the court that "this opinion and Order is to be posted on the school bulletin board in a prominent place, and copies of this opinion and Order are to be made available to the students in the school library."[1]

This was a reminder to students, teachers, and school board members—but especially to the students—that First Amendment rights applied to them. As the United States Supreme Court had put it exactly thirty years earlier in *Barnette,* the First Amendment rights need to be practiced in our schools "if we are not to strangle the free mind at its source and teach youth to discount important principles of our government as mere platitudes."[2]

While the actual decisions in the cases involving the First Amendment rights of students and teachers in the classroom are crucial, the arguments and reasoning in the opinions are equally important. *Why* did the court decide that students could not be prohibited from distributing their literature? *Why* did the court decide that students could not be compelled to salute the flag? *Why* could the teacher not be dismissed for using books containing "offensive" language? *Why* could not the school board dismiss the teacher for using "unorthodox" teaching methods? *Why* could not parents have sex education banned from the school? *Why* did the court decide that prayer in the classroom was unconstitutional? Understanding the "whys" leads to an understanding of the workings of a democratic society.

In 1937, when throughout the world democratic institutions were being threatened and some were being destroyed, John Dewey observed that wherever political democracy has fallen, "it was too exclusively political in nature. It had not become part of the bone and blood of the people in daily conduct of life. Democratic forms were limited to Parliament, elections, and combats between parties. What is happening proves conclusively, I think, that unless democratic habits of thought and action are part of the fibre of a people, political democracy is insecure. It cannot stand in isolation. It must be buttressed by the presence of democratic methods in all social relationships."[3]

When the students, teachers, school boards, and parents involved in these cases insisted on exercising their First Amendment freedoms, they learned that the principles of our democracy are not "mere platitudes." For the students especially, the cases helped demonstrate that the Bill of Rights and "democratic habits of thought and action are part of the fibre of a people." These cases show political democracy "buttressed by the presence of democratic methods" in one realm of our society—the classroom.

It has been clearly established at several levels of our judicial system that protecting the First Amendment freedoms of teachers and students is crucial in a free society. In *Barnette,* the United States Supreme Court declared: "The Fourteenth Amendment, as now applied to the States, protects the citizen against the State itself and all of its creatures—Boards of Education not excepted. These have, of course, important, delicate, and highly discretionary functions, but none that they may not perform within the limits of the Bill of Rights. That they are educating the young for citizenship is reason for scrupulous protection of Constitutional freedoms of the individual, if we are not to to strangle the free mind at its source and teach youth to discount important principles of our government as mere platitudes."

In giving First Amendment protection to junior and senior high school students who had worn black armbands to school to protest U.S. involvement in the Vietnam War, the United States Supreme Court spoke most clearly in *Tinker* on the issue of the First Amendment rights of teachers and students. Justice Abe Fortas, delivering the opinion of the Court, said in 1969: "First Amendment rights, applied in light of the special characteristics of the school environment, are available to teachers and students. It can hardly be argued that either students or teachers shed their constitutional rights to freedom of speech or expression at the schoolhouse gate. This has been the unmistakable holding of this Court for almost 50 years."[4]

When in 1978 United States District Court Judge Joseph Tauro ordered school authorities to return to the high school library a book which had been removed because it contained a "dirty, filthy" poem, he reiterated in his own words what had been declared in *Tinker:* ". . . the First Amendment is not merely a mantle which students and faculty doff when they take their places in the classroom."[5]

On these pages are the stories of students and teachers who risked much to fight for their First Amendment rights in the classroom, who did not "shed their constitutional rights to freedom of speech or expression at the schoolhouse gate" and did not see the First Amendment as "merely a mantle which students and teachers doff when they take their places in the classroom." What is encouraging is that in almost all the cases appearing in this series, students and teachers have been given First Amendment protection by the courts.

The reasons given in the opinions on these pages are applicable to many of those First Amendment controversies which may never reach the courts. Edward Jenkinson, who has done much research and writing on censorship in the schools and who chaired the National Council of Teachers of English Committee Against Censorship has reported: "During the early seventies, approximately one hundred censorship incidents were reported to the ALA [American Library Association]'s Office for Intellectual Freedom each year. By 1976, the number had risen to slightly less than two hundred and climbed to nearly three hundred in 1977." Shortly after the 1980 Presidential election, Judith Krug of the American Library Association estimated a threefold increase in reported censorship incidents, "which would mean roughly nine hundred reported incidents a year." But as Jenkinson points out, the reported incidents "are only a small part of the censorship attempts each year. . . . After talking with teachers, librarians and administrators in meetings in 33 states, I believe that for every reported incident of censorship at least fifty go unreported."[6]

The First Amendment in the Classroom makes available the many substantial arguments that can be used by students, teachers, and parents involved in First Amendment controversies surrounding teachers and students in the classroom. The reasons given by the judges on these pages are there for students, teachers, and parents to use in their efforts to persuade school boards and others that the First Amendment applies to the school environment and that the "Fourteenth Amendment, as now applied to the States, protects the citizen against the State itself and all of its creatures—Boards of Education not excepted."

In his discussion of the nature and function of the judicial court opinion, legal scholar Piero Calamandrei has observed that "the most important and most typical indication of the rationality of the judicial function is the reasoned opinion." Of the need for the judge to present the reasoned opinion, Calamandrei says that

> "ever since justice descended from heaven to earth and the idea gained ground that the judge is a human being and not a supernatural and infallible oracle to be adored, whose authority is beyond question, man has felt the need of a rational explanation to give validity to the word of the judge." [The major function of the reasoned opinion, explains Calamandrei,] "is an explanatory or, one might say, a pedagogical one. No longer content merely to command, to proclaim a *sic volo, sic iubeo* [So I wish, so I command] from his high bench, the judge descends to the level of the parties, and although still commanding, seeks to impress them with the reasonableness of the command. The reasoned opinion is above all the justification of the decision and as such it attempts to be as persuasive as it can."[7]

Like the judge, neither supernatural nor infallible, we are asked for rational explanations to justify our decisions. The judicial opinions on these pages provide useful and persuasive reasons.

I hope that readers of the books in this series—students, teachers, school board members, parents, and others—will develop their appreciation for and commitment to the First Amendment rights of students and teachers in the classroom and will recognize the variety of arguments available to counter those who would not have the First Amendment apply to teachers and students. The First Amendment freedoms were put into the Bill of Rights to be used; the court opinions in this book demonstrate that teachers and students usually get First Amendment protection from the courts. We must recognize, however, that freedoms not exercised by the citizenry lose their vitality. Teachers and students, said Chief Justice Earl Warren, "must always remain free to inquire, to study and to evaluate, to gain new maturity and understanding; otherwise our civilization will stagnate and die."[8]

NOTES

1. *Vail* v. *Bd. of Ed. of Portsmouth School Dist.,* 354 F. Supp. 592 (1973).
2. *West Virginia State Bd. of Ed.* v. *Barnette,* 319 U.S. 624 (1943).
3. John Dewey, "Democracy and Educational Administration," *School and Society,* 45(April 3, 1937), p. 462.
4. *Tinker* v. *Des Moines School Dist.,* 393 U.S. 503 (1969).
5. *Right to Read Defense Committee* v. *School Committee, Etc.,* 454 F. Supp. 703 (1978).
6. Edward Jenkinson, "Protecting Holden Caulfield and His Friends from the Censors," *English Journal,* 74(January 1985), p. 74.
7. Piero Calamandrei, *Procedure and Democracy,* trans. John C. Adams and Helen Adams (New York: New York University Press, 1956), p. 53.
8. *Sweezy* v. *New Hampshire,* 354 U.S. 234 (1957).

Constitutional Amendments

ARTICLE I

Congress shall make no law respecting an establishment of religion, or prohibiting the free exercise thereof; or abridging the freedom of speech, or of the press; or the right of the people peaceably to assemble, and to petition the government for a redress of grievances.

ARTICLE XIV

All persons born or naturalized in the United States, and subject to the jurisdiction thereof, are citizens of the United States and of the State wherein they reside. No State shall make or enforce any law which shall abridge the privileges or immunities of citizens of the United States; nor shall any State deprive any person of life, liberty or property, without due process of law; nor deny to any person within its jurisdiction the equal protection of the law.

Judicial Circuits

Circuits	*Composition*
District of Columbia	District of Columbia
First	Maine, Massachusetts, New Hampshire, Puerto Rico, Rhode Island
Second	Connecticut, New York, Vermont
Third	Delaware, New Jersey, Pennsylvania, Virgin Islands
Fourth	Maryland, North Carolina, South Carolina, Virginia, West Virginia
Fifth	Alabama, Canal Zone, Florida, Georgia, Louisiana, Mississippi, Texas
Sixth	Kentucky, Michigan, Ohio, Tennessee
Seventh	Illinois, Indiana, Wisconsin
Eighth	Arkansas, Iowa, Minnesota, Missouri, Nebraska, North Dakota, South Dakota
Ninth	Alaska, Arizona, California, Idaho, Montana, Nevada, Oregon, Washington, Guam, Hawaii
Tenth	Colorado, Kansas, New Mexico, Oklahoma, Utah, Wyoming

[28 U.S.C.A. §41]

Foreword

by Ken Donelson

W ITH some pain and a little amusement, I can remember my first run-in with a censor. I was in my second year of teaching English in a small Western Iowa town, I had finished my last class for the day, and I saw my superintendent coming down the hall, beaming at me. He beamed for only one reason. I was in trouble, again. He never beamed at me for any other reason.

I found the mother of one of my students waiting for me. Sincere, dedicated, moral, patriotic, religious, helpful, omniscient—in short, the sum of all that is noble about parenthood and dangerous about censors. She began by announcing, "I've come to help you, Mr. Donelson, to find better books than the ones you've been recommending to our innocent young people."

That should have been enough warning, but I was naive about such parents and censorship. I'd graduated from the University of Iowa barely more than a year before, sanctified by a Master's degree in English, but I knew nothing of censorship except for two graduate papers I'd written, one on the 1737 English Licensing Act that ended Henry Fielding's dramatic career, and one on Milton's *Areopagitica.* Neither paper, nor anything else for that matter, had prepared me for this encounter. After announcing the agenda, she alternately placated and admonished me, confiding that she'd heard some unhappy rumors about me and the literature I'd talked about in class and assuring me that she didn't intend anything she said to be misunderstood as censorship. Since she repeated that several times, I assumed others before me had mistaken her for a censor. I had trouble reminding myself that she wasn't a censor. She certainly sounded like one, even if I'd never met one before.

After more advice on the dangers of allowing young people to read books like *A Farewell to Arms, 1984, The Grapes of Wrath,* and *The Great Gatsby*—all without telling me exactly what was wrong with these "dangerous" books—she concluded the first part of her monologue by asking me, "Why let children read books that tell about the nastiness of the world? Why not encourage them to read, as a good English teacher would, some clean, happy, classic, wholesome books without violence and without anything offensive?"

Since I was as unsure as only a new English teacher could be and since she obviously expected me to ask her for details or examples of these better books, I played the part she had written for me and asked if she had any titles she'd like to recommend. Thus began the second part of her monologue.

I have no idea what I expected her to say, but I was surprised and puzzled by her examples. She was only too happy to recommend some of these "clean, happy, classic, wholesome books without violence and without anything offensive." Her first choice, she said, would be *Huckleberry Finn.* Ignoring for the moment the problems Twain's book later had with the NAACP and other social critics, I'd reread *Huck* not all that long before, and I remembered how bitter and violent those scenes involving the Shepherdson-Grangerford feud were, maybe the most violent words about humanity's inhumanity in American literature.

Her second choice was equally curious—Swift's *Gulliver's Travels.* When she announced the title, I knew she must have read it in an emasculated children's edition or she'd seen the stupefyingly awful film Disney had made of the book. In any case, as I tried to keep my face straight, all I could remember of the book was the section about Gulliver's overindulging in spirits, his discovery of the palace fire, and his unique way of putting out the blaze. I doubt she'd read that section, and I decided not to tell her about it.

Her final choice, the epitome, I gathered, of greatness because it was Shakespeare, was *Macbeth.* That did it for me. I was able, barely, to keep my face composed and my voice ungiggly, but the thought of a play in which the major character's head appears on stage at the end, sans body, seemed to suggest a tiny bit of violence.

But even as I chuckled to myself, I felt impotent and unsure of what to do about her and her ideas. I'm sure she would have been offended if she had known that I would refer to the meeting as a run-in. She clearly saw her visit as a mission to save a poor misguided teacher from himself. For me, it was far worse than a run-in. She had been totally in control of our conversation. Cower-in or stun-in might be demeaning words, but they would have far more accurately described my part of the meeting.

That visit was not the only such visit I had in the small town, nor was the meeting much different from many I had when I moved to Cedar Rapids, Iowa. All the visits from parents—or school board members or school administrators or ministers or "representatives" from this or that organization—had one thing in common. All suggested that someone else knew more about teaching English and helping my students than I did. No matter how the book protesters (a currently fashionable and possibly more accurate term for censors) came to me, and some were jovial and confiding and others were antagonistic and untrusting, they all challenged my right as a teacher to select books for students.

But if that wasn't the last visit, I was better prepared for the ones that followed. I learned what I should have known before, that parents weren't necessarily going to trust my judgment simply because I was a teacher. I recognized that I must be able to explain and justify what I was doing and why I was doing it. That should have been obvious to me, but it wasn't. I also learned that some people can't be placated. For them, teaching or recommending *The Catcher in the Rye* or *To Kill a Mockingbird* or *Othello* or *Go Ask Alice* or *Of Mice and Men* or *Slaughterhouse-Five* (to mention only a few currently popular titles on the censors' hit lists) is inherently wrong and not arguable. I learned to respect the sincerity and honesty of the protestor without giving in, though I have always believed that any parent has the right to control the reading of his or her child and no one else. I learned that I caused many of the problems that I labeled censorship by not communicating with parents about both what I taught and, more important, why I taught as I did. I learned that there are rarely only two sides to an issue and that my early efforts to simplify, simplify (as Thoreau had taught me) rarely did justice to anyone involved and usually led to confusion and anger (I should have remembered that Thoreau was a flop at teaching).

And while I'm a slow learner, I'm not certainly hopeless. That first visit forced me to learn much more about censors and censorship, partly out of naive curiosity, partly to protect myself as a teacher, partly to atone for the sense of inadequacy that I felt.

In the years that followed, I learned that some authors and books are high on the censors' list of targets. Steinbeck was the most popular author on the hit list when I began teaching, though Judy Blume is likely to overtake him soon. Salinger's *Catcher in the Rye* was and is the most widely attacked book. I sometimes wonder if his book, good as it is, isn't kept alive for today's students because censors insist on making him virtually mandatory reading for young people by keeping his name in the newspapers. I learned that some titles popped up over and over on censors' lists—Vonnegut's *Slaughterhouse-Five,* Kesey's *One Flew Over the Cuckoo's Nest,* Lee's *To Kill a Mockingbird,* Twain's *Huckleberry Finn,* Terkel's *Working, Go Ask Alice* (the nearest rival to *The Catcher in the Rye* for the most times attacked), and Heller's *Catch-22.*

I learned that other teachers, not just English teachers, were sometimes under attack for their ideas or books, and I recognized what I wish more teachers would see, that we all ought to band together to face attacks. Science teachers worried about teaching evolution in some communities, and today they worry about evolution *and* scientific creationism (if those last two words aren't mutually contradictory). Home economics teachers and physical education teachers worry about sex education. Social science teachers worry about how much they should mention of McCarthyism or the union movement or non-heroic actions of some of our patriotic heroes.

I learned that no matter how ugly some censorship battles could be, the censors provided us with humor if we were willing to search for it. And those occasional bits of humor gave me the chance to laugh, and that's rare enough on something as somber and frightening as censorship. I learned that censors may have little interest in literary merit, but they have an abiding passion for mathematics. In Issaquah, Washington, in August 1978, an objector to *The Catcher in the Rye* told the school board that she'd counted "785 profanities." I learned that some censors were funny, inadvertently I assume. In Eldon, Missouri, in April 1977, the school board banned *The American Heritage Dictionary* because it contained several four-letter words. A Missouri Highway Patrolman said, "If people learn words like that, it ought to be where you and I learned them—in the streets and in the gutter."

I learned that doublespeak is the standard language for some censors. In Cotati-Rohnert Park School District (near San Francisco) in October 1982, Judy Blume's *Deenie* was banned from elementary schools even though many parents favored keeping the book. A trustee of the school pointed out a higher wisdom— "the real down-to-earth parents who have lived in the district for quite awhile didn't want it in the elementary school," proof that Orwell's "All animals are equal but some animals are more equal than others" holds true in some schools. The Rev. Vincent Strigas, attacking girlie magazines in Mesa, Arizona, in July 1981 said "Some people are saying that we are in violation of First Amendment Rights. I do not think that the First Amendment protects people [who sell] pornographic materials. The Constitution protects only the freedom to do what's right," surely an original reading of the Constitution.

I learned that some educators favor indoctrination and not education. An adminstrative aide at Mark Twain Intermediate School in Fairfax, Virginia, in April 1983 announced that *Huckleberry Finn* was "racist trash" and should be removed from the county system's curriculum. And a California Board President announced in 1986 that Gardner's *Grendel* and Garcia Marquez's *One Hundred Years of Solitude* didn't meet standards set by the board. "It is not our intention to convert public classrooms into Sunday school classes, and students are entitled to a liberal arts education as much as possible. But we also have a duty to the community and we must guard against the use of garbage being passed off as literature."

And I learned that some English teachers are gutless wonders, incapable of fighting or unwilling to fight for education and against censorship. When I edited the *Arizona English Bulletin* a few years ago, I surveyed censorship conditions in the state in 1969 and 1975. The questionnaire several hundred teachers in 1969 completed was long and involved, but I assumed that I might have missed something worth pursuing, so a final question encouraged them to put down whatever they needed to say but I had forgotten to ask. Here are few scary responses. "The Board of Education knows what parents in our area want their children to read. If teachers don't feel they can teach what the parents approve, they should move on." "I would not recommend any book any parent might object to." "The English teacher is hired by the school board which represents the public. The public, therefore, has the right to ask any English teacher to avoid using any material repugnant to any parent or student." I've wondered ever since I read those comments whether the writers had any idea what they were saying. Unfortunately, I'm sure they meant precisely what they said. That frightens me. I suspect it comforts them.

I knew from my first experience with a censor that I could expect no support from my superintendent. I soon learned that I was typical. When I asked English teachers in Arizona what their administrators would do if someone objected to a book, the answers were depressingly similar. "He would agree with the parents and demand that I remove the offensive material." "The principal would go into utter panic." "His decision would be based on the pressure put on him." "After an investigation of both sides, the principal might agree with the parents since we have been warned by the school board that as far as book selection is concerned, we are on shaky ground. In other words, we cannot force the issue because we will not get *any* support."

And I learned to expect censorship and not to be frightened if it came. In a strange and perhaps perverted way, censorship ought to reassure us that we're sometimes doing something right. Books are ideas, as censors recognize—sometimes more often than English teachers do—and ideas can be dangerous if taken seriously. If censors recognize that and publicize it, maybe there's hope that students might recognize it as well. And whatever else censors do, they never fail to spread the word that certain titles are "immoral" or "unpatriotic" or "anti-Christian" or "perverted" or somesuch. No English teacher, or collection of teachers, could do as fine a job of alerting young people about titles that sound appealing. For that, if nothing else, we ought to be grateful to the censors.

But I was much slower at learning about court decisions involving teachers and censorship. That wouldn't have helped me way back in 1952, mostly because there were few judicial precedents about teachers like me, partly because most of the trials were extralegal. Teachers came under attack, and teachers were tried in the court of public opinion and sometimes before a school board. The attackers worried not at all about niceties like fairness or impartiality or solid evidence, but the trial—fair or no—was soon over and the matter rapidly disposed of.

Later, much later, I learned about *Epperson* v. *Arkansas* and *Keefe* v. *Geanakos* and *Parducci* v. *Rutland* and more. They reassured me that teachers had someplace to turn to for relief other than the untrustworthy court of public opinion and the school board. With Haig Bosmajian's help, the court cases of most interest to teachers are here gathered together. Not all of them will be comforting to teachers, but all of them deserve to be better known and their lessons, such as they are, noted.

Introduction

IN 399 B.C., Socrates was condemned to death for corrupting the minds of youth and not believing in the gods of the state. In the twentieth century, books, films, plays, and speakers are banned and censored because, it is claimed, they corrupt the minds of our youth and blaspheme the gods of the state. Those who argue that the challenged materials should be kept out of the classroom contend that they are "vulgar," "coarse," "offensive," and "indecent" and that students need to be protected from them.

As the cases in this volume reveal, the courts are still concerned with the "gods of the state." In the now famous *Scopes* case of 1927, the Tennessee Supreme Court upheld the constitutionality of Tennessee's "Anti-Evolution Act" which made it illegal "to teach any theory that denies the story of divine creation of man as taught in the Bible and to teach instead that man has descended from a lower order of animals." The "gods of the state" were the concern in 1968 in *Epperson,* in which the United States Supreme Court declared unconstitutional the Arkansas "anti-evolution" statute which prohibited "the teaching in its public schools and universities of the theory that man evolved from other species of life." In 1982, the United States District Court in Arkansas declared unconstitutional the Arkansas statute which required that the public schools give "balanced treatment" to creation-science and to evolution; District Court Judge Overton had to remind us that "no group, no matter how large or small, may use the organs of government, of which the public schools are the most conspicuous and influential, to foist its religious beliefs on others."

Over the centuries the "gods" and terms have changed, but Socrates' battle to defend freedom of thought and expression is still being fought today. In his speech of defense, *The Apology,* Socrates dealt not only with his right and obligation to speak, but he also recognized the nexus between the right to speak and the right to receive information:

> And now, Athenians, I am not going to argue for my own sake, as you may think, but for yours, that you may not sin against God by condemning me, who am his gift to you. For if you kill me you will not easily find a successor to me, who, if I may use such a ludicrous figure of speech, am a sort of gadfly, given to the state by God; and the state is a great and noble steed who is tardy in his motions owing to his very size, and requires to be stirred into life. I am that gadfly which God has attached to the state, and all day long and in all places am always fastening upon you, arousing and persuading and reproaching you. You will not easily find another like me, and therefore I would advise you to spare me.

Socrates died, but his philosophy survived.

In 1633, Galileo's *Dialogue Concerning the Two Chief Systems of the World* was banned by the Church, but his ideas prevailed. In ordering that Galileo be silenced and his book banned, the Church declared:

> We say, pronounce, sentence, declare that you, the said Galileo, by reason of the matters adduced at trial, and by you confessed as above, have rendered yourself in the judgment of this Holy Office vehemently suspected of heresy, namely of having believed and held the doctrine—which is false and contrary to the sacred and divine Scriptures—that the Sun is the center of the world and does not move from east to west, and that the Earth moves and is not the center of the world; and that an opinion may be held and defended as probable after it has been declared and defined to be contrary to Holy Scripture. . . . And in order that this your grave and pernicious error and transgression may not remain altogether unpunished, and that you may be more cautious for the future and an example to others, that they may abstain from similar delinquencies—we ordain the book of the Dialogue of Galileo Galilei be prohibited by public edict.

One result of this censorship and persecution was that the center of scientific learning moved from the Mediterranean area to Northern Europe.

Ten years later, John Milton, who had met Galileo, wrote his famous attack on censorship and licensing, *Areopagitica.* Several of Milton's arguments condemning censorship appear in some of the opinions in this volume. For example, Milton argued that censorship discourages learning and hinders the discovery of new truths; that weighing worthy ideas against unworthy ones develops wisdom; that evil manners are learned from sources other than books. He wrote:

> Good and evil we know in the field of this world grow up together almost inseparably; and the knowledge of good is so involved and interwoven with the knowledge of evil, and in so many cunning resemblances hardly to be discerned, that those confused seeds which imposed upon Psyche as an incessant labor to cull out and sort asunder, were not more intermixed. . . . He that can apprehend and consider vice with all her baits and seeming pleasures, and yet abstain, and yet distinguish, and yet prefer that which is truly better, he is the true warfaring Christian. I cannot praise a fugitive and cloistered virtue, unexercised and unbreathed, that never sallies out and sees her adversary, but slinks out of the race, where that immortal garland is to be run for, not without dust and heat. . . . Many there be that complain of divine Providence for suffering Adam to transgress. Foolish Tongues! When God gave him reason, he gave him freedom to choose, for reason is but choosing; he had been else a mere artificial Adam. . . .

Over three centuries later, a Michigan judge decided in *Todd* that Kurt Vonnegut's *Slaughterhouse-Five* could not be banned from the classrooms and libraries of Michigan schools and in so deciding he argued that the students should be free to choose: "Vonnegut's literary dwellings on war, religion, death, Christ, God, government, politics, and any other subject should be as welcome in the public schools of this state as those of Machiavelli, Chaucer, Shakespeare, Melville, Lenin, Hitler, Joseph McCarthy, or Walt Disney. The students of Michigan are free to make of *Slaughterhouse-Five* what they will."

While Milton did not use the "marketplace of ideas" metaphor which appears so often in the judicial opinions giving First Amendment protection to classroom materials, he did have truth and falsity competing: "And though all the winds of doctrine were let loose to play upon the earth, so Truth be in the field, we do injuriously by licensing and prohibiting to misdoubt her strength. Let her and Falsehood grapple; who ever knew Truth put to the worse in a free and open combat? Her confuting is the best and surest suppressing. . . . For who knows not that Truth is strong next to the Almighty? She needs no policies, nor stratagems, nor licensings to make her victorious; those are the shifts and the defences that error uses against her power: give her but room and do not bind her when she sleeps, for then she speaks not true. . . .''

More than one opinion in this volume includes the now classic statement from the United States Supreme Court's 1967 *Keyishian* opinion: "Our nation is deeply committed to safeguarding academic freedom, which is of transcendent value to all of us and not merely to the teachers concerned. That freedom is therefore a special concern of the First Amendment which does not tolerate laws that cast a pall of orthodoxy over the classroom. . . . The classroom is peculiarly the 'marketplace of ideas.' . . . The Nation's future depends upon leaders trained through wide exposure to that robust exchange of ideas which discovers truth 'out of a multitude of tongues, [rather] than through any kind of authoritative selection.' "

Like Milton, John Stuart Mill defended freedom of thought and discussion, but unlike Milton he focused in his essay *On Liberty* on censorship imposed not so much by the state as by the citizenry; he feared the populace's silencing unorthodox views. Said Mill: "If all mankind minus one were of one opinion, and only one person were of the contrary opinion, mankind would be no more justified in silencing that one person, than he, if he had the power, would be justified in silencing mankind." While Mill was concerned with defending the right of the speaker, he was more concerned with what society lost as a result of censorship. Those who censor, said Mill, are assuming their infallibility: "All silencing of discussion is an assumption of infallibility. . . . " But "it is not the feeling sure of a doctrine . . . which I call an assumption of infallibility. It is the undertaking to decide that question *for others*, without allowing them to hear what can be said on the contrary side."

The harm done by suppressing opinions is greatest to those denied access to the unorthodox ideas: " . . . it is not the minds of heretics that are deteriorated most, by the ban placed on all inquiry which does not end in the orthodox conclusions. The greatest harm done is to those whose whole mental development is cramped, and their reason cowed, by the fear of heresy. Who can compute what the world loses in the multitude of promising intellects combined with timid characters, who dare not follow out any bold, vigorous independent train of thought, lest it should land them in something which would admit of being considered irreligious or immoral?"

Summarized, Mill's arguments against censorship are: (1) If the silenced opinion is true, we have denied ourselves the opportunity of exchanging our error for that truth; (2) If the silenced opinion is false, we "lose what is almost as great a benefit, the clearer perception and livelier impression of truth, produced by its collision with error; (3) Even if the received opinion be not only true, but the whole truth, unless it is suffered to be, and actually is, vigorously and earnestly contested, it will, by most of those who receive it, be held in the manner of a prejudice, with little comprehension or feeling of its rational grounds; (4) . . . the meaning of the doctrine itself will be in danger of being lost, or enfeebled, and deprived of its vital effect on the character and conduct: the dogma becoming a mere formal profession, inefficacious for good, but cumbering the ground, and preventing the growth of any real and heartfelt conviction, from reason or personal experience."

Freedom of thought and expression, articulated and defended by Socrates, Milton, and Mill, has prevailed in the twentieth century. In his 1982 *Pratt* opinion, United States Court of Appeals Judge Gerald Heaney presented reason after reason for deciding that the school board's decision to remove from classroom use the film "The Lottery" and its trailer film, based on Shirley Jackson's short story, had violated the First Amendment rights of the students. The judge asserted that "the school board cannot constitutionally ban the films because a majority of its members object to the film's religious and ideological content and wish to prevent the ideas contained in the material from being expressed in the school." The arguments and reasons Judge Heaney presents to support his judgment are similar to those presented in other school censorship cases. As other courts have repeatedly argued, "notwithstanding the power and discretion accorded them, school boards do not have an absolute right to remove materials from the curriculum."

Next, "students do not 'shed their constitutional rights to freedom of speech or expression at the schoolhouse gate.'" Further, "at the very least, the First Amendment precludes local authorities from imposing a 'pall of orthodoxy' on classroom instruction which implicates the state in the propagation of a particular religious or ideological viewpoint." Thus, the judge concluded, "the students here had a right to be free from official conduct that was intended to suppress the ideas expressed in these films."

Addressing school authorities' practice of excluding from the schools books and ideas with which they disagree, Judge Heaney noted that "opponents of 'The Lottery' focused primarily on the purported religious and ideological impact of the films. They contended that the movies must be removed from the curriculum because they posed a threat to the students' religious beliefs and family values." It is obvious, he said, that the school board, "in response to the citizens' objections and without offering any reasons for its action, decided to remove the films from all of the District's schools." Clearly, "the board banned the films because the majority of its members objected to the ideas expressed in them." Therefore, reasoned Judge Heaney, "to avoid a finding that it acted unconstitutionally, the board must establish that a substantial and reasonable governmental interest exists for interfering with the students' right to receive information."

In response to the school board's rationale for banning "The Lottery"—that the film placed "an exaggerated and undue emphasis on violence and bloodshed which is not appropriate or suitable for showing in a high school classroom" and hence distorted the original short story—Judge Heaney asserted that "the contention that the films graphically emphasize violence is simply not supported by the facts. The two films contain but a single scene showing any physical violence—and that scene in the final brief frames of the main film is faithfully adapted from the short story."

Judge Heaney also deals with the apparent selective enforcement, declaring that "no systematic review of violence in the curriculum has been undertaken by the board. Indeed, there is no evidence that the board ever removed from the high school curriculum any materials other than the films in dispute here because of their violent content."

Reviewing the sequence of events that led to the banning of the films, the judge concluded that "we must agree with the District Court that the board eliminated the films not because they distort the short story, but rather it so acted because the majority of the board agreed with those citizens who considered the films' ideological and religious themes to be offensive."

The First Amendment, said Judge Heaney, "requires, in a situation such as the instant one, that the school board act so that the reasons for its decision are apparent to those affected." In this case, "only after the district court asked for an explanation of the board's actions did it offer its violence rationale. Even then, the board failed to specify why the films were too violent and how they distorted the short story. This approach inevitably suggests that the Board acted not out of its concern about violence, but rather to express an 'official policy with respect to God and country of uncertain and indefinite content which is to be ignored by pupils, librarians and teachers at their peril.' . . . Consequently, the board failed to 'clearly inform' students and teachers what it was proscribing as the constitution requires."

As for the argument, as often presented by those who support banning books, that the censored materials are still available to teachers and students in other forms and from other sources, Judge Heaney responded (as so many other judges have) that "restraint on protected speech generally cannot be justified by the fact that there may be other times, places or circumstances for such expression."

Recognizing the "symbolic effect of removing the films from the curriculum" as "more significant than the resulting limitation of access to the story," Judge Heaney observed: "The board has used its official power to perform an act clearly indicating that the ideas contained in the films are unacceptable and should not be discussed or considered. This message is not lost on students and teachers, and its chilling effect is obvious."

"For these reasons," said Judge Heaney, "the appellant has failed to carry its burden of establishing that a substantial governmental interest existed for interfering with the students' right to receive information. Hence, the board's action violated the First Amendment."

The judge admitted that "The Lottery" is not a "comforting film. But there is more at issue here than the sensibilities of those viewing the films. What is at stake is the right to receive information and to be exposed to controversial ideas—a fundamental First Amendent right. If these films can be banned by those opposed to their ideological theme, then a precedent is set for the removal of any such work." Judge Heaney's opinion provides a lesson in democracy, the limits of state power, the rights of students, and the impermissibility of selective enforcement and arbitrary censorship by school boards.

Many of these arguments and reasons are found in Judge Frank Johnson's decision giving First Amendment protection to a teacher who was dismissed for assigning Kurt Vonnegut's short story "Welcome to the Monkey House" to her eleventh grade class over the principal's objections. Early in his opinion, Judge Johnson wrote, " . . . the safeguards of the First Amendment will quickly be brought into play to protect the right of academic freedom because any unwarranted invasion of this right will tend to have a chilling effect on the exercise of the right by other teachers."

The first question to be answered, wrote Judge Johnson in Section One of his opinion, "is whether 'Welcome to the Monkey House' is inappropriate reading for high school juniors." In answering this question, he contended: "While the story contains several vulgar terms and a reference to an involuntary act of sexual intercourse, the Court, having read the story very carefully, can find nothing that would render it obscene. . . ." As for the slang words, he observed that they "are less ribald than those found in many of Shakespeare's plays. The reference in the story to an act of sexual intercourse is no more descriptive than the rape scene in Pope's 'Rape of the Lock.' As for the theme of the story, this Court notes that the anthology in which the story was published was reviewed by several of the popular weekly magazines, none of which found the subject-matter of any of the stories to be offensive."

Having argued that the book was not inappropriate for high school juniors, Judge Johnson concluded that the assignment of the book did not "materially and substantially interfere with reasonable requirements of discipline in the school." Then quoting from a 1969 censorship case involving the classroom use of an article containing offensive language, he said: "We do not question the good faith of the defendants in believing that some parents have been offended. With the greatest of respect to such parents, their sensibilities are not the full measure of what is proper education." Judge Johnson concluded Section One of his opinion by asserting that the teacher's "dismissal constituted an unwarranted invasion of her First Amendment right to academic freedom."

In Section Two, the judge addressed the teacher's allegation that she was denied "the right to use the short story in question as extra reading without a clear and concise written standard to determine which books are obscene." Since there was no written policy, "the only question before this Court on this point, therefore, is whether plaintiff was entitled, under the Due Process Clause, to prior notice that the conduct for which she was punished was prohibited." A basic constitutional right is involved here: "Our laws in this country have long recognized that no person should be punished for conduct unless such conduct has been proscribed in clear and precise terms. . . . When the conduct being punished involves First Amendment rights, as is the case here, the standards for judging permissible vagueness will be even more strictly applied."

"In the case now before this Court," Johnson continued, "we are concerned not merely with vague standards, but with the total absence of standards. When a teacher is forced to speculate as to what conduct is permissible and what conduct is proscribed, he is apt to be overly cautious and reserved in the classroom. Such a reluctance on the part of the teacher to investigate and experiment with new and different ideas is anathema to the entire concept of academic freedom."

Finally, in Section Three of his opinion, Judge Johnson focused on the kind of selective enforcement found in so many book banning incidents. He pointed out: "One of the recommended novels on the 'Junior English Reading List' is J.D. Salinger's *Catcher in the Rye*. This novel, while undisputedly a classic in American literature, contains far more offensive and descriptive language than that found in plaintiff's assigned story. The 'Senior English Reading List' contains a number of works, such as Huxley's *Brave New World* and Orwell's *1984* which have highly provocative and sophisticated themes. Furthermore, the school library contains a number of books with controversial words and philosophies."

On the danger of school boards wielding absolute power, the judge observed: "This situation illustrates how easily arbitrary discrimination can occur when public officials are given unfettered discretion to decide what books should be taught and what books should be banned. While not questioning either the motives or good faith of the defendants, this Court finds their inconsistency to be not only enigmatic but also grossly unfair."

At the end of his opinion Judge Johnson declares: "With these several basic constitutional principles in mind it inevitably follows that the defendants in this case cannot justify the dismissal of this plaintiff under the guise of insubordination." The judge ordered that the teacher be reinstated, that the school authorities "expunge from plaintiff's employment records and transcripts any and all references relating to her suspension and dismissal" and finally, "It is further ordered that the court costs incurred in this cause be and they are hereby taxed against the defendants."

As *Pratt* and *Parducci* and other decisions on these pages indicate, one can conclude that:

• School boards do not have absolute power and unfettered discretion. "These [school boards] have, of course, important, delicate and highly discretionary functions, but none that they may not perform within the limits of the Bill of Rights."

• Students and teachers do not "shed their constitutional rights to freedom of speech or expression at the schoolhouse gate."

• Books and other classroom materials cannot be banned simply because school board members or parents find them ideologically, linguistically, or religiously offensive.

• The board of education must establish a substantial and reasonable governmental interest before interfering with the student's right to receive information.

• Selective enforcement is not to be tolerated. Why is this book, film, or play banned when other materials used in the classroom also contain "offensive" language?

• School boards must clearly explain to students and teachers what is proscribed. Vague standards, or no standards, force teachers and students to speculate about what speech and conduct are permissible, leading to a chilling effect on expression.

• The fact that the banned materials are available elsewhere in the community does not justify censorship. "Restraint on protected speech generally cannot be justified by the fact that there may be other times, places or circumstances for such expression."

• In order for the state, including school boards and school authorities, to restrict the First Amendment rights of a student, it must demonstrate that the "forbidden conduct would 'materially and substantially' interfere with the requirements of appropriate discipline in the operation of the school."

• Materials charged with being "obscene" must be shown to be obscene under the standards established by the Supreme Court. It should be noted that none of the books, films, or plays in these cases was ever found to be obscene, even though the censors charged that they were vulgar, offensive, and distasteful.

These principles have served to protect the First Amendment rights of students and teachers in almost all the cases in this volume. The arguments tend to verify Supreme Court Justice Jackson's often quoted and eloquently stated principles asserted in *Barnette:*

> The very purpose of a Bill of Rights was to withdraw certain subjects from the vicissitudes of political controversy, to place them beyond the reach of majorities and officials and to establish them as legal principles to be applied by the courts. One's right to life, liberty, and property, to free speech, a free press, freedom of worship and assembly, and other fundamental rights may not be submitted to vote; they depend on the outcome of no election. . . .
>
> If there is any fixed star in our constitutional constellation, it is that no official, high or petty, can prescribe what shall be orthodox in politics, nationalism, religion, or other matters of opinion or force citizens to confess by word or act their faith therein. If there are any circumstances which permit an exception, they do not now occur to us.

Justice Jackson's sentiments have prevailed to protect the First Amendment rights of students and teachers over the decades since *Barnette.* They have prevailed in the courts, and if they have not prevailed in the many book, film, and drama censorship controversies that go unreported, the fault may be not with our courts but in ourselves. In a free society, it is ultimately the citizenry—teachers, parents, students, voters, school board members—who will determine whether the First Amendment freedoms will be protected in the schools.

THE United States Supreme Court decides that a Nebraska statute forbidding the teaching of a foreign language to any child who has not passed the eighth grade invades the liberty guaranteed by the Fourteenth Amendment. In deciding for a teacher who had been tried and convicted for teaching German to a ten year old child enrolled in a parochial school, the Court declared: "No emergency has arisen which renders knowledge by a child of some language other than English so clearly harmful as to justify its inhibition with the consequent infringement of rights long freely enjoyed. We are constrained to conclude that the statute as applied is arbitrary and without reasonable relation to any end within the competency of the State.

As the statute undertakes to interfere only with teaching which involves a modern language, leaving complete freedom as to other matters, there seems no adequate foundation for the suggestion that the purpose was to protect the child's health by limiting his mental capacities. It is well known that proficiency in a foreign language seldom comes to one not instructed at an early age, and experience shows that this is not injurious to the health, morals or understanding of the ordinary child."

Meyer v. *Nebraska,* 262 U.S. 390 (1923)

Mr. Justice McReynolds delivered the opinion of the Court.

Plaintiff in error was tried and convicted in the District Court for Hamilton County, Nebraska, under an information which charged that on May 25, 1920, while an instructor in Zion Parochial School, he unlawfully taught the subject of reading in the German language to Raymond Parpart, a child of ten years, who had not attained and successfully passed the eighth grade. The information is based upon "An act relating to the teaching of foreign languages in the State of Nebraska," approved April 9, 1919, which follows [Laws 1919, c. 249.]:

"Section 1. No person, individually or as a teacher, shall, in any private, denominational, parochial or public school, teach any subject to any person in any language other than the English language.

"Sec. 2. Languages, other than the English language, may be taught as languages only after a pupil shall have attained and successfully passed the eighth grade as evidenced by a certificate of graduation issued by the county superintendent of the county in which the child resides.

"Sec. 3. Any person who violates any of the pro-

visions of this act shall be deemed guilty of a misdemeanor and upon conviction, shall be subject to a fine of not less than twenty-five dollars ($25), nor more than one hundred dollars ($100) or be confined in the county jail for any period not exceeding thirty days for each offense.

"Sec. 4. Whereas, an emergency exists, this act shall be in force from and after its passage and approval."

The Supreme Court of the State affirmed the judgment of conviction. 107 Neb. 657. It declared the offense charged and established was "the direct and intentional teaching of the German language as a distinct subject to a child who had not passed the eighth grade," in the parochial school maintained by Zion Evangelical Lutheran Congregation, a collection of Biblical stories being used therefor. And it held that the statute forbidding this did not conflict with the Fourteenth Amendment, but was a valid exercise of the police power. The following excerpts from the opinion sufficiently indicate the reasons advanced to support the conclusion.

"The salutary purpose of the statute is clear. The legislature had seen the baneful effects of permitting foreigners, who had taken residence in this country, to rear and educate their children in the language of their native land. The result of that condition was found to be inimical to our own safety. To allow the children of foreigners, who had emigrated here, to be taught from early childhood the language of the country of their parents was to rear them with that language as their mother tongue. It was to educate them so that they must always think in that language, and, as a consequence, naturally inculcate in them the ideas and sentiments foreign to the best interests of this country. The statute, therefore, was intended not only to require that the education of all children be conducted in the English language, but that, until they had grown into that language and until it had become a part of them, they should not in the schools be taught any other language. The obvious purpose of this statute was that the English language should be and become the mother tongue of all children reared in this state. The enactment of such a statute comes reasonably within the police power of the state. *Pohl* v. *State*, 132 N.E. (Ohio) 20; *State* v. *Bartels*, 181 N.W. (Ia.) 508.

"It is suggested that the law is an unwarranted restriction, in that it applies to all citizens of the state and arbitrarily interferes with the rights of citizens who are not of foreign ancestry, and prevents them, without reason, from having their children taught foreign languages in school. That argument is not well taken, for it assumes that every citizen finds himself restrained by the statute. The hours which a child is able to devote to study in the confinement of school are limited. It must have ample time for exercise or play. Its daily capacity for learning is comparatively small. A selection of subjects for its education, therefore, from among the many that might be taught, is obviously necessary. The legislature no doubt had in mind the practical operation of the law. The law affects few citizens, except those of foreign lineage. Other citizens, in their selection of studies, except perhaps in rare instances, have never deemed it of importance to teach their children foreign languages before such children have reached the eighth grade. In the legislative mind, the salutary effect of the statute no doubt outweighed the restriction upon the citizens generally, which, it appears, was a restriction of no real consequence."

The problem for our determination is whether the statute as construed and applied unreasonably infringes the liberty guaranteed to the plaintiff in error by the Fourteenth Amendment. "No State shall . . . deprive any person of life, liberty, or property, without due process of law."

While this Court has not attempted to define with exactness the liberty thus guaranteed, the term has received much consideration and some of the included things have been definitely stated. Without doubt, it denotes not merely freedom from bodily restraint but

also the right of the individual to contract, to engage in any of the common occupations of life, to acquire useful knowledge, to marry, establish a home and bring up children, to worship God according to the dictates of his own conscience, and generally to enjoy those privileges long recognized at common law as essential to the orderly pursuit of happiness by free men. *Slaughter-House Cases*, 16 Wall. 36; *Butchers' Union Co.* v. *Crescent City Co.*, 111 U.S. 746; *Yick Wo* v. *Hopkins*, 118 U.S. 356; *Minnesota* v. *Barber*, 136 U.S. 313; *Allgeyer* v. *Louisiana*, 165 U.S. 578; *Lochner* v. *New York*, 198 U.S. 45; *Twining* v. *New Jersey*, 211 U.S. 78; *Chicago, Burlington & Quincy R.R. Co.* v. *McGuire*, 219 U.S. 549; *Truax* v. *Raich*, 239 U.S. 33; *Adams* v. *Tanner*, 244 U.S. 590; *New York Life Ins. Co.* v. *Dodge*, 246 U.S. 357; *Truax* v. *Corrigan*, 257 U.S. 312; *Adkins* v. *Children's Hospital*, 261 U.S. 525; *Wyeth* v. *Cambridge Board of Health*, 200 Mass. 474. The established doctrine is that this liberty may not be interfered with, under the guise of protecting the public interest, by legislative action which is arbitrary or without reasonable relation to some purpose within the competency of the State to effect. Determination by the legislature of what constitutes proper exercise of police power is not final or conclusive but is subject to supervision by the courts. *Lawton* v. *Steele*, 152 U.S. 133, 137.

The American people have always regarded education and acquisition of knowledge as matters of supreme importance which should be diligently promoted. The Ordinance of 1787 declares, "Religion, morality, and knowledge being necessary to good government and the happiness of mankind, schools and the means of education shall forever be encouraged." Corresponding to the right of control, it is the natural duty of the parent to give his children education suitable to their station in life; and nearly all the States, including Nebraska, enforce this obligation by compulsory laws.

Practically, education of the young is only possible in schools conducted by especially qualified persons who devote themselves thereto. The calling always has been regarded as useful and honorable, essential, indeed, to the public welfare. Mere knowledge of the German language cannot reasonably be regarded as harmful. Heretofore it has been commonly looked upon as helpful and desirable. Plaintiff in error taught this language in school as part of his occupation. His right thus to teach and the right of parents to engage him so to instruct their children, we think, are within the liberty of the Amendment.

The challenged statute forbids the teaching in school of any subject except in English; also the teaching of any other language until the pupil has attained and successfully passed the eighth grade, which is not usually accomplished before the age of twelve. The

Supreme Court of the State has held that "the so-called ancient or dead languages" are not "within the spirit or the purpose of the act." *Nebraska District of Evangelical Lutheran Synod* v. *McKelvie,* 187 N.W. 927. Latin, Greek, Hebrew are not proscribed; but German, French, Spanish, Italian and every other alien speech are within the ban. Evidently the legislature has attempted materially to interfere with the calling of modern language teachers, with the opportunities of pupils to acquire knowledge, and with the power of parents to control the education of their own.

It is said the purpose of the legislation was to promote civic development by inhibiting training and education of the immature in foreign tongues and ideals before they could learn English and acquire American ideals; and "that the English language should be and become the mother tongue of all children reared in this State." It is also affirmed that the foreign born population is very large, that certain communities commonly use foreign words, follow foreign leaders, move in a foreign atmosphere, and that the children are thereby hindered from becoming citizens of the most useful type and the public safety is imperiled.

That the State may do much, go very far, indeed, in order to improve the quality of its citizens, physically, mentally and morally, is clear; but the individual has certain fundamental rights which must be respected. The protection of the Constitution extends to all, to those who speak other languages as well as to those born with English on the tongue. Perhaps it would be highly advantageous if all had ready understanding of our ordinary speech, but this cannot be coerced by methods which conflict with the Constitution—a desirable end cannot be promoted by prohibited means.

For the welfare of his Ideal Commonwealth, Plato suggested a law which should provide: "That the wives of our guardians are to be common, and their children are to be common, and no parent is to know his own child, nor any child his parent . . . The proper officers will take the offspring of the good parents to the pen or fold, and there they will deposit them with certain nurses who dwell in a separate quarter; but the offspring of the inferior, or of the better when they chance to be deformed, will be put away in some mysterious, unknown place, as they should be." In order to submerge the individual and develop ideal citizens, Sparta assembled the males at seven into barracks and intrusted their subsequent education and training to official guardians. Although such measures have been deliberately approved by men of great genius, their ideas touching the relation between individual and State were wholly different from those upon which our institutions rest; and it hardly will be affirmed that any legislature could impose such restrictions upon the people of a State without doing violence to both letter and spirit of the Constitution.

The desire of the legislature to foster a homogeneous people with American ideals prepared readily to understand current discussions of civic matters is easy to appreciate. Unfortunate experiences during the late war and aversion toward every characteristic of truculent adversaries were certainly enough to quicken that aspiration. But the means adopted, we think, exceed the limitations upon the power of the State and conflict with rights assured to plaintiff in error. The interference is plain enough and no adequate reason therefor in time of peace and domestic tranquility has been shown.

The power of the State to compel attendance at some school and to make reasonable regulations for all schools, including a requirement that they shall give instructions in English, is not questioned. Nor has challenge been made of the State's power to prescribe a curriculum for institutions which it supports. Those matters are not within the present controversy. Our concern is with the prohibition approved by the Supreme Court. *Adams* v. *Tanner, supra,* p. 594, pointed out that mere abuse incident to an occupation ordinarily useful is not enough to justify its abolition, although regulation may be entirely proper. No emergency has arisen which renders knowledge by a child of some language other than English so clearly harmful as to justify its inhibition with the consequent infringement of rights long freely enjoyed. We are constrained to conclude that the statute as applied is arbitrary and without reasonable relation to any end within the competency of the State.

As the statute undertakes to interfere only with teaching which involves a modern language, leaving complete freedom as to other matters, there seems no adequate foundation for the suggestion that the purpose was to protect the child's health by limiting his mental activities. It is well known that proficiency in a foreign language seldom comes to one not instructed at an early age, and experience shows that this is not injurious to the health, morals or understanding of the ordinary child.

The judgment of the court below must be reversed and the cause remanded for further proceedings not inconsistent with this opinion.

Reversed.

THE Supreme Court of Tennessee upholds the constitutionality of Tennessee's "Anti-Evolution Act" which read: "Be it enacted by the general assembly of the state of Tennessee, that it shall be unlawful for a teacher in any of the universities, normals and all other public schools of the state which are supported in whole or in part by the public school funds of the state, to teach any theory that denies the story of the divine creation of man as taught in the Bible and to teach instead that man has descended from a lower order of animals." In declaring the act constitutional, the Court said: "If the Legislature thinks that, by reason of popular prejudice, the cause of education and the study of science generally will be promoted by forbidding the teaching of evolution in the schools of the state, we can conceive of no ground to justify the court's interference. The courts cannot sit in judgment on such acts of the Legislature or its agents and determine whether or not the omission or addition of a particular course of study tends 'to cherish science.' " The Court's opinion concludes with the following observations and suggestion: "The court is informed that the plaintiff [Scopes] in error is no longer in the service of the state. We see nothing to be gained by prolonging the life of this bizarre case. On the contrary, we think the peace and dignity of the state, which all criminal prosecutions are brought to redress, will be the better conserved by the entry of a nolle prosequi [an agreement not to continue the proceedings against Scopes] herein. Such a course is suggested to the Attorney General."

Scopes v. *State*, 289 S.W. 363 (1927)

GREEN, C.J. Scopes was convicted of a violation of chapter 27 of the Acts of 1925, for that he did teach in the public schools of Rhea county a certain theory that denied the story of the divine creation of man, as taught in the Bible, and did teach instead thereof that man had descended from a lower order of animals. After a verdict of guilty by the jury, the trial judge imposed a fine of $100, and Scopes brought the case to this court by an appeal in the nature of a writ of error.

The bill of exceptions was not filed within the time fixed by the court below, and, upon motion of the state, at the last term, this bill of exceptions was stricken from the record. *Scopes* v. *State*, 152 Tenn. 424, 278 S.W. 57.

A motion to quash the indictment was seasonably made in the trial court raising several questions as to the sufficiency thereof and as to the validity and construction of the statute upon which the indictment rested. These questions appear on the record before us and have been presented and debated in this court with great elaboration.

Chapter 27 of the Acts of 1925, known as the Tennessee Anti-Evolution Act is set out in the margin.[1]

While the act was not drafted with as much care as could have been desired, nevertheless there seems to be no great difficulty in determining its meaning. It is entitled:

"An act prohibiting the teaching of the evolution theory in all the Universities, normals and all other public schools in Tennessee, which are supported in whole or in part by the public school funds of the state, and to provide penalties for the violations thereof."

Evolution, like prohibition, is a broad term. In recent bickering, however, evolution has been understood to mean the theory which holds that man has developed from some preexisting lower type. This is the popular significance of evolution, just as the popular significance of prohibition is prohibition of the traffic in intoxicating liquors. It was in that sense that evolution was used in this act. It is in this sense that the word will be used in this opinion, unless the context otherwise indicates. It is only to the theory of the evolution of man from a lower type that the act before us was intended to apply, and much of the discussion we have heard is beside this case. The words of a statute, if in common use, are to be taken in their natural and ordinary sense. O'Neill v. State, 115 Tenn. 427, 90 S. W. 627, 3 L. R. A. (N. S.) 762; State ex rel. v. Turnpike Co., 2 Sneed (34 Tenn.) 90.

Thus defining evolution, this act's title clearly indicates the purpose of the statute to be the prohibition of teaching in the schools of the state that man has developed or descended from some lower type or order of animals.

When the draftsman came to express this purpose in the body of the act, he first forbade the teaching of "any theory that denies the story of the divine creation of man, as taught in the Bible"—his conception evidently being that to forbid the denial of the Bible story would ban the teaching of evolution. To make the purpose more explicit, he added that it should be unlawful to teach "that man has descended from a lower order of animals."

Supplying the ellipsis in section 1 of the act, it reads that it shall be unlawful for any teacher, etc.—

"to teach any theory that denies the story of the divine creation of man as taught in the Bible, and to teach instead [of the story on the divine creation of man as taught in the Bible] that man has descended from a lower order of animals."

The language just quoted illustrates what is called in rhetoric exposition by iteration. The different form of the iterated idea serves to expound the first expression of the thought. The undertaking of the statute was to prevent teaching of the evolution theory. It was considered this purpose could be effected by forbidding the teaching of any theory that denied the Bible story, but to make the purpose clear it was also forbidden to teach that man descended from a lower order of animals.

This manner of expression in written instruments is common, and gives use to the maxim of construction noscitur a sociis. Under this maxim subordinate words and phrases are modified and limited to harmonize with each other and with the leading and controlling purpose or intention of the act. For example, see Lewis' Southerland Stat. Const. § 415 et seq.; Caldwell & Co. v. Lea, 152 Tenn. 48, 272 S. W. 715.

It thus seems plain that the Legislature in this enactment only intended to forbid teaching that men descended from a lower order of animals. The denunciation of any theory denying the Bible story of creation is restricted by the caption and by the final clause of section 1.

So interpreted, the statute does not seem to be uncertain in its meaning nor incapable of enforcement for such a reason, notwithstanding the argument to the contrary. The indictment herein follows the language of the statute. The statute being sufficiently definite in its terms, such an indictment is good. State v. Odam, 2 Lea (70 Tenn.) 220; Villines v. State, 96 Tenn. 141, 33 S. W. 922; Griffin v. State, 109 Tenn. 17, 70 S. W. 61. The assignments of error, which challenge the sufficiency of the indictment and the uncertainty of the act, are accordingly overruled.

It is contended that the statute violates section 8 of article 1 of the Tennessee Constitution, and section 1 of the Fourteenth Amendment of the Constitution of the United States—the law of the land clause of the state Constitution, and the due process of law clause of the federal Constitution, which are practically equivalent in meaning.

We think there is little merit in this contention. The plaintiff in error was a teacher in the public schools of Rhea county. He was an employee of the state of Tennessee or of a municipal agency of the state. He was under contract with the state to work in an institution of the state. He had no right or privilege to serve the state except upon such terms as the state prescribed. His liberty, his privilege, his immunity to teach and proclaim the theory of evolution, elsewhere than in the service of the state, was in no wise touched by this law.

The statute before us is not an exercise of the police power of the state undertaking to regulate the conduct and contracts of individuals in their dealings with each other. On the other hand, it is an act of the state as a corporation, a proprietor, an employer. It is a declaration of a master as to the character of work the master's servant shall, or rather shall not, perform. In dealing with its own employees engaged upon its own work, the state is not hampered by the limitations of section 8 of article 1 of the Tennessee Constitution, nor of the Fourteenth Amendment to the Constitution of the United States.

In People v. Crane, 214 N. Y. 154, 108 N. E. 427, L. R. A. 1916D, 550, Ann. Cas. 1915B, 1254, the validity of a statute of that state, providing that citizens only should be employed upon public works was sustained. In the course of opinion (page 175 [108 N. E. 434]), it was said:

"The statute is nothing more, in effect, than a resolve by an employer as to the character of his employees. An individual employer would communicate the resolve to his subordinates by written instructions or by word of mouth. The state, an incorporeal master, speaking through the Legislature, communicates the resolve to its agents by enacting a statute. Either the private employer or the state can revoke the resolve at will. Entire liberty of action in these respects is essential unless the state is to be deprived of a right which has heretofore been deemed a constituent element of the relationship of master and servant, namely, the right of the master to say who his servants shall (and therefore shall not) be."

A case involving the same statute reached the Supreme Court of the United States, and the integrity of the statute was sustained by that tribunal. Heim v. McCall, 239 U. S. 175, 36 S. Ct. 78, 60 L. Ed. 207, Ann. Cas. 1917B, 287. The Supreme Court referred to People v. Crane, supra, and approvingly quoted a portion of the language of Barrett, Chief Judge, that we have set out above.

At the same term of the Supreme Court of the United States an Arizona statute, prohibiting individuals and corporations with more than five workers from employing less than 80 per cent. thereof of qualified electors or native-born citizens of the United States was held invalid. Truax v. Raich, 239 U. S. 33, 36 S. Ct. 7, 60 L. Ed. 131, L. R. A. 1916D, 545, Ann. Cas. 1917B, 283.

These two cases from the Supreme Court make plain the differing tests to be applied to a statute regulating the state's own affairs and a statute regulating the affairs of private individuals and corporations.

A leading case is Atkin v. Kansas, 191 U. S. 207, 24 S. Ct. 124, 48 L. Ed. 148. The court there considered and upheld a Kansas statute making it a criminal offense for a contractor for a public work to permit or require an employee to perform labor upon that work in excess of eight hours each day. In that case it was laid down:

"... For, whatever may have been the motives controlling the enactment of the statute in question, we can imagine no possible ground to dispute the power of the state to declare that no one undertaking work for it or for one of its municipal agencies, should permit or require an employee on such work to labor in excess of eight hours each day, and to inflict punishment upon those who are embraced by such regulations and yet disregard them.

"It cannot be deemed a part of the liberty of any contractor that he be allowed to do public work in any mode he may choose to adopt, without regard to the wishes of the state. On the contrary, it belongs to the state, as the guardian and trustee for its people, and having control of its affairs, to prescribe the conditions upon which it will permit public work to be done on its behalf, or on behalf of its municipalities. No court has authority to review its action in that respect. Regulations on this subject suggest only considerations of public policy. And with such considerations the courts have no concern."

In Ellis v. United States, 206 U. S. 246, 27 S. Ct. 600, 51 L. Ed. 1047, 11 Ann. Cas. 589, Atkins v. Kansas was followed, and an act of Congress sustained which prohibited, under penalty of fine or imprisonment, except in case of extraordinary emergency, the requiring or permitting laborers or mechanics employed upon any of the public works of the United States or of the District of Columbia to work more than eight hours each day.

These cases make it obvious that the state or government, as an incident to its power to authorize and enforce contracts for public services, "may require that they shall be carried out only in a way consistent with its views of public policy, and may punish a departure from that way." Ellis v. United States, supra.

To the same effect is Waugh v. Board of Trustees, 237 U. S. 589, 35 S. Ct. 720, 59 L. Ed. 1131, in which a Mississippi statute was sanctioned that prohibited the existence of Greek letter fraternities and similar societies in the state's educational institutions, and deprived members of such societies of the right to receive or compete for diplomas, class honors, etc.

This court has indicated a like view in Leeper v. State, 103 Tenn. 500, 53 S. W. 962, 48 L. R. A. 167, in which the constitutionality of chapter 205 of the Acts of 1899, known as the Uniform Text Book Law, was sustained. In the opinion in that case Judge Wilkes observed:

"If the authority to regulate and control schools is legislative, then it [is] must have an unrestricted right to prescribe methods, and the courts cannot interfere with it unless some scheme is devised which is contrary to other provisions of the Constitution. ..."

In Marshall & Bruce Co. v. City of Nashville, 109 Tenn. 495, 71 S. W. 815, the charter of the city of Nashville required that all contracts for goods and supplies furnished the city, amounting to over $50, must be let out at competitive bidding to the lowest responsible bidder. In the face of such a charter provision, an ordinance of the city, which provided that all city printing should bear the union label, was held unauthorized—necessarily so. The lowest bidder, provided he was responsible, was entitled to such a contract, whether he employed union labor, and was empowered to affix the union label to his work or not. Other things said in that case were not necessary to the decision.

Traux v. Raich, supra, Meyer v. Nebraska, 262 U. S. 390, 43 S. Ct. 625, 67 L. Ed. 1042, 29 A. L. R. 1446, Pierce v. Society of Sisters of the Holy Names of Jesus and Mary, 268 U. S. 510, 45 S. Ct. 571, 69 L. Ed. 1070,

39 A. L. R. 468, and other decisions of the Supreme Court of the United States, pressed upon us by counsel for the plaintiff in error, deal with statutes affecting individuals, corporations, and private institutions, and we do not regard these cases as in point.

Since the state may prescribe the character and the hours of labor of the employees on its works, just as freely may it say what kind of work shall be performed in its service, what shall be taught in its schools, so far at least as section 8 of article 1 of the Tennessee Constitution, and the Fourteenth Amendment to the Constitution of the United States, are concerned.

But it is urged that chapter 27 of the Acts of 1925 conflicts with section 12 of article 11, the educational clause, and section 3 of article 1, the religious clause, of the Tennessee Constitution. It is to be doubted if the plaintiff in error, before us only as the state's employee, is sufficiently protected by these constitutional provisions to justify him in raising such questions. Nevertheless, as the state appears to concede that these objections are properly here made, the court will consider them.

The relevant portion of section 12 of article 11 of the Constitution is in these words:

" . . . It shall be the duty of the General Assembly in all future periods of this government, to cherish literature and science."

The argument is that the theory of the descent of man from a lower order of animals is now established by the preponderance of scientific thought and that the prohibition of the teaching of such theory is a violation of the legislative duty to cherish science.

While this clause of the Constitution has been mentioned in several of our cases, these references have been casual, and no act of the Legislature has ever been held inoperative by reason of such provision. In one of the opinions in Green v. Allen, 5 Humph. (24 Tenn.) 170, the provision was said to be directory. Although this court is loath to say that any language of the Constitution is merely directory (State v. Burrow, 119 Tenn. 376, 104 S. W. 526, 14 Ann. Cas. 809; Webb v. Carter, 129 Tenn. 182, 165 S. W. 426), we are driven to the conclusion that this particular admonition must be so treated. It is too vague to be enforced by any court. To cherish science means to nourish, to encourage, to foster science.

In no case can the court directly compel the Legislature to perform its duty. In a plain case the court can prevent the Legislature from transgressing its duty under the Constitution by declaring ineffective such a legislative act. The case, however, must be plain, and the legislative act is always given the benefit of any doubt.

If a bequest were made to a private trustee with the avails of which he should cherish science, and there was nothing more, such a bequest would be void for uncertainty. Green v. Allen, 5 Humph. (24 Tenn.) 170, Ewell v. Sneed, 136 Tenn. 602, 191 S. W. 131, 5 A. L. R. 303, and cases cited. It could not be enforced as a charitable use in the absence of prerogative power in this respect which the courts of Tennessee do not possess. A bequest in such terms would be so indefinite that our courts could not direct a proper application of the trust fund nor prevent its misapplication. The object of such a trust could not be ascertained.

If the courts of Tennessee are without power to direct the administration of such a trust by an individual, how can they supervise the administration of such a trust by the Legislature? It is a matter of far more delicacy to undertake the restriction of a co-ordinate branch of government to the terms of a trust imposed by the Constitution than to confine an individual trustee to the terms of the instrument under which he functions. If language be so indefinite as to preclude judicial restraint of an individual, such language could not possibly excuse judicial restraint of the General Assembly.

If the Legislature thinks that, by reason of popular prejudice, the cause of education and the study of science generally will be promoted by forbidding the teaching of evolution in the schools of the state, we can conceive of no ground to justify the court's interference. The courts cannot sit in judgment on such acts of the Legislature or its agents and determine whether or not the omission or addition of a particular course of study tends "to cherish science."

The last serious criticism made of the act is that it contravenes the provision of section 3 of article 1 of the Constitution, "that no preference shall ever be given, by law, to any religious establishment or mode of worship."

The language quoted is a part of our Bill of Rights, was contained in the first Constitution of the state adopted in 1796, and has been brought down into the present Constitution.

At the time of the adoption of our first Constitution, this government had recently been established and the recollection of previous conditions was fresh. England and Scotland maintained state churches as did some of the Colonies, and it was intended by this clause of the Constitution to prevent any such undertaking in Tennessee.

We are not able to see how the prohibition of teaching the theory that man has descended from a lower order of animals gives preference to any religious establishment or mode of worship. So far as we know, there is no religious establishment or organized body that has in its creed or confession of faith any article denying or affirming such a theory. So far as we know, the denial or affirmation of such a theory does not enter into any recognized mode of worship. Since this cause has been pending in this court, we have been favored, in addition to briefs of counsel and various amici curiæ, with a multitude of resolutions, addresses, and communications from scientific bodies, religious factions, and individuals giving us the benefit of their views upon the theory of evolution. Examination of these contributions indicates that Protestants, Catholics, and Jews are divided among themselves in their beliefs, and that there is no unanimity among the members of any religious establishment as to this subject. Belief or unbelief in the theory of evolution is no more a characteristic of any religious establishment or mode of worship than is belief or unbelief in the wisdom of the prohibition laws. It would appear that members of the same churches quite generally disagree as to these things.

Furthermore, chapter 277 of the Acts of 1925 *requires* the teaching of nothing. It only *forbids* the teaching of the evolution of man from a lower order of animals. Chapter 102 of the Acts of 1915 requires that ten verses from the Bible be read each day at the opening of every public school, without comment, and provided the teacher does not read the same verses more than twice during any session. It is also provided in this act that pupils may be excused from the Bible readings upon the written request of their parents.

As the law thus stands, while the theory of evolution of man may not be taught in the schools of the state, nothing contrary to that theory is required to be taught. It could scarcely be said that the statutory scriptural reading just mentioned would amount to teaching of a contrary theory.

Our school authorities are therefore quite free to determine how they shall act in this state of the law. Those in charge of the educational affairs of the state are men and women of discernment and culture. If they believe that the teaching of the science of biology has been so hampered by chapter 27 of the Acts of 1925 as to render such an effort no longer desirable, this course of study may be entirely omitted from the curriculum of our schools. If this be regarded as a misfortune, it must be charged to the Legislature. It should be repeated that the act of 1925 deals with nothing but the evolution of man from a lower order of animals.

It is not necessary now to determine the exact scope of the religious preference clause of the Constitution and other language of that section. The situation does not call for such an attempt. Section 3 of article 1 is binding alike on the Legislature and the school authorities. So far we are clear that the Legislature has not crossed these constitutional limitations. If hereafter the school authorities should go beyond such limits, a case can then be brought to the courts.

Much has been said in argument about the motives of the Legislature in passing this act. But the validity of a statute must be determined by its natural and legal effect, rather than proclaimed motives. Lochner v. New York, 198 U. S. 45, 25 S. Ct. 539, 49 L. Ed. 937, 3 Ann. Cas. 1133; Grainger v. Douglas Park Jockey Club (C. C. A) 148 F. 513, 8 Ann. Cas. 997; R. C. L. III, 81.

Some other questions are made, but in our opinion they do not merit discussion, and the assignments of error raising such questions are overruled.

This record discloses that the jury found the defendant below guilty, but did not assess the fine. The trial judge himself undertook to impose the minimum fine of $100 authorized by the statute. This was error. Under section 14 of article 6 of the Constitution of Tennessee, a fine in excess of $50 must be assessed by a jury. The statute before us does not permit the imposition of a smaller fine than $100.

Since a jury alone can impose the penalty this act requires, and as a matter of course no different penalty can be inflicted, the trial judge exceeded his jurisdiction in levying this fine, and we are without power to correct his error. The judgment must accordingly be reversed. Upchurch v. State, 153 Tenn. 198, 281 S. W. 462.

The court is informed that the plaintiff in error is no longer in the service of the state. We see nothing to be gained by prolonging the life of this bizarre case. On the contrary, we think the peace and dignity of the state, which all criminal prosecutions are brought to redress, will be the better conserved by the entry of a nolle prosequi herein. Such a course is suggested to the Attorney General.

Mr. Justice SWIGGART took no part in the decision. He came on this bench upon the death of Mr. Justice HALL, after the argument and submission hereof.

COOK, J., concurs.

CHAMBLISS, J. (concurring). While I concur in the conclusions announced by Chief Justice GREEN, and agree, as so ably shown by him, that it is within the power of the Legislature to so prescribe the public school curriculum as to prohibit the teaching of the evolution of man from a lower order of animal life, even though the teaching of some branches of science may be thereby restricted, I am of opinion that the constitutional objections urged do not apply for yet other reasons, and in another view.

Two theories of organic evolution are well recognized, one the theistic, which not only concedes, but maintains, consistently with the Bible story, that "the Lord God formed man of the dust of the earth, and breathed into his nostrils the breath of life, and man became a living soul." This is the theory advanced eloquently by learned counsel for Scopes, and held to by numerous outstanding scientists of the world. The other theory is known as the materialistic, which denies that God created man, that He was the first cause, and seeks in shadowy uncertainties for the origin of life. The act before us, as I view it, prohibits the teaching in public schools of the state of this latter theory, inconsistent, not only with the common belief of mankind of every clime and creed and "religious establishment," even those that reject Christ or Judaism, and look through Buddha or Mohammed to God, but inconsistent also with our Constitution and the fundamental declaration lying back of it, through all of which runs recognition of and appeal to "God," and a life to come. The Declaration of Independence opens with a reference to "the laws of nature and nature's God," and holds this truth "to be self-evident, that all men are created equal, that they are endowed by their Creator," etc., and concludes "with a firm reliance on the protection of Divine Providence." The Articles of Confederation and Perpetual Union read, "And whereas, it hath pleased the Great Governor of the world." And so section 3 of article 1 of the Constitution of this state, which declares that "no preference shall ever be given, by law, to any religious establishment," opens with the declaration "that all men have a natural and indefeasible right to worship Almighty God," while section 2 of article 9 declares that "no person who denies the being of God, or a future state of rewards and punishments, shall hold any office in the civil department of this state." That the Legislature may prohibit the teaching of the future citizens and office holders to the state a theory which denies the Divine Creator will hardly be denied.

Now I find it conceded in an exceptionally able brief for Scopes, devoted exclusively to the question of uncertainty, that "the act might be construed as only aimed at materialists." This is my view of it. As I read it, the act makes no war on evolution, except in so far as the evolution theory conflicts with the recognition of the divine in creation.

While it is conceded that the language is in some respects ambiguous, analysis of the caption and body of the act as a whole appears to sustain this view. The variance between the caption and the body of the act is significant. The caption refers broadly to "the evolution theory," but it is clear that the act itself, as finally framed and passed, was expressly limited and restricted in its body to the prohibition of the teaching—not of any theory of evolution at all, but of any theory only that denies or controverts "the divine creation of man." While the language used is "any theory that denies *the story of* the divine creation of man as *taught in the Bible,*" the italicized phraseology may be said to be descriptive only of the essential matter. It may be insisted that these words, when given their proper

force, serve to narrow the meaning of the act so as to confine its operation to prohibition against the denial of the divine creation of man to the story taught in the Bible as interpreted by those liberalists who hold to the instantaneous creation view. In reply, it may be said that, however plausible may be this construction or application of this language, it must be rejected on the very grounds emphasized by learned counsel, who adopt it and then proceed to predicate thereon their argument for the unconstitutionality of the act. The courts may go far to avoid a construction which will destroy the act. This is axiomatic. One may not consistently contend for a construction of language, at all open to construction, which, if applied, will make void the act. Moreover, it would seem that, since "the story as taught in the Bible" of man's creation by God from the dust of the earth is readily susceptible of the construction given it by those known as liberalists, this language is consistent with the conclusion that what the act aims at and effects is the prohibition of the teaching of any such theory only as denies that man was *divinely created* according to the Bible story, *however this story may be interpreted as to details.* So long as the story as told in the Bible is so construed as to recognize the divine creation of man, these words have no limiting effect upon the central and essential object of the act as hereinbefore suggested—to restrain the inculcation into the minds of pupils of the public schools of any theory that denies the divine creation of man, and on the contrary traces his origin, *in exclusion of the divine,* to a lower order of animal life. It is this materialistic teaching which is denounced, and, so construed, the act may clearly be sustained, negative only as it is, first, of the right to teach in the public schools a denial of the existence, recognized by our Constitution, of the Creator of all mankind; and, second, of the right to teach any theory which involves the support or advocacy of either, or any, religious dogma or view.

The concluding phrase, "and to teach instead that man has descended from a lower order of animals," is added on the apparent assumption that such teaching involves a denial, which the preceding clause prohibits, of divine creation. The use of this language, aptly defined by our learned Chief Justice as a species of iteration, for the purpose of emphasis, indicates an intention to set over, one against the other, the theory, or "story," of man's divine creation, and the antagonistic and materialistic theory, or "story," of his origin in the animal kingdom, to the exclusion of God. The phraseology is antithetical—a favorite form of strengthening statement—"measures, not men;" springing from God, not animals. The two theories of man's origin are placed in direct opposition; the manifest purpose being to emphasize the essence of the thing prohibited, the teaching of a denial of man's divine creation.

The following statement of Dr. E. N. Reinke, professor of biology in Vanderbilt University, is repeatedly quoted in briefs of counsel for the defense:

"The theory of evolution is altogether essential to the teaching of biology and its kindred sciences. To deny the teacher of biology the use of this most fundamental generalization of his science would make his teaching as chaotic as an attempt to teach astronomy without the law of gravitation or physics without assuming the existence of the ether."

Conceding that "the theory of evolution is altogether essential to the teaching of biology and its kindred sciences," it will not be contended by Dr. Reinke, or by learned counsel quoting from him, that the theory of evolution essentially involves the denial of the divine creation of man, and that, when construed to prohibit such a denial only, the act is objectionable as denying to "the teacher of biology the use of the most fundamental generalization of his science."

Now, in this view, it is clear that the constitutional direction to cherish education and science is not disregarded. The teaching of all sciences may have full legitimate sway, with the restriction only that the teaching shall not convey a denial of man's divine origin—God as his Creator. The theories of Drummond, Winchell, Fiske, Hibbens, Millikan, Kenn, Merriam, Angell, Cannon Barnes, and a multitude of others, whose names are invoked in argument and brief, do not deny the story of the divine creation of man as taught in the Bible, evolutionists though they be, but, construing the Scripture for themselves in the light of their learning, accept it as true and their teaching would not come under the ban of this act.

Much that has been said here bears directly upon the contention that section 3, art. 1, of our Constitution is violated, in that a preference is given by law to those "religious establishments which have as one of their tenets or dogmas the instantaneous creation of man." As was said by Chief Justice GREEN, the act gives no preference to any particular religious establishment. The doctrine or tenet of the instantaneous creation of man is not set forth or preferred over other conceptions. It is too well established for argument that "the story of the divine creation of man as taught in the Bible" is accepted—not "denied"—by millions of men and women who do not interpret it as teaching instantaneous creation, who hold with the Psalmist that "a thousand years in thy sight are but as yesterday when it is past," as but a day. It follows that to forbid the teaching of a denial of the biblical account of divine creation does not, expressly or by fair implication, involve acceptance or approval of instantaneous creation, held to by some literalists. One is not prohibited by this act from teaching, either that "days," as used in the book of Genesis, means days of 24 hours, the literalist view, or days of "a thousand years" or more, as held by liberalists, so long as the teaching does not exclude God as the author of human life.

Considering the caption and body of this act as a whole, it is seen to be clearly negative only, not affirmative. It requires nothing to be taught. It prohibits merely. And it prohibits, not the teaching of any theory of evolution, but that theory (of evolution) only that denies, takes issue with, positively disaffirms, the creation of man by God (as the Bible teaches), and that, instead of being so created, he is a product of, springs from, a lower order of animals. No authority is recognized or conferred by the laws of this state for the teaching in the public schools, on the one hand, of the Bible, or any of its doctrines or dogmas, and this act prohibits the teaching on the other hand of any denial thereof. It is purely an act of neutrality. Ceaseless and irreconcilable controversy exists among our citizens and taxpayers, having equal rights, touching matters of religious faith, and it is within the power of the Legislature to declare that the subject shall be excluded from the tax-supported institutions, that the state shall stand neutral, rendering "unto Caesar the things which be Caesar's and unto God the things which be God's," and insuring the completeness of separation of church and state.

In the light of this interpretation, is the act void for uncertainty? I think not. If the act were affirmative in its requirements, calling for the teaching of some theory, the objection would be more plausible. A clear chart is more necessary when one must move, over matter or in mind, then when one is required merely not to teach or act. Any reasonable intelligence should be able to understand and observe the plain prohibition against instilling into the minds of the pupils a denial that he is a creation of God, but rather a product of the beast of the field; against teaching, and the term is here employed in the sense of seeking to convince, the pupil affirmatively that his origin is not divine, but material through the animal. He who runs may read. He need do no guessing as to what particular conception or view of the Bible account he shall teach. The act does not require that he choose between the fundamentalist and the modernist, the literalist and the liberalist. Our laws approve no teaching of the Bible at all in the public schools, but require only that no theory shall be taught which denies that God is the Creator of man—that his origin is not thus to be traced.

In brief, as already indicated, I concur with the majority in the conclusion (1) that this case must be reversed for the error of the judge in fixing the fine; (2) that a nolle prosequi should be entered; and (3) that the act is constitutional as within the power of the Legislature as the employer of its teachers. However, I go further and find the act constitutional for additional reasons, rested upon the view that the act fairly construed is limited to the prohibition of the teaching of any theory of evolution only which denies the divine creation of man, without regard to details of religious belief, or differing interpretations of the story as taught in the Bible. In this view the constitutionality of the act is sustained, but the way is left open for such teaching of the pertinent sciences as is approved by the progressive God recognizing leaders of thought and life.

McKINNEY, J. (dissenting). An elemental rule of statutory construction, which is well stated by Mr. Justice Sutherland in delivering the opinion of the Supreme Court of the United States in Connally v. General Construction Co., 269 U.S. 385, 46 S. Ct. 126, 70 L. Ed. 322, is as follows:

"That the terms of a penal statute creating a new offense must be sufficiently explicit to inform those who are subject to it what conduct on their part will render them liable to its penalties is a well-recognized requirement, consonant alike with ordinary notions of fair play and the settled rules of law; and a statute which either forbids or requires the doing of an act in terms so vague that men of common intelligence must necessarily guess at its meaning and differ as to its application violates the first essential of due process of law. International Harvester Co. v. Kentucky, 234 U. S. 216, 221, 34 S. Ct. 853,

58 L. Ed. 1284; Collins v. Kentucky, 234 U. S. 634, 638, 34 S. Ct. 924, 58 L. Ed. 1510."

Applying the foregoing rule to the statute here invoked, I am of the opinion that it is invalid for uncertainty of meaning. I therefore respectfully dissent from the contrary holding of my associates.

NOTES

1.   "An act prohibiting the teaching of the evolution theory in all the Universities, normals and other public schools of Tennessee, which are supported in whole or in part by the public school funds of the state, and to provide penalties for the violations thereof.

"Section 1. Be it enacted by the General Assembly of the state of Tennessee, that it shall be unlawful for any teacher in any of the Universities, normals and all other public schools of the state which are supported in whole or in part by the public school funds of the state, to teach any theory that denies the story of the divine creation of man as taught in the Bible and to teach instead that man has descended from a lower order of animals.

"Sec. 2. Be it further enacted, that any teacher found guilty of the violation of this act, shall be guilty of a misdemeanor and upon conviction shall be fined not less than one hundred ($100.00) dollars nor more than five hundred ($500.00) dollars for each offense.

"Sec. 3. Be it further enacted, that this act take effect from and after its passage, the public welfare requiring it."

THE Arkansas "Anti-Evolution" statute, which prohibited "the teaching in its public schools and universities of the theory that man evolved from other species of life," is declared unconstitutional by the United States Supreme Court. Delivering the opinion of the Court, Justice Fortas stated: "The State's undoubted right to prescribe the curriculum for its public schools does not carry with it the right to prohibit, on pain of criminal penalty, the teaching of a scientific theory or doctrine where that prohibition is based upon reasons that violate the First Amendment. It is much too late to argue that the State may impose upon the teachers in its schools any conditions that it chooses, however restrictive they may be of constitutional guarantees. . . . Arkansas' law cannot be defended as an act of religious neutrality. Arkansas did not seek to excise from its curricula of its schools and universities all discussion of the origin of man. The law's effort was confined to an attempt to blot out a particular theory because of its supposed conflict with the Biblical account, literally read. Plainly, the law is contrary to the mandate of the First, and in violation of the Fourteenth, Amendment to the Constitution."

Epperson v. *Arkansas*, 393 U.S. 97 (1968)

MR. JUSTICE FORTAS delivered the opinion of the Court.

I

This appeal challenges the constitutionality of the "anti-evolution" statute which the State of Arkansas adopted in 1928 to prohibit the teaching in its public schools and universities of the theory that man evolved from other species of life. The statute was a product of the upsurge of "fundamentalist" religious fervor of the twenties. The Arkansas statute was an adaptation of the famous Tennessee "monkey law" which that State adopted in 1925.[1] The constitutionality of the Tennessee law was upheld by the Tennessee Supreme Court in the celebrated *Scopes* case in 1927.[2]

The Arkansas law makes it unlawful for a teacher in any state-supported school or university "to teach the theory or doctrine that mankind ascended or descended from a lower order of animals," or "to adopt or use in any such institution a textbook that teaches" this theory. Violation is a misdemeanor and subjects the violator to dismissal from his position.[3]

The present case concerns the teaching of biology in a high school in Little Rock. According to the testimony, until the events here in litigation, the official textbook furnished for the high school biology course did not have a section on the Darwinian Theory. Then, for the academic year 1965-1966, the school administration, on recommendation of the teachers of biology in the school system, adopted and prescribed a textbook which contained a chapter setting forth "the theory about the origin . . . of man from a lower form of animal."

Susan Epperson, a young woman who graduated from Arkansas' school system and then obtained her master's degree in zoology at the University of Illinois, was employed by the Little Rock school system in the fall of 1964 to teach 10th grade biology at Central High School. At the start of the next academic year, 1965, she was confronted by the new textbook (which one surmises from the record was not unwelcome to her). She faced at least a literal dilemma because she was supposed to use the new textbook for classroom instruction and presumably to teach the statutorily condemned chapter; but to do so would be a criminal offense and subject her to dismissal.

She instituted the present action in the Chancery Court of the State, seeking a declaration that the Arkansas statute is void and enjoining the State and the defendant officials of the Little Rock school system from dismissing her for violation of the statute's provisions. H. H. Blanchard, a parent of children attending the public schools, intervened in support of the action.

The Chancery Court, in an opinion by Chancellor Murray O. Reed, held that the statute violated the Fourteenth Amendment to the United States Constitution.[4] The court noted that this Amendment encompasses the prohibitions upon state interference with freedom of speech and thought which are contained in the First Amendment. Accordingly, it held that the challenged statute is unconstitutional because, in violation of the First Amendment, it "tends to hinder the quest for knowledge, restrict the freedom to learn, and restrain the freedom to teach."[5] In this perspective, the Act, it held, was an unconstitutional and void restraint upon the freedom of speech guaranteed by the Constitution.

On appeal, the Supreme Court of Arkansas reversed.[6] Its two-sentence opinion is set forth in the margin.[7] It sustained the statute as an exercise of the State's power to specify the curriculum in public schools. It did not address itself to the competing constitutional considerations.

Appeal was duly prosecuted to this Court under 28 U. S. C. § 1257 (2). Only Arkansas and Mississippi have such "anti-evolution" or "monkey" laws on their books.[8] There is no record of any prosecutions in Arkansas under its statute. It is possible that the statute is presently more of a curiosity than a vital fact of life in these States.[9] Nevertheless, the present case was brought, the appeal as of right is properly here, and it is our duty to decide the issues presented.

II

At the outset, it is urged upon us that the challenged statute is vague and uncertain and therefore within the condemnation of the Due Process Clause of the Fourteenth Amendment. The contention that the Act is vague and uncertain is supported by language in the brief opinion of Arkansas' Supreme Court. That court, perhaps reflecting the discomfort which the statute's quixotic prohibition necessarily engenders in the modern mind,[10] stated that it "expresses no opinion" as to whether the Act prohibits "explanation" of the theory of evolution or merely forbids "teaching that the theory is true." Regardless of this uncertainty, the court held that the statute is constitutional.

On the other hand, counsel for the State, in oral argument in this Court, candidly stated that, despite the State Supreme Court's equivocation, Arkansas would interpret the statute "to mean that to make a student aware of the theory . . . just to teach that there was such a theory" would be grounds for dismissal and for prosecution under the statute; and he said "that the

Supreme Court of Arkansas' opinion should be interpreted in that manner." He said: "If Mrs. Epperson would tell her students that 'Here is Darwin's theory, that man ascended or descended from a lower form of being,' then I think she would be under this statute liable for prosecution."

In any event, we do not rest our decision upon the asserted vagueness of the statute. On either interpretation of its language, Arkansas' statute cannot stand. It is of no moment whether the law is deemed to prohibit mention of Darwin's theory, or to forbid any or all of the infinite varieties of communication embraced within the term "teaching." Under either interpretation, the law must be stricken because of its conflict with the constitutional prohibition of state laws respecting an establishment of religion or prohibiting the free exercise thereof. The overriding fact is that Arkansas' law selects from the body of knowledge a particular segment which it proscribes for the sole reason that it is deemed to conflict with a particular religious doctrine; that is, with a particular interpretation of the Book of Genesis by a particular religious group.[11]

III

The antecedents of today's decision are many and unmistakable. They are rooted in the foundation soil of our Nation. They are fundamental to freedom.

Government in our democracy, state and national, must be neutral in matters of religious theory, doctrine, and practice. It may not be hostile to any religion or to the advocacy of no-religion; and it may not aid, foster, or promote one religion or religious theory against another or even against the militant opposite. The First Amendment mandates governmental neutrality between religion and religion, and between religion and nonreligion.[12]

As early as 1872, this Court said: "The law knows no heresy, and is committed to the support of no dogma, the establishment of no sect." Watson v. Jones, 13 Wall. 679, 728. This has been the interpretation of the great First Amendment which this Court has applied in the many and subtle problems which the ferment of our national life has presented for decision within the Amendment's broad command.

Judicial interposition in the operation of the public school system of the Nation raises problems requiring care and restraint. Our courts, however, have not failed to apply the First Amendment's mandate in our educational system where essential to safeguard the fundamental values of freedom of speech and inquiry and of belief. By and large, public education in our Nation is committed to the control of state and local authorities. Courts do not and cannot intervene in the resolution of conflicts which arise in the daily operation of school systems and which do not directly and sharply implicate basic constitutional values.[13] On the other hand, "[t]he vigilant protection of constitutional freedoms is nowhere more vital than in the community of American schools," *Shelton* v. *Tucker*, 364 U. S. 479, 487 (1960). As this Court said in *Keyishian* v. *Board of Regents*, the First Amendment "does not tolerate laws that cast a pall of orthodoxy over the classroom." 385 U. S. 589, 603 (1967).

The earliest cases in this Court on the subject of the impact of constitutional guarantees upon the classroom were decided before the Court expressly applied the specific prohibitions of the First Amendment to the States. But as early as 1923, the Court did not hesitate to condemn under the Due Process Clause "arbitrary" restrictions upon the freedom of teachers to teach and of students to learn. In that year, the Court, in an opinion by Justice McReynolds, held unconstitutional an Act of the State of Nebraska making it a crime to teach any subject in any language other than English to pupils who had not passed the eighth grade.[14] The State's purpose in enacting the law was to promote civic cohesiveness by encouraging the learning of English and to combat the "baneful effect" of permitting foreigners to rear and educate their children in the language of the parents' native land. The Court recognized these purposes, and it acknowledged the State's power to prescribe the school curriculum, but it held that these were not adequate to support the restriction upon the liberty of teacher and pupil. The challenged statute, it held, unconstitutionally interfered with the right of the individual, guaranteed by the Due Process Clause, to engage in any of the common occupations of life and to acquire useful knowledge. *Meyer* v. *Nebraska*, 262 U. S. 390 (1923). See also *Bartels* v. *Iowa*, 262 U. S. 404 (1923).

For purposes of the present case, we need not re-enter the difficult terrain which the Court, in 1923, traversed without apparent misgivings. We need not take advantage of the broad premise which the Court's decision in *Meyer* furnishes, nor need we explore the implications of that decision in terms of the justiciability of the multitude of controversies that beset our campuses today. Today's problem is capable of resolution in the narrower terms of the First Amendment's prohibition of laws respecting an establishment of religion or prohibiting the free exercise thereof.

There is and can be no doubt that the First Amendment does not permit the State to require that teaching and learning must be tailored to the principles or prohibitions of any religious sect or dogma. In *Everson* v. *Board of Education*, this Court, in upholding a state law to provide free bus service to school children, including those attending parochial schools, said: "Neither [a State nor the Federal Government] can pass laws which aid one religion, aid all religions, or prefer one religion over another." 330 U. S. 1, 15 (1947).

At the following Term of Court, in *McCollum* v. *Board of Education*, 333 U. S. 203 (1948), the Court held that Illinois could not release pupils from class to attend classes of instruction in the school buildings in the religion of their choice. This, it said, would involve the State in using tax-supported property for religious purposes, thereby breaching the "wall of separation" which, according to Jefferson, the First Amendment was intended to erect between church and state. *Id.*, at 211. See also *Engel* v. *Vitale*, 370 U. S. 421 (1962); *Abington School District* v. *Schempp*, 374 U. S. 203 (1963). While study of religions and of the Bible from a literary and historic viewpoint, presented objectively as part of a secular program of education, need not collide with the First Amendment's prohibition, the State may not adopt programs or practices in its public schools or colleges which "aid or oppose" any religion. *Id.*, at 225. This prohibition is absolute. It forbids alike the preference of a religious doctrine or the prohibition of theory which is deemed antagonistic to a particular dogma. As Mr. Justice Clark stated in *Joseph Burstyn, Inc.* v. *Wilson*, "the state has no legitimate interest in protecting any or all religions from views distasteful to them. . . ." 343 U. S. 495, 505 (1952). The test was stated as follows in *Abington School District* v. *Schempp, supra*, at 222: "[W]hat are the purpose and the primary effect of the enactment? If either is the advancement or inhibition of religion then the enactment exceeds the scope of legislative power as circumscribed by the Constitution."

These precedents inevitably determine the result in the present case. The State's undoubted right to prescribe the curriculum for its public schools does not carry with it the right to prohibit, on pain of criminal penalty, the teaching of a scientific theory or doctrine where that prohibition is based upon reasons that violate the First Amendment. It is much too late to argue that the State may impose upon the teachers in its schools any conditions that it chooses, however restrictive they may be of constitutional guarantees. *Keyishian* v. *Board of Regents*, 385 U. S. 589, 605-606 (1967).

In the present case, there can be no doubt that Arkansas has sought to prevent its teachers from discussing the theory of evolution because it is contrary to the belief of some that the Book of Genesis must be the exclusive source of doctrine as to the origin of man. No suggestion has been made that Arkansas' law may be justified by considerations of state policy other than the religious views of some of its citizens.[15] It is clear that fundamentalist sectarian conviction was and is the law's reason for existence.[16] Its antecedent, Tennessee's "monkey law," candidly stated its purpose: to make it unlawful "to teach any theory that denies the story of the Divine Creation of man as taught in the Bible, and to teach instead that man has descended from a lower order of animals."[17] Perhaps the sensational publicity attendant upon the *Scopes* trial induced Arkansas to adopt less explicit language.[18] It eliminated Tennessee's reference to "the story of the Divine Creation of man" as taught in the Bible, but there is no doubt that the motivation for the law was the same: to suppress the teaching of a theory which, it was thought, "denied" the divine creation of man.

Arkansas' law cannot be defended as an act of religious neutrality. Arkansas did not seek to excise from the curricula of its schools and universities all discussion of the origin of man. The law's effort was confined to an attempt to blot out a particular theory because of its supposed conflict with the Biblical account, literally read. Plainly, the law is contrary to the mandate of the First, and in violation of the Fourteenth, Amendment to the Constitution.

The judgment of the Supreme Court of Arkansas is   *Reversed.*

NOTES

1. Chapter 27, Tenn. Acts 1925; Tenn. Code Ann. § 49-1922 (1966 Repl. Vol.).

2. *Scopes* v. *State,* 154 Tenn. 105, 289 S. W. 363 (1927). The Tennessee court, however, reversed Scopes' conviction on the ground that the jury and not the judge should have assessed the fine of $100. Since Scopes was no longer in the State's employ, it saw "nothing to be gained by prolonging the life of this bizarre case." It directed that a *nolle prosequi* be entered, in the interests of "the peace and dignity of the State." 154 Tenn., at 121, 289 S. W., at 367.

3. Initiated Act No. 1, Ark. Acts 1929; Ark. Stat. Ann. § § 80-1627, 80-1628 (1960 Repl. Vol.). The text of the law is as follows:

   "§80-1627.—Doctrine of ascent or descent of man from lower order of animals prohibited.—It shall be unlawful for any teacher or other instructor in any University, College, Normal, Public School, or other institution of the State, which is supported in whole or in part from public funds derived by State and local taxation to teach the theory or doctrine that mankind ascended or descended from a lower order of animals and also it shall be unlawful for any teacher, textbook commission, or other authority exercising the power to select textbooks for above mentioned educational institutions to adopt or use in any such institution a textbook that teaches the doctrine or theory that mankind descended or ascended from a lower order of animals.

   "§80-1628.—Teaching doctrine or adopting textbook mentioning doctrine—Penalties—Positions to be vacated.—Any teacher or other instructor or textbook commissioner who is found guilty of violation of this act by teaching the theory or doctrine mentioned in section 1 hereof, or by using, or adopting any such textbooks in any such educational institution shall be guilty of a mis-

demeanor and upon conviction shall be fined not exceeding five hundred dollars; and upon conviction shall vacate the position thus held in any educational institutions of the character above mentioned or any commission of which he may be a member."

4. The opinion of the Chancery Court is not officially reported.

5. The Chancery Court analyzed the holding of its sister State of Tennessee in the *Scopes* case sustaining Tennessee's similar statute. It refused to follow Tennessee's 1927 example. It declined to confine the judicial horizon to a view of the law as merely a direction by the State as employer to its employees. This sort of astigmatism, it held, would ignore overriding constitutional values, and "should not be followed," and it proceeded to confront the substance of the law and its effect.

6. 242 Ark. 922, 416 S. W. 2d 322 (1967).

7. "Per Curiam. Upon the principal issue, that of constitutionality, the court holds that Initiated Measure No. 1 of 1928, Ark. Stat. Ann. § 80-1627 and § 80-1628, (Repl. 1960), is a valid exercise of the state's power to specify the curriculum in its public schools. The court expresses no opinion on the question whether the Act prohibits any explanation of the theory of evolution or merely prohibits teaching that the theory is true; the answer not being necessary to a decision in the case, and the issue not having been raised.

   "The decree is reversed and the cause dismissed.

   "Ward, J., concurs. Brown, J., dissents.

   "Paul Ward, Justice, concurring. I agree with the first sentence in the majority opinion.

   "To my mind, the rest of the opinion beclouds the clear announcement made in the first sentence."

8. Miss. Code Ann. § § 6798, 6799 (1942). Ark. Stat. Ann. § § 80-1627, 80-1628 (1960 Repl. Vol.) The Tennessee law was repealed in 1967. Oklahoma enacted an anti-evolution law, but it was repealed in 1926. The Florida and Texas Legislatures, in the period between 1921 and 1929, adopted resolutions against teaching the doctrine of evolution. In all, during that period, bills to this effect were introduced in 20 States. American Civil Liberties Union (ACLU), The Gag on Teaching 8 (2d ed., 1937).

9. Clarence Darrow, who was counsel for the defense in the *Scopes* trial, in his biography published in 1932, somewhat sardonically pointed out that States with anti-evolution laws did not insist upon the fundamentalist theory in all respects. He said: "I understand that the States of Tennessee and Mississippi both continue to teach that the earth is round and that the revolution on its axis brings the day and night, in spite of all opposition." The Story of My Life 247 (1932).

10. R. Hofstadter & W. Metzger, in The Development of Academic Freedom in the United States 324 (1955), refer to some of Darwin's opponents as "exhibiting a kind of phylogenetic snobbery [which led them] to think that Darwin had libeled the [human] race by discovering simian rather than seraphic ancestors."

11. In *Scopes* v. *State,* 154 Tenn. 105, 126, 289 S. W. 363, 369 (1927), Judge Chambliss, concurring, referred to the defense contention that Tennessee's anti-evolution law

gives a "preference" to "religious establishments which have as one of their tenets or dogmas the instantaneous creation of man."

12. *Everson* v. *Board of Education,* 330 U. S. 1, 18 (1947); *McCollum* v. *Board of Education,* 333 U. S. 203 (1948); *Zorach* v. *Clauson,* 343 U. S. 306, 313-314 (1952); *Fowler* v. *Rhode Island,* 345 U. S. 67 (1953); *Torcaso* v. *Watkins,* 367 U. S. 488, 495 (1961).

13. See the discussion in Developments in The Law— Academic Freedom, 81 Harv. L. Rev. 1045, 1051-1055 (1968).

14. The case involved a conviction for teaching "the subject of reading in the German language" to a child of 10 years.

15. Former Dean Leflar of the University of Arkansas School of Law has stated that "the same ideological considerations underlie the anti-evolution enactment" as underlie the typical blasphemy statute. He says that the purpose of these statutes is an "ideological" one which "involves an effort to prevent (by censorship) or punish the presentation of intellectually significant matter which contradicts accepted social, moral or religious ideas." Leflar, Legal Liability for the Exercise of Free Speech, 10 Ark. L. Rev. 155, 158 (1956). See also R. Hofstadter & W. Metzger, The Development of Academic Freedom in the United States 320-366 (1955) (*passim*); H. Beale, A History of Freedom of Teaching in American Schools 202-207 (1941); Emerson & Haber, The *Scopes* Case in Modern Dress, 27 U. Chi. L. Rev. 522 (1960); Waller, The Constitutionality of the Tennessee Anti-Evolution Act, 35 Yale L. J. 191 (1925) (*passim*); ACLU, The Gag on Teaching 7 (2d ed., 1937); J. Scopes & J. Presley, Center of the Storm 45-53 (1967).

16. The following advertisement is typical of the public appeal which was used in the campaign to secure adoption of the statute:

"THE BIBLE OR ATHEISM, WHICH?

"All atheists favor evolution. If you agree with atheism vote against Act No. 1. If you agree with the Bible vote for Act No. 1. . . . Shall conscientious church members be forced to pay taxes to support teachers to teach evolution which will undermine the faith of their children? The Gazette said Russian Bolshevists laughed at Tennessee. True, and that sort will laugh at Arkansas. Who cares? Vote FOR ACT NO. 1." The Arkansas Gazette, Little Rock, Nov. 4, 1928, p. 12, cols. 4-5.

Letters from the public expressed the fear that teaching of evolution would be "subversive of Christianity," *id.,* Oct. 24, 1928, p. 7, col. 2; see also *id.,* Nov. 4, 1928, p. 19, col. 4; and that it would cause school children "to disrespect the Bible," *id.,* Oct. 27, 1928, p. 15, col. 5. One letter read: "The cosmogony taught by [evolution] runs contrary to that of Moses and Jesus, and as such is nothing, if anything at all, but atheism. . . . Now let the mothers and fathers of our state that are trying to raise their children in the Christian faith arise in their might and vote for this anti-evolution bill that will take it out of our tax supported schools. When they have saved the children, they have saved the state." *Id.,* at cols. 4-5.

17. Arkansas' law was adopted by popular initiative in 1928, three years after Tennessee's law was enacted and one year after the Tennessee Supreme Court's decision in the *Scopes* case, *supra.*

18. In its brief, the State says that the Arkansas statute was passed with the holding of the *Scopes* case in mind. Brief for Appellee 1.

A United States District Court in Maryland decides against school children and their parents who sought to have the District Court declare unconstitutional a state board of education bylaw that provided: "It is the responsibility of the local school system to provide a comprehensive program of family life and sex education in every elementary and secondary school for all students as an integral part of the curriculum including a planned and sequential program of health education." In deciding against the children and parents who sought to prevent the implementation of the "sex education program," the Court stated: ". . . It is quite clear to this Court that the purpose and primary effect of the bylaw here is not to establish any particular religious dogma or precept, and that the bylaw does not directly or substantially involve the state in religious exercises or in the favoring of religion or any particular religion. The bylaw may be considered quite simply as a public health measure."

Cornwell v. *State Bd. of Education,* 314 F. Supp. 340 (1969)

HARVEY, District Judge:

In this civil action, Baltimore County taxpayers are suing the Maryland State Board of Education seeking to prevent the implementation in the Baltimore County Schools of a program of sex education. In particular, the plaintiffs, who are school children and their parents, seek to have this Court declare unconstitutional a bylaw duly adopted by the State Board. The provision in question is By-Law 720, Section 3, Subsection 4, which provides as follows:

"It is the responsibility of the local school system to provide a comprehensive program of family life and sex education in every elementary and secondary school for all students as an integral part of the curriculum including a planned and sequential program of health education."

The plaintiffs ask for the following relief (paragraph 14 of the complaint):

"Wherefore, plaintiffs demand judgment that the defendants . . . be perpetually and permanently enjoined and restrained from promulgating, teaching, initiating or enforcing any of the tenets found within Sub-section 4 of By-Law 720:3 as they pertain to non-pregnant children, as such By-Law was enacted in July, 1967; and plaintiffs further pray for a preliminary injunction . . . and . . . other . . . relief."

The plaintiffs claim that jurisdiction exists here because the by-law in question violates the First Amendment, the Equal Protection Clause of the Fourteenth Amendment and the Due Process Clause of the Fourteenth Amendment. Defendants have filed motions to dismiss the complaint.

At the outset, it should be noted that the plaintiffs have not requested in this complaint the convening of a three-judge court. However, it would appear that this is a proper case for such a court. See 28 U. S. C. Section 2281; also American Federation of Labor v. Watson, 327 U. S. 582, 592, 66 S.Ct. 761, 90 L.Ed. 873 (1946), quoting from Phillips v. United States, 312 U. S. 246, 251, 61 S.Ct. 480, 85 L. Ed. 800 (1941). But, the mere fact that plaintiffs have not requested a three-judge court does not mean that the action is subject to summary dismissal. In this connection, see Aaron v. Cooper, 261 F.2d 97, 105 (8th Cir. 1958). Therefore, this action will be treated as one in which a three-judge court was requested but with respect to which the suit has been referred to one judge to make the initial determination whether the suit is subject to dismissal.

It is clear that one judge may dismiss if he finds that a constitutional claim is so insubstantial that there is no jurisdiction. As the Supreme Court noted in Ex parte Poresky, 290 U. S. 30, 54 S.Ct. 3, 78 L.Ed. 152 (1933), for jurisdiction to exist in a three-judge court case there must be a substantial question of constitutionality. The Court further said the following (at page 32, 54 S.Ct. at page 4):

"The question may be plainly unsubstantial, either because it is 'obviously without merit' or because 'its unsoundness so clearly results from the previous decisions of this court as to foreclose the subject . . .' ."

See also the Fourth Circuit decision of Jacobs v. Tawes, 250 F.2d 611 (4th Cir. 1957); Bailey v. Patterson, 369 U. S. 31, 33, 82 S.Ct. 549, 7 L.Ed.2d 512 (1962), and a recent decision of Judge Kaufman in this Court, Chester v. Kinnamon, 276 F. Supp. 717 (D. Md. 1967). Judge Kaufman, at page 720, said this:

"Under 28 U. S. C. § § 2281 and 2284 (1) this Court is required to ask the Chief Judge of the United States Circuit Court for the Fourth Circuit to convene a three-judge District Court *only* if there is a substantial, nonfrivolous attack upon the constitutionality of a Maryland statute, but not otherwise." (Emphasis in original)

In determining whether there is here a substantial question of constitutionality, this Court concludes initially that no question whatsoever arises under the Fourteenth Amendment. There is first no denial of substantive due process to the plaintiffs. Under Section 6 of Article 77 of the Maryland Code (as amended and recodified by Chapter 405 of the Acts of 1969), the State Board is directed to determine the educational policies of the state and to enact bylaws for the administration of the public school system, which when enacted and published shall have the force of law. Assuredly it cannot be said that the by-law here is an arbitrary or unreasonable exercise of the authority vested in the State Board to determine a teaching curriculum, nor that there is no basis in fact for the legislative policy expressed in the bylaw. Furthermore, it does not appear that the bylaw denies equal protection of the laws, as on its face it applies to all pupils equally.

Plaintiffs allege that the enactment of this bylaw was based on a study made in reference to pregnant pupils. But whatever the genesis of the bylaw, it is not the study that is being attacked here but the bylaw itself, and it is being attacked on its face. It is the provisions of the bylaw then that must be examined in the light of the United States Constitution. The plaintiffs' argument that the bylaw is defective because it applies to non-pregnant as well as to pregnant pupils is difficult to follow. There would appear to be just as much reason for the State Board to provide sex education for the non-pregnant (and, incidentally, for the non-impregnating) as for those students who, because of a lack of information on the subject (or for other reasons), have become pregnant or who have caused pregnancy.

The plaintiffs further assert that they have the exclusive constitutional right to teach their children about sexual matters in their own homes, and that such exclusive right would prohibit the teaching of sex in the schools. No authority is cited in support of this novel proposition, and this Court knows of no such constitutional right. This Court, then, is satisfied that the claims asserted in this complaint under the Fourteenth Amendment are so insubstantial that they do not confer jurisdiction here.

In support of their First Amendment claim, the plaintiffs assert that they have been denied the free exercise of their religious concepts and that the teaching of sex in the Baltimore County Schools will in fact establish religious concepts. In Everson v. Board of Education, 330 U. S. 1, 67 S.Ct. 504, 91 L.Ed. 711 (1947), the Supreme Court said that the Establishment Clause meant the following (at page 15, 67 S.Ct. at page 511):

"Neither a state nor the Federal Government can set up a church. Neither can pass laws which aid one religion, aid all religions, or prefer one religion over another."

In the more recent case of School District of Abington Township v. Schempp, 374 U. S. 203, 225, 83 S.Ct. 1560, 1573, 10 L.Ed.2d 844 (1963), the Supreme Court said that the actual study of the Bible and of religion, "when presented objectively as part of a secular program of education" would not offend the Establishment Clause. Earlier in that opinion, at page 222, 83 S. Ct. at page 1571, the Court formulated a basic test for determining the validity of a legislative provision under the Establishment Clause of the First Amendment as follows:

"[W]hat are the purpose and the primary effect of the enactment? If either is the advancement or inhibition of religion then the enactment exceeds the scope of legislative power as circumscribed by the Constitution."

It is clear from the cases that the First Amendment does not say that in every and all respects there shall be a separation of church and state. See Zorach v. Clauson, 343 U.S. 306, 312, 72 S.Ct. 679, 96 L.Ed. 954 (1952). As Mr. Justice Brennan said, concurring in the *Schempp* case, the Framers meant only to foreclose "those involvements of religious with secular institutions which (a) serve the essentially religious activities of religious institutions; (b) employ the organs of government for essentially religious purposes; or (c) use essentially religious means to serve governmental ends, where secular means would suffice." 374 U.S. at 295, 83 S.Ct. at 1609.

Here it is helpful to look at those cases in which the

Supreme Court has found an establishment of religion in violation of the First Amendment. I would note Engel v. Vitale, 370 U.S. 421, 82 S.Ct. 1261, 8 L.Ed.2d 601 (1962), where official prayers to be recited in the classroom were held unconstitutional. I would further note Chamberlin v. Dade County Board of Public Instruction, 377 U.S. 402, 84 S.Ct. 1272, 12 L.Ed.2d 407 (1964), and the *Schempp* case to which I have previously referred, where devotional Bible reading and recitation of the Lord's Prayer were held to be in violation of the First Amendment. I would note People of State of Illinois ex rel. McCollum v. Board of Education, 333 U.S. 203, 68 S.Ct. 461, 92 L.Ed. 649 (1948), where the employment of teachers by private religious groups to give religious instruction in the schools to those children whose parents desired it was held to be proscribed.

On the other hand, where such overt religious activities have been absent, the Supreme Court has upheld governmental programs even though they had some religious connection. Here I would refer to the *Everson* case, *supra,* where the reimbursement of parents for transportation expenses to parochial schools was upheld, Zorach v. Clauson, *supra,* where a released-time program allowing students to attend religious instruction centers off school grounds during the school day was upheld, and Board of Education v. Allen, 392 U.S. 236, 88 S.Ct. 1923, 20 L.Ed.2d 1060 (1968), where the loan by the state of textbooks to students in parochial schools was also upheld.

A very recent and pertinent decision of the Supreme Court is Epperson v. Arkansas, 393 U.S. 97, 89 S.Ct. 266, 21 L.Ed.2d 228 (1968). There the Arkansas anti-evolution statute was under challenge. That act made it a criminal offense to teach the theory that man evolved from a lower form of animal life. The Supreme Court found the act to be an unconstitutional violation of the Establishment and Free Exercise Clauses and held that a state may not proscribe the teaching of a particular segment of knowledge solely because it conflicts with a particular doctrine of a particular religious group. In that case, the Court said this (at page 104, 89 S.Ct. at page 270):

"Judicial interposition in the operation of the public school system of the Nation raises problems requiring care and restraint. . . . By and large, public education in our Nation is committed to the control of state and local authorities. Courts do not and cannot intervene in the resolution of conflicts which arise in the daily operation of school systems and which do not directly and sharply implicate basic constitutional values."

The Court further asserted in that case that the state may neither prefer any religion nor prohibit any theory just because it be deemed antagonistic to the principles or prohibitions of any religious sect or dogma. The Court quoted in the *Epperson* case from Joseph Burstyn, Inc. v. Wilson, 343 U.S. 495, 505, 72 S.Ct. 777, 782, 96 L.Ed. 1098 (1952), as follows:

"[T]he state has no legitimate interest in protecting any or all religions from views distasteful to them. . . . "

Rather, the test is that enumerated in the *Schempp* case, which I have previously cited, namely, what are the purpose and the primary effect of the enactment. And I would interpolate in the quotation from the *Burstyn* case to say that this Court likewise has no legitimate interest in protecting any or all religions from views distasteful to them.

Applying these principles that have been established by these various cases, it is quite clear to this Court that the purpose and primary effect of the bylaw here is not to establish any particular religious dogma or precept, and that the bylaw does not directly or substantially involve the state in religious exercises or in the favoring of religion or any particular religion. The bylaw may be considered quite simply as a public health measure. As the Supreme Court indicated in Prince v. Massachusetts, 321 U.S. 158, 64 S.Ct. 438, 88 L.Ed. 645 (1944), the State's interest in the health of its children outweighs claims based upon religious freedom and the right of parental control. The Court in that particular case said this (at pages 168-169, 64 S.Ct. at page 443):

"A democratic society rests . . . upon the healthy, well-rounded growth of young people into full maturity as citizens. . . . It is too late now to doubt that legislation appropriately designed to reach such evils is within the state's police power, whether against the parent's claim to control of the child or one that religious scruples dictate contrary action."

In summary, then, the Court concludes that the federal question here is plainly insubstantial. Construing the allegations in a light most favorable to the plaintiffs, as the Court must do on these motions to dismiss, this Court finds that the constitutional questions relied upon are obviously without merit. The unsoundness and insubstantiality of the plaintiffs' position is clearly indicated by the various decisions of the Supreme Court to which I have alluded.

For these reasons then, the two motions to dismiss are granted.

THE United States Court of Appeals, First Circuit, decides for a high school English teacher who had been suspended for assigning to his senior English class an *Atlantic Monthly* article which contained "a vulgar word for an incestuous son" and who had refused to agree never to use "the word" again in the classroom. The Court stated: " . . . the question in this case is whether a teacher may, for demonstrated educational purposes, quote a 'dirty' word currently used in order to give special offense, or whether the shock is too great for high school seniors to stand. If the answer were that the students must be protected from such exposure, we would fear for their future. We do not question the good faith of the defendants in believing that some parents have been offended. With the greatest of respect to such parents, their sensibilities are not the full measure of what is proper education."

Keefe v. *Geanakos*, 418 F.2d 359 (1969)

ALDRICH, Chief Judge.

Plaintiff, who unsuccessfully sought from the district court a temporary injunction pendente lite, requests a stay, or more precisely, a temporary injunction, from us pending our determination of his appeal from the district court's refusal.[1] The matter is before us on the complaint, the answer, affidavits and exhibits introduced by both sides, certain statements of counsel, and the findings of the district court as contained in its opinion dated November 6, 1969.

The plaintiff is the head of the English department and coordinator for grades 7 through 12 for the Ipswich (Massachusetts) Public School System, with part-time duties as a teacher of English. He has tenure, pursuant to Mass.G.L. c. 71, § 41. The defendants are the members of the Ipswich School Committee.[2] Briefly, after some preliminaries, five charges were furnished the plaintiff as grounds for dismissal, and a hearing was scheduled thereon, which plaintiff seeks to enjoin as violating his civil rights. 42 U.S.C. § 1983. Jurisdiction is asserted under 28 U.S.C. § 1343(3) (4). In order to preserve the status quo, this hearing has not yet been held, and the defendants await our decision. The district court, in its opinion denying temporary relief, dealt with only one of the five charges, the third. We will hereafter refer to this as the charge.[3]

Reduced to fundamentals, the substance of plaintiff's position is that as a matter of law his conduct which forms the basis of the charge did not warrant discipline. Accordingly, he argues, there is no ground for

any hearing. He divides this position into two parts. The principal one is that his conduct was within his competence as a teacher, as a matter of academic freedom, whether the defendants approved of it or not. The second is that he had been given inadequate prior warning by such regulations as were in force, particularly in the light of the totality of the circumstances known to him, that his actions would be considered improper, so that an ex post facto ruling would, itself, unsettle academic freedom. The defendants, essentially, deny plaintiff's contentions. They accept the existence of a principle of academic freedom to teach,[4] but state that it is limited to proper classroom materials as reasonably determined by the school committee in the light of pertinent conditions, of which they cite in particular the age of the students. Asked by the court whether a teacher has a right to say to the school committee that it is wrong if, in fact, its decision was arbitrary, counsel candidly and commendably (and correctly) responded in the affirmative. This we consider to be the present issue. In reviewing the denial of interlocutory injunctive relief, the test that we of course apply is whether there is a probability that plaintiff will prevail on the merits. Automatic Radio Mfg. Co., Inc. v. Ford Motor Co., 1 Cir., 1968, 390 F.2d 113, cert. denied 391 U.S. 914, 88 S.Ct. 1807, 20 L.Ed.2d 653.

On the opening day of school in September 1969 the plaintiff gave to each member of his senior English class a copy of the September 1969 Atlantic Monthly magazine, a publication of high reputation, and state.] that the reading assignment for that night was the first article therein.[5] September was the educational number, so-called, of the Atlantic, and some 75 copies had been supplied by the school department. Plaintiff discussed the article, and a particular word that was used therein, and explained the word's origin and context, and the reasons the author had included it. The word, admittedly highly offensive, is a vulgar term for an incestuous son. Plaintiff stated that any student who felt the assignment personally distasteful could have an alternative one.

The next evening the plaintiff was called to a meeting of the school committee and asked to defend his use of the offending word. Following his explanation, a majority of the members of the committee asked him informally if he would agree not to use it again in the classroom. Plaintiff replied that he could not, in good conscience, agree. His counsel states, however, without contradiction, that in point of fact plaintiff has not used it again. No formal action was taken at this meeting. Thereafter plaintiff was suspended, as a matter of discipline, and it is now proposed that he should be discharged.[6]

The Lifton article, which we have read in its entirety, has been described as a valuable discussion of "dissent, protest, radicalism and revolt." It is in no sense pornographic. We need no supporting affidavits to find it scholarly, thoughtful and thought-provoking. The single offending word, although repeated a number of times, is not artificially introduced, but, on the contrary, is important to the development of the thesis and the conclusions of the author. Indeed, we would find it difficult to disagree with plaintiff's assertion that no proper study of the article could avoid consideration of this word. It is not possible to read the article, either in whole or in part, as an incitement to libidinous conduct, or even thoughts. If it raised the concept of incest, it was not to suggest it, but to condemn it; the word was used, by the persons described, as a superlative of opprobrium. We believe not only that the article negatived any other concept, but that an understanding of it would reject, rather than suggest, the word's use.

With regard to the word itself, we cannot think that it is unknown to many students in the last year of high school, and we might well take judicial notice of its use by young radicals and protesters from coast to coast.[7] No doubt its use genuinely offends the parents of some of the students—therein, in part, lay its relevancy to the article.

Hence the question in this case is whether a teacher may, for demonstrated educational purposes, quote a "dirty" word currently used in order to give special offense, or whether the shock is too great for high school

seniors to stand. If the answer were that the students must be protected from such exposure, we would fear for their future. We do not question the good faith of the defendants in believing that some parents have been offended.[8] With the greatest of respect to such parents, their sensibilities are not the full measure of what is proper education.

We of course agree with defendants that what is to be said or read to students is not to be determined by obscenity standards for adult consumption. Ginsberg v. New York, 1968, 390 U.S. 629, 88 S.Ct. 1274, 20 L.Ed.2d 195. At the same time, the issue must be one of degree. A high school senior is not devoid of all discrimination or resistance. Furthermore, as in all other instances, the offensiveness of language and the particular propriety or impropriety is dependent on the circumstances of the utterance.

Apart from cases discussing academic freedom in the large, not surprisingly we find no decisions closely in point. The district court cited what it termed the well-reasoned opinion of the district court in Parker v. Board of Education, D.Md., 1965, 237 F.Supp. 222, aff'd 4 Cir., 348 F.2d 464, cert. denied 382 U.S. 1030, 86 S.Ct. 653, 15 L.Ed.2d 543, regarding it "strikingly similar on its facts to the instant case, in that it too involved a high school teacher challenging his dismissal from employment in a public school system because of his assigning 'Brave New World' to a class as an infringement of his claimed First Amendment right to free speech. . . . " We do not find ourselves impressed by the *Parker* court's reasoning, or by the similarity of the facts. As to the latter, *Parker* was not a case where the teacher was dismissed. As the court of appeals pointed out, Parker, unlike plaintiff, did not have tenure, and his only complaint was that his contract was not renewed. With regard to the reasoning, we think it significant that the court of appeals affirmed the district court only on this distinguishing ground, and disclaimed approval of the balance of the opinion. We accept the conclusion of the court below that "some measure of public regulation of classroom speech is inherent in every provision of public education." But when we consider the facts at bar as we have elaborated them, we find it difficult not to think that its application to the present case demeans any proper concept of education. The general chilling effect of permitting such rigorous censorship is even more serious.[9]

We believe it equally probable that the plaintiff will prevail on the issue of lack of any notice that a discussion of this article with the senior class was forbidden conduct. The school regulation upon which defendants rely,[10] although unquestionably worthy, is not apposite. It does not follow that a teacher may not be on notice of impropriety from the circumstances of a case without the necessity of a regulation. In the present case, however, the circumstances would have disclosed that no less than five books, by as many authors, containing the word in question were to be found in the school library. It is hard to think that any student could walk into the library and receive a book, but that his teacher could not subject the content to serious discussion in class.

Such inconsistency on the part of the school has been regarded as fatal. Vought v. Van Buren Public Schools, E.D.Mich., 6/13/69, 38 Law Week 2034. We, too, would probably so regard it. At the same time, we prefer not to place our decision on this ground alone, lest our doing so diminish our principal holding, or lead to a bowdlerization of the school library.

Finally, we are not persuaded by the district court's conclusion that no irreparable injury is involved because the plaintiff, if successful, may recover money damages. Academic freedom is not preserved by compulsory retirement, even at full pay.

The immediate question before us is whether we should grant interlocutory relief pending appeal. This question, as defendants point out, raises the ultimate issue of the appeal itself. The matter has been extensively briefed and argued by both sides. We see no purpose in taking two bites, and believe this a case for action under Local Rule 5. The order of the district court denying an interlocutory injunction pending a decision on the merits is reversed and the case is remanded for further proceedings consistent herewith.

NOTES

1. Plaintiff did not seek a stay order from the district court pending appeal, but was excused from doing so because of the court's unavailability.
2. Two school officials are also named, but may be disregarded for purposes of this opinion.
3. The defendants agree that charges 1, 2 and 4 are dependent on charge 3. They do, however, wish to press separately charge 5. (Insubordination). The district

court did not deal with this charge, and the record does not permit us to do so. We do suspect, though, that however separate it may be, it is to some extent tied in with charge 3, and we believe that it would be better for all concerned to postpone consideration thereof until the disposition of the issue as to charge 3. We accordingly will make the same order, so far as temporary relief is concerned.

4. For a recent discussion of the cases see Developments in the Law—Academic Freedom, 81 Harv.L.Rev. 1048 (1968); cf. Wright, The Constitution on the Campus, 22 Vand.L.Rev. 1027 (1969).
5. "The Young and the Old," by Robert J. Lifton, a psychiatrist and professor at a noted medical school.
6. The question must be considered whether this suit is premature, at least so far as an injunction against holding the meeting is concerned, since conceivably the vote might be in plaintiff's favor. We intimated as much during oral argument, but defendants' counsel did not respond. Very possibly counsel recognize that dismissal is a foregone conclusion, as plaintiff suggests, or defendants feel that if, in fact, there is no cause for dismissal, they would prefer a declaratory decision in advance. Under the circumstances we accept jurisdiction as a matter of discretion.
7. E.g., "Up against the wall, motherfucker."
8. It is appropriate in this connection to consider what, exactly, is the charge with which plaintiff is presently faced. "3. Use of offensive material in the classroom on September 3, 1969, and subsequently, which use would undermine public confidence and react unfavorably upon the public school system of Ipswich. . . . "
9. "Such unwarranted inhibition upon the free spirit of teachers affects not only those who, like the appellants, are immediately before the Court. It has an unmistakable tendency to chill that free play of the spirit which all teachers ought especially to cultivate and practice. . . . " Frankfurter, J., concurring, in Wieman v. Updegraff, 1952, 344 U.S. 183, 194, 195, 73 S.Ct. 215, 221, 97 L.Ed. 216.
10. "1. Teachers shall use all possible care in safeguarding the health and moral welfare of their pupils, discountenancing promptly and emphatically: vandalism, falsehood, profanity, cruelty, or other form of vice." See also, Mass.G.L. c.71, § 30, "Moral Education."

THE Supreme Court of Hawaii decides against parents who had sought to enjoin school authorities from continuing to show to fifth and sixth graders a film series entitled "Time of Your Life" which was a "family living and sex education program." In deciding against the parents of the fifth and sixth graders, the Court said: "If we were to hold that the "family life and sex education" program adopted by the State is contrary to certain religious beliefs of some of our citizens and therefore unconstitutional on the grounds that it prevents the free exercise of their religion, we would come dangerously close to approving that which is prohibited by *Epperson*. We must be equally protective of the freedoms of speech, inquiry and belief as we are of the freedom of religion. Inasmuch as we have found no compulsion or coercion related to the educational Program in question, we find no violation of the First Amendment's Free Exercise of Religion Clause."

Medeiros v. *Kiyosaki,* 478 P.2d 314 (1970)

RICHARDSON, Chief Justice.

Plaintiffs-appellants, residents of the City and County of Honolulu and parents of 5th and 6th grade children in the public school system, sought to enjoin the defendants-appellees, Ralph H. Kiyosaki, the State Superintendent of Education, the members of the State Board of Education, and Alice M. Doyle, Program Specialist of the Department of Education, from continuing with a film series entitled "Time of Your Life." The film series was being shown in the 5th and 6th grade levels of the public school system as part of a newly adopted curriculum for family life and sex education. The plaintiffs based their action on the constitutional grounds that the program is an invasion of privacy and a violation of their religious freedom. Plaintiffs further alleged that the program was illegal because it was adopted by an improper delegation of authority by the State Board of Education to the administrative staff of the State Department of Education. The trial court dismissed the complaint and denied the request for injunctive relief.

Before turning to the issues involved in this appeal, a further description of the film series entitled "Time of Your Life" is warranted. In 1968 the legislature approved the Department of Education's intent to devote resources toward the planning and programming of instruction in the area of social problems.[1] These problems included, but were not limited to, family living and sex education.[2] Pursuant to this legislative approval, the Superintendent of Education, as chief executive officer of the Department, upon the recommendation of his staff, selected the program "Time of Your Life." It was developed for and is successfully being used on instructional television in San Francisco, California. The program involved has been described as a "family living and sex education program" for the 5th and 6th grades and may be characterized as a socio-physiological educational program.[3] It consists of 15 lessons covering subject areas of interpersonal relationships, self-understanding, family structure and sex education. Lessons 1 through 10 are psychologically and sociologically oriented. Lessons 11 through 15 concern sexuality and sexual development. Each lesson consists of a twenty minute film designed for viewing over Educational Television. It is supplemented with preparatory and follow-up activities planned by the individual classroom teacher and is geared to the needs of the individual class. Although it is primarily lessons 11 through 15 to which plaintiffs object, they seek to enjoin the entire program for reasons of unconstitutionality and illegal delegation of power. Therefore, we turn first to the constitutional issues raised by this appeal.

I. Constitutional Issues.

Plaintiffs contend that the basic and underlying issue of this case is whether parents are free to educate their offspring in the intimacies of sexual matters according to their own moral and religious beliefs without undue interference by the State. More specifically, they argue that the sex education program (hereinafter referred to as "Program") adopted by the State is unconstitutional because it unduly interferes with their right of privacy and freedom of religion.

A. Right of Privacy.

There is no question that the citizens of this State have been afforded the specific right of privacy. Section 5 of Article I of our State Constitution provides that " . . . the right of the people to be secure . . . against invasions of privacy shall not be violated." And although the right of privacy is not specifically afforded in the First Amendment of the United States Constitution, the Supreme Court of the United States has held that the Amendment " . . . has a penumbra where privacy is protected from governmental intrusion." Griswold v. Connecticut, 381 U.S. 479, 483, 85 S.Ct. 1678, 1681, 14 L.Ed.2d 510 (1968).

Plaintiffs cite Griswold v. Connecticut, *supra,* in support of their position. In *Griswold,* a Connecticut statute which made the use of contraceptives a criminal offense was held invalid as being an invasion of marital privacy. As stated by Justice Douglas in delivering the opinion of the Court at pages 485-486, 85 S.Ct. at page 1682:

The present case, then, concerns a relationship lying within the zone of privacy created by several fundamental constitutional guarantees. And it concerns a law which, in forbidding the *use* of contraceptives rather than regulating their manufacture or sale, seeks to achieve its goals by means having a maximum destructive impact upon that relationship. Such a law cannot stand in light of the familiar principle, so often applied by this Court, that a "governmental purpose to control or prevent activities constitutionally subject to state regulation may not be achieved by means which sweep unnecessarily broadly and thereby invade the area of protected freedoms." NAACP v. Alabama, 377 U.S. 288, 307, 84 S.Ct. 1302, 1314, 12 L.Ed.2d. 325. Would we allow the police to search the sacred precincts of marital bedrooms for telltale signs of the use of contraceptives? The very idea is repulsive to the notions of privacy surrounding the marriage relationship.

Thus, the Supreme Court held where the zone of privacy is invaded by the state by unnecessarily broad means, its action is in contravention of the First Amendment. Connecticut had forbidden the *use* of contraceptives rather than merely regulating their

manufacture or sale. This interdiction, the Court held, was unnecessarily broad.

The question we now face is this: Can this State through its proper agencies adopt and initiate a curriculum of family life and sex education for use in the fifth and sixth grades without invading its citizens' constitutional right to privacy? We must not look to see if there has been a possible or technical invasion of privacy but instead whether the government has by "unnecessarily broad means" contravened the plaintiffs' right of privacy.

The State in formulating policies for the adoption of the Program anticipated possible objections by parents and guardians of fifth and sixth grade children to the context of the film series, especially the treatment of the subject matter in lessons numbered 11 through 15.[4] The State, therefore, established an "excusal system" whereby parents and guardians had the option of withholding or withdrawing their children from the Program by submitting a written excuse to the school. Furthermore, in order to allow parents and guardians an opportunity to view the 15 lessons of the film series before they were shown to their children at school, the lessons were shown each Monday evening at 10 p.m. on Educational Television. The Monday night telecasts enabled the parents to consider the content of the lesson and then submit a written excuse if they found it objectionable. We view this "excusal system" as an effort by the defendants to allow those parents or guardians who might object to the Program or parts thereof on moral or religious grounds to have their children excused. The Program was in no way compulsory, and, therefore, we cannot see how the State by "unnecessarily broad means" contravened plaintiffs' right of privacy.

Presumably in support of their invasion of privacy theory, plaintiffs cite two other cases: Meyer v. Nebraska, 262 U.S. 390, 43 S.Ct. 625, 67 L.Ed. 1042 (1923), which upheld the rights of parents to have their children learn a foreign language, and Pierce v. Society of Sisters, 268 U.S. 510, 45 S.Ct. 571, 69 L.Ed. 1070 (1925), which upheld the rights of parents to have their children educated in private elementary schools. *Meyer* and *Pierce* are supportive of the explicit freedoms of speech and press rather than the penumbral right of privacy. Citing these two cases, the Supreme Court drew the following conclusion in Griswold v. Connecticut, supra, 381 U.S. at 482, 85 S.Ct. at 1680: "In other words, the State may not, consistently with the spirit of the First Amendment, contract the spectrum of available knowledge." Yet, this is the very thing that the plaintiffs would have this court do. They seek to "contract the spectrum of available knowledge" by enjoining the State from continuing with its family life and sex education program. In light of the *Gris-*

wold, Pierce, and *Meyer* cases, we cannot, under the circumstances of this case, sustain plaintiffs' position that the Program should be enjoined on the basis that their constitutional right of privacy has been violated.

B. Freedom of Religion.

We turn next to plaintiffs' contention that the Program in question is a violation of their First Amendment right of religious freedom. The First Amendment to the United States Constitution provides in relevant part:

Congress shall make no law respecting an establishment of religion, or prohibiting the free exercise thereof. . . .

The counterpart of the First Amendment is found in Article I, Section 3, of the Hawaii State Constitution.

Plaintiffs assert that the instant case basically involves a "free exercise of religion" situation in that the program enacted by the Department of Education is claimed to infringe upon plaintiffs' rights to educate their children in sexual matters pursuant to their particular religious beliefs. There was testimony by some parents that the Program violated basic religious and moral beliefs that they have instilled in their children. Other parents, however, testified to the desirability of having the series continued and generally took views opposite to those of the plaintiffs. Clergymen from various faiths, including Catholic, Mormon, Baptist and independent Protestant groups testified that certain aspects of the series violated their religious beliefs and doctrines. On the other hand, clergymen of other faiths, including Episcopalian, Methodist, Buddhist, Presbyterians and other independent denominations testified that they saw no violation of religious or moral principles in the series.

It has been argued that *requiring* attendance at sex education courses would burden the free exercise of religion of those who honestly believe that exposure to certain subjects covered within those courses is sinful or that sex education must be accompanied by moral instruction.[5] However, in view of the fact that the program to which the plaintiffs now seek a permanent injunction is not compulsory, we fail to find any direct or substantial burden on their "free exercise" of religion.

Nevertheless, plaintiffs argue that availability of the "excusal system" is not constitutionally sufficient, citing People of State of Ill. ex rel. McCollum v. Board of Education, 333 U.S. 203, 68 S.Ct. 461, 92 L.Ed. 649 (1948), and Justice Brennan's concurring opinion in

School Dist. of Abington v. Schempp, 374 U.S. 203, 83 S.Ct. 1560, 10 L.Ed.2d 844 (1963).[6] The *Schempp* case concerned Pennsylvania law requiring that at least ten verses from the Holy Bible should be read, without comment, at the opening of each public school day, and that any child shall be excused from such Bible reading, or attending such Bible reading, upon the written request of his parent or guardian. Justice Clark, in delivering the opinion of the Court, held that the reading from the Holy Bible and the recitation of the Lord's Prayer were religious in character and were, therefore, *ipso facto,* violative of the Establishment Clause. As the Court pointed out at page 223, 83 S.Ct. at page 1572: "The distinction between the two clauses is apparent—a violation of the Free Exercise Clause is predicated on coercion while the Establishment Clause violation need not be so attended." Inasmuch as plaintiffs have available the excusal system, they are under no direct governmental compulsion.

Furthermore, unlike the case at bar, both *McCollum* and *Schempp* involved the direct use of tax supported public school systems for *religious instruction,* and both were held to clearly violate the *Establishment Clause.* Our case is distinguishable in that we are asked to decide the constitutionality of a State-wide program of "family life and sex education" based upon a complaint that certain subjects covered therein are objectionable from a moral and religious standpoint.

Equally pertinent to our discussion is the Supreme Court's holding in Epperson v. Arkansas, 393 U.S. 97, 89 S.Ct. 266, 21 L.Ed.2d 228 (1968), in which an Arkansas statute prohibiting the teaching of the Darwinian theory of evolution because such theory was contrary to the religious views of some of its citizens was held unconstitutional. At page 104, 89 S.Ct. at page 270, the Court stated:

. . . Our courts, however, have not failed to apply the First Amendment's mandate in our educational system where essential to safeguard the fundamental values of freedom of speech and inquiry and of belief. . . .

And at 106, 89 S.Ct. at 271:

There is and can be no doubt that the First Amendment does not permit the State to require that teaching and learning must be tailored to the principles or prohibitions of any religious sect or dogma.

If we were to hold that the "family life and sex education" program adopted by the State is contrary to certian religious beliefs of some of our citizens and therefore unconstitutional on the grounds that it prevents the free exercise of their religion, we would come dangerously close to approving that which is prohibited by *Epperson*. We must be equally protective of the freedoms of speech, inquiry and belief as we are of the freedom of religion.

Inasmuch as we have found no compulsion or coercion related to the educational Program in question, we find no violation of the First Amendment's Free Exercise of Religion Clause.

II. Improper Delegation of Authority.

Plaintiffs also seek reversal on the argument that the Program in question is illegal because it was adopted by an improper delegation of authority by the State Board of Education to the administrative staff of the State Department of Education. They argue that the Board of Education's power is based upon law and since no legislative authority was granted for such a program, either the Board's action, or lack thereof, or defendant Ralph Kiyosaki's action in accepting and adopting this program was an unlawful delegation of power. In other words, plaintiffs contend that in order for curriculum dealing with family life and sex education to be used in the public school system, the State Board of Education must have specific authorization from the legislature before it can establish policies or adopt programs. We do not agree.

There is no question that the Board of Education, as the executive head of the State Department of Education, is granted broad discretionary powers in formulating and enacting educational programs for the State's public schools. Section 3 of Article IX of our constitution (as amended) provides:

The board of education shall have power, in accordance with law, to formulate policy, and to exercise control over the public school system through its executive officer, the superintendent of education. . . .

The same language is incorporated into Section 296-2 of the Hawaii Revised Statutes pertaining to the powers of the Board and its Superintendent. The duties of the Superintendent are set out in Section 296-11 and read, in part, as follows:

§ 296-11 *Duties of superintendent.* Under policies established by the board of education, the superintendent of education shall administer programs of education and public instruction throughout the State, including education at the preschool, primary, and secondary school levels, health educa-

tion and instruction, and such other programs as may be established by law.

The Program in question was adopted in response to the appropriation for the operating budget of the Department of Education for the fiscal year ending June 30, 1969, as set forth in a lump sum in Act 74, Session Laws of Hawaii 1968. With reference to such appropriation, House Conf. Comm. Rep. No. 3 (1968 Budget Session, Hawaii State Legislature) contains, *inter alia,* the following, on page 8:

10. *Program for instruction of social problems.* The rapidly expanding population, expanding and changing economy, and a change in social mores, are conditions which call for a program of instruction related to social problems. These problems include, but are not limited to, family living and sex education. . . . The department presently has a program offering courses in the area of social problems. However, this program is spotty and it has not been planned in a comprehensive fashion or programmed in a manner which would allow articulation of levels of expectation from the beginning to the terminal point of instruction. The Committee approves of the department's intent to devote resources toward the planning and programming of instruction in the area of social problems.

As the trial court correctly ruled, the cited passage indicates the legislative intent as to what direction sex education programs in the schools should take. Pursuant to such expressed intent, the Department of Education recommended for adoption the Program in question.

However, plaintiffs argue that even if such a program is deemed to be within the discretionary powers of the Board of Education or that there was a sufficient mandate by the legislature for the adoption of such program, there was, nevertheless, a clear abuse of such discretionary powers. Reference is again made by plaintiffs to HRS § 296-11, which states in relevant part: "Under policies established by the board of education, the superintendent of education shall administer programs of education and public instruction throughout the State. . . . " The plaintiffs contend that the Program was formally adopted before any policies were established by the Board of Education. There is no validity to such a contention since the actions of the administrative staff were merely recommendatory, the actual adoption being made by Superintendent Kiyosaki as executive officer of the Board. The Board meeting of January 9, 1969, reaffirmed the policy which Mr. Kiyosaki understood to be in effect at the time he adopted the program.

Affirmed.

NOTES

1. House Conf.Comm.Rep. No. 3, p. 8 (1968 Budget Session, Hawaii State Legislature).
2. *Supra.*
3. Decision—Exhibit "A": Findings of Fact, p. 1, April 21, 1969.
4. These lessons deal specifically with sexuality and sexual development. They are entitled as follows: Lesson 11—"The Male"; Lesson 12—"The Female"; Lesson 13—"A New Life"; Lesson 14—"Questions, Please"; Lesson 15—"Growing Up."
5. Recent Developments, The Constitutionality Under the Religion Clauses of the First Amendment of Compulsory Sex Education in Public Schools, 68 Mich. L. Rev. 1050 (1970). "The free exercise clause has often been invoked by religious groups to gain exemptions from laws of general applicability." *Supra* at 1053. *See, e.g.,* Sherbert v. Verner, 374 U.S. 398, 83 S.Ct. 1790, 10 L.Ed.2d 965 (1963) (which required South Carolina to carve out of its unemployment compensation laws an exemption for petitioner, a Seventh-Day Adventist, who refused on religious grounds to accept a job which required her to work on Saturdays); Martin v. City of Struthers, 319 U.S. 141, 63 S.Ct. 862, 87 L.Ed. 1313 (1943) (concurring opinion of Murphy, J., which held a municipal ordinance forbidding the distribution of handbills or circulars—as applied to a person distributing advertisements for a religious meeting—invalid under the Federal Constitution as a denial of freedom of religion); Murdock v. Pennsylvania, 319 U.S. 105, 63 S.Ct. 870, 87 L.Ed. 1292 (1943) (which held a municipal ordinance that, as construed and applied, required colporteurs to pay a license tax as a condition to the pursuit of their activities, was invalid under the Federal Constitution as a denial of freedom of speech, press and religion.)
6. It should be noted that Justice Brennan's opinion was not shared by any other member of the Court while Justice Douglas took the opposite view. Justice Brennan reasoned that the evils inherent in the "excusal system" are just as much present regardless of whether the action complained of concerns Establishment or Free Exercise clauses. 374 U.S. 203, 288, 83 S.Ct. 1560.

Justice Douglas in his concurring opinion reasons that the Free Exercise Clause "is written in terms of what the State may not require of the individual" and lack of any compulsion by the school district effectively disposes of any issue relating to the "free exercise" of religion. 374 U.S. 203, 227, 83 S.Ct. 1560.

A United States District Court in Alabama decides for a high school English teacher who had been dismissed from her teaching position because she had assigned her eleventh grade class to read, over the principal's objections, Kurt Vonnegut's story *Welcome to the Monkey House,* a work described by the principal and associate superintendent as "literary garbage." The Court declares: "Since the defendants [school officials] have failed to show either that the assignment was inappropriate reading for high school juniors, or that it created a significant disruption to the educational processes of this school, this Court concludes that plaintiff's dismissal constituted an unwarranted invasion of her First Amendment right to academic freedom."

Parducci v. *Rutland,* 316 F.Supp. 352 (1970)

JOHNSON, Chief Judge.

Plaintiff was dismissed from her position as a high school teacher in the Montgomery public schools for assigning a certain short story to her junior (eleventh grade) English classes. In her complaint, which was filed with this Court on April 27, 1970, plaintiff alleges that defendants, in ordering her dismissal, violated her First Amendment right to academic freedom and her Fourteenth Amendment right to due process of law. Plaintiff's claim for damages and request for jury trial as contained in her initial complaint were stricken by amendment. The defendants are the members of the Montgomery County Board of Education, the Superintendent of Schools of the county, the Associate Superintendent, and the Principal of plaintiff's high school. Plaintiff's request for injunctive relief is authorized under the Civil Rights Act of 1871, 42 U.S.C. § 1983. The jurisdiction of this Court is invoked pursuant to 28 U.S.C. § 1343(3) and (4).

Plaintiff was graduated with high honors from Troy State University in June, 1969. Upon graduation, she entered into a one-year contract to teach English and Spanish at Jefferson Davis High School in Montgomery, such contract to commence in October, 1969.

On April 21, 1970, plaintiff assigned as outside reading to her junior English classes a story, entitled "Welcome to the Monkey House." The story, a comic satire, was selected by plaintiff to give her students a better understanding of one particular genre of western literature—the short story. The story's author, Kurt Vonnegut, Jr., is a prominent contemporary writer who

has published numerous short stories and novels, including *Cat's Cradle* and a recent best seller, *Slaughterhouse-Five.*

The following morning, plaintiff was called to Principal Rutland's office for a conference with him and the Associate Superintendent of the school system. Both men expressed their displeasure with the content of the story, which they described as "literary garbage," and with the "philosophy" of the story, which they construed as condoning, if not encouraging, "the killing off of elderly people and free sex."[1] They also expressed concern over the fact that three of plaintiff's students had asked to be excused from the assignment and that several disgruntled parents had called the school to complain. They then admonished plaintiff not to teach the story in any of her classes.

Plaintiff retorted that she was bewildered by their interpretation of and attitude toward the story, that she still considered it to be a good literary work, and that, while not meaning to cause any trouble, she felt that she had a professional obligation to teach the story. The Associate Superintendent then warned plaintiff that he would have to report this incident to the Superintendent who might very well order her dismissal. Plaintiff, who by this time had become very emotionally upset, responded to this threat by tendering her resignation.

On April 27, a hearing was held before this Court on plaintiff's motion for a temporary restraining order. Although plaintiff's motion for a temporary restraining order was subsequently denied, defendants agreed at the hearing to allow plaintiff to withdraw her resignation and to accord plaintiff a hearing before the Montgomery County Board of Education on the question of dismissal.[2] The School Board hearing, in which both sides participated, was held the following day. On May 6, the School Board notified plaintiff that she had been dismissed from her job for assigning materials which had a "disruptive" effect on the school and for refusing "the counselling and advice of the school principal." The School Board also advised the plaintiff that one of the bases for her dismissal was "insubordination" by reason of a statement that she made to the Principal and Associate Superintendent that "regardless of their counselling" she "would continue to teach the eleventh grade English class at the Jeff Davis High School by the use of whatever material" she wanted "and in whatever manner" she thought best.

Having exhausted all her remedies within the school system, plaintiff immediately renewed her motion for a preliminary injunction in which she sought her immediate reinstatement as a teacher. The present submission is upon this motion, the response thereto by the defendants, the evidence taken orally before the Court, including the testimony of several witnesses and exhibits thereto, and the briefs and arguments of the parties.

At the outset, it should be made clear that plaintiff's teaching ability is not in issue. The Principal of her school has conceded that plaintiff was a good teacher and that she would have received a favorable evaluation from him at the end of the year but for the single incident which led to her dismissal.

I

Plaintiff asserts in her complaint that her dismissal for assigning "Welcome to the Monkey House" violated her First Amendment right to academic freedom.

That teachers are entitled to First Amendment freedoms is an issue no longer in dispute. "It can hardly be argued that either students or teachers shed their constitutional rights to freedom of speech or expression at the schoolhouse gate." Tinker v. Des Moines Independent Community School District, 393 U.S. 503, 506, 89 S.Ct. 733, 736, 21 L.Ed.2d 731 (1969); see Pickering v. Board of Education, etc., 391 U.S. 563, 568, 88 S.Ct. 1731, 20 L.Ed.2d 811 (1968); Pred v. Board of Public Instruction, etc., 415 F.2d 851, 855 (5th Cir. 1969). These constitutional protections are unaffected by the presence or absence of tenure under state law. McLaughlin v. Tilendis, 398 F.2d 287 (7th Cir. 1968); Johnson v. Branch, 364 F.2d 177 (4th Cir. 1966), cert. denied, 385 U.S. 1003, 87 S.Ct. 706, 17 L.Ed.2d 542 (1967).

Although academic freedom is not one of the enumerated rights of the First Amendment, the Supreme Court has on numerous occasions emphasized that the right to teach, to inquire, to evaluate and to study is fundamental to a democratic society.[3] In holding a New York loyalty oath statute unconstitutionally vague, the Court stressed the need to expose students to a robust exchange of ideas in the classroom:

Our nation is deeply committed to safeguarding academic freedom, which is of transcendant value to all of us and not merely to the teachers concerned. That freedom is therefore a special concern of the First Amendment, which does not tolerate laws that cast a pall of orthodoxy over the classroom. . . . The classroom is peculiarly the "marketplace of ideas."[4]

Furthermore, the safeguards of the First Amendment will quickly be brought into play to protect the right of academic freedom because any unwarranted invasion of this right will tend to have a chilling effect on the exercise of the right by other teachers. Cf. Wieman v. Updegraff, 344 U.S. at 194, 195, 73 S.Ct. 215 (Frankfurter, J., concurring); Pickering v. Board of Education, etc., *supra* 391 U.S. at 574, 88 S.Ct. 1731.

The right to academic freedom, however, like all other constitutional rights, is not absolute and must be balanced against the competing interests of society. This Court is keenly aware of the state's vital interest in protecting the impressionable minds of its young people from *any* form of extreme propagandism in the classroom.

A teacher works in a sensitive area in a schoolroom. There he shapes the attitudes of young minds towards the society in which they live. In this, the state has a vital concern.[5]

While the balancing of these interests will necessarily depend on the particular facts before the Court, certain guidelines in this area were provided by the Supreme Court in Tinker v. Des Moines Independent Community School District, *supra*. The Court there observed that in order for the state to restrict the First Amendment right of a student, it must first demonstrate that:

[T]he forbidden conduct would *"materially* and *substantially* interfere with the requirements of appropriate discipline in the operation of the school." [Emphasis added.][6]

The Court was, however, quick to caution the student that:

[Any] conduct . . . in class or out of it, which for any reason—whether it stems from time, place or type of behavior—materially disrupts classwork or involves substantial disorder or invasion of the rights of others is, of course, not immunized by the constitutional guarantee of freedom of speech.[7]

Thus, the first question to be answered is whether "Welcome to the Monkey House" is inappropriate reading for high school juniors. While the story contains several vulgar terms and a reference to an involuntary act of sexual intercourse, the Court, having read the story very carefully, can find nothing that would render it obscene either under the standards of Roth v. United States,[8] or under the stricter standards for minors as set forth in Ginsberg v. New York.[9]

The slang words are contained in two short rhymes which are less ribald than those found in many of Shakespeare's plays. The reference in the story to an act of sexual intercourse is no more descriptive than the rape scene in Pope's "Rape of the Lock." As for the theme of the story, the Court notes that the anthology in which the story was published was reviewed by several of the popular national weekly magazines, none of which found the subject matter of any of the stories to be offensive. It appears to the Court, moreover, that the author, rather than advocating the "killing off of old people," satirizes the practice to symbolize the increasing depersonalization of man in society.

The Court's finding as to the appropriateness of the story for high school students is confirmed by the reaction of the students themselves. Rather than there being a threatened or actual substantial disruption to the educational processes of the school, the evidence reflects that the assigning of the story was greeted with apathy by most of the students. Only three of plaintiff's students asked to be excused from the assignment. On this question of whether there was a material and substantial threat of disruption, the Principal testified at the School Board hearing that there was no indication that any of plaintiff's other 87 students were planning to disrupt the normal routine of the school. This Court now specifically finds and concludes that the conduct for which plaintiff was dismissed was not such that "would materially and substantially interfere with" reasonable requirements of discipline in the school.

A recent First Circuit case lends further support to this Court's conclusion. There a high school teacher was suspended for assigning and discussing a magazine article which contained several highly offensive words. The court, finding the article to be well-written and thought-provoking, formulated the issues thusly,

Hence the question in this case is whether a teacher may, for demonstrated educational purposes, quote a "dirty" word currently used in order to give special

offense, or whether the shock is too great for high school seniors to stand. If the answer were that the students must be protected from such exposure, we would fear for their future. We do not question the good faith of the defendants in believing that some parents have been offended. With the greatest of respect to such parents, their sensibilities are not the full measure of what is proper education.[10]

Since the defendants have failed to show either that the assignment was inappropriate reading for high school juniors, or that it created a significant disruption to the educational processes of this school, this Court concludes that plaintiff's dismissal constituted an unwarranted invasion of her First Amendment right to academic freedom.

II

Plaintiff also alleges that she was denied "the right to use the short story in question as extra reading without a clear and concise written standard to determine which books are obscene."

The record shows that prior to plaintiff's dismissal, there was no written or announced policy at Jefferson Davis High School governing the selection and assignment of outside materials. One of the defendants testified at the School Board hearing that the selection of outside readings was a matter determined solely by the good taste and good judgment of the individual teacher. The only question before this Court on this point, therefore, is whether plaintiff was entitled, under the Due Process Clause, to prior notice that the conduct for which she was punished was prohibited.[11]

Our laws in this country have long recognized that no person should be punished for conduct unless such conduct has been proscribed in clear and precise terms. See Connally v. General Constr. Co., 269 U.S. 385, 391, 46 S.Ct. 126, 70 L.Ed. 322 (1926). When the conduct being punished involves First Amendment rights, as is the case here, the standards for judging permissible vagueness will be even more strictly applied.[12]

In the case now before the Court, we are concerned not merely with vague standards, but with the total absence of standards. When a teacher is forced to speculate as to what conduct is permissible and what conduct is proscribed, he is apt to be overly cautious and reserved in the classroom.[13] Such a reluctance on the part of the teacher to investigate and experiment with new and different ideas is anathema to the entire concept of academic freedom.

This Court is well aware of the fact that "school officials should be given wide discretion in administering their schools" and that "courts should be reluctant to interfere with or place limits on that discretion." Such legal platitudes should not, however, be allowed to become euphemisms for "infringement upon" and "deprivations of" constitutional rights. However wide the discretion of school officials, such discretion cannot be exercised so as to arbitrarily deprive teachers of their First Amendment rights. See Johnson v. Branch, *supra,* 364 F.2d at 180. This Court cannot, on the facts of this case, find any substantial interest of the schools to be served by giving defendants unfettered discretion to decide how the First Amendment rights of teachers are to be exercised. Cf. Niemotko v. Maryland, 340 U.S. 268, 71 S.Ct. 325, 328, 95 L.Ed. 267, 280 (1951).

It should be emphasized, however, that because of the special circumstances present in this case this Court does not feel any necessity to comment upon the advisability of requiring school administrators to promulgate rules and regulations under any other circumstances.

III

The English Department at Jefferson Davis High School publishes "English Reading Lists" for the benefit of its teachers and students. Each list (the lists are compiled separately for each grade) contains the names of approximately twenty-five recommended works.

One of the recommended novels on the "Junior English Reading List" is J. D. Salinger's *Catcher in The Rye.* This novel, while undisputedly a classic in American literature, contains far more offensive and descriptive language than that found in plaintiff's assigned story. The "Senior English Reading List" contains a number of works, such as Huxley's *Brave New World* and Orwell's *1984* which have highly provocative and sophisticated themes. Furthermore, the school library contains a number of books with controversial words and philosophies.

This situation illustrates how easily arbitrary discrimination can occur when public officials are given unfettered discretion to decide what books should be taught and what books should be banned. While not questioning either the motives or good faith of the defendants, this Court finds their inconsistency to be not only enigmatic but also grossly unfair.[14]

With these several basic constitutional principles in mind it inevitably follows that the defendants in this case cannot justify the dismissal of this plaintiff under the guise of insubordination. The facts are clear that plaintiff's "insubordination" was not insubordination in any sense and was not, in reality, a reason for the School Board's action. Dickey v. Alabama State Board of Education, 273 F.Supp. 613 (D.C.).

In accordance with the foregoing, it is the order, judgment and decree of this Court that the plaintiff be reinstated as a teacher for the duration of her contract, with the same rights and privileges which attached to her status prior to her illegal suspension.

It is further ordered that plaintiff be paid her regular salary for both the period during which she was suspended and for the remaining period of her contract.

It is further ordered that defendants expunge from plaintiff's employment records and transcripts any and all references relating to her suspension and dismissal.

It is further ordered that the court costs incurred in this cause be and they are hereby taxed against the defendants.

NOTES

1. Both Mr. Rutland and Mr. Garrett later testified that neither of them was much of a reader, had any special expertise in the field of literature, or had ever taught an English course.
2. Since plaintiff was only a probationary teacher, she was not entitled under state law to a hearing before the School Board. Code of Alabama, Tit. 52 § 351 et seq.
3. See e.g., Sweezy v. New Hampshire by Wyman, 354 U.S. 234, 77 S.Ct. 1203, 1 L.Ed.2d 1311 (1957); Wieman v. Updegraff, 344 U.S. 183, 73 S.Ct. 215, 97 L.Ed. 216 (1952).
4. Keyishian v. Board of Regents, etc., 385 U.S. 589, 603, 87 S.Ct. 675, 683, 17 L.Ed.2d 629 (1967). Cf. Meyer v. Nebraska, 262 U.S. 390, 43 S.Ct. 625, 67 L.Ed. 1042 (1923).
5. Shelton v. Tucker, 364 U.S. 479, 485, 81 S.Ct. 247, 250, 5 L.Ed.2d 231 (1960).
6. 393 U.S. at 509, 89 S.Ct. at 738, quoting Burnside v. Byars, 363 F.2d 744, 749 (5th Cir. 1966).
7. 393 U.S. at 513, 89 S.Ct. at 740; see Pred v. Board of Public Instruction, etc., *supra,* 415 F.2d 859.
8. 354 U.S. 476, 77 S.Ct. 1304, 1 L.Ed.2d 1498 (1957).
9. 390 U.S. 629, 88 S.Ct. 1274, 20 L.Ed.2d 195 (1968).
10. Keefe v. Geanakos, 418 F.2d 359, 361-362 (1st Cir. 1969).
11. Since the court has found earlier in this opinion that plaintiff's conduct was constitutionally protected, that is, was not "hard-core," she has standing to raise this Due Process question. Cf. Dombrowski v. Pfister, 380 U.S. 479, 491-492, 85 S.Ct. 1116, 14 L.Ed.2d 22 (1965).
12. NAACP v. Button, 371 U.S. 415, 432, 83 S.Ct. 328, 9 L.Ed. 2d 405 (1963); Winters v. New York, 333 U.S. 507, 509-510, 68 S.Ct. 665 , 92 L.Ed. 840 (1948); see Brooks v. Auburn University, 296 F.Supp. 188 (M.D. Ala.), aff'd 412 F.2d 1171 (5th Cir. 1969).
13. Cf. Keyishian v. Board of Regents, etc., *supra,* 385 U.S. at 604, 87 S.Ct. 675.
14. See Keefe v. Geanakos, *supra,* 418 F.2d at 362; Vought v. Van Buren Public Schools, 306 F.Supp. 1388, 1395-1396 (E.D.Mich. 1969).

In deciding that *Slaughterhouse-Five* could not be banned from the classrooms and libraries of Michigan schools, the Court of Appeals of Michigan declares: "We hold that, as a matter of law, *Slaughterhouse-Five* is not obscene in the constitutional sense ... we find as a matter of fact that *Slaughterhouse-Five* is not obscene, profane, or vulgar in the constitutional sense. We believe it to be a serious work of quasi-fiction by an acknowledged legitimate writer. The book's dominant theme is anti-war. The subject, war, slaughter, bombing, may be obscene; the telling of the tale is not ... Vonnegut's literary dwellings on war, religion, death, Christ, God, government, politics, and any other subject should be as welcome in the public schools of this state as those of Machiavelli, Chaucer, Shakespeare, Melville, Lenin, Hitler, Joseph McCarthy, or Walt Disney. The students of Michigan are free to make of *Slaughterhouse-Five* what they will."

Todd v. *Rochester Community Schools,* 200 N. W. 2d 90 (1972)

BRONSON, Presiding Judge.

On March 24, 1971, plaintiff, Bruce Livingston Todd, filed a complaint for a writ of mandamus against the defendant, Rochester Community Schools, in the Oakland County Circuit Court. Mr. Todd's complaint alleged that one of his minor children was enrolled in a course of instruction referred to as "Current Literature" which was being taught in a Rochester public high school. Plaintiff averred that part of the curriculum in said course was the study of *Slaughterhouse-Five or The Children's Crusade,*[1] a novel by the contemporary American author, Kurt Vonnegut, Jr.

The gravamen of plaintiff's complaint was that *Slaughterhouse-Five* "contains and makes reference to religious matters" and, therefore, "the use of such book as a part or in connection with any course of instruction by a public school district or system is illegal and contrary to the laws of the land; namely, the First and Fourteenth Amendments of the United States Constitution."[2] Predicated on these factual allegations, Mr. Todd requested that the Oakland County Circuit Court issue a writ of mandamus compelling the defendant school district to cease utilizing *Slaughterhouse-Five* "as a part of a course of instruction in the Rochester Community Schools." In his complaint, Mr. Todd did not allege that *Slaughterhouse-Five* was obscene nor that it had no literary value.

On March 31, 1971, defendant answered plaintiff's complaint. In its pleading the Rochester Community

Schools affirmatively stated that the novel at issue, along with several others, "is used in connection with a general secular course of instruction entitled 'Current Literature' and the fact that the same might incidentally refer to religious matters does not render its use in violation of the First and Fourteenth Amendments of the Constitution of the United States." Defendant further contended that the selection of books to be used in its course of instruction was a matter exclusively within its administrative power and not subject to judicial supervision nor review.[3]

Subsequent to answering, defendant filed a motion for summary judgment of no cause of action on the basis that there was no genuine issue as to any material fact and that the Rochester Community School District was entitled to judgment as a matter of law. GCR 1963, 117.2(3). A hearing on this motion was held on April 7, 1971, before the Honorable Arthur E. Moore, Circuit Judge for the County of Oakland. At this time the parties stipulated to allow the novel into evidence, formally waived pretrial, and agreed to accept the court's decision predicated upon the pleadings, briefs and motions, with the book itself constituting the sole evidence.

On May 13, 1971, the court filed a nine-page opinion granting plaintiff's requested relief "if necessary." On May 20, 1971, in the trial judge's temporary absence, the Presiding Judge of the Oakland County Circuit Court entered a judgment of mandamus. However, on May 28, 1971, the trial judge, on his own motion, set aside the May 20, 1971 judgment so he could make more appropriate findings of fact and law. GCR 1963, 517.1. A new hearing was held before Judge Moore on June 5, 1971. On June 9, 1971, a final opinion and order granting plaintiff a judgment of mandamus was issued.[4]

On June 18, 1971, defendant filed a claim of appeal as a matter of right. On July 16, 1971, this Court granted the American Civil Liberties Union of Michigan permission to file a brief *amicus curiae*.[5]

After thorough study of the proceedings below, including a careful scrutiny of *Slaughterhouse-Five*, and aware that some of the legal questions suggested by these proceedings have apparently never been squarely passed upon by any other court in this country, we are constrained to reverse the trial court's judgment and permanently dissolve the previously issued judgment of mandamus. The reasons for our actions follow.

Initially we consider what we believe should have been the proper disposition of this matter in the court below. As previously indicated on March 31, 1971, defendant filed a motion for summary judgment pursuant to GCR 1963, 117.2(3). Technically, defendant's requested relief was more properly predicated upon the authority of GCR 1963, 117.2(1). For reasons we are about to delineate, we hold that even if all the factual allegations pleaded in the instant complaint are taken to be true, Bielski v. Wolverine Insurance Co., 379 Mich. 280, 283, 150 N.W.2d 788, 789 (1967), plaintiff still has "failed to state a claim upon which relief can be granted" and defendant should prevail as a matter of law.

Our Court considered the nature of GCR 1963, 117.2(1) in Major v. Schmidt Trucking Co., 15 Mich. App. 75, 166 N.W.2d 517 (1968). In *Major*, Judge Charles Levin, writing for a unanimous panel, observed that:

"A motion under GCR 1963, 117.2(1) asserts that the opposing party's pleading fails to state a claim upon which relief can be granted. The motion may be granted only where it appears on the face of the challenged pleading that the pleader cannot recover." *Major, supra*, at 78, 166 N.W.2d at 518.

See, also, Bloss v. Williams, 15 Mich.App. 228, 231, 166 N.W.2d 520 (1968); Johnston's Administrator v. United Airlines, 23 Mich.App. 279, 286, 178 N.W.2d 536 (1970). The fact that defendant chose to support its motion by appending an affidavit is perfectly proper inasmuch as the combining of subparts of GCR 1963, 117 has been approved. Durant v. Stahlin, 375 Mich. 628, 644, 135 N.W.2d 392 (1965). But it was not

necessary for defendant to affix an affidavit with its motion for summary judgment to prevail inasmuch as plaintiff's complaint pleads an alleged cause of action heretofore unknown to our law.[6] Plaintiff's theory will remain an unwelcome stranger to our jurisprudence unless and until the United States Supreme Court or our State Supreme Court dictate otherwise.

Pursuant to GCR 1963, 820.1(1) and (7) we grant defendant's requested summary judgment of no cause of action and reverse the trial court's judgment of mandamus.

Plaintiff's complaint specifically pleads only that *Slaughterhouse-Five* is used in a public school and "contains and makes reference to religious matters." We have been cited to no authority, nor has our own research uncovered any, which holds that *any* portion of *any* constitution is violated simply because a novel, utilized in a public school "contains and makes reference to religious matters." This concept is legally repugnant to what we believe is the time-tested rationale underlying the First and Fourteenth Amendments. By couching a personal grievance in First Amendment language, one may not stifle freedom of expression. Vigorously opposed to such a suggestion, we stand firm in rendering plaintiff's theory constitutionally impermissible.

If plaintiff's contention was correct, then public school students could no longer marvel at Sir Galahad's saintly quest for the Holy Grail, nor be introduced to the dangers of Hitler's *Mein Kampf* nor read the mellifluous poetry of John Milton and John Donne. Unhappily, Robin Hood would be forced to forage without Friar Tuck and Shakespeare would have to delete Shylock from *The Merchant of Venice*. Is this to be the state of our law? Our Constitution does not command ignorance; on the contrary, it assures the people that the state may not relegate them to such a status and guarantees to all the precious and unfettered freedom of pursuing one's own intellectual pleasures in one's own personal way.

We hasten to point out that plaintiff did not allege that the Rochester public schools were intentionally taking action which was derogatory to Christianity. Nor did plaintiff aver that defendant was attempting to "establish" any specific religious sect in preference over another; nor one over all others; nor none at all. Had plaintiff's complaint suggested such a state of affairs, the question before the Court would be substantially different. But in this case the evidence is undisputed that the novel in question, and the Bible, were being utilized as literature. There is no allegation nor proof that *Slaughterhouse-Five* was being taught subjectively, or that the religious or antireligious view contained therein were espoused by the teachers.

Portions of the trial court's rulings were as follows:

"40. It is hereby ordered that the book, 'Slaughterhouse-Five or The Children's Crusade,' be forthwith removed from the defendant's school library.

"41. It is further ordered that the book may not be fostered, promoted or recommended for use in the defendant's school system; and defendant is ordered to desist accordingly.

"42. It is further ordered that the book is banned from the school library only so long as is necessary to prevent its use as promoted or recommended reading material in the course of study in defendant's school system.

"43. The book may be returned to the library shelves of the defendant school if and when the defendant has definitely and conclusively withdrawn and desisted from the promotion, recommendation and use of the book in educational courses of the defendant school system. This mandamus order may then be amended for that specific purpose on appropriate motion of counsel."

In rendering his decision the trial court relied solely upon School District of Abington Tp. v. Schempp, 374 U.S. 203, 83 S.Ct. 1560, 10 L.Ed.2d 844 (1963). *Schempp* held that a statute requiring daily Bible reading without comment in public schools violated the First Amendment, even though participation by each pupil was voluntary. *Schempp* is totally dissimilar to the case at bar. *Schempp* turned upon the fact that reciting a prayer in public schools had no connection whatsoever with secular education. Saying the prayer was an end in itself. Such conduct had as its primary purpose the advancement of religion; the relationship between prayer and education was nonexistent.[7] This cannot be said about *Slaughterhouse-Five*. In our opinion, Mr. Vonnegut's novel is an antiwar allegory which dwells on the horror of the Allied fire-bombing of Dresden[8] and which makes ancillary use of religious matter only for literary reasons. But whatever our insight or ability as critics, we are strongly persuaded that, as judges, we are correct in holding that *Slaughterhouse-Five* is not violative of the *Schempp* test:

"The test may be stated as follows: what are the purpose and the primary effect of the enactment? If either is the advancement or inhibition of religion then the enactment exceeds the scope of legislative power as circumscribed by the Constitution. That is to say that to withstand the strictures of the Establishment Clause there must be a secular legislative purpose and a primary effect that neither advances nor inhibits religion. . . ." Abington School District v. Schempp, 374 U.S. 203, 222, 83 S.Ct. 1560, 1571, 10 L.Ed.2d 844, 858 (1963).

See, also, Board of Education of Central School District No. 1 v. Allen, 392 U.S. 236, 243, 88 S.Ct. 1923, 1926, 20 L.Ed.2d 1060, 1065 (1968); Walz v. Tax Commission of City of New York, 397 U.S. 664, 90 S.Ct. 1409, 25 L.Ed.2d 697 (1970). Mr. Justice Brennan's concurring opinion in *Schempp* is highly instructive as to the proper interpretation of that decision:

"The holding of the Court today plainly does not foreclose teaching *about* the Holy Scriptures or about the differences between religious sects in classes in literature or history. Indeed, whether or not the Bible is involved, it would be impossible to teach meaningfully many subjects in the social sciences or the humanities without some mention of religion. *To what extent, and at what points in the curriculum, religious materials should be cited are matters which the courts ought to entrust very largely to the experienced officials who superintend our Nation's public schools. They are experts in such matters, and we are not.* We should heed Mr. Justice Jackson's *caveat* that any attempt by this Court to announce curricular standards would be 'to decree a uniform, rigid and, if we are consistent, an unchanging standard for countless school boards representing and serving highly localized groups which not only differ from each other but which themselves from time to time change attitudes.' . . ." (Emphasis supplied.) Abington School District v. Schempp, *supra*, 374 U.S. at 300-301, 83 S.Ct. at 1612 (Brennan, J., concurring).

Our scrutiny of Zorach v. Clauson, 343 U.S. 306, 72 S.Ct. 679, 96 L.Ed. 954 (1952); Illinois ex rel. McCollum v. Champaign County Board of Education, 333 U.S. 203, 68 S.Ct. 461, 92 L.Ed. 649 (1948); Torcaso v. Watkins, 367 U.S. 488, 81 S.Ct. 1680, 6 L.Ed.2d 982 (1961); Engel v. Vitale, 370 U.S. 421, 82 S.Ct. 1261, 8 L.Ed.2d 601 (1962), and the famous Everson v. Board of Education of Ewing Township, 330 U.S. 1, 67 S.Ct. 504, 91 L.Ed. 711 (1947), all of which authoritatively construe the First Amendment's religion clauses, leads us to conclude that the learned trial judge misapplied the teachings of the First Amendment and the specific holding of *Schempp*.[9]

Obscenity, although not raised in the pleadings, and declared not to be at issue in the trial court's June 9, 1971 judgment, is pervasive in the lower court's opinion.

In his findings of fact, the trial judge did indeed cite many words which, if standing alone, would offend some person's sensibilities. Yet each and every example advanced by the trial court was taken totally out of context. This is constitutional error. Ackerman v. United States, 293 F.2d 449 (C.A. 9, 1961); Haldeman v. United States, 340 F.2d 59 (C.A. 10, 1965); People v. Stabile, 58 Misc.2d 905, 296 N.Y.S.2d 815 (1969). To be constitutionally obscene, the matter scrutinized must be judged in its entirety. Roth v. United States, 354 U.S. 476, 77 S.Ct. 1304, 1 L.Ed.2d 1498 (1957); Excellent Publications, Inc. v. United States, 309 F.2d 362 (C.A. 1, 1962); State v. Hudson County News Co., 41 N.J. 247, 196 A. 2d225 (1963). As *amicus curiae* correctly points out, even the Bible may be considered profane or vulgar if certain passages are considered piecemeal and without due regard given to the entire text.[10]

The Supreme Court has clearly held that it is incumbent upon a court to employ a constitutional test to determine whether a given work is "obscene" in the legal sense. A Book Named "John Cleland's Memoirs" v. Massachusetts, 383 U.S. 413, 86 S.Ct. 975, 16 L.Ed. 2d 1 (1966). In Jacobellis v. Ohio, 378 U.S. 184, 84 S.Ct. 1676, 12 L.Ed.2d 793 (1964), the Court eloquently articulated the dangers of a Balkanized obscenity standard. Neither the trial court nor this Court has any legal prerogative to refuse to follow the rulings of the United States Supreme Court when it decides a question which requires interpretation of the Federal Constitution. Scholle v. Secretary of State, 360 Mich. 1, 104 N.W.2d 63 (1960); Union Central Life Insurance Co. v. Peters, 361 Mich. 283, 105 N.W.2d 196 (1960). See, also, People v. Gonzales, 356 Mich. 247, 262-263, 97 N.W.2d 16 (1959); People v. Temple, 23 Mich.App. 651, 661, 179 N.W.2d 200 (1970).

Although the trial court did not expressly rule that *Slaughterhouse-Five* was obscene, his June 9, 1971 judgment strongly suggests that possibility. We are constrained to hold that *Slaughterhouse-Five* is clearly not obscene under present constitutional tests. Roth v. United States, *supra;* Jacobellis v. Ohio, *supra;* Redrup v. New York, 386 U.S. 767, 87 S.Ct. 1414, 18 L.Ed.2d 515 (1967); People v. Wasserman, 27 Mich. App. 16, 183 N.W.2d 313 (1970); People v. Billingsley, 20 Mich.App. 10, 173 N.W.2d 785 (1969); Wayne County Prosecutor v. Doerfler, 14 Mich.App. 428, 165 N.W.2d 648 (1968).

Courts cannot permit themselves the luxury of refusing to adhere to a constitutional standard of review. When a court momentarily forgets this fact, as we did in Grand Rapids City Attorney v. Bloss, 17 Mich.App. 318, 169 N.W.2d 367 (1969), a higher court usually terminates this judicial forgetfulness. Bloss v. Dykema, 398 U.S. 278, 90 S.Ct. 1727, 26 L.Ed.2d 230 (1970).

Judges are mortal and therefore are heir to the delightful differences which make up the human species. Nevertheless, when passing upon an alleged obscenity issue, we must strive to put aside our personal predilections and strictly adhere to the authoritative United States Supreme Court decisions.[11]

In *Redrup, supra,* the Court found the paperback books *Lust Pool* and *Shame Agent* not to be obscene.

We believe that it is ludicrous to consider *Slaughterhouse-Five* in the same literary niche as *Lust Pool* and *Shame Agent.* If the latter are not convicted because of their alleged profanity, then the former should never even stand trial. *Slaughterhouse-Five* is Sunday school reading compared to these paperbacks. We do not wish to demean Mr. Vonnegut by making such ridiculous comparisons. That he is a serious writer has been attested to by those whose literary credentials are more impressive than our own.[12]

"Obscenity" is a mercurial matter. As Mr. Justice Harlan recently said for the Court in Cohen v. California, 403 U.S. 15, 25, 91 S.Ct. 1780, 1788, 29 L.Ed.2d 284, 294 (1971):

"[I]t is nevertheless often true that one man's vulgarity is another's lyric. Indeed, we think it is largely because governmental officials cannot make principled distinctions in this area that the Constitution leaves matters of taste and style so largely to the individual."

We concur.

We hold that, as a matter of law, *Slaughterhouse-Five* is not obscene in the constitutional sense. Under the authority granted us by GCR1963, 820.6, we find as a matter of fact that *Slaughterhouse-Five* is not obscene, profane, or vulgar in the constitutional sense. We believe it to be a serious work of quasi-fiction by an acknowledged legitimate writer. The book's dominant theme is anti-war. The subject, war, slaughter, bombing, may be obscene: the telling of the tale is not.[13]

Defendant and *amicus curiae* urge that the real issue underlying this case is that a circuit judge, or any government official, has no lawful right to impose his own particular value judgments on our citizenry in matters which are traditionally protected by the penumbra of the First Amendment. They argue that that, in fact, is what happened here and meticulously cite the trial record for factual support. For the reasons outlined below we entertain no doubt that defendant and *amicus curiae* are legally correct and that the trial court abused its discretion in entering this traditionally sacred area.

One of the reasons that our constitutions have wisely precluded sovereign interference with an individual's right to read, think, speak, observe, and pray as he desires is the fact that these concepts are so arbitrary and diverse that they are foreign to standardization and any possible test of right-wrong. Government has no legitimate interest in controlling or tabulating the human mind nor the fuel that feeds it.

In his May 11, 1971 opinion, the trial judge stated:

"The Court did read the book as requested for determination of factual matters and issues of law alike, and unfortunately did thus waste considerable time. At points, the Court was deeply disgusted. How any educator entrusted during school hours with the educational, emotional and moral welfare and healthy growth of children could do other than reject such cheap, valueless reading material, is incomprehensible. Its repetitious obscenity and immorality, merely degrade and defile, teaching nothing. Contemporary literature, of real educational value to youth abounds, contains scientific, social and cultural facts, of which youth need more to know, today.

"Certainly, it is unnecessary for any school system to search out and select obscenity, pornography, or deviated immorality in order to teach modern literature.

"Modern desire for complete licentious freedom has evidently led some educators into the fallacy that degradation of subject matter in reading and thought, is a necessary part of freedom in modern education. Does the modern trend of education permit mental prostitution, and encourage mental deviation? If so, this is a sad distortion of educational purpose."

While the May 11, 1971 opinion was subsequently superseded by a later one, the former is instructive insomuch as it allows this Court the opportunity to follow the trial judge's judicial thought process. Clearly, the trial judge found *Slaughterhouse-Five* to be a "bad" book, totally worthless and utterly lacking in any merit, literary or otherwise. But as Shakespeare reminds us in language antedating almost all of our sacred precedent, "There is nothing either good or bad, but thinking makes it so." (Hamlet, Act II, Scene 2, line 259). This Court cannot, in good conscience, nor in adherence to our constitutional oath of office, allow a non-educational public official the right, in absence of gross constitutional transgressions, to regulate the reading material to which our students are exposed. Our Constitution will tolerate no supreme censor nor allow any man to superimpose his judgment on that of others so that the latter are denied the freedom to decide and choose for themselves.

The reasons for such a philosophy are basic to the American system of jurisprudence. Judges pass on the law not upon morals. It is, then, perhaps ironic that the most able articulation of judicial non-intervention in matters of conscience and personal conviction was penned by the distinguished English playwright Robert Bolt. In *A Man for All Seasons,* Sir Thomas More, the sacred ancestor of our judiciary, is infused by Mr. Bolt with the following language:

"More: ... The law, Roper, the law. I know what's legal not what's right. And I'll stick to what's legal.

Roper: Then you set man's law above God's!

More: No, far below; but let *me* draw your attention to a fact—I'm *not* God. The currents and eddies of right and wrong, which you find such plain sailing, I can't navigate. I'm no voyager. But in the thickets of the law, oh, there I'm a forester. I doubt if there's a man alive who could follow me there, thank God...." *A Man for All Seasons,* 37 (Vintage Books, N.Y., 1960).

What does the law say when it speaks to this precise issue? No American jurist ever stated the basic premise better than Mr. Justice Jackson in his now classical opinion in West Virginia State Board of Education v. Barnette, 319 U.S. 624, 642, 63 S.Ct. 1178, 1187, 87 L.Ed. 1628, 1639 (1943):

"If there is any fixed star in our constitutional constellation, it is that no official, high or petty, can prescribe what shall be orthodox in politics, nationalism, religion or other matters of opinion...."

It is clear from the trial court's May 11, 1971 opinion that he viewed reading *Slaughterhouse-Five* as a "waste (of) considerable time." He found the novel to be "deeply disgust(ing)," "cheap, valueless reading material," repetitious in its obscenity, "incomprehensible," "immoral," "defil(ing)" and totally non-instructive. He further said "Certainly, it is unnecessary for any school system to search out and select obscenity, pornography, or deviated immorality in order to teach modern literature." Capsulized, the trial judge found *Slaughterhouse-Five* to be "rubbish."

Turning again for guidance to Mr. Justice Jackson,[14] we approvingly cite and adopt the following language from his scholarly dissent in United States v. Ballard, 322 U.S. 78, 95, 64 S.Ct. 882, 890, 88 L.Ed. 1148, 1158 (1944):

"But that is precisely the thing the Constitution put beyond the reach of the prosecutor, for the price of freedom of religion or of speech or of the press is that we must put up with, and even pay for, a good deal of rubbish."[15]

We are concerned that in this case the trial court, in attempting to adjudicate this matter, substituted its own judgment of what is "right" and "moral" for that of the student, the teacher, and the duly constituted school authority.[16] Such action is resolutely forbidden by the Constitution. It is for the lawfully elected school board, its supervisory personnel and its teachers to determine the local schools' curriculum. The judicial censor is *persona non grata* in formation of public education. Epperson v. Arkansas, 393 U.S. 97, 104, 89 S.Ct. 266, 270, 21 L.Ed.2d 228, 234 (1968). "The vigilant protection of constitutional freedoms is nowhere more vital than in the community of American schools," Shelton v. Tucker, 364 U.S. 479, 487, 81 S.Ct. 247, 251, 5 L.Ed.2d 231, 236 (1960), but the trial court's actions in this case abridge these priceless, guaranteed academic freedoms and "cast a pall of orthodoxy over the classroom." Keyishian v. Board of Regents, 385 U.S. 589, 603, 87 S.Ct. 675, 683, 17 L.Ed.2d 629, 640 (1967). We cannot approve such action by the judiciary nor any other government official. U.S.Const., art. VI, cl. 2; Sweezy v. New Hampshire, 354 U.S. 234, 250, 77 S.Ct. 1203, 1211-1212, 1 L.Ed.2d 1311, 1324-1325 (1957). Schools are an institution, indeed the only institution, in which our youth is exposed to exciting and competing ideas, varying from antiquity to the present.

It is the trial court's right to select the reading matter which he personally consumes. That is a matter purely for his own conscience, preference and appetite. On the other hand, the judicial garb should never be mistaken for the accoutrements of a censor and the black robes of the trial court may not exclude, from public school students, the light of ideas—irrespective of their varied hues. See, American Bar Association "Statement on the Freedom to Read," reprinted in *The First Freedom*, Robert B. Downs, ed. (American Library Association, 1960). Sweezy v. New Hampshire, *supra;* Shelton v. Tucker, *supra*.

The Supreme Court has clearly indicated that book censorship is an odious practice. In Hannegan v. Esquire, Inc., 327 U.S. 146, 157-158, 66 S.Ct. 456, 462, 90 L.Ed. 586, 593 (1946), the Court observed:

"Under our system of government there is an accommodation for the widest varieties of tastes and ideas. What is good literature, what has educational value, what is refined public information, what is good art, varies with individuals as it does from one generation to another. There doubtless would be a contrariety of views concerning Cervantes' Don Quixote, Shakespeare's Venus and Adonis or Zola's Nana. *But a requirement that literature or art conform to some norm prescribed by an official smacks of an ideology foreign to our system.*" (Emphasis supplied.)

The Court has characterized the classroom as "the 'marketplace of ideas.' The Nation's future depends upon leaders trained through wide exposure to that robust exchange of ideas which discovers truth 'out of a multitude of tongues, [rather] than through any kind of authoritative selection.'" Keyishian v. Board of Regents, *supra,* 385 U.S. at 603, 87 S.Ct. at 683, 17 L.Ed.2d at 640. See, also, Tinker v. Des Moines Community School District, 393 U.S. 503, 512, 89 S.Ct. 733, 739, 21 L.Ed.2d 731, 741 (1969).

Vonnegut's literary dwellings on war, religion, death, Christ, God, government, politics, and any other subject should be as welcome in the public schools of this State as those of Machiavelli, Chaucer, Shakespeare, Melville, Lenin, Hitler, Joseph McCarthy, or Walt Disney. The students of Michigan are free to make of *Slaughterhouse-Five* what they will.

Reversed. Summary judgment of no cause of action is entered in this Court in favor of defendant Rochester Community Schools.

No costs, a public question being involved.

O'HARA, Judge (concurring in result).

Judge Brennan and I concur only in the result reached by Judge Bronson. We are not prepared to endorse his opinion.

We feel the basic point involved here is not whether the book in question is *per se* obscene or pornographic as those terms have been judicially defined by the United States Supreme Court. This is made clear by the following finding of the trial judge.

"The issues in this case have to do solely with the doctrine of separation of religion and state, and there is nothing before the court on which to rule concerning mere obscenity, pornography...."

There is no doubt, as the trial court noted, that certain *characters* in the novel express sentiments that are derogatory of the religious beliefs of a very sizable segment of our society. However, the novel in question is merely listed as one of a number of books reflective of a current literary style. It is not alleged that the teacher of the course advocated, approved or promulgated concepts offensive to established religious beliefs or organized religious sects.

This, of course, is precisely the point. Writings, contemporary as well as of ages past, have attributed to characters beliefs and expressions highly antagonistic to established religious beliefs. Manifestly, many of these writings have attained classical status. As we view the constitutional test, a public educational institution cannot espouse as part of its teaching program such expressions of belief *pro* or *contra* as representative of the beliefs of the institution. In the presentation of reading material, the public institution is well within its teaching function to list the particular books the faculty regards as valuable to the full exposure of the student to conflicting views of religious beliefs. To advocate the views doctrinally as those of the institution is quite another thing. It is not alleged that defendant in this case espoused any antireligious views as opposed merely to making available course material.

We find no violation of the "establishment" clause of the First Amendment.

The judgment granting mandamus against defendant school system is reversed. The case is remanded to the trial court for entry under directions to grant defendant motion for summary judgment.

No costs.

NOTES

* MICHAEL D. O'HARA, former Supreme Court Justice, sitting on the Court of Appeals by assignment pursuant to Const. 1963, art. 6, § 23 as amended in 1968.

1. The novel was published in 1969 by the Delacorte Press, Inc., of New York.

2. The quoted textual passages in this paragraph of the opinion are taken verbatim from paragraphs 4 and 5 of plaintiff's complaint.

3. The "Current Literature" course offered by the Rochester Community Schools was not part of the prescribed curriculum but was an elective. Some of the other literature which was required reading for the course was: *Arsenic and Old Lace, The Detective Story,* Herman Hesse's *Steppenwolf, The American Dream,* short stories by J.D. Salinger, and selected poetry by James Dickey, Allen Ginsberg, Lawrence Ferlinghetti, and Howard Nemerov. The supplemental reading list for the course included: *Love Story* by Erich Segal, *Walden II* by B.F. Skinner, *Catch-22* by Joseph Heller, *Waiting for Godot* by Samuel Beckett, *Catcher in the Rye* by J.D. Salinger, *The Andromeda Strain* by Michael Crichton, *Who's Afraid of Virginia Woolf?* by Edward Albee and *The Power and the Glory* by Graham Greene. Since plaintiff apparently did not find these writings to violate the First and Fourteenth Amendments, we express no judicial opinion as to their constitutional validity. Nor is such necessary.

4. The May 13, 1971 and June 9, 1971 opinions by Judge Moore are meticulous and thorough. We commend him for his steadfast adherence to GCR 1963, 517.1. Relevant portions of both opinions will be set out later in this opinion.

5. This Court wishes to express its gratitude to the American Civil Liberties Union of Michigan for its valued assistance as *amicus curiae.*

6. The complaint is herein set out in full: "NOW COMES, BRUCE LIVINGSTON TODD, a resident of the County of Oakland, residing at 753 Charlesina, Oakland Township, Oakland County, Michigan, and complaint [*sic*] of the ROCHESTER COMMUNITY SCHOOLS, A Body Corporate, Defendant herein, named pursuant to RJA 600.4401 and GCR [1963] 710, as follows:

   "1) One of Plaintiff's children is lawfully enrolled in the Rochester Community Schools and is attending the prescribed classes of instruction pursuant to the curriculum requirements and specifications.

   "2) As a part of said curriculum is a course of study referred to as 'Current Literature'.

   "3) As a part of said 'Current Literature' course of instruction is the offered reading of a book titled, 'Slaughterhouse-Five' or 'The Children's Crusade' believed to have been authored by one Kurt Von-

negut, Jr. and published by Dell Publishing Company, Inc. of New York, New York.

   "4) Said book contains and makes reference to religious matters.

   "5) The use of such book as a part of or in connection with any course of instruction by a Public School District or System is illegal and contrary to the laws of this land; namely, the First and Fourteenth Amendments of the Constitution of the United States, pursuant to the determinations of the Supreme Court of the United States, to-wit: Engel v. Vitale, 370 U.S. 421; 82 S.Ct. 1261; 8 L.Ed.2d 601 (1962), and DeSpain v. DeKalb County Community School District, 7 Cir., 384 F.2d 836 (1967), *et al.*

   "6) Plaintiff herein has often requested of Defendant herein that said book, to wit: 'Slaughterhouse-Five' or 'The Children's Crusade', be withdrawn from and as a part of the curriculum offered by Defendant has failed and refused to do so, and Defendant continues to employ said book as a part of its offered course of instruction contrary to the laws of this land.

   "WHEREFORE, Plaintiff prays that a Writ of Mandamus be issued adjudging said book, 'Slaughterhouse-Five' or 'The Children's Crusade' to be unlawful and unfit for use as a part of a course of instruction offered by Defendant, The Rochester Community Schools; or

"In the Alternative

   "That this Court issue its Order to Show Cause pursuant to the Petition and Affidavit of Bruce Livingston Todd, Plaintiff herein, the originals of which are attached hereto and made a part of this Complaint and that said matter be brought on for an immediate hearing and determination by this Honorable Court."

7. As Mr. Justice Brennan so ably articulated in his concurring opinion in *Schempp, supra:*

   "... What the Framers meant to foreclose, and what our decisions under the Establishment Clause have forbidden, are those involvements of religious with secular institutions which (a) serve the essentially religious activities of religious institutions; (b) employ the organs of government for essentially religious purposes; or (c) use essentially religious means to serve governmental ends, where secular means would suffice. ..." 374 U.S. at 294-295, 83 S.Ct. at 1609-1610, 10 L.Ed.2d at 899.

   "The holding of the Court today plainly does not foreclose teaching *about* the Holy Scriptures or about the differences between religious sects in classes in literature or history. Indeed, whether or not the Bible is involved, it would be impossible to teach meaningfully many subjects in the social sciences or the humanities without some mention of religion. To what extent, and at what points in the curriculum, religious materials should be cited are matters which the courts ought to entrust very largely to the experienced officials who superintend our Nation's public schools. They are experts in such matters, and we are not. We should heed Mr. Justice Jackson's caveat that any attempt by this Court to announce curricular standards would be 'to decree a uniform, rigid and, if we are consistent, an unchanging standard for countless school boards representing and serving highly localized groups which not only differ from each other but which themselves from time to time change attitudes.'..." 374 U.S. at 300-301, 83 S.Ct. at 1612-1613; 10 L.Ed.2d at 902-903.

8. Kurt Vonnegut, Jr. personally witnessed this carnage while in a Nazi prisoner of war camp. See, Slaughterhouse-Five at 1; 93 Time 108-109 (April 11, 1969).

9. The Michigan Supreme Court apparently stands foursquare with the *Schempp* test. See, Advisory Opinion re: Constitutionality of P.A. 1970, No. 100, 384 Mich. 82, 180 N.W.2d 265 (1970), which has been overruled on the issue of "parochiaid." See, generally, Downey and Roberts, Freedom From Federal Establishment (1964) and Church, State and Freedom (1967), by Leo Pfeffer.

10. See, *e.g.,* Genesis 19:33.

11. To insure objective, rather than subjective, review the Fifth Circuit Court of Appeals has held that expert testimony is required on community obscenity standards. United States v. Groner (C.A. 5, Jan. 11, 1972) rehearing en banc granted March 28, 1972.

12. See, *e.g.,* Granville Hicks, Saturday Review (March 27, 1969).

13. The following sentiment of Kurt Vonnegut, Jr. is perhaps self-explanatory:

"Addressing his editor, Seymour Lawrence, Vonnegut says: 'Sam—here's the book, It is so short and jumbled and jangled, Sam, because there is nothing intelligent to say about a massacre.' " Saturday Review, p. 25 (March 27, 1969).

14. Lest it be thought that somehow Justice Robert Jackson was incapable of taking a firm, "moral" stance on an issue, we have not forgotten that it was this legal giant, perhaps the most eloquent man ever to wear the robes of a Justice of the United States Supreme Court, who successfully headed the prosecution of the chief Nazi war criminals at Nuremberg.

15. Similarly, see the recent decision in United States v. Head, D.C., 317 F.Supp. 1138, 1146 (1970), in which the Court said:

"The whole thrust of the First Amendment is to shelter expression from the value judgments of those in power; when any judge or prosecutor attempts to assess speech, he must do so in his own coin—a coin that is by definition suspect."

16. "The law knows no heresy, and is committed to the support of no dogma...." Watson v. Jones, 80 U.S. (13 Wall.) 679, 728, 20 L.Ed. 666, 676 (1872).

T HE California Supreme Court decides for a tenth grade English teacher not rehired because of his reading to his class a short story he had written, a story containing language deemed "objectionable" by the principal, "including a slang expression for an incestuous son."

Lindros v. *Governing Bd. of Torrance U. Sch. Dist.*, 510 P.2d 361 (1972)

TOBRINER, Justice.

In this case we examine Education Code section 13443,[1] which establishes the conditions under which the governing boards of local school districts may decline to rehire probationary teachers. At the end of the 1969-1970 academic year, the Governing Board of the Torrance Unified School District[2] terminated petitioner Stanley Lindros, a probationary teacher, because he read a theme to his English class which contained controversial language, and because he allegedly on one occasion allowed students to return needed books to the library without proper authorization.

For the reasons set forth below, we hold that these incidents fail to establish "cause" for termination which is reasonably "relate[d] to the welfare of the schools and pupils thereof" as required by section 13443, subdivision (d); in so doing we note that in both incidents Lindros acted in the good faith pursuit of concededly legitimate educational objectives, and that the Board demonstrated no significant adverse impact on the students or the school.

The Torrance Board employed petitioner as a tenth-grade probationary English teacher at South High School for the 1969-1970 school year. Petitioner's record attested to his eminent qualification for the position. Not only did he hold a California teacher credential but also he had studied for, or obtained, advanced degrees in philosophy, theology, and the communication arts. A Catholic priest on leave of absence from the Church, petitioner had enjoyed a wide range of experience: he had served as a parish priest, prison chaplain, resident counselor, and secondary level teacher. Nothing in the record suggests that petitioner had failed to fulfill his promise as an effective English instructor or had been unable to relate well with young people; indeed "teacher evaluation" records indicated that he proved himself "above average" in both competency in subject matter and in rapport with students.

The incident which constituted the main charge against the petitioner occurred early in the school year. In mid-October 1969 petitioner assigned his tenth-grade English classes the task of preparing a short story relating a personal emotional experience. The purpose of this assignment, as later described by petitioner, was to stress "the relationship between good creative writing and personal experience. I believe this to be the key in communicating with students and encouraging better writing."

At the request of several students that he present them with an example of his own work, Lindros read a short story, "The Funeral," which he originally wrote as a rough draft for a television play at Loyola University. Autobiographical in nature, the story recorded petitioner's emotions at the funeral of one of his students who, during the time Lindros taught at a predominantly black high school in Watts, died of a heroin overdose. The theme contained language later deemed objectionable by South High's principal—including a slang expression for an incestuous son. We set forth the full text below:

"The Funeral"

I was mad, disgusted . . . tense. If Agnes hadn't reminded me I'd still be watching *Shoes of a Fisherman* at the film director's studio. But whether it was guilt or concern, I knew I should be at Ed's funeral at 2 p.m.

"The highway provided me with nothing but a blanket of mist and melancholy. Splashing past 110-th and Compton Ave. I caught sight of Greater Antioch Baptist Church just as four of my students were carrying Ed's body into the dismal looking building.

"Water dripped from the ceiling as the small choir intoned, *Come Sweet Jesus*. . . . Only the appearance of plump Rev. Black, Bible in hand, saved us from their uncoordinated efforts.

"I couldn't catch what Black was reading but it was unimportant. I was here, somber, moody, thoughtful; and all to the testimony that I as a white man did care for a young black hipe who died too young . . . too soon.

"Lloyd made it . . . Larry, Fred, Benard, Fuzzy—they were all there. Seemed like every addict in the community was on the scene with his leather jacket and shades, as if to collect . . . or to pay off to Ed. What a lineup! Sargent [*sic*] Masterson from Precinct 77 would have raised a brow or two at this gathering.

"Kelly had tears streaming down his face; perpetually high . . . who could blame him; deserted father, bitch mother; in and out of jail since thirteen. He shot with Ed for the last time that Saturday night.

"The wailing, so characteristic at a Black funeral did not begin until the second stanza of *I Believe,* delivered by Hessie Jones. The little Black kid next to me stared at the solitary tear that rolled down my cheek.

"Why are women so goddam hysterical? Did they really know Ed? Did they care? Were they using Ed's 'time' from their own shackles of welfare and project living? I do not know. I do not live in Watts; but I feel for them now, in their strange melodramatic way.

"Only the obituary read by Sister Maebelle shook me out of my depression. 'Ed Leavy Pollard. Born in Greenwood, Miss., 1952; Died Jan. 11, 1969 . . . , She droned on in a pitifully low, uneducated tone.

"Curley, a steady shooter with Ed was moved to bellow out, 'Louder Lady, I can't hear ya.' Choresetta in the fourth pew from the front responded to this abrupt remark with a deep shaking sob. The storm grew louder. I noticed at least three leaks from the roof now. God, what a depressing hole; wet, dam [*sic*] pictureless, peeling paint, worn, dam pews; only the cossack of Ed and us. 'Only us O Lord,' I thought 'but what the hell are we here for?'

"I sit here white, middleclass, secure, while the goddam system rapes these poor people of every vestage [*sic*] of dignity.

"Rev. Galine, a slick looking 'Tom' began the eulogy; Jeremiah was the scapegoat. First there was the woman in the back row. She was joined by three others; then another . . . and another; soon everyone in the drama had his chance to chant a response back to the Baptist Preacher; 'Oh Lord' . . . 'That's right' . . . 'I'm listnin' . . . 'Speak God.' . . . Only the periodic gasping signs (sobs) interrupted the Rev's show.

"Ed would have rolled over and grimaced if he would have heard the hysterics when David, his classmate, opened his cossack for the finale. The weeping and gnashing lasted long enough for all of us to troop past Ed and glance at his ashen, black face.

"I felt whipped out; this was a strange two hours; strange to a white who had no blackness in him; strange to a white who knew no such poverty and desperation; even stranger outside when I greeted a young Black in a Panther-like outfit: 'White-mother-fuckin Pig.' . . .' "

Before reading the controversial words at the end of "The Funeral," petitioner pondered their appropriateness for the classroom, and decided in good faith that their use was permissible in some, but not all, of his classes.[3] As petitioner stated, although he recognized that "a few words in 'The Funeral' [were] not acceptable in common usage . . . [he] felt that even if one student was to give up or think less of drugs, the reason for reading the play was justified." Lindros read the young black's objectionable and defiant remark at the end of the story only in college preparatory classes, which he considered most mature; in other classes he substituted the initials "W.M.F.P." While petitioner did not preliminarily consult with school administrators as to whether he should read the story, his conduct accorded with the prevailing policy of the school that instructors could select outside instructional material. According to the hearing officer "There [was] widespread use of outside instructional material selected by the instructors and not submitted for approval." Moreover, school administrators had promulgated "no clear statement of the criteria or standards [to be] applied in selecting this material."

Furthermore, the prevailing practices and conditions at the high school strongly indicated that the inclusion of the language in a literary composition would evoke no concern. The library shelved books, readily available to students, which contained words identical to all of those found in "The Funeral"; school administrators, moreover, as part of the curriculum, had permitted instructors to take students to theatrical performances in which the lines spoken by the actors contained the same or similar words.

No disruption of classroom activities followed petitioner's reading of "The Funeral." As the hearing officer noted, "In considering the seriousness of the use of the offending material . . . these words were presented fully or by their initial letters to five classes of a total of approximately 150 students. No complaint arose from the students and none arose from the parents of these students. This will not establish that the material was appropriate for classroom use but does tend to establish that the context and manner of presentation was not nearly so startling to the students who heard it . . . as the disembodied restatement of the offending words makes it appear."

Despite this seemingly indifferent reaction, the principal of the high school learned of the incident and reprimanded Lindros. The principal counseled Lindros that the language of the short story did not accord with established classroom usage and that further use of vulgar material should be avoided; petitioner agreed to abide by this directive and signed a statement to that effect. This meeting closed the incident until the end of the school year, some eight months later, when the Torrance Board announced that it would not rehire Lindros. As both the hearing officer and the superior court later found, the reading of "The Funeral" constituted the "gravamen" of the Torrance Board's complaint against Lindros.[4]

In addition to the incident involving "The Funeral," the hearing officer found Lindros to have permitted students to leave class on one occasion without the authorization normally required by school regulations.[5] On February 6, 1970, petitioner allowed students in one class to depart a few minutes before the "sounding of the bell signalling the close of the class session." Lindros "had instructed those of his students who were in possession of a book entitled *Zorba the Greek* to depart from class early, secure the book from their lockers, and return the book to the library so that it could be redistributed when needed by the students of another English instructor . . . It was not established that all of those students who departed were leaving to complete this errand."

After the superintendent of the Torrance School District served notice of an intention not to rehire Lindros because of the aforementioned incidents, the Board held an administrative hearing pursuant to subdivision (b) of section 13443. At this proceeding the hearing officer found that " 'The Funeral' is not within the generally accepted standard and that its use would violate the policy of the school in regard to the introduction of objectionable language into the classroom." He further found that although "[t]he school does sanction the use of literary work and current periodical material in which socially unacceptable words and phrases appear . . . [The Funeral] is not a generally accepted literary work and does not appear within a generally accepted periodical. [Petitioner's] lapse of judgment and violation of standards is a factor relating to the welfare of the students and the school." Though he found that the incident involving "The Funeral" was the "gravamen" of the complaint, the hearing officer also declared that the February 6, 1970, incident involving early dismissal of students from class constituted "cause" under section 13443.

The Torrance Board, without examining the record of the administrative hearing, adopted the hearing officer's report as its own: the Board further declared that each charge "separately and collectively" constitute[d] . . . sufficient cause not to reemploy [petitioner].

Following the Torrance Board's final decision, Lindros petitioned the Los Angeles Superior Court for a writ of mandate under Code of Civil Procedure section 1094.5. In denying the petition the superior court declared that the language of "The Funeral" is "manifestly coarse and vulgar" and that "[p]etitioner should have known that such language by a teacher was totally unacceptable in a Tenth Grade English class." The superior court then noted that the charges relating to both "The Funeral" and the February 6, 1970, incident involving early dismissal of students "were found to be related to the welfare of the school and the pupils thereof, and the Governing Board's determination of sufficiency is conclusive." We believe that this holding cannot be sustained because petitioner's conduct did not, as a matter of law, constitute cause for termination within the meaning of Education Code section 13443. We turn now to an analysis of section 13443, and of the errors which we perceive in the superior court's denial of the writ of mandate.

I. *The question whether alleged misconduct establishes "cause" under section 13443, subdivision (d), constitutes a question of law.*

Education Code section 13443, subdivision (d) defines the conditions under which a local school board can refuse to rehire a probationary teacher. The statute provides that: "The Governing Board's determination not to reemploy a probationary employee for the ensuing school year shall be for cause only. The determination of the Governing Board as to the sufficiency of the cause pursuant to this section shall be conclusive, but the cause shall relate solely to the welfare of the schools and the pupils thereof. . . . "

The precedents clearly establish that the question whether a particular cause for refusal to rehire relates "solely to the welfare of the schools and the pupils thereof" presents a matter of law that must be determined by the courts, and, ultimately, by this court. The Board determines the *facts* and their sufficiency to support the Board's determination but the court decides whether the facts as found—in our case, the conduct of the teacher—reasonably could be said to have adversely affected the welfare of the school or its pupils.

In the fountainhead case of Griggs v. Board of Trustees (1964) 61 Cal.2d 93, 37 Cal.Rptr. 194, 389 P.2d 722, a school board refused to rehire a probationary teacher for "lack of self-restraint and tact in dealing with co-workers, pupils, and parents." (*Id.* at p. 97, 37 Cal. Rptr. at p. 197, 389 P.2d at p.725.) We interpreted section 13443 (then § 13444) to mean that "where there is evidence to support the board's findings of fact *and where the cause for dismissal found by the board can reasonably be said to relate to the 'welfare of the schools and pupils thereof,'* the reviewing court may not consider whether the facts found are sufficiently serious to justify dismissal." (*Id.* at p. 96, 37 Cal.Rptr. at p. 197, 389 P.2d at p. 275.) (Emphasis added.) The *Griggs* court then itself found a reasonable relationship between the "cause" (lack of tact) and the "welfare of the schools." (*Id.* at p. 97, 37 Cal.Rptr. 194, 389 P.2d 722.)

We more recently examined the division of responsibilities between courts and governing boards under section 13443 in Bekiaris v. Board of Education (1972) 6 Cal. 3d 575, 100 Cal.Rptr. 16, 493 P.2d 480. "It is to be emphasized . . . that [under section 13443] the general applicability of the rule of substantial evidence in light of the entire record does not affect the power and duty of the trial court to make an independent determination of questions having a legal character. Thus, [n]othing . . . prevents the reviewing court from determining whether the board has proceeded in excess of jurisdiction, whether there has been a fair trial, and whether the board's findings of fact are supported by substantial evidence.' [Citation.] Moreover, it is for the *court to determine whether a particular cause for dismissal 'relate[s] solely to the welfare of the schools and the pupils thereof'* as required by section 13443. [Citations.]" (*Id.* at p. 587, 100 Cal.Rptr. at p. 22, 493 P.2d at p. 486.) (Emphasis added.)

We further explained that "although the reviewing court must accept evidentiary facts shown by substantial evidence and the sufficiency of those facts to constitute a stated cause, still it remains for the court to determine *as a matter of law* whether such cause relates to the welfare of the school and its pupils and is therefore adequate under the provisions of section 13443 to justify dismissal." (*Id.* at p. 589, 100 Cal.Rptr. at p. 24, 493 P.2d at p. 488.) (Emphasis in the opinion.)

The Courts of Appeal have consistently followed this approach. Thus, the court in Blodgett v. Board of Trustees (1971) 20 Cal.App.3d 183, 97 Cal.Rptr. 406, held that refusal to rehire a probationary teacher solely because she was overweight was not a "cause" reasonably related to school welfare; the "physical condition unrelated to the plaintiff's fitness [to teach] was used as a pretext for refusing [re-employment]." (*Id.* at p. 193, 97 Cal.Rptr. at p. 412.) In Thornton v. Board of Trustees (1968) 262 Cal.App.2d 761, 68 Cal.Rptr. 842, the Court of Appeal held refusal to rehire solely because a probationary teacher was 65 years old was not "cause"[6] reasonably related to the welfare of the school.

In sum, whether particular conduct establishes cause under section 13443, poses a pure question of law. This question must be sharply distinguished from two other types of questions which arise under section 13443: (1) questions of *fact* and (2) questions as to the *sufficiency* of the "cause" to warrant dismissal in light of all the circumstances. Past cases have held that findings of fact, developed by the hearing officer and the governing board, will be upheld by the courts so long as supported by substantial evidence on the whole record. (Griggs v. Board of Trustees, *supra*, 61 Cal.2d at p. 96, 37 Cal.Rptr. 194, 389 P.2d 722.)[7] Similarly, the determination as to the "sufficiency of the cause"—whether the "cause" warrants a refusal to rehire despite the teacher's redeeming qualities as a teacher, his attitude, and the particular needs of the school district—lies solely in the discretion of the governing board *so long as*

section 1344's requirement of "cause . . . relate[d] solely to the welfare of the schools and the pupils thereof . . . " has been met. (Bekiaris v. Board of Education, *supra*, 6 Cal. 3d at p. 589, 100 Cal.Rptr. 16, 24, 493 P.2d 480, 488.)

Having demonstrated that the determination of "cause" under section 13443 constitutes a question of law, we turn to an examination of that issue in light of the two charges of misconduct against petitioner Lindros.

II. *The reading of "The Funeral" did not constitute "cause" under section 13443.*

Lindros' reading of the composition did not constitute "cause" under section 13443 because, first, in presenting it to his pupils petitioner sought to pursue a bona fide educational purpose and in so doing did not adversely affect "the welfare of the schools or the pupils thereof"; second, the composition was used as teaching material without prior reasonable notice that such use would later be deemed impermissible by school authorities. We shall separately analyze each of these propositions.

A. *In reading "The Funeral" petitioner sought to pursue a bona fide educational purpose and in so doing did not adversely affect the welfare of the school or the pupils thereof.*

Erroneously applying a per se approach to the controversial epithet at the end of "The Funeral," the superior court declared that its use was "manifestly coarse and vulgar." The court, however, apparently failed to make the crucial distinction between unrestricted use of such words in the classroom and their inclusion in teaching material for a class in creative writing.

Petitioner is the first to concede that it would be "outrageous . . . if a teacher simply shouts 'motherfucking-pigs' to his students." Obviously teachers are not to sanction the use of words as blatantly offensive as these in classroom discussion or even in the personal banter of students. But here the words were used by a character in a story; the story, in turn, was presented as an example of expressive writing. The black character utters the words in "The Funeral" as a mark of his anger and disgust at a white's presence at the funeral; the words were employed for a definite literary objective. Thus, Lindros read the story to his students as part of a quite obvious teaching technique.

Many classic works seeking to capture the anger of blacks against a society that they consider inexcusably oppressive are peppered with epithets that express outrage in terms at least as violent as that used here. Malamud's "The Tenants" is a recent example; "Man-Child in a Promised Land" by Claude Brown is another. Baldwin's "The Fire Next Time," written, as it is, by a black, is the most virulent; we could cite innumerable other examples. The writer of "The Funeral" could not properly convey the fury of the young black at the apparent condescension of a white man in attending the funeral except by the use of an expletive. The outrage of the black *had* to be mirrored in language that outraged.

Lindros was obviously trying to teach his students that in writing creative compositions the author must attempt to put those words in the mouths of his characters that belong there. The blasphemous epithet must fit the emotional outburst of the speaker. To isolate the epithet and to condemn the teacher is to miss the function of expressive writing. In sum, we could not impose upon teachers of writing, as a matter of law, that they must tell and teach their students that in depicting the jargon of the ghetto, the slum, or the barrack room, characters must speak in the pedantry of Edwardian English.

The record shows that neither student nor parent complained about this use of the lurid words in Lindros' composition. The students had been exposed to identical language in books and periodicals in the school library; their teachers had taken them to dramatic productions that used these and other obnoxious terms. That the students were not "shocked" can come as no surprise.

Finally, the United States Supreme Court has recognized the widespread use of current, divergent and distasteful patterns of speech, such as those involved here; indeed, in some situations that court has accorded constitutional protection to similarly shocking and offensive language. For example, the Supreme Court recently held the phrase "fuck the draft" protected by the First Amendment when portrayed on a jacket worn in a courthouse corridor. (Cohen v. California (1971) 403 U.S. 15, 91 S.Ct. 1780, 29 L.Ed.2d 284.) Although *Cohen* involved a controversial term in expressing a political view in a public forum and is thus distinguishable from the instant situation, we note its reasoning: "How is one to distinguish this from any other offensive word? Surely the State has no right to cleanse public debate to the point where it is grammatically palatable to the most squeamish among us. Yet no readily ascertainable general principle exists for stopping short of that result were we to affirm the judgment below. For, while the particular four-letter word being litigated here is perhaps more distasteful than most others of its genre, it is nevertheless often true that one man's vulgarity is another's lyric." (Cohen v. California, *supra*, 403 U.S. at p. 25, 91 S.Ct. at p. 1788.)

Three recent cases in which the Supreme Court vacated criminal convictions for offensive speech and remanded in light of Cohen v. California, *supra*, 403 U.S. 15, 91 S.Ct. 1280, 29 L.Ed.2d 284, illustrate the same point. In Rosenfeld v. New Jersey (1972) 408 U.S.

901, 92 S.Ct. 2483, 33 L.Ed.2d 321 the defendant was convicted of disturbing the peace by indecent and offensive language; he had addressed a school board meeting, attended by some 40 children, using, on several occasions in his speech, the words "mother fucker"; in Brown v. Oklahoma (1972) 408 U.S. 914, 92 S.Ct. 2507, 33 L.Ed.2d 326, the defendant, during a speech before a group of men and women in the University of Tulsa chapel, referred to policemen as "mother fucking fascist pig cops"; in Lewis v. City of New Orleans (1972) 408 U.S. 913, 92 S.Ct. 2499, 33 L.Ed.2d 321, a mother addressed police officers who had arrested her son as "god-damned-mother-fucking-police."

These cases illustrate both the use of such speech in sections of our multifarious society and an increasing immunity from criminal sanction for such expressions. While these rulings by no means legitimize the general use of offensive language in the classroom, they do explain the background and reasons for the use of such words in literary works depicting realistically the coarse and strident forms of communication that so often attend public dialogue today.[8]

We conclude that the Board has failed to show that the inclusion of opprobrious language currently used in many subcultures, in a single composition, presented solely for teaching purposes, rises to the level of a legal cause for severance of a teacher from his employment.

B. *The reading was only a single incident in the presentation of teaching material which, although later deemed objectionable, was used in the absence of prior reasonable notice that such use would be deemed impermissible by the school authorities.*

As we have pointed out, the accepted policy at South High School permitted the selection of instructional material by teachers without submission to administrators for advanced approval. Moreover, as we have explained, books and periodicals at the school library contained language as controversial as that found in "The Funeral"; further, students with the sponsorship of their teachers attended plays in which such language was employed. In the previous section we have alluded to the unfortunate current prevalence of language as repulsive as that we face here. The record shows no specific disapproval of the use of written material containing such expressions. Under these circumstances we must conclude that petitioner acting in good faith, presented the composition to the class without prior reasonable notice that such presentation would contravene the governing policies of the high school.[9]

We do not believe that one isolated classroom usage of material later deemed objectionable by school administrators, without reasonable prior notice, can constitute "cause" for termination reasonably "relate[d] solely to the welfare of the schools and the pupils thereof." "Cause" under section 13443 requires that the teacher must have failed to exercise such reasonable judgment as would be expected of a member of his profession under the same circumstances. "Teachers, particularly in the light of their professional expertise, will normally be able to determine what kind of conduct indicates unfitness to teach. Teachers are further protected by the fact that they cannot be disciplined merely because they made a reasonable, good faith, professional judgment in the course of their employment with which higher authorities later disagreed." (Morrison v. State Board of Education (1969) 1 Cal.3d 214, 233, 82 Cal.Rptr. 175, 189, 461 P.2d 375, 389.)[10]

III. *The incident involving dismissal of students on one school day fails to establish "cause" reasonably related to the welfare of the schools and was not the true reason for the Board's refusal to rehire Lindros.*

We turn to the remaining charge that on one occasion during the school year Lindros permitted students to leave one of his classes "without proper authorization." A close review of the findings pertinent to the incident reveals that it was not conclusively established that Lindros violated any school rule, and that, in any event, the isolated *de minimis* violation charged was a mere makeweight that did not constitute the true reason for the Board's refusal to rehire Lindros.

The hearing officer's findings of fact, later adopted by both the Torrance Board and the superior court, contain ambiguities which cast doubt on the assertion that Lindros improperly dismissed his class;[11] these ambiguities strengthen our conclusion that the charge of improper dismissal of students did not trigger the action against Lindros. The record indicates that on February 6, 1970, Lindros dismissed some students for the legitimate educational purpose of returning needed copies of the book, *Zorba the Greek,* to the library. Nothing suggests that this action, by itself, violated any school rule. Although it "was not established that all of those students who departed" actually followed petitioner's instructions, Lindros could hardly be dismissed merely because he failed to prove that all of the students obeyed his instructions and went to the library after leaving his classroom. Thus the findings of fact could not support a conclusion that Lindros failed to "authorize" his students to go to the library.[12]

As the hearing officer found, however, de facto school policy required a teacher to provide a *written* authorization when sending more than five students to the library; conceivably, Lindros violated a school regulation, not by dismissing his students, but by failing on this single occasion to furnish a written "hall pass." The hearing officer's decision, however, omitted any findings about this vital fact. The findings therefore do not directly support even the conclusion that

Lindros dismissed the students without proper *written* authorization. (Cf. Almaden-Santa Clara Vineyards v. Paul (1966) 239 Cal.App.2d 860, 867-868, 49 Cal. Rptr. 256.)

In any event, the record makes clear that the reading of "The Funeral" comprised the "gravamen" of the charges, and that the refusal to rehire rested upon this foundation. We are reminded here of the incisive language of Bekiaris v. Board of Education, *supra,* 6 Cal.3d 575, 592-593, 100 Cal.Rptr. 16, 26, 493 P.2d 480, 490 that "a dismissed public employee is entitled to a judicial determination of the *true* reason for his dismissal . . . " (emphasis in the original). Although *Bekiaris* condemned a dismissal involving constitutional rights, its logic equally applies in the instant situation involving statutory rights. Since both the hearing officer and superior court found that "The Funeral" comprised the "gravamen" of the complaint against petitioner, we believe that charge was the "true reason" for the refusal to rehire.[13]

Furthermore, to assume that the Torrance Board would have refused to rehire Lindros based *solely* on the incident of February 6 stretches the credible. The incident at most involved a single, unrepeated infraction of a minor regulation in mid-year, with no showing of any adverse impact on the educational process, and with no showing that it occurred by other than mere inadvertence. We doubt that the Torrance Board would have acted so harshly as to ignore Shakespeare's common sense observation that "men are men; the best sometimes forget." (Shakespeare, Othello, II (1604).[14]

Summarizing the case as a whole, we conclude that the Board's refusal to rehire petitioner was invalid because it was not for cause reasonably related to the Welfare of the school.[15] We heed Judge Wyzanski's characterization of fundamental public policy: that education must "foster open minds, creative imagination, and adventurous spirits. Our national belief is that the heterodox as well as the orthodox are a source of individual and of social growth. We do not confine academic freedom to conventional teachers or to those who can get a majority vote from their colleagues. Our faith is that the teacher's freedom to choose among options for which there is any substantial support will increase his intellectual vitality and his moral strength. The teacher whose responsibility has been nourished by independence, enterprise, and free choice becomes for his student a better model of the democratic citizen." (Mailloux v. Kiley (D.Mass 1971) 323 F.Supp. 1387, 1391.)

The judgment of the superior court denying the writ of mandate is reversed, and the cause is remanded to the superior court for proceedings consistent with this opinion.

WRIGHT, C.J., MOSK and SULLIVAN, JJ., and ROTH, J. pro tem*, concur.

BURKE, Justice (dissenting).

I dissent. The majority have wholly emasculated the provisions of section 13443, subdivision (d), of the Education Code which, until now, assured that a local school board's decision as to the sufficiency of the cause for failing to reemploy a probationary teacher was *conclusive* and free from judicial interference. The "cause" which led defendant district to refuse to reemploy Lindros was his *classroom* use of improper, indecent language. Since the use of such language in the tenth-grade classroom obviously is a matter of relating to "the welfare of the schools and the pupils thereof," (Ed.Code, § 13443, subd. (d), the district's determination concerning the sufficiency of that cause should have been "conclusive." *(Id.)* Instead, the majority have rendered that determination wholly *inclusive,* by relying upon a variety of supposedly mitigating factors (such as Lindros' asserted "good faith") which more properly were matters of sole concern to the district in appraising the sufficiency of the cause for terminating Lindros' services. More importantly, however, and wholly apart from the particular circumstances surrounding this case, the majority's approach can be employed in future cases involving probationary teachers to undermine and defeat the clear legislative intent to vest in the local school board plenary control over these matters.

Section 13443, subdivision (d), carefully allocates the respective responsibilities of the school boards and the courts in cases involving refusals to rehire probationary teachers. That section expressly makes the governing board's determination as to the sufficiency of the cause "conclusive," so long as that cause relates to the welfare of the school or its pupils. As stated in Griggs v. Board of Trustees, 61 Cal.2d 93, 96, 37 Cal.Rptr. 194, 197, 389 P.2d 722, 725, the landmark case in this area, "Nothing in the language of section 13444 [now § 13443] prevents the reviewing court from determining whether the board has proceeded in excess of jurisdiction, whether there has been a fair trial, and whether the board's findings of fact are supported by substantial evidence. However, *where there is evidence to support the board's findings of fact and where cause for dismissal found by the board can reasonably be said to relate to the 'welfare of the schools and the pupils thereof,' the reviewing court may not consider whether the facts found are sufficiently serious to justify dismissal.*" (Italics added.)

In *Griggs,* the "cause" for the board's decision was the teacher's "lack of self-restraint and tact in dealing with co-workers, pupils and parents." Since substantial evidence existed to support the existence of that cause, and since that cause "is clearly a matter which relates to the welfare of the school and its pupils," this court held that "the trial court could not properly substitute its own judgment for that of the board on the question of the sufficiency of the cause for Mrs. Griggs' dismissal." (P. 97, 37 Cal.Rptr. p. 197, 389 P.2d p. 725.) I stress the fact that this court did not purport to reappraise the "good faith," "lack of significant adverse impact," or other possible mitigating factors in Mrs. Griggs' favor, unlike the majority's approach in this case, for such matters were exclusively within the domain of the school board.[1]

Subsequent cases have uniformly employed the Griggs' approach, namely, to determine only whether or not the type of conduct at issue (e.g., lack of tact) can be said to reasonably relate to the welfare of the school and its pupils. For example, in Raney v. Board of Trustees, 239 Cal.App. 2d 256, 48 Cal.Rptr. 555, the "cause" relied upon by the school board was the teacher's severe grading techniques and poor rapport with students. The court explained that were it at liberty to supervise the judgment of the board on the matter, the court "might well reach an opposite conclusion. . . . *[B]ut our theory of government gives to the school trustees, for better or for worse, an almost absolute choice either to 'hire or fire' teachers who have not yet attained tenure.*" (Italics added; p. 260, 48 Cal.Rptr. p. 557.)

Similarly, in American Federation of Teachers v. San Lorenzo, etc., Sch. Dist., 276 Cal.App.2d 132, 136, 80 Cal.Rptr. 758, 760, the court held that a probationary teacher's inability to accept responsibility and inadequate supervision of students "certainly relate to the welfare of the schools and the pupils. . . ." Accordingly, the court explained that it "cannot consider whether the charges justify dismissal." (See also Governing Board v. Brennan, 18 Cal. App.3d 396, 95 Cal.Rptr. 712 [teacher advocated marijuana use]; McGlone v. Mt. Diablo Unified Sch. Dist., 3 Cal.App.3d 17, 82 Cal.Rptr. 225 [failure to supervise students]; Feist v. Rowe, 3 Cal.App.3d 404, 83 Cal. Rptr. 465.)

The two cases which reversed school board decisions in this area are not on point for they merely established that physical characteristics of a teacher, such as advanced age or obesity, cannot constitute "cause" under section 13443 since neither factor standing alone could involve the welfare of the school or students. In the instant case, on the other hand, the cause for Lindros' termination was his *classroom* use of indecent language, a matter which (like the lack of tact in *Griggs,* the severe grading techniques in *Raney,* or the inadequate supervision in *San Lorenzo*) by its very nature relates to the welfare of the school and its pupils. Of course, depending upon the underlying circumstances in each case, including the teacher's "good faith" or the lack of any "significant adverse impact," the school board might determine that particular act or impropriety is excusable and insufficient cause for refusal to reemploy. Yet that decision lies with the school board not the courts.

As I interpret section 13443, the Legislature intended to vest the school board with sole discretion in appraising the sufficiency of the cause, but to assure that the cause asserted has some reasonable relation to the school and its pupils rather than pertaining solely to the teacher's private life, unrelated to school affairs. For example, a court might properly hold that a teacher's persistent refusal to obey his parents, his inability to teach his wife how to drive, his failure to keep timely dental appointments, or his intemperate language with his neighbors, were acts of a type which could not reasonably relate to the welfare of the school or its pupils under section 13443. Yet similar acts of insubordination, incompetence, tardiness or use of indecent language, when occurring in a classroom setting or otherwise affecting school affairs, clearly would meet the statutory test.

In the instant case, Lindros used language *in his classroom* which many persons deem objectionable in any context.[2] Indeed, it is well established that even permanent, tenured teachers are subject to appropriate discipline, including dismissal, on account of their classroom use of indecent or profane language. (See Board of Trustees v. Metzger, 8 Cal.3d 206, 212, 104 Cal.Rptr. 452, 501 P.2d 1172; Palo Verde, etc., Sch. Dist. v. Hensey, 9 Cal.App. 3d 967, 88 Cal.Rptr. 570.) Accordingly, the district certainly had statutory authority to refuse to reemploy Lindros for the coming year.

The majority stress such factors as Lindros' "good faith," his "bona fide educational purpose," the lack of complaints from his students, and the absence of school rules or regulations prohibiting the use of crude and vulgar language by teachers. Once again, it is apparent to me that consideration of such allegedly mitigating factors is for the school board, not the courts. If the board, in the exercise of its discretion and expertise, chooses not to reemploy a probationary teacher who uses such language, on what basis can this court interfere with that decision? Certainly there is no rule of law, statutory or otherwise, which would require advance publication of elaborate regulations and guidelines anticipating all possible infractions or misconduct which a probationary teacher might commit.[3] As the trial court pointed out, Lindros' language was "manifestly coarse and vulgar ... [P]etitioner should have known that such language by a teacher was totally unacceptable in a Tenth Grade English class."

The Court of Appeal, Second District, in the vacated opinion in this case written by Presiding Justice Ford (103 Cal.Rptr. 188), aptly disposed of plaintiff's contention regarding lack of notice: 'There is no iron-clad rule of law that regulations or rules be promulgated which specify in minute detail the various kinds of misconduct which will subject a teacher to disciplinary action. It is not unreasonable to assume that a person engaged in the profession of teaching will have a reasonable concept of generally accepted standards relating to propriety of conduct, including the avoidance of vulgarity, and will adhere to such standards in his relationship with his pupils. . . .

"Adhering to an objective standard, in the present case it was not unreasonable to determine that the plaintiff was on notice that in teaching his tenth grade English classes the art of writing a short story and in affording his students aid by using as a model a short story written by him, resort to a particular story embodying vulgarity would not serve a substantial educational purpose but would constitute a serious impropriety because of the extraneous matter of an unexemplary nature. Since manifestly inherent in such conduct was the probability of an effect adverse to the welfare of students, it was reasonable to assume that the teacher was aware that he was thereby subjecting himself to the hazard of disciplinary measures. Consequently, his contention as to the lack of adequate notice to satisfy the concept of due process is untenable."

I would conclude that the trial court properly denied mandate in this case, and, accordingly, would affirm the judgment.

McCOMB, J., concurs.

Rehearing denied; McCOMB, CLARK and BURKE, JJ., dissenting.

COURT'S OPINION NOTES

1. Except as otherwise noted, all statutory references herinafter are to the Education Code.

   Section 13443 provides probationary teachers with a panoply of procedural and substantive rights. The statute requires school administrators to give notice by March 15, with a statement of reasons, of an intent to recommend against reemployment for the following academic year. It also provides for a hearing upon request before a hearing officer appointed under Government Code section 11500 et seq., for discovery, and for a final decision by the governing board by May 15. The substantive protection afforded by the statute appears in subdivision (d) which declares in relevant part that *"The governing board's determination not to reemploy a probationary employee for the ensuing school year shall be for cause only. The determination of the governing board as to the sufficiency of the cause pursuant to this section shall be conclusive, but the cause shall relate solely to the welfare of the schools and the pupils thereof. . . . "* (Emphasis added.)

2. The Governing Board of the Torrance Unified School District will hereinafter be designated as the "Torrance Board" or "Board."

3. Although the hearing officer did not find expressly that Lindros acted in good faith in pursuit of bona fide educational purposes, we believe that such a finding is implicit in the final paragraph of the hearing officer's proposed decision: "Another relevant consideration is the problem of judgment and professionalism. It should require no argument to support the proposition that the District's Governing Board, as the ultimate employer of the teacher on behalf of the citizens of the district, has the right to control the teacher by promulgating the standards of conduct which it deems appropriate. These standards may allow broad discretion or may be explicit. Here, as is true of much in the field of education, a latitude has been allowed for the exercise of the professional judgment of the educational administrators and the teachers.

Whenever latitude for judgment is granted there will be inevitable variances in its exercise by the individuals involved. The superior may reasonably anticipate that the subordinate's exercise of judgment will vary from his own and, particularly in the case of a beginning employee, that it will be at times erroneous."

4. The superior court declared that "the substantive charge involved, as the hearing officer said, and I agree with him, the gravamen of these proceedings [was] the use of this short story, 'The Funeral,' with its coarse language at the end"; the hearing officer, however, found that the "gravamen" of the charges against Lindros included not only the reading of "The Funeral" but also use of copies of the lyrics from the song "The Pusher" in one of Lindros' classes on January 30, 1970. These lyrics were distributed by one of Lindros' students who presented a class report on drug use. "The Pusher," according to the findings of the hearing officer, was a popular score taken from the motion picture "Easy Rider" and was at the time widely disseminated in radio broadcasts and readily available in phonographic record shops. In fact, the lyrics of "The Pusher" had been used by other instructors at South High School. The hearing officer concluded that "The Pusher" was a work of "established usage" and that its use did not constitute "cause" within the meaning of Education Code section 13443. The Torrance Board later adopted this finding as its own; thus this alleged incident of "misconduct" is not before us here. Other minor charges against petitioner—not discussed in the text—were rejected by the hearing officer or the superior court. (See fn. 5, *infra*.)

5. Lindros was originally charged with three additional isolated incidents of misconduct. First, he allegedly permitted students to write vulgar phrases on their desks and on the bulletin board on a single day in December. As to this charge, the hearing officer found that "The necessarily alleged element of permission was not established" since "[i]t was affirmatively established that [petitioner] had neither by word nor by deed caused the inscribing of these words."

In addition, Lindros was charged with, on one occasion, uttering a swear word at a fellow teacher in the presence of a third teacher. He apologized the next day. The hearing officer found that "while objectionable" this incident occurred "privately between two men in disagreement and has had no substantial impact upon the school or the pupils therof, and therefore, does not constitute a cause not to rehire . . . within the meaning of section 13443." The Torrance Board ultimately accepted this conclusion as its own.

Finally, petitioner was charged with leaving his classroom unattended for a few minutes on a single day in October in violation of school regulations. The superior court found this allegation unsupported by substantial evidence and the Torrance Board has not challenged that determination here.

6. In 1969 the Legislature, in response to the *Thornton* holding amended Education Code section 13325 to make it apply to probationary, as well as permanent, employees (Stats.1969, ch. 795, p. 1613 § 1); section 13325 provides that upon reaching age 65 "employment shall be from year to year at the discretion of the governing board." In extending to governing boards this plenary power over probationary teachers reaching the age of 65 (Taylor v. Board of Education (1939) 31 Cal.App.2d 734, 89 P.2d 148), the Legislature impliedly recognized that the authority of governing boards is not as extensive under section 13443. (Ladd v. Board of Trustees (1972) 23 Cal.App.3d 984, 989-991, 100 Cal.Rptr. 571.)

7. Since neither party has challenged the applicability of the substantial evidence scope of review to this proceeding, we have not addressed the question whether a higher standard of review should apply.

8. "If standards of taste of future generations are to be elevated it will not be accomplished by those who seek to sweep distasteful matters under the rug, or by self-embarrassed school trustees who discharge as unfit those who would bring the problem out in the open for discussion." (Oakland Unified Sch. Dist. v. Olicker (1972) 25 Cal.App.3d 1098, 1112, 102 Cal.Rptr. 421, 431 (Sims, J., concurring).) Several federal cases illustrate the serious constitutional questions which arise when school authorities seek to curb the academic freedom of teachers to employ techniques supported by substantial opinion in the teaching profession. (Keefe v. Geanakos (1st Cir. 1969) 418 F.2d 359; Parducci v. Rutland (M.D.Ala. 1970) 316 F.Supp. 352.)

9. We reject the assertion of the respondent Torrance Board that because petitioner refrained from actually reading the controversial words in question in some of his classes, he necessarily knew their use would be considered objectionable. To the contrary, Lindros' discriminating use of the controversial language in his more mature college prep classes only demonstrates his good faith effort to discern when the usage would serve a bona fide educational purpose.

10. See Oakland Unified Sch. Dist. v. Olicker (1972) 25 Cal.App. 3d 1098, 1110, 102 Cal.Rptr. 421, applying the same reasoning as to lack of notice to a teacher dismissal case under Education Code section 13403. Several federal cases, moreover, have accepted the notice argu-

ment in the context of constitutional due process and academic freedom challenges to teacher dismissals. (See Mailloux v. Kiley (D. Mass.1971) 323 F.Supp. 1387, affd. 448 F.2d 1242 (1st Cir.); Keefe v. Geanakos (1st Cir. 1969) 418 F.2d 359, 362; Webb v. Lake Mills Community School Dist. (N.D.Iowa 1972) 344 F.Supp. 791, 800-801, 804-805; Parducci v. Rutland (M.D. Ala. 1970) 316 F.Supp. 352, 357;cf. President's Council, Dist. 25 v. Community School Board (2d Cir. 1972) 457 F.2d 289, 293-294.)

11. We set forth the full findings pertinent to this issue:

"F. On approximately February 6, 1970, at the close of a class session the students in the class then being instructed by respondent departed from the room with few exceptions and without being dismissed by respondent and prior to the sounding of the bell signalling the close of the class session. It was established that on this date respondent had instructed those of his students who were in possession of a book entitled "Zorba the Greek" to depart from class early, secure the book from their lockers, and return the book to the library so that it could be redistributed on the morning of February 19th when it was needed by the students of another English instructor. It was not established that all of those students who departed were leaving to complete this errand. It is contrary to school policy to permit students to be out of class during the class time without a proper pass, with the limited exception that five students at a time may be permitted to be in the hallway for the purpose of obtaining or returning books at the bookroom in the library."

12. One of petitioner's supervisors, the sole witness for the Board on the charge of early dismissal of students, testified that he observed students leave Lindros' class *without any authorization.* Petitioner's testimony contradicted that of his supervisor; petitioner attested that he authorized his students to leave class to return copies of *Zorba the Greek* to the library. Testimony of other teachers indicated that Lindros had been asked to arrange for the return of these books. Though the findings of the hearing officer (*supra,* fn. 11) contain ambiguities, apparently the hearing officer accepted petitioner's version that he *did not* dismiss his class early, but rather authorized his students to go to the library.

13. As the superior court declared, "That brings us to what I suppose might be called *the substantive charge* involved, as the hearing officer said, and I agree with him, the *gravamen* of these proceedings, that is, the use of this short story, 'The Funeral'." (Emphasis added.) The meaning of "gravamen" is clear; "gravamen" means the "material part of a grievance, charge, etc." (Webster's New Internat. Dict. (2d ed. 1957) unabridged.)

This conclusion of the hearing officer and superior court was supported by substantial evidence. The principal of South High School testified that he would not have recommended against rehiring Lindros based solely on the alleged dismissal of students without proper authorization.

"Q: [hearing officer] 'The Funeral' was the most compelling incident?

"A: [the principal] Yes. "...

"Q: ... That's not a very good question, but would you have based a recommendation of not to rehire a teacher upon an incident [of] permitting students to leave?

"A: Perhaps not."

14. We find further support for our conclusion that the gravamen for the refusal to rehire was the reading of "The Funeral" in the action of the Torrance Board itself; the Board, in effect, agreed that the incident involving "The Funeral" constituted the material complaint. Although the Board declared that the charges "separately and collectively constitute[d] ... sufficient cause not to reemploy," the Board also accepted the position of the hearing officer that the charge relating to "The Funeral" formed the real basis for the action against petitioner. As the Board concedes, under section 13443, subdivision (c) the hearing officer conducts a hearing and prepared a proposed decision; based on the record of this hearing and the "proposed decision" the Board then makes its determination; under the Government Code the Board can *either* adopt the "proposed decision" *in its entirety* (Gov.Code. § 11517, subd. (b)) or make further findings "upon the record" of the administrative hearing (Gov. Code. § 11517, subd. (c)). Here the Board did *not* examine the record of the administrative hearing or make further findings: accordingly it adopted the officer's determination *in its entirety* under section 11517, subdivision (b)—including the finding that "The Funeral" constituted the gravamen of the complaint.

15. We therefore need not reach petitioner's other contention that his discharge was invalid on various procedural grounds as well.

JUSTICE BURKE'S OPINION NOTES

1. The majority have substantially misstated the test set forth in section 13443 and the *Griggs* case. Although correctly explaining that the role of the courts is limited to determining whether the cause for termination *relates* to the welfare of the school or its pupils (pp. 190-191), the majority purport to apply that test by inquiring whether in fact the teacher's conduct *adversely affected* the welfare of the school or its pupils. (*Id.,* at p. 186, p. 190, p. 191, pp. 191-193.) Yet the question of adverse effect is precisely the question reserved to the school board by section 13443—otherwise a court could in every case reverse the board's decision by finding that particular conduct had no "significant adverse impact" (*id,* at p. 186) on the school or its pupils.

2. Since the district's action in this case can be sustained on the basis of Lindros' improper language in his classroom, I do not reach the question whether that action could also be upheld on the independent ground that Lindros permitted unauthorized departure of students from his class.

3. The majority's reliance upon the so-called "free-speech

cases (e.g., Cohen v. California, 403 U.S. 15, 91 S.Ct. 1780., 29 L.Ed.2d 284), seems wholly misplaced, for no attempt is made to subject Lindros to criminal liability for his conduct. As conceded by the majority (p. 193), "these rulings by no means legitimize the general use of offensive language in the classroom. . . ."

A United States District Court in Iowa decides for a ninth grade English-drama teacher who had been dismissed from her drama coaching position because of the "drinking and profanity" which she allowed in the student drama productions and to which the principal and superintendent had objected. In deciding for the teacher, the Court stated: "Miss Webb allowed nothing in her plays or rehearsals that is so inherently repugnant to good teaching practices or to community standards of decency that she should have known that such activity was unequivocally not in the best interests of the Lake Mills Schools: that is, so much so that she would automatically lose her job. . . . The school library is replete with books containing vulgarity far more extreme than any vulgarity uttered or performed under Miss Webb's supervision; these books can be freely assigned to and read by high school students. Superintendent Mitchell testified that teachers in the Lake Mills High School can and have assigned and discussed materials containing vulgarity . . . All evidence before this Court indicates that Miss Webb was fired in direct reprisal to her proper exercise of academic freedom—her freedom to employ methods of teaching reasonably relevant to the subject matter she was employed to teach. . . . The termination of Miss Webb without giving her prior notice that the teaching method she employed was not allowed denied her due process of law, and cannot but have had a chilling effect upon the academic freedom of Miss Webb and the other teachers of Lake Mills to innovate and to develop new and more effective teaching methods which are reasonably relevant to the subject matter they are assigned to teach."

Webb v. *Lake Mills Community School Dist.*, 344 F. Supp. 791 (1972)

HANSON, District Judge.

Martha Webb brings this action against the Lake Mills Community School District and the superintendent and the board members of the district, both in their individual and official capacities. Miss Webb alleges that these defendants have acted under color of State law in refusing to allow her to carry out her functions as drama coach pursuant to her employment contract. She alleges that this action by these defendants has violated the constitutional rights guaranteed her by the Fourteenth and First Amendments to the Constitution of the United States. The suit is based upon 42 U.S.C., Section 1983, the Civil Rights Act of 1871; the Court has jurisdiction over the subject matter of this action by reason of 28 U.S.C., Section 1343 (3).

Miss Webb seeks a permanent injunction from the Court barring the defendants from interfering with her activities as drama instructor at Lake Mills High School, and from refusing to permit her to conduct, coach and head the dramatics activities at the school. She further prays that the defendants be required to place all high school plays under her immediate supervision, direction and control, and that they be required to grant her the increments in salaries that would have been hers had the Board adhered to the salary schedule they have established. She also seeks back pay she has lost. She further seeks damages of $30,000 for lost reputation and for mental pain and anguish. Finally, she seeks her reasonable attorneys fees and court costs.

In addition to generally denying the allegations of the complaint, the defendants assert that the Court lacks subject matter jurisdiction over plaintiff's complaint, that the plaintiff's complaint fails to state a claim upon which relief can be granted, and that plaintiff has failed to join an indispensible party.

The Motion for Temporary Injunction in this matter was heard on October 13, 1971. The Motion was denied in an Order filed January 14, 1972. This matter came on for trial on February 2, 1972. From all of the evidence heard in this case the Court finds the following facts:

FINDINGS OF FACT

1. The plaintiff, Martha Webb, and all of the individual defendants are citizens of the United States of America and are residents of Winnebago County, Iowa. Defendant Lake Mills Community School District is a public school district organized and existing under the laws of the State of Iowa and accredited by the Department of Public Instruction for the State of Iowa. Defendants Harris Honsey, Stanley Helgeson, Dr. C. S. Nelson, Clarence Willand, and Gordon Anderson are each members of the Board of Directors of the Lake Mills Community School District and collectively constitute the entire Board of Directors of that school district. Defendant Burton Mitchell is superintendent of Schools of the Lake Mills Community School District.

2. In May, 1969, Miss Webb was employed as a school teacher by the Lake Mills Community School District for the school year 1969-70. She was assigned as instructor in Junior High School English for that term, which duties she satisfactorily performed.

3. Towards the end of the 1969-70 term, Miss Webb informed Principal Raymond Six that she was interested in teaching Ninth Grade English, a position then open for the 1970-71 term. Principal Six stated that the Ninth Grade English position was to be assigned only to a person also willing and qualified to coach high school drama. Negotiations subsequently took place between Miss Webb and Superintendent Mitchell and Principal Six. One concern of the administration was that Miss Webb become certified with the State Department of Public Instruction to teach dramatics. Miss Webb indicated that she would attend summer classes in dramatics at a university to enable her to secure certification. A further concern of Superintendent Mitchell and Principal Six was that the plays produced by Miss Webb not contain profanity, drinking, or other depictions distasteful to the public. The precise nature of the agreement with respect to this item between Miss Webb and the administration is the central factual issue of this lawsuit.

4. Testimony of the various board members indicates that the Board did have some vague and generally unarticulated policy concerning profanity and drinking in school sponsored activities. With respect to the use of profanity or drinking scenes in public dramatic productions, most board members felt that at some time they had discussed the matter and that they had generally agreed that profanity and drinking on stage should not be allowed. No board member could recall clearly when the matter had been discussed and the Board Minutes do not reflect any record of such a discussion prior to the Martha Webb incident. The rules and regulations of the school promulgated by the Board and in effect at the time Miss Webb agreed to become drama coach did not contain a specific policy on the use of profanity and drinking scenes in plays. The Board did not meet with Miss Webb to discuss her employment as drama coach. All discussions over this job were between Miss Webb and Superintendent Mitchell and Principal Six.

5. During the school year 1969-70, the school produced the plays "Brigadoon" and "I Remember Mama." "Brigadoon" contained scenes in which a drunk appeared and drank to excess on stage. "I Remember Mama" contained a scene in which an old man taught a nine-year-old boy to swear in order to relieve the boy's pain from a knee operation. The swear words consisted of "damn" and "damn it to hell." The plays contained many other irreverent references to the deity. Some of the citizenry objected to the immoral nature of these scenes; the drama coach was criticized for producing these objectionable plays. Miss Webb was aware of these productions and the criticism they generated. The drama coach was not fired, but resigned at the end of the school year for reasons not related to these productions.

6. During the Spring, 1970, negotiations with Miss Webb about the drama coach job for 1970-71, Superintendent Mitchell and Principal Six told Miss Webb that they did not want drinking and profanity in high school plays. Miss Webb believes that the discussion was with reference to the kind of profanity and drinking found in "Brigadoon" and "I Remember Mama." Superintendent Mitchell and Principal Six believe they said that absolutely no drinking or swearing was to be shown in plays before the public, but they do not remember exactly what they said. They testified that the discussion may have had reference to the plays produced in 1969-70. The Court finds that the rule with respect to this matter given to Miss Webb by Superintendent Mitchell was not a precise one, but was rather ambiguous. There is no writing showing what the precise nature of the rule was. Miss Webb entered into the drama coach job with the understanding that unnecessary and excessive drinking and vulgarity, such as was contained in "Brigadoon" and "I Remember Mama", were not to be contained in plays performed before the public. There was no discussion about whether profanity and simulated drinking could take place in play rehearsals. Superintendent Mitchell also told Miss Webb that she would be required to present a synopsis of all plays to the administration prior to his ordering them.

7. There has never been a policy in the Lake Mills Schools concerning the use or discussion of materials containing profanity, vulgarity, or drinking by teachers in the classroom. The school library contains books with much more profane and vulgar material than any material ever presented on stage at Lake Mills. These books can be and are assigned and read by students in the school.

The play "I Remember Mama" was read and discussed by a seventh grade class with the apparent approval of the administration. Superintendent Mitchell stated that he would have no objection to the reading and discussion in the classroom of the plays produced by Miss Webb during the 1970-71 term. Any prohibition against profanity and drinking, simulated or otherwise, in the Lake Mills Schools apparently is with respect to public utterances and acts only.

8. In 1969, the Lake Mills Schools and Miss Webb entered into a continuing contract for teaching services. This contract can be modified yearly to provide for such things as a different salary or a change in teaching duties. On April 27, 1970, Miss Webb and the Lake Mills Schools entered into an "Agreement to Modify Teacher's Continuing Contract." This agreement provided for a salary of $7,004.00 and the assignment of Miss Webb as instructor in high school English. In the left hand margin of this agreement are the words: "If college work is obtained in Dramatics and Dramatics is added to the contract, the salary will be $7412."

9. During the summer of 1970, Miss Webb successfully completed six semester hours of course work in dramatics at the University of Iowa. Miss Webb was the drama coach at Lake Mills Schools during the 1970-71 term. She coached the junior class play, two one-act plays, the senior class play, the freshmen students who participated in the state speech competition, and the school's entry in the state large group dramatics competition. She was also second in charge of the high school speech department.

10. In the fall of 1970, Miss Webb chose "The Haunting of Hill House" for the junior class play. She presented a synopsis of this play to the administration, and sometime prior to the performance of the play, she met with Superintendent Mitchell and Principal Six to discuss some drinking scenes in the play. "The Haunting of Hill House" concerns itself with the supernatural and ends with one of the principals being the fatal victim of supernatural forces. The play as written contains some scenes depicting repetitive drinking (one of the characters is a rather heavy drinker), some dialogue which could be frightening to small children, some dialogue about possible criminal acts, and some dialogue containing language which could be considered vulgar or at least not suitable to be uttered before small children. Sometime prior to public performance of the play, Miss Webb either deleted or suitably modified all of these potentially offensive passages except two. She left one passage in which the principal characters drank a toast of welcome to the haunted house to ease their nerves, and another in which the same people drank a shot of brandy after several shocking supernatural phenomena had occurred. Before the performance, however, Miss Webb discussed performing these scenes with Superintendent Mitchell and Principal Six. Superintendent Mitchell told Miss Webb that his feeling was that the scenes probably should be omitted, but that she should exercise her own judgment as to whether the scenes were necessary and whether the plays would be presentable with those scenes excluded. Miss Webb decided that the scenes were necessary for proper dramatic effect and that the play would conform with Superintendent

Mitchell's rule with respect to drinking scenes in high school plays. The Court finds that the play did not violate the rule as Miss Webb understood it. The actors actually used tea on stage; alcoholic beverages were never used in the rehearsals or in the performances, which occurred on November 13, 1970. Superintendent Mitchell attended a performance of "The Haunting of Hill House." He testified that he felt at the time that the drinking scenes violated the rule he had stated to Miss Webb. He, however, did not mention this to Miss Webb until after the performance of the one act plays in January of 1971.

11. Later in the winter Miss Webb selected two one-act plays which were to be performed in the latter part of January of 1971. The plays were entitled "Bridges . . . Are When You Cross Them" and "The Great Choice." "Bridges" concerns itself with the problems an independent thinking teenage girl has in coping with her "typical" American family. The controversial scenes in this play involve the situation in which the father, after reaching his saturation point of frustration over the odd ideas of his daughter, feels that he must swear in order to relieve his frustration. Before swearing, however, he orders his family into the bedroom so they cannot hear him. At one point in the play he utters "damn", and at another point, when extremely frustrated, he utters "son of a bitch." The family, of course, hears him; hence, the supposed comedy of the scene. Miss Webb allowed the play to be rehearsed with these words, but changed "damn" to "darn" and "son of a bitch" to "son of a gun" and then, at the student's request, to "son of a biscuit" a week prior to the public performance. The play was performed using this modified script. One night during rehearsals, while "son of a bitch" was still being used, Superintendent Mitchell walked past the open auditorium doors. He heard the offending phrase, "son of a bitch", ring out from the stage. This annoyed and disturbed him, but he did not approach Miss Webb until after the matinee performance of the one-act plays on January 27, 1971.

12. The other one-act play, "The Great Choice," had as its subject matter the United States under martial law during World War III and a citizen's conflict between duty to God and duty to country. Several times in the play various characters invoked the deity in prayerful, but forceful, manner.

13. In the afternoon of January 27, after the dress rehearsal-matinee, Superintendent Mitchell approached Miss Webb in the hallway. He had received a complaint from a certain unnamed elementary teacher that the students in the plays that afternoon had taken the Lord's name in vain and had used other profanity—in particular "son of a biscuit," which the teacher felt was "too close to the real thing." The teacher complained to Superintendent Mitchell that such language was unfit for her elementary students to hear. Superintendent Mitchell had not attended the afternoon performance. In the hallway, he criticized Miss Webb severely for not following the rules they had previously established. He further told Miss Webb that she had violated his rule with respect to "The Haunting of Hill House." He

ended the conversation by stating that she could not be trusted to properly carry out her duties as drama coach. At Superintendent Mitchell's request, Miss Webb changed "son of a biscuit" to "son of a gun" for the public performance of "Bridges."

14. The two one-act plays were performed in the main by members of the junior and senior classes, with a few sophomores participating. None of the students or their parents complained about the material contained in any of the three plays discussed above. In fact, from the evidence in the case, the only complaint about the plays anyone could remember as specifically coming from the public was the complaint of the unnamed elementary teacher. The defendants do not complain that the plays in general were unsuitable for performance by students of upper high school level; rather they complain only of particular small passages in the scripts of the plays as not conforming to Lake Mills community standards of morality.

15. On March 10, 1971, Principal Six informed Miss Webb that Superintendent Mitchell intended to replace her as drama coach because of the drinking and profanity in her plays. Miss Webb confronted Principal Six on March 12 and told him that she was not going to let this happen. On Monday, March 15, 1971, Superintendent Mitchell called Miss Webb into his office to inform her that she would not have the dramatics job at Lake Mills for the 1971-72 term. He told her that she had been completely inadequate in fulfilling her drama duties in that she had gone against everything that he had said. The sum and substance of her disobedience was with respect to the play passages which Superintendent Mitchell deemed as being not in accord with his profanity instructions. He further told Miss Webb that he had already hired a replacement for her and that she had no right to appear before the board to discuss the matter because the board knew about her case and had approved Mitchell's actions. Miss Webb then contacted representatives of the Iowa State Education Association (ISEA), the state teachers' organization. The ISEA apparently expressed some concern about the matter to Superintendent Mitchell, and subsequently Miss Webb was told that she could meet with the Board on April 12.

16. Sometime prior to the April 12 meeting Miss Webb was tendered a new contract modification agreement stating that she would be assigned only Ninth Grade English duties, but with the usual annual salary increment for teachers at Lake Mills. Miss Webb did not sign and has not signed this contract modification to date.

17. The day before the April 12 meeting with the Board, Miss Webb told her students that the meeting was to take place. She asked students to encourage parents with views either way on the matter to attend the meeting and express their views. She discouraged students from attending. The students came to the meeting anyway, but were orderly for the most part, with only one student making a discourteous remark to a board member. A local minister expressed his view to the Board that their actions with respect to Miss Webb constituted unbridled censorship. Other citizens spoke before the

Board, two in support of the Board's position, and the rest in support of Miss Webb. The Board went into closed session after hearing the public. The Board never formally voted on Miss Webb's termination as drama coach, but the members all testified that they supported Superintendent Mitchell's decision. None of the individual board members had personal knowledge of what Miss Webb had done and none had personally received any complaints from the public concerning Miss Webb. The members testified in court that, although they found some of the passages in the plays offensive, they would have followed Superintendent Mitchell's decision not to terminate Miss Webb as drama coach, had he so decided. They decided to support Superintendent Mitchell's decision to terminate solely because that was what their superintendent had decided was the proper thing to do. All board members agreed that the predominant reason for Miss Webb's termination was that she disobeyed Superintendent Mitchell's instructions and thus created intolerable disorder in the school. Both the Superintendent and the Board agreed that Miss Webb's violation of school rules was not flagrant enough to warrant complete dismissal; hence, the decision to keep her on as English teacher. Neither the Board or Superintendent Mitchell has ever questioned Miss Webb's competency and effectiveness as a drama coach or as an English teacher.

18. On April 13, the day following the Board meeting, many students boycotted classes in protest to the Board's handling of Miss Webb. Miss Webb did not encourage the walkout. At first she warned the students of their duties as responsible individuals; later she told them that they belonged in school and were not accomplishing anything constructive by their walkout. Later the Board met with four student representatives, Miss Webb, and her attorney, but took no further action with respect to Miss Webb's termination as drama coach.

19. Miss Webb coached the senior class play in the spring of 1971. There was no complaint about that play.

20. In August of 1971, the ISEA told Miss Webb and Lake Mills school officials that it would provide legal assistance to Miss Webb to enable her to sue for her reinstatement. The Board then told the ISEA and Miss Webb that they would discuss Miss Webb's situation at the September 17 meeting. The Board took no further action and this lawsuit was instituted in October of 1971.

21. Miss Webb is receiving the same salary for the term 1971-72 that she did for the term 1970-71, i. e., $7412.00. Had she received the usual salary increment for the English teacher-drama coach position, her salary for 1971-72 would have been $7797.00.

22. Miss Webb is performing duties as high school English teacher for Lake Mills Schools during the 1971-72 term. She has not seriously looked for another job as drama coach with another school district. She has made a few inquiries, but no jobs were available. There is no evidence before the Court that any school district has refused Miss Webb a position as drama coach because of the Lake Mills problem.

I.

The defendants acted for the state when they discharged Miss Webb from her drama coaching job and are therefore subject to the Fourteenth Amendment's command. Pickering v. Board of Education, 391 U.S. 563, 88 S.Ct. 1731, 20 L.Ed.2d 811 (1968); Moore v. Board of Education, 448 F.2d 709 (8th Cir. 1971); Hegler v. Board of Education, 447 F.2d 1078 (8th Cir. 1971).

Courts have recognized that under the Fourteenth Amendment a public school teacher has not only a civic right to freedom of speech both outside, Pickering, supra, and inside, Tinker v. Des Moines Independent Comm. School Dist., 393 U.S. 503, 506, 89 S.Ct. 733, 21 L.Ed.2d 731 (1969), the school house, but also some measure of academic freedom in the classroom as well. Bartels v. Iowa, 262 U.S. 404, 43 S.Ct. 628, 67 L.Ed. 1047 (1923); Meyer v. Nebraska, 262 U.S. 390, 43 S.Ct. 625, 67 L.Ed. 1042 (1923); Keefe v. Geanakos, 418 F.2d 359 (1st Cir. 1969); Mailloux v. Kiley, 323 F.Supp. 1387 (D.Mass.1971); Parducci v. Rutland, 316 F.Supp. 352 (M.D.Ala. 1970). See Tinker, supra.

Keyishian v. Board of Regents, 385 U.S. 589, 603, 87 S.Ct. 675, 683, 17 L.Ed. 2d 629 (1967), describes the Constitutional guarantee surrounding classroom activity of teachers in the following terms:

"Our Nation is deeply committed to safeguarding academic freedom, which is of transcendant value to all of us and not merely to the teachers concerned. That freedom is therefore a special concern of the First Amendment, which does not tolerate laws that cast a pall of orthodoxy over the classroom.... The classroom is peculiarly the 'marketplace of ideas.'"

Although Keyishian is concerned with college teachers, the rationale must extend to high school and even elementary teachers. The state interest in limiting the discretion of teachers grows stronger, though, as the age of the students decreases; thus, the Fourteenth and First Amendments do not necessarily give teachers of younger students the same "academic freedom" that they give to teachers of college students. See Ginsberg v. New York, 390 U.S. 629, 88 S.Ct. 1274, 20 L.Ed.2d 195 (1968).

With respect to the academic freedom of teachers of high school students of the age of those involved in the instant case, federal courts dealing with the subject have upheld two kinds of academic freedom: the substantive right of a teacher to choose a teaching method which in the court's view served a demonstrated educational purpose; and the procedural right of a teacher not to be discharged for the use of a teaching method which was not proscribed by a regulation, and as to

which it was not shown that the teacher should have had notice that its use was prohibited. Keefe, supra; Mailloux, supra; Parducci, supra. The Court of Appeals for the Eighth Circuit has simply declared, in cases of this nature, that the actions of school officials shall not be arbitrary and capricious. McConnell v. Anderson, 451 F.2d 193 (8th Cir. 1971), cert. denied, 405 U.S. 1046, 92 S.Ct. 1312, 31 L.Ed.2d 588 (1972). In the Court's mind, this articulation of the Eighth Circuit means much the same as the articulation in Keefe, Mailloux, and Parducci. See Mailloux v. Kiley, 436 F.2d 565 (1st Cir. 1971); Close v. Lederle, 424 F.2d 988 (1st Cir. 1970).

II.

Defendants assert that the Lake Mills School Board had promulgated a rule proscribing profanity or drinking scenes in school-sponsored plays produced for the public on the school stage. They allege that Miss Webb had notice of the rule and violated it by producing plays containing profanity and drinking scenes. Defendants further contend that, irrespective of the rule, Miss Webb agreed with Superintendent Mitchell not to produce plays containing profanity and drinking scenes. This agreement, they allege, was part of her contract, which agreement she subsequently disregarded. Hence, defendants claim that Miss Webb breached her employment contract.

The preponderance of the evidence before the Court indicates that the "rule" Superintendent Mitchell announced to Miss Webb was as Miss Webb remembers it and not as Superintendent Mitchell remembers it. The Court must initially consider the circumstances surrounding the discussions between Miss Webb and Superintendent Mitchell and Principal Six. The plays "Brigadoon" and "I Remember Mama" were the topic of the day in the school and the community. It is not unreasonable to believe Miss Webb's testimony that the discussion about profanity and drinking in plays centered around the plays produced in the 1969-1970 term. Superintendent Mitchell and Principal Six testified that the plays could have been discussed in their conversations with Miss Webb, although they do not remember mentioning them in the discussion. Subsequent events, however, indicate more strongly that the rule Superintendent Mitchell declared to Miss Webb was that profanity and drinking in plays produced during the 1970-71 term should not be as conspicuously evident as they were in "Brigadoon" and "I Remember Mama." Superintendent Mitchell was aware of the intention of Miss Webb to allow the two cocktail scenes in "The Haunting of Hill House." He and Miss Webb discussed the matter and he told her to use her discretion, but to conform the scenes to the rule. If the rule had been an absolute prohibition against any drinking scenes, as Superintendent Mitchell remembers it, he would never have said, "Use your own judgment." Superintendent Mitchell saw the play, but said nothing about the drinking to Miss Webb for two months.

Defendants assert that Miss Webb was contractually bound to the rule as Superintendent Mitchell stated it. The written agreement between Miss Webb and the Board mentions nothing about profanity and drinking in plays. Defendants correctly assert, however, that the written contract is not the complete or integrated agreement of the parties, and that, therefore, the Court must examine matters outside of the written agreement to determine the whole agreement between the parties. 32A C.J.S. Evidence § 1013(1). There is a disagreement between the parties with respect to the agreement between Miss Webb and Superintendent Mitchell about the performance of plays containing profanity or drinking scenes. Three rules of construction of contracts control in a situation such as the present one, where there is some uncertainty about what the agreement actually was. First, in construing an oral contract, courts must take into consideration the circumstances surrounding both parties at the time the contract was made. Gildner Bros. v. Ford Hopkins Co., 235 Iowa 191, 16 N.W. 2d 229 (1944). The circumstances at the time of the agreement between Miss Webb and Superintendent Mitchell indicate that the concern of Superintendent Mitchell was that vulgarity to the degree of that produced on stage during the 1969-70 term not be allowed. Second, a contract is strictly construed against the party stating the terms which are ambiguous. *E. g.,* Archibald v. Midwest Paper Stock Co., 176 N.W.2d 761 (Iowa, 1970); Walnut Street Baptist Church v. Oliphant, 257 Iowa 879, 135 N.W.2d 97 (1965); Freese v. Town of Alburnett, 255 Iowa 1264, 125 N.W.2d 790 (1964); Pazawich v. Johnson, 241 Iowa 10, 39 N.W.2d 590 (1949). Here Superintendent Mitchell stated the terms of the agreement concerning the use of profanity and drinking in the plays; by his own admission the terms could have been interpreted as Miss Webb interpreted them. Iowa law, therefore, dictates that Miss Webb's interpretation must be the correct one. Third, the practical construction given the ambiguous terms of an agreement will usually be adopted by the courts. *E. g.,* Goering v. Jefferson, 159 N.W.2d 409 (Iowa, 1968); Keding v. Barton, 261 Iowa 327, 154 N.W.2d 172 (Iowa, 1967); Hamilton v. Wosepka, 261 Iowa 299, 154 N.W.2d 164 (Iowa, 1967). The conduct of both Miss Webb and Superintendent Mitchell with respect to the drinking scenes in "The Haunting of Hill House" indicates that Miss Webb's interpretation of the agreement was the interpretation the parties lived by, at least until January of 1971 when Superintendent Mitchell decided that the agreement prohibition should be stricter. When all of these rules of contract law are taken in aggregate, the Court must conclude that the agreement with respect to profanity and drinking in plays was as Miss Webb interpreted it, and that Miss Webb did not in fact violate that agreement.

Moving now to defendants' contention that an absolute rule against any profanity or drinking scenes in plays produced for the Lake Mills Schools was in effect at the time Miss Webb agreed to become drama coach, the Court will assume for the moment that such a rule was duly promulgated by the Board in accordance with Iowa law and its own bylaws. The board members could not recall any specific discussions about such a rule; the Minutes of the Board do not reflect that the Board ever passed such a rule. Nevertheless, Superintendent Mitchell announced to Miss Webb a rule with respect to profanity and drinking scenes in plays. The Court finds that Superintendent Mitchell's statement of the rule was vague and ambiguous; "profanity" and "drinking" have different meanings to different people. Especially considering the context of the discussion between Miss Webb and Superintendent Mitchell, Superintendent Mitchell could not but have been aware that a rule absolutely prohibiting profanity and drinking scenes could easily be subject to misinterpretation unless stated clearly. The Board and Superintendent Mitchell state that the rule has been in effect for many years at Lake Mills. He conveyed this impression to Miss Webb. The plays "Brigadoon" and "I Remember Mama" produced just prior to the discussions violated the rule, but the drama coach was not terminated as a result. Thus, Miss Webb could easily assume that those plays, although being in violation of the rule, were not in flagrant violation, and that her plays should maintain a standard of decency somewhat higher than that contained in those plays. Miss Webb's job as drama coach was terminated because she failed to obey the rule under discussion. It is the prevailing law of the land that no person shall be punished for conduct unless such conduct has been proscribed in clear and precise terms. *See* Connolly v. General Constr. Co., 269 U.S. 385, 391, 46 S.Ct. 126, 70 L.Ed. 322 (1926). This is especially true when the conduct involves First Amendment rights, such as in the instant case. NAACP v. Button, 371 U.S. 415, 432, 83 S.Ct. 328, 9 L.Ed. 2d 405 (1963); Winters v. New York, 333 U.S. 507, 509-510, 68 S.Ct. 665, 92 L.Ed. 840 (1948). The Court need not reach the question of whether the rule stated by Superintendent Mitchell was constitutionally invalid; it suffices to say that the rule must be construed as narrowly as possible. Welsh v. United States, 398 U.S. 333, 90 S.Ct. 1792, 26 L.Ed.2d 308 (1970). The narrow construction given the rule by

Miss Webb was a reasonable construction under the circumstances. The Court concludes that Miss Webb's statement of the rule gives the true legal meaning of the rule. None of Miss Webb's plays, as produced on stage, violated this rule.

The Court is not saying that the School Board cannot prohibit the use of vulgar speech and mannerisms in school-sponsored plays on its stage. Social acceptable speech and conduct are proper concerns of our elementary and secondary schools. Small children are in attendance at the school plays produced at Lake Mills; the Board has a legitimate concern that they not be subjected to vulgarity emanating from the stage of the school. The Board, moreover, has a legitimate concern about the reputation of the school; vulgar speech and conduct performed on the school stage during a school-sponsored play could well suggest to the public that the school is doing an inadequate job of imparting principles of socially acceptable speech and conduct to the students. *See* McConnell v. Anderson, *supra.* This does not mean that the Board or any other arm of the State can regulate profanity as such, for "profanity" is legally very closely related to "blasphemy." 12 Am. Jur.2d, Blasphemy and Profanity, Section 10. State regulation of "profanity" may well be in collision with Establishment of and Free Exercise of Religion Clauses of the Constitution. *See* State v. West, 9 Md.App. 270, 263 A.2d 602, 41 A.L.R.3d 512 (1970). The Court takes no position with respect to state regulation of "profanity".

III.

Drama coaching in public high schools in Iowa is characterized by Iowa law as a classroom activity. An accredited Iowa high school must offer dramatic activities to its students and must hire a teacher certified by the Department of Public Instruction to coach drama.[1] The facts that most dramatic activity is conducted after school hours, that students are not graded for their dramatic capabilities, and that students are not required to participate in drama do not detract from the conclusion that a drama coach performs academic, classroom-type duties.

Lake Mills Schools have no regulation with respect to discussion of profanity or vulgarity in the classroom. Superintendent Mitchell testified that Miss Webb would not have been fired had she discussed the words found in her plays in the classroom.

The Court has no Board findings or reasons in support of Miss Webb's termination before it. In fact, testimony of the board members indicates that they never even officially voted to terminate Miss Webb as drama coach, but rather ratified Superintendent Mitchell's decision by their tacit acquiescence. Thus, this Court cannot merely look for substantial evidence to support the Board's decision, for the Board made no formal decision. *See* McConnell v. Anderson, *supra.*

All board members testified that they approved of Miss Webb's termination as drama coach because she had disobeyed Superintendent Mitchell. The Court finds no substantial evidence that Miss Webb ever disobeyed Superintendent Mitchell; rather, she made a conscientious, good faith effort to follow his wishes. Miss Webb at no time told Superintendent Mitchell that because of her conscience and professional ideals, she would not obey a rule with respect to vulgarity, either on stage or in the classroom. Superintendent Mitchell's desires were simply not articulated well enough for Miss Webb to properly understand them.

The Court has already concluded that Miss Webb violated no rule of the Lake Mills Schools. Nevertheless, she did allow the terms "son of a bitch" and "damn" to be used in rehearsals. The Court finds that Miss Webb was in good faith in allowing this language in the rehearsals and that she believed that the use of the words, in the context in which they were spoken, had a legitimate, good faith purpose in imparting knowledge of drama to her students. The defendants have made no effort to deny that the use of the words in context were in accord with legitimate, good faith teaching practices, their contention being that drama coaching is not a classroom activity, and that, therefore, the concept of "academic freedom" has no application. The Court will not hold, just from the testimony of Miss Webb, however that the use of such vulgarity as "son of a bitch" or "damn" is so necessary to the proper teaching of drama that a formal or informal regulation proscribing its use would be repugnant to the Constitution.

The Supreme Court of the United States has found proscriptions against the teaching of foreign languages in public schools, Meyer v. Nebraska, 262 U.S. 390, 43 S.Ct. 625, 67 L.Ed. 1042 (1923); Bartels v. Iowa, 262 U.S. 404, 43 S.Ct. 628, 67 L.Ed. 1047 (1923); and against teaching the theory of evolution, Epperson v. Arkansas, 393 U.S. 97, 89 S.Ct. 266, 21 L.Ed.2d 228 (1968); to be repugnant to the Constitution because the teaching of these matters are legitimate academic concerns and there is no compelling state interest dictating that they not be taught. In the instant case there is no proof that the use of vulgar terms is a legitimate academic concern; no case has ever held that vulgarity is a legitimate academic concern. *See* Mailloux v. Kiley, 323 F.Supp. 1387 (D.Mass. 1971). And there is at least some legitimate state interest in prohibiting the teaching and use of vulgarity in secondary public schools. *See* Section II *supra*. The Court finds that the use of "son of a bitch" and "damn" in rehearsals did have relevancy to the proper teaching of drama, although the use of the terms is not at all essential to the proper teaching of drama.

The Court notes that no student or parent complained about the use of "son of a bitch" or "damn" in rehearsals, although the terms were used for a number of weeks. Defendants agree that Miss Webb's students have heard the terms often during their lives and that the terms are used commonly in Lake Mills, although perhaps not to the liking of some or even a majority of the residents. The only person offended by the use of the terms in rehearsal was Superintendent Mitchell. He felt that their use was improper, but only because of the possibility that small children could overhear them. He testified that the kindergarten classroom is near the auditorium in which the rehearsals took place, that the public is allowed to attend the rehearsals, and that students are sometimes in the building after hours when the rehearsals usually take place. There is no evidence, however, that small children were ever in or near the auditorium when the rehearsals for "Bridges" occurred. And Superintendent Mitchell apparently was not overly concerned about the words in the rehearsals; when he heard "son of a bitch" he did not walk into the auditorium and tell Miss Webb to disallow the use of the term; he did not even shut the doors of the auditorium as a precaution against small children, wandering through the school halls at night, hearing the word.

Miss Webb allowed nothing in her plays or rehearsals that is so inherently repugnant to good teaching practices or to community standards of decency that she should have known that such activity was unequivocally not in the best interests of the Lake Mills Schools; that is, so much so that she would automatically lose her job.[2] In two instances, occurring in the school terms 1969-70 and 1970-71, teachers had either uttered vulgarity or allowed vulgarity in public, school-sponsored activities, and had not lost their jobs for it. One instance involved the drama coach for 1969-70, and the other, the basketball coach for 1970-71. The school library is replete with books containing vulgarity far more extreme than any vulgarity uttered or performed under Miss Webb's supervision; these books can be freely assigned to and read by high school students. Superintendent Mitchell testified that teachers in the Lake Mills High School can and have assigned and discussed materials containing vulgarity.

Courts have held that a teacher cannot be discharged from using a method relevant to the proper teaching of the subject matter involved unless the state, or arm thereof, proves that he was put on notice either by regulation or otherwise that he should not use that method. Keefe v. Geanakos, 418 F.2d 359 (1st Cir. 1969); Parducci v. Rutland, 316 F.Supp. 352 (M.D.Ala. 1970); Mailloux v. Kiley, 323 F.Supp. 1387 (D.Mass 1971). Mailloux v. Kiley, 323 F.Supp. at 1392, reasons:

"This exclusively procedural protection is afforded to a teacher not because he is a state employee, or because he is a citizen, but because in his teaching capacity he is engaged in the exercise of what may plausibly be considered 'vital First Amendment rights.' Keyishian v. Board of Regents, 385 U.S. 589, 604, 87 S.Ct. 675, 684, 17 L.Ed.2d 629. In his teaching capacity he is not required to 'guess what conduct or utterance may lose him his position.' *Ibid.* If he did not have the right to be warned before he was discharged, he might be more timid than it is in the public interest that he should be, and he might steer away from reasonable methods with which it is in the public interest to experiment. *Ibid.* "

Miss Webb's plays were in conformity with the rules stated to her by Superintendent Mitchell. She was not given any notice that she would be fired for allowing vulgarity to be used in rehearsals. All circumstances indicated that such actions on her part would be permissible. After considering the total circumstances surrounding Miss Webb's termination as drama coach, this Court concludes that the action of the defendants was arbitrary, capricious, and unreasonable. Miss Webb was not insubordinate, and the defendants admit that she is a good teacher; indeed, she is still employed by the defendants as English teacher, and was offered for 1971–72 the ordinary increment awarded teachers whose performance has been satisfactory. Miss Webb's character is good and she has not caused disruption to the affairs of the school. Indeed, the only disruption shown in the evidence was precipitated by the defendants' own actions.

All evidence before this Court indicates that Miss Webb was fired[3] in direct reprisal to her proper exercise of academic freedom—her freedom to employ methods of teaching reasonably relevant to the subject matter she was employed to teach. Although the defendants would be justified in proscribing all vulgarity in the classroom or on the stage, they did not give adequate notice to Miss Webb that they had done so; the circumstances led Miss Webb to believe that they had not done so. The termination of Miss Webb without giving her prior notice that the teaching method she employed was not allowed denied her due process of law, and cannot but have had a chilling effect upon the academic freedom of Miss Webb and the other teachers of Lake

Mills to innovate and to develop new and more effective teaching methods which are reasonably relevant to the subject matter they are assigned to teach.

IV.

Because the Court concludes that Miss Webb's constitutional rights have been violated by the defendants while acting under color of State law, permanent injunctive relief may properly issue under 42 U.S.C., Sections 1983 and 1988. This injunction shall order Miss Webb's reinstatement as drama coach with all rights and privileges appurtenant thereto, including all increments in salary awarded to persons satisfactorily performing their teaching duties.

Defendants assert that the Court cannot reinstate Miss Webb as drama coach because the present drama coach, Karen Koch, is an indispensable party, under F.R.Civ.P. 19, to such an order, and Miss Koch has not been named as a defendant to this action. The Court concludes that Miss Koch is not an indispensable party to this action. The Court is not ordering that Miss Koch not be allowed to coach drama. Rather, it appears to the Court that as a result of its order reinstating Miss Webb as drama coach, Lake Mills High School will have two drama coaches, just as it probably has more than one history or English teacher. How drama coaching duties are to be allocated between Miss Webb and Miss Koch is a matter lying solely within the discretion of the school administration. The Court is simply saying this: Miss Webb must be reinstated as a drama coach, for she was terminated from that job in violation of the Constitution of the United States.

At this point it is appropriate to discuss defendants' contention that the equitable doctrine of laches precludes Miss Webb from obtaining relief in this Court. The doctrine of laches is often employed when the party seeking relief has lulled the opposing party into security because of the time that has passed since the events complained of occurred; relying on the complaining party's inaction, the opposing party has altered its position to the extent that to give the complaining party relief at such a late date would impose unconscionable burden on the opposing party. Defendants contend that, at the time this action commenced, over six months after the events complained of took place, they had hired a new drama coach and were proceeding with plans for drama activities under the new coach's supervision. The Court notes, however, that the new coach, Miss Koch, was hired at the same time Miss Webb was fired, and before Miss Webb was given her hearing before the Board. In addition, the Board promised Miss Webb as late as August of 1971 that it would review its decision to terminate her as

drama coach. The facts in this case do not show that Miss Webb lulled the defendants to such security that they changed their position materially as a result of her inaction. Accordingly, the doctrine of laches has no applicability here.

Miss Webb is receiving a salary of $7,412.00 for the school year 1971-72, the same salary she received for the previous year. Had she received the usual salary increments for an English teacher-drama coach with her teaching experience, she would be receiving $7,797.00 for the year 1971-72. The Court concludes that Miss Webb has been damaged in the sum of $385.00 as the result of the unconstitutional action taken against her.

The Court finds no substantial evidence that Miss Webb has suffered any loss of reputation. Many of the citizens of Lake Mills have supported her in her fight with the defendants. Nearly all of the newspaper publicity, most of it coming as the result of the institution of this lawsuit, has been favorable to Miss Webb. There has been no convincing showing that Miss Webb will not be hired as drama coach in another school because of the incident at Lake Mills. The Court further finds that there has been no showing that Miss Webb suffered any grievous mental pain and anguish because of the defendants' unconstitutional action.

V.

Defendants assert that this Court does not have subject matter jurisdiction over this action because Miss Webb has failed to exhaust her state administrative remedies. There has been a deluge of recent cases from the Supreme Court of the United States and the Court of Appeals for the Eighth Circuit stating that exhaustion of state administrative remedies is not a prerequisite to the proper institution of a lawsuit under 42 U.S.C., Section 1983. E. g., Carter v. Stanton, 405 U.S. 669, 92 S.Ct. 1232, 31 L.Ed.2d 569 (April 3, 1972); Gilliam v. City of Omaha, 459 F.2d 63 (8th Cir., April 25, 1972); McClelland v. Sigler, 456 F.2d 1266 (8th Cir., March 22, 1972).

Defendants further contend that this Court should abstain to allow Iowa courts to decide this case under state law. It has long been held that plaintiff's remedy under 42 U.S.C., Section 1983 is in addition to any remedy he might have under State law, and that the availability of a remedy in State court is no bar to an action under the Civil Rights Act of 1871. Monroe v. Pape, 365 U.S. 167, 81 S.Ct. 473, 5 L.Ed.2d 492 (1961). Here there is no knotty question of Iowa law to be unraveled before federal law can be applied. In such a case, a federal court should not abstain from deciding a cause of action under 42 U.S.C., Section 1983. Wiscon-

sin v. Constantineau, 400 U.S. 433, 439, 91 S.Ct. 507, 27
L.Ed.2d 515 (1971); Stradley v. Anderson, 456 F.2d
1063 (8th Cir. 1972).

Defendant Lake Mills Community School District
asserts that the Court does not have subject matter
jurisdiction to grant relief against it because it is not a
"person" within the contemplation of 42 U.S.C., Section 1983. Monroe v.Pape, *supra,* holds that a municipality is not a "person" under 42 U.S.C., Section 1983,
and that, therefore, no relief at law or at equity can be
had against a municipality under the Civil Rights Act
of 1871. The Court can find only one case deciding the
status of a school district under 42 U.S.C., Section
1983, and it held that the district was a "person."
Harkless v. Sweeney Ind. Sch. Dist., 427 F.2d 319 (5th
Cir. 1970), cert. denied, 400 U.S. 991, 91 S.Ct. 451, 27
L.Ed.2d 439 (1971). Many decisions from both the Supreme Court of the United States and the Court of
Appeals for the Eighth Circuit have allowed both legal
and equitable relief against school districts under 42
U.S.C., Section 1983. *E g.,* Tinker v. Des Moines Ind.
Sch. Dist., 393 U.S. 503, 89 S.Ct. 733, 21 L.Ed.2d 731
(1969); Hegler v. Board of Education, 447 F.2d 1078
(8th Cir. 1971). This Court concludes, however, that
were the issue before the Supreme Court or the Eighth
Circuit, they would hold that the Lake Mills Community School District is not a "person" under 42
U.S.C., Section 1983, following the reasoning of Monroe v. Pape.[4] This Court so holds.

VI.

Miss Webb seeks to recover from the defendants her
reasonable attorneys' fees. Cases from the Eighth Circuit indicate that attorneys' fees are only to be awarded
as a punitive measure where a defendant has acted
with obdurant recalcitrance.[5] These defendants, although somewhat stubborn, did not willfully seek to
withhold from Miss Webb her constitutional guarantees. They sought and received the advice of an attorney for the Department of Public Instruction before
proceeding to terminate Miss Webb as drama coach.

Accordingly, it is ordered that the foregoing shall
constitute the findings of fact and conclusions of law of
this Court in accordance with F.R.C.P. 52(a).

NOTES

1. Iowa Code Section 280.17 provides in part:

> "The board [of directors of the school] may establish
> graded and high schools and determine what branches
> shall be taught therein, but the course of study shall
> be subject to the approval of the state board of pub-
> lic instruction."

The Rules of the Department of Public Instruction are
set out in Iowa Departmental Rules, p. 386 et seq. (1966).
Rule 3.50 (257) provides in part:

> "Each school district maintaining elementary and
> secondary schools through grade twelve, and com-
> munity or junior colleges, if operated, shall provide a
> program of pupil activities sufficiently broad and
> varied to offer opportunity for all pupils to participate.
> The activity program shall be co-operatively planned
> by pupils and teachers and be supervised by qualified
> school personnel. . . . "

Iowa Departmental Rules at 395 (1966). Rule 3.55 (257)
provides in part:

> "[T]he senior high school shall provide an activities
> program based on mutual as well as individual pupils
> needs, interests, abilities and enthusiasms. The pro-
> gram shall be so organized and administered that
> broad and varied experiences will be available which
> will contribute to the enrichment of the total educa-
> tional program. Opportunities in the following areas
> shall be provided: . . . speech activities and dramatics.
> . . . "

Iowa Departmental Rules at 396 (1966). Rule 19.10 (257)
provides in part:

> "The department of public instruction makes no dis-
> tinction for approval purposes between physical edu-
> cation and athletics; between curricular and extra-
> curricular activities; or between credit and noncredit
> courses. If the teacher directs pupils in any part of the
> school program, it is assumed that he is paid for such
> service and he must meet approval standards."

Iowa Departmental Rules at 424 (1966).

2. Federal courts have found certain activities of teachers so
repugnant and contrary to the best interests of the
institution that a teacher should know what he was doing
was wrong. These cases fall into two basic categories: (1)
Cases in which the teacher used his position with the
school to proselyte views in public on issues in which the
school should remain neutral; Long v. Board of Education, 456 F.2d 1058 (8th Cir. 1972); McConnell v. Anderson, 451 F.2d 193 (8th Cir. 1971), cert. denied, 405 U.S.
1046, 92 S.Ct. 1312, 31 L.Ed.2d 588 (1972); and, (2) cases
in which the teacher was teaching matters not within
subject area he was supposed to be teaching. Ahern v.
Board of Education, 456 F.2d 399 (8th Cir. 1972). This
instant fact situation reflects no act by Miss Webb that
falls within the categories just described, that is, activity
so apparently contrary to the best interests of the school
that she could not but know that she was doing wrong.

3. This is not a simple case of reassignment of a teacher as
defendants suggest. Miss Webb was specially hired as
drama coach and was paid additionally for that job.
When the defendants fired Miss Webb as drama coach,
they proposed to take away the additional pay she was
receiving for that position. Thus, the cases of McGuffin

v. Willow Creek Comm. Sch. Dist., 182 N.W.2d 165
(Iowa, 1970), and Griffin v. Red Oak Comm. Sch. Dist.,
167 N.W.2d 166 (Iowa, 1969), holding that a school board
can substitute new teaching duties for old ones as long as
the teacher receives the same pay are not applicable.
Here the defendants did not substitute new duties for former ones; instead, they terminated a teaching duty and
diminished Miss Webb's pay.

4. Iowa Code Section 274.1 provides:

    "Each school district shall continue a body politic as a
    school corporation, unless changed as provided by law,
    and as such may sue and be sued, hold property, and
    exercise all the powers granted by law, and shall have
    exclusive jurisdiction in all school matters over the
    territory therein contained."

1 U.S.C., Section 1. defining generally the word "person," does not in terms apply to bodies politic. Monroe v.
Pape, 365 U.S. at 190 n. 47, 81 S.Ct. 473. A holding that a
school board is a "person" would violate the apparent
intendment of Congress when it enacted 42 U.S.C., Section 1983. Monroe v. Pape, 365 U.S. at 187-192, 81 S.Ct.
473. Absent some explicit law to the contrary, this Court
cannot conclude that Congress intended the term "person" in 42 U.S.C., Section 1983, to include school
boards.

5. Clark v. Board of Education, 449 F.2d 493, 502 (8th Cir.
1971); Arkansas Educational Association v. Board of
Education, 446 F.2d 763, 770 (8th Cir. 1971); Cato v.
Parham, 403 F.2d 12, 16 (8th Cir. 1968); Kemp v.
Beasley, 352 F.2d 14, 23 (8th Cir. 1965); Rogers v. Paul,
345 F.2d 117, 125-126 (8th Cir. 1965).

THE United States Court of Appeals, Seventh Circuit, decides against three eighth grade public school teachers who had been discharged by the board of education for distributing to their eighth grade pupils allegedly obscene and improper reading materials dealing with the 1969 Woodstock rock festival. In deciding against the teachers, the Court said: "We do not believe that however much the reach of the First Amendment has been extended and however eager today's courts have been to protect the many varieties of claims of civil rights, the appellee school board had to put up with the described conduct of appellants. . . . We consider that these teachers should have known better than to hand to their young students something that invited the use of the described drugs. Additionally, appellants had been aware of and had participated in previously presented teaching programs expounding upon the baleful consequences of the use of drugs and alcohol."

Judge Fairchild argues in his dissenting opinion that "the Woodstock brochure was not so offensive that its classroom use was obviously improper. The school board had not promulgated any standards against which plaintiffs could measure this type of literature to determine whether board policy forbade its use. . . . Whether the board could constitutionally have promulgated specific rules which would have prohibited the classroom use of this literature by eighth grade students is not the issue presented. I cannot conclude that these materials are so clearly improper as to justify the mid-term discharge of an instructor who elected to use them in his teaching."

Brubaker v. *Bd. of Education,* 502 F.2d 973 (1974)

O'SULLIVAN, Senior Circuit Judge.

This appeal concerns the discharge by defendant Board of Education of three public school teachers—plaintiff-appellants—for distributing or causing to be distributed to their eighth grade pupils allegedly obscene and improper reading materials. Action was brought against the appellees, Board of Education, its members and agents, in the United States District Court for the Northern District of Illinois, Eastern Division. For their cause of action, plaintiffs charged that defendants' action abridged their civil rights secured to them by 42 U.S.C. § 1983, and their rights under the First and Fourteenth Amendments. Jurisdiction of the Court was based upon 28 U.S.C. §§ 1332 and 1343(3) and (4). The litigation was concluded in the District Court by an order granting defendant-appellees' motion for summary judgment. From such order, plaintiffs appeal.

We affirm.

Clara S. Brubaker, John W. Brubaker and Ronald K. Sievert were teachers of eighth grade students in public schools operated by the Board of Education of District 149, Cook County, Illinois. They were all non-tenured, and their respective one-year contracts were to expire on June 12, 1970. Prior to the events here involved, the Brubakers had been advised that they would not be rehired, while Sievert had been notified that he would be retained for the 1970-71 school year.

In April, 1970, Clara Brubaker and another teacher, not involved here, attended the movie "Woodstock" which documented the 1969 rock festival by the same name. A number of relevant brochures were acquired at the theatre. These contained various articles, poems and pictures. One article—or poem—entitled "Getting Together" contained material which brought about the discharge of the plaintiffs. Its total content is set out in the brochure "Woodstock" a copy of which is made an appendix hereto. Those parts relating to drugs, sexual behavior and what might be called vulgarities are as follows:

"Woodstock felt like home. *A place to take acid. A place to make love.* Felt a little like a place we'd been before, but hard to remember, like yesterday's vision, like last night's dream. But now it's all now, *and it feels like we're never turning back.*

* * *

Woodstock felt like a swell of energy, wave of elation that fills the heart *and flows on over the lover beside you.*

Woodstock was freedom. Don't ever forget that. Don't ever settle for less.

* * *

Oh joy overflowing, *oh lover caressing,* I am what I have to share, oh take me completely!

* * *

Grass smoked together.[1]
Stink of our shit; Music of Laughter.
Gathering together.
Bodies naked into the water, touching each other, opening hearts into greater awareness of being together
of living on the planet
   of being part of something—a movement, a motion, like a drop of water in the crest of the tide, moving together *we're a big fucking wave . . . !*

* * *

Its only the beginning.

* * *

Old world crumbling, new world being born."

(Emphasis supplied.)

As a message to the minds of eighth graders, the brochure's poetry can and probably must be fairly read as an alluring invitation and a beckoning for them to throw off the dull discipline imposed on them by the moral environment of their home life, and in exchange to enter into a new world of love and freedom—freedom to use acid and grass, freedom to take their clothes off and to get an early start in the use of such vulgarities as "shit," "fucking," and their companions.

It is probably a fair inference that by second or third year high school most American males have become familiar with, and at times employ, these and like words. Is it only a forlorn hope, however, that most of our young ladies will never employ that kind of speech?

Clara Brubaker, who taught French at various primary grade schools, placed some of these brochures in the teachers' lounges and also gave copies to her husband, John Brubaker, and to Ronald Sievert, allegedly

for use in their classes. She did not herself distribute any brochures to students, but did display one of the brochure's posters in her classroom.

Copies of the brochure were then made available to the eighth grade students in John Brubaker's and Ronald Sievert's classes. In due time, these brochures found their way into the homes of some of the students. When parents complained to the principal, appellee John Condon, (especially about the poem "Getting Together"), appellants were asked by Superintendent James R. Albert whether they had made copies of the brochure available to the students. He was told that appellants had done so, and Albert reported his findings to the appellee Board of Education members at a closed session on April 30, 1970. The next day the Board resolved to dismiss appellants as of May 4, 1970. Each teacher received a letter advising of the Board's adoption of the following Resolution:

"Resolve that [teacher's name] be dismissed as a teacher of the District effective May 4, 1970 for circulating within the schools of the District certain promotional material entitled "Woodstock" which material is of an obscene and suggestive nature, promotes a viewpoint contrary to the requirements of the laws of the State in regard to teaching about the harmful effects of alcoholic drinks and narcotics, and was distributed contrary to the provisions of policy 3547 of the Policies and By-Laws of School District 149, Cook County, Illinois, prohibiting the distribution within the schools or on school property of any material other than material purchased, procurred [sic] or furnished under the initiative and with the approval of the Board of Education of the District for distribution and use in its Educatonal Program.[2]

"Be It Further Resolved that the secretary of the Board be authorized and directed to prepare a letter to the teacher notifying him [or her] of this action and that the Superintendent be authorized and directed to deliver said letter to the teacher in person as soon as convenient."

Before the effective date of discharge, an attorney contacted the School District, asking for "the setting of a hearing date with regard to the charges pursuant to which they [plaintiffs] were dismissed." This request was reiterated in a letter of May 15, 1970, from a staff attorney for the American Civil Liberties Union to the School District's attorney. The letter concluded:

"I also hereby demand a written bill of particulars, a list of witnesses who may or may not be called to testify on behalf of the school board, and copies of any written statements heretofore made by such witnesses in writing or made orally and committed to writing."

In this letter, plaintiffs' attorney also observed:

"There is a recent case, Roth v. Board of Regents, decided on March 9, 1970 in the federal court district for the Western District of Wisconsin, which, I am told, summarizes the procedural requirements for dismissal of non-tenured university professors at state institutions. However, I have not had time as yet to track down that opinion. Of course, it is our position that the same procedural due process standards apply to teachers in the public school system as to teachers in the public university system."

On May 28, 1970, the School District attorney replied that the Board had considered plaintiffs' request but declined to grant such a hearing. No further action was taken, nor address made to the School Board for about a year, and then on April 22, 1971, this lawsuit was started. The District Court decision of Roth v. Board of Regents, 310 F.Supp. 972 (W.D. Wisc.1970), referred to in counsel for plaintiffs' letter of May 15, 1970, was then pending on appeal in this Court.

In their complaint, appellants charged that appellees had abridged their First and Fourteenth Amendment freedoms and their civil rights and in addition had breached their contracts and defamed them. Appellants each sought reinstatement, together with an award of back salary and compensatory and punitive damages for willful defamation in the amount of $200,000 each. An award of attorney fees was also sought.[3]

The complaint set out that Clara Brubaker had placed a number of the brochures in the teachers' lounges at four or five schools where she taught French, gave a number of copies to plaintiffs John Brubaker and Ronald K. Sievert, and "display[ed] the poster contained therein [in the brochure] in her classroom." She made no allegation that the brochure or its contents were in any way relevant to what she was teaching. It was further alleged that plaintiffs John Brubaker and Ronald K. Sievert had placed the brochures on their desks to be available to their students.

Appellants claim that the brochure had relevancy to what was being taught to the eighth grade students. Appellant Sievert said it had relevancy to his teaching assignment—Language Arts—because under his guidance his class was studying the history of rock music. We are not advised what rock music has to do with Language Arts, but appellant Sievert testified:

"We were to begin a new unit that day, but since we had just finished the other unit on the evolution of music I took out a brochure and I opened it up and instead of showing it I said, 'I have a brochure here which might be of interest to you because it seems to pertain specifically to what we just studied.'

"And I said, 'It has a very colorful poster in it as well, which I think you may well be interested in,' and so I held up the poster part and got ooh's and ahh's from the class."

* * *

"So most of them were rather impressed, I think, by the colorful poster, and after showing this to them I said they could have one after the class period."

* * *

"Nobody took any until after the class period, when I said, 'Okay. Now you can come up and get the poster,' where they just rushed literally to the file cabinet and were just grabbing like crazy, trying to get as many as they could."

He testified that the brochure was not given to him by the school authorities; also that examination of it would quickly disclose that its material had not been prepared for classroom use.

He said that as to the poem "Getting Together" he felt that the young people could handle it quite well—"I was fearing mainly the reaction of parents and administrators."

Appellant John Brubaker's teaching assignment was solely "Industrial Arts." As to the relevancy of the Woodstock brochure to that subject, he said: "I think that this whole thing contributed to the interest of my class in musical instruments." He added that such would be true of the poetry also, saying that as to the words of the poem, "there was nothing wrong with them . . . they were part of the regular vocabulary of youngsters of this age." Neither Brubaker not Sievert explained to their students any claimed relevancy of the Woodstock brochure.

In due course appellees made a Motion to Dismiss the Complaint, averring that plaintiffs had no constitutional right to a hearing concerning the reasons for their discharge; that plaintiffs had admitted the misconduct which had brought on their discharge; that furnishing eighth grade students brochures containing the language set out above was not an activity protected by the First or Fourteenth Amendments or an exercise of civil rights; and that such material was without relevancy to the classes taught by plaintiffs. Appellees further contended that dismissal of plaintiffs was not a breach of their teaching contracts, that the truth of the alleged defamatory language had been admitted by plaintiffs, and that the allegedly defamatory statements were privileged.

This motion was denied by District Judge Hubert

L. Will by order entered September 16, 1971, as follows:

"Order defendants' motion to dismiss the complaint is denied. Order defendants to answer complaint within 10 days."

Following appellees' ordered answer, plaintiffs on November 22, 1971, moved for a summary judgment as to its claims of "Violation of 1st and 14th Amendments" (Count I of their complaint) and "Violations of the Employment Agreements" (Count II). On December 21, 1971, District Judge William J. Bauer, to whom the case had been transferred, and upon the authority of this Court's decision in Roth v. Board of Regents, 446 F.2d 806 (7th Cir. 1971) (Reversed thereafter in 1972 by the Supreme Court, Board of Regents v. Roth, 408 U.S. 564, 92 S.Ct. 2701, 33 L.Ed.2d 548), ordered the Board to provide appellants with a hearing and a statement of the reasons for their discharges.

The ordered hearings were held in early 1972 at which appellants were represented by counsel. Prior to such hearings each plaintiff was provided with a statement of the reasons for dismissal. The one given to John Brubaker included the following:

"1. That on or about April 20, 1970 John Brubaker, while employed as an industrial arts teacher of School District 149, made available to students of the district a brochure entitled 'No one who was there will ever be the same' with the knowledge and intention that students would take and retain copies of the brochure for their personal reading and inspection.
"2. That among the written material contained within said Woodstock brochure was a poem entitled 'Getting Together' containing language of an obscene and suggestive nature and promoting or otherwise favorably portraying the use of drugs and other hallucinogens."

Reasons 3, 4 and 5 stated that the distributed brochure had not been approved for distribution and had not been prepared as a tool for school instruction; that appellants knew, or should have known, the contents of the brochure, and that Brubaker knew, or should have known, that:

"[T]he patent purpose of the brochure was to publicize a motion picture about and recorded music from the 1969 rock music festival known as the Woodstock Festival which festival was widely reported in newspapers and on television and criticized for the purported sexual promiscuity and drug use of its participants, and also since the film promoted by said brochure had been assigned and advertized as having

an R rating by its distributors which rating provided that persons under 17 years of age were not to be admitted unless accompanied by a parent or adult guardian."

Reasons 6 to 10 were as follows:

"6. That the language of the poem Getting Together contained in said brochure promoted a viewpoint contrary to the requirements of the laws of the State of Illinois in regard to teaching about the harmful effects of alcoholic drinks and narcotics as contained in Ill.Rev.Stat.1969, ch. 122, § 27-10.
"7. That the language in the poem Getting Together was contradictory and counteractant to the generally accepted objective of discouraging the use of drugs and other hallucinogens by young persons.
"8. That the language of the poem Getting Together contained in the brochure violates what are called the proprieties or the standards of what is socially acceptable in conduct, behavior and speech, especially as between adult and elementary school age children.
"9. That making the poem Getting Together as a part of the brochure available to elementary school age children without comment or criticism served no legitimate educational objective and that the language of the poem is not consistent with generally approved and professionally acceptable classroom material or generally accepted educational standards and practices.
"10. That the language and subject matter of the poem Getting Together contained in the brochure had no relevance or in any way related to the courses of study which John Brubaker was assigned to present nor which he was, in fact, giving."

Those furnished Clara Brubaker and Ronald Sievert were of similar substance; the assigned reasons were substantially those originally given to appellants with notice of their dismissals.

At the relevant public hearings, testimony was presented by plaintiffs and by the Board. Plaintiffs produced two eminently educated men who expressed the view that the poem "Getting Together" was proper material to be given to eighth grade students. Both had received Ph.D's from important American universities, and had studied and were currently active in the field of education.

The attention of these expert witnesses was called to the poem's reference to the apparent joys of smoking grass—marijuana—and its invitation to Woodstock as "a place to take acid"—LSD—and to make love. They knew of the transports and ecstasies suggested by:

"Oh joy overflowing, *Oh lover caressing* . . . Oh take

me completely . . . *Grass smoked together. Stink of our shit;* music of laughter. . . . *Bodies naked* into the water, touching each other, opening hearts into greater awareness. . . . Of being part of something—a movement, a motion . . . moving together *we're a big fucking wave.*" (Emphasis supplied.)

Of the total work containing the above, one of such witnesses made the following comments:

"For all its apparent looseness as to Whitman, it has quality, it's very tightly constructed, and it seems not too bad a poem."

Further:

"I think there's a good deal of artistic imagination and integrity in that poem."

and, again,

"It would be very hard, I think to suggest that any of it is there for shock value, for crude and gross shock value. He does get some shock value out of the literary contrast, but *for my money, it shows a great awareness of the literary tradition, a great sensitivity to language,* to the development of English and American poetry." (Emphasis supplied.)

and:

"You want a criticism, and I think myself that 'Oh lover caressing' is a little bit sentimental, but then you get from 'Oh lover caressing' down to the 'Bodies naked into the water,' where he plays the romantic sentimentality against the—well, the realism of 'Bodies naked into the water' is an actual knowledge of each other, *the opening of hearts into greater awareness.*"(Emphasis supplied.)

*   *   *

"I think the gentleness of this pose of lovemaking would be also of *very educational value.* It might well have a considerable impression on them."

This same witness also considered the furnishing of the poem to eighth grade children and stated that he thought the teaching methods of Brubaker and Sievert, employed in their Industrial Arts and Language Arts classes "are admirable." He expanded this compliment by observing:

"It seems to me that they establish quite clearly that they had a good deal of sensitivity with the children and knew precisely what children are interested in."

He said of the words used in the poem that,

"there are perhaps better words than seem to have been suggested, but I think that, you know, in a way, *these are sort of beautiful.*" (Emphasis supplied.)

When asked whether the distribution of the brochure *Woodstock* would fit the "preponderant" opinion of the teaching profession, he answered, "it is the kind of material that is in public circulation and is, therefore, part of the material of the classroom." He thought also that providing such material to the students would help to develop a "rapport with these students . . . as this all increases the general fluidity and realism of the classrooms."

One of the experts also expressed himself as follows:

"[T]his is the real vision of the Woodstock thing, a whole notion of *a new sense of community* which I, for one, can deplore as having lost." (Emphasis supplied)

This witness also testified as follows:

"Q. I kind of get the feeling, Doctor, that what you are saying is that life is different really from what we adults and educators would like it to be and that we had better really attune our educational program to what it is really like as against what we prefer it to be.
"A. If we are to serve the children instead of our own anxieties, yes, by all means."

Both of plaintiffs' experts disclosed current activities having to do with training the minds of today's children. One said he was,

"Engaged in the activity of the schooling and service training of teachers, to a degree watching them work with children."

The other referred to his research for the National Institute of Child Health and Human Development. Thus the above quoted excerpts portray the attitudes and beliefs of some of the *teachers of the teachers* of today's children. It was their opinion that teachers should not be required to get approval from school authorities before distributing such materials as the Woodstock brochure to their students. Such a requirement it was said, "demeans the teacher" and would,

"rigidify the teaching . . . it would simply make it at least difficult if not impossible to bring forth the kind of imaginative improvisation that . . . is especially important in a subject or a learning area like English."

Questioned as to whether the poem's suggestion of the joys of using drugs would offend the school's obedience to an Illinois statute requiring the teaching of the effects of the use of narcotics, one of the experts disposed of the subject as follows:

"Q. Referring to the reference to drugs in that poem, do you think this poem ... would tend to glorify that use?
"A. I think it may in part, that the latter would be true."

And after some reference to what he described as our "drug addicted society," the witness concluded:

" ... so this additional exposure of the drug experience [its joyful use at Woodstock] I can't conceive of it again as being anything but a *trivial* plus on the side of drug use."

He later gave emphasis to the above by referring to the poem's invitation to drugs as being "exceedingly trivial."

One of plaintiffs' experts found hypocrisy in the contrast between contemporary society's professed notions of morality and the total conduct of that society. He said,

"but as a social scientist it is my considered opinion that society in the form and conduct of that society is indeed a *sick society*."

We ponder, then, whether a vaccine or therapy to be given to our eighth graders for this sickness—hypocrisy of their seniors—may be found in exposure to Woodstock and its invitations.

At the hearing, appellants Brubaker and Sievert said they had not read the poem "Getting Together" before they first made it available to their students. There was testimony by the Board's representative, however, that when these teachers were approached by him, they did not rely on such excuse. Rather, Brubaker and Sievert indicated that what was in the poem was something that the students "could handle." At the ordered hearing they reiterated such a view.

Relevant to the testimony of appellants Brubaker and Sievert that they had not read the quoted poetry when they gave it to their classes, it should be emphasized that a substantial interval of time elapsed between their claimed tardy reading of it, the Board's reaction to its distribution, and their termination. Neither of them, however, employed this interval to make an explanation or to express to their students disapproval of the poem.

A member of the staff of the Superintendent of Public Instruction for the State of Illinois testified in support of the action of the defendant Board. He was director of the state program for gifted children. By education and experience he was qualified to express his view that the Woodstock brochure and its poetry had no educational value and was inappropriate for distribution to grammar school children. He found invalid the offered excuse that appellants had not read the brochure's poem "Getting Together" before distributing it. We share this view. Parents of children who had brought the Woodstock brochure home also testified in support of the Board's action.

We think it right also to observe that upon learning of the Board's reaction to what had happened, none of the plaintiffs expressed any regret over the matter; neither did any of them seek reinstatement by assurance that corrective measures would be taken. They made no effort to come to a friendly solution with the Board. Their first step was employment of a lawyer who demanded a plenary hearing. This lawsuit followed almost a year thereafter. Whatever their ambivalence as to whether what they did was at most an innocent mistake or done after deliberation, their lawsuit insists and relies solely upon a position that what they did—providing, with their apparent approval, the Woodstock poetry—was but an exercise of the academic freedom guaranteed them by the United States Constitution.

After the hearing, the Board, by resolution adopted April 8, 1972, ratified and confirmed the dismissal of plaintiff-appellants. The resolution stated in part:

"WHEREAS, the Board of Education has heard the evidence presented by and on behalf of the teachers, and on behalf of the School Administration and has heard the arguments of counsel

*   *   *

the Board ... finds that each of the reasons for the dismissal of the teachers served upon them on January 14, 1972 by service on their attorneys has been sustained by evidence; ... "

Plaintiffs and defendants thereafter filed renewed cross-motions for summary judgment, and on August 21, 1972, District Judge William Bauer denied plaintiffs' motion and granted defendants' motion. In deciding the legality of plaintiffs' discharge, the Court felt that the question before it was: "have the plaintiffs herein been discharged for a basis wholly unsupported in fact or for a basis wholly without reason?" It would appear that by this expression District Judge Bauer was employing the language used by the District Judge in the case of Roth v. Board of Regents, 310 F.Supp. at 979. Upon a review of the proceedings before the Board, the Court concluded:

"It is this Court's opinion that the distribution of the brochure is a basis for discharge that is not wholly without reason. The brochure contains a poem entitled 'Getting Together' which contains profane words and favorable references to drugs; this Court cannot say that all reasonable men would find that this poem was suitable reading material for elementary school children.

"Accordingly, this Court holds that there was a basis for discharge of the plaintiffs which was not wholly unsupported in fact or wholly without reason."

That part of the District Court order which reads, "this Court cannot say *that all reasonable men* would find that this poem was suitable reading material for elementary school children," is unknown to us as a rule controlling the District Court's disposition of the matter. We consider, however, that his order's total language constituted a finding adequate to sustain the final judgment.

The Issues Presented for Review,[4] as set out in appellants' brief, are:

That the District Court erred,
"1.   In failing to find that plaintiffs' constitutional rights, including particularly their academic freedom rights as protected by the First Amendment, were infringed by defendants' action in dismissing plaintiffs from their employment as teachers.
"2.   In failing to award plaintiffs back pay and attorneys' fees based on the district court's earlier ruling that plaintiffs had been denied procedural due process in that they had not been given notice and a hearing prior to their discharge.
"3.   In summarily dismissing plaintiffs' claim relating to defamation of character, when said claim raised genuine issues as to material fact which were incapable of resolution on a motion for summary judgment."

I.   *First Amendment and Civil Rights.*

We have set out the factual background of this case at the above length because we believe that such recitation exposes the correctness of our affirmance of the District Court's holding that the School Board's action was not arbitrary or capricious, and was not an invasion of appellants' constitutional rights. Appellants assert that making available to their eighth grade students the Woodstock brochure's poem "Getting Together" was an exercise of free speech guaranteed to them by the First Amendment and an exercise of their Civil Rights, protection of which is vouchsafed to them by 42 U.S.C. § 1983. They said that their dismissal invaded their Right of Academic Freedom, and they

suggest that what was done would have a "chilling effect" on the exercise of academic freedom by other teachers.

We do not believe that however much the reach of the First Amendment has been extended and however eager today's courts have been to protect the many varieties of claims to civil rights, the appellee school board had to put up with the described conduct of appellants.

Appellants' address to us includes this statement:

"[I]nquiry should be made by the court as to whether the publication in question was inappropriate reading for the students involved and whether a serious educational purpose was sought to be achieved. Plaintiffs' expert testimony at the hearing before the School Board, and defendants' lack of testimony concerning this issue, established beyond any reasonable doubt that the use of the Woodstock brochure by plaintiffs was not only appropriate, *but admirable as a teaching tool.*" (Emphasis supplied.)

Relevant to this assertion, we observe that neither the appellants nor their experts emphasized with any degree of specificity what parts of the brochure, other than the poetry, could be classified as "admirable as a teaching tool." The experts primarily addressed their applause to the poem.

Appellants further argue that they were denied due process,

"because there existed a lack of ascertainable standards by which they could measure their conduct."

They do not attempt definition of the relevant and ascertainable standards which they say the School Board should have promulgated. We will not fault a school board for not anticipating that eighth grade teachers might distribute to their students, without explanation or assigned reason therefor, poetry of the caliber of "Getting Together." Appellants say that the Board was wrong because it reached a conclusion as to the poetry's impropriety,

"[w]ithout the benefit of any supporting expert testimony in the fields of literature, obscenity or drugs."

Experts should not be needed to support a conclusion that is obvious. Moreover, the Supreme Court, in Paris Adult Theatre I v. Slaton, 413 U.S. 49, 56, 93 S.Ct. 2628, 2634, 37 L.Ed.2d 446 (1973), rejected the contention that " 'expert' affirmative evidence that the materials were obscene," was necessary when the alleged obscene material was itself placed in evidence. Similarly in this case no "expert" testimony was required.

Relative to the brochure's admitted invitation to the use of drugs, the evidence disclosed that Ill.Rev. Stat. ch. 122, § 27-10 required that the "Nature and effect of alcoholic drinks and narcotics and their effects on the human system" be taught to pupils below the second year of high school and above the third year of elementary school work. Appellants argue that they were not aware of such statute, and that, therefore, it "did not constitute the kind of constitutionally permissible ascertainable standard which should have placed plaintiffs on notice that their conduct in distributing the Woodstock brochure [with its glorification of grass and acid] would subject them to dismissal." Whether they knew of the statute or not, we consider that these teachers should have known better than to hand to their young students something that invited the use of the described drugs. Additionally, appellants had been aware of and had participated in previously presented teaching programs expounding upon the baleful consequences of the use of drugs and alcohol.

In rejecting appellants' claim of academic freedom, we note the following from the First Circuit's opinion in Mailloux v. Kiley, 436 F.2d 565 (1st Cir. 1971), where a claim of academic freedom was similarly raised. There the Court said:

"The court in no way regrets its decision in Keefe v. Geanakos, 1 Cir., 1969, 418 F.2d 359, but it did not intend thereby to do away with what, to use an old-fashioned term, are considered the proprieties, *or to give carte blanche in the name of academic freedom* to conduct which can reasonably be deemed both offensive and unnecessary to the accomplishment of educational objectives. *Cf.* Close v. Lederle, 1 Cir., 1970, 424 U.S. 988, cert. denied, 400 U.S. 903, 91 S.Ct. 141, 27 L.Ed.2d 140. Here, particularly, such questions are mattters of degree involving judgment on such factors *as the age and sophistication of students, relevance of the educational purpose, and context and manner of presentation.*" 436 F.2d at 566. (Emphasis supplied.)

In affirming the District Court order on remand, the First Circuit also said in Mailloux v. Kiley, *supra,*

"With all respect to the district court's sensitive effort to devise guidelines for weighing those circumstances, 323 F.Supp. 1387, we suspect that any such formulation would introduce more problems than it would resolve. At present we see no substitute for a case-by-case inquiry into whether the legitimate interests of the authorities are demonstrably sufficient to circumscribe a teacher's speech." 448 F.2d at 1243.

The validity of our conclusion that the District Court properly found no violation of appellants' First Amendment or Civil Rights emerges so clearly that we decline to add, by our own extended dissertation, to the already abundant literature on the subject we deal with.

II. *Back Pay and Attorney Fees.*
1) *Back pay.*

Appellants argue that in all events the Brubakers are entitled to an award for the pay that they would have received from the date of their termination—May 4, 1970—to the end of the school year—June 12, 1970. Appellant Sievert seeks back pay for the above period and for the pay he would have received for the school year 1970-1971. As noted previously, all appellants were non-tenured teachers: the Brubakers had been advised before May 4, 1970, that they would not be employed for the following year. Sievert, however, had been advised before May 4, 1970, that they [sic] the 1970-71 school year. Appellants' position is that notwithstanding that they had been given the reasons for their termination, they were also entitled to, but initially refused, a hearing. They argue that the court-ordered hearing did not provide them with due process.

Cases cited by appellants to support their claims for an award of back pay are distinguishable from the present case. Horton v. Orange County Bd. of Educ., 464 F.2d 536, 538 (4th Cir. 1972); Rolfe v. County Bd. of Educ., 391 F.2d 77, 81 (6th Cir. 1968); Jackson v. Wheatley School Dist. No. 28, 464 F.2d 411 (8th Cir. 1972); Bates v. Hinds, 334 F.Supp. 528, 533 (N.D.Tex. 1971); Callaway v. Kirkland, 334 F.Supp. 1034, 1038 (N.D.Ga.1971). In so distinguishing, we emphasize that the notices of termination given to appellants each set out the reasons therefor. As ordered, a plenary hearing was had before the School Board. The District Court held, and this Court now holds, that there was good cause for termination of each of the appellants.

In Horton v. Orange County Board of Education, *supra*, the court emphasized that:

"In none of the letters advising her [the discharged teacher] of the termination was she told of the grounds therefor." 464 F.2d at 537.

Such failure is not present in our case.

Back pay was also allowed in Rolfe v. County Board of Education, *supra*, where the Sixth Circuit affirmed a District Court judgment, "holding that the discharge of two schoolteachers, [plaintiffs] appellees herein, was discriminatory because it was based on consideration of race." 391 F.2d at 78.

Also in Jackson v. Wheatley School District, No. 28 *supra,* the Eighth Circuit recited that in an earlier hearing of the same case,

"we held that the Wheatley School Board had unlawfully discharged three black teachers [the plaintiffs in the above cited case]." 464 F.2d at 412.

In Bates v. Hinds, supra, the District Judge's opinion does not consider, nor rule upon, whether there were valid grounds for dismissal of the involved teacher. Although Bates was awarded back pay and attorney fees, the court's ruling and award appear to have been bottomed upon the failure of the school authorities to give the discharged teacher a fair hearing or adequate notice of the reasons for his discharge. The District Judge said, *inter alia*:

"Plaintiff never received official word of his termination." 334 F.Supp. at 531.

* * *

"The teacher . . . was not given written notice of the charges against him . . . ." 334 F.Supp. at 532.

* * *

"The Court concludes that Bates' hearing satisfied neither the procedural due process standards set out by the Fifth Circuit nor the rudiments of fair play." 334 F.Supp. at 533.

The case of Callaway v. Kirkland, *supra,* presented some procedural novelties inasmuch as the parties did agree upon a settlement. A District Judge, however, awarded back pay over and above the amount received by the teacher upon the settlement. In doing so, the District Court said:

"Since there has been no correction of the procedural defects connected with plaintiffs' dismissal *and no adjudication of the basis for the dismissal,* the court need look no further than its ruling of December 29, 1970, to find that defendants unlawfully interfered with plaintiff's expectancy of reemployment by summarily dismissing him without affording him procedural due process. Therefore, plaintiff is entitled to recover the back pay which he seeks."

* * *

"Plaintiff has consistently denied defendants' allegations of misconduct and has never been provided with a meaningful opportunity to counteract those allegations." 334 F.Supp. at 1038. (Emphasis supplied.)

It is clear that none of the above cases are in point here where written notice of the reasons for termination were given, a court-ordered plenary hearing on the matter was had and the school board, a District Court, and this Court, hold that appellants were terminated for just cause.

We are essentially being asked to rule that where school authorities are made aware of a non-tenured teacher's misconduct, they must continue such teacher in service until a full-dress hearing has been provided, or pay the terminated teacher's salary until such hearing can be arranged. We decline to do so in this case where the propriety of the termination has been fully vindicated by the record made upon such hearing. It should also be emphasized that the attorney early engaged by appellants was promptly advised that his request for a hearing had been submitted to and declined by the Board. At the time of these events, no decision of the United States Supreme Court, a United States Court of Appeals, or the courts of Illinois, had held that a hearing had to precede termination.

We mention, too, that appellants waited for almost a year from the time they received the reasons for their termination before instituting this lawsuit. At that time there was pending before this Court an appeal from a District Court holding that two non-tenured college professors were entitled to a hearing before they were refused reemployment for another year. The decision of this Court affirming such holding was announced July 1, 1971, after this suit was started, Roth v. Board of Regents of State Colleges, 446 F.2d 806 (7th Cir. 1971). Such decision was reversed by the Supreme Court in Board of Regents v. Roth, 408 U.S. 564, 92 S.Ct. 2701, 33 L.Ed. 2d 548 (1972). The Supreme Court there held that non-tenured teachers are not entitled to a hearing upon a decision of school authorities not to reemploy them. That decision, however, held that termination of such teachers *during* an existing school year had to be accompanied by obedience to due process, 408 U.S. at 576-577, 92 S.Ct. 2701. But it did not say that termination had to await a hearing regardless of whether such hearing ultimatley disclosed that the termination was for good cause.

We are aware of decisions which, under their facts, have said that a due process hearing should have preceded the challenged action. Such cases were referred to in footnote seven in Board of Regents of State Colleges v. Roth, 408 U.S. at 570, 92 S.Ct. 2701, cited to consider the need for a hearing "*before* the termination becomes effective." Bell v. Burson, 402 U.S. 535, 542, 91 S.Ct. 1586, 29 L.Ed.2d 90 (1971). In *Bell,* a Georgia statute allowed suspension of the driver's license of an uninsured motorist "involved in an accident . . . unless he posts security to cover the amount of damages claimed *by aggrieved parties in reports of the accident.*" (Emphasis supplied.) Such action would take place without reference to whether the public authorities had, or claimed to have, made any investigation as to whether the driver in question was at fault. In the present case, however, the school authorities had investigated the charged misconduct, and such misconduct was admitted to have occurred. The School Board's decision to discharge appellants and their reasons therefor were made known to appellants. In the other case cited in Roth, Cafeteria & Restaurant Workers Union, Local 473 v. McElroy, 367 U.S. 886, 81 S.Ct. 1743, 6 L.Ed.2d 1230 (1961), the Court stated the following:

"The Fifth Amendment does not require a trial-type hearing in every conceivable case of government impairment of private interest, 'For, though "due process of law" generally implies and includes *actor, reus, judex,* regular allegations, opportunity to answer, and a trial according to some settled course of judicial proceedings, . . . yet, this is not universally true.' Murray's Lessee v. Hoboken Land and Improvement Co., 18 How. 272, 280 [15 L.Ed. 372.] The very nature of due process negates any concept of inflexible procedures universally applicable to every imaginable situation. Communications Comm'n v. WJR, 337 U.S. 265, 275-276 [69 S.Ct. 1097, 1103, 93 L.Ed. 1353]; Hannah v. Larche, 363 U.S. 420, 440, 442 [80 S.Ct. 1502, 1513-1514, 4 L.Ed.2d 1307]; Hagar v. Reclamation District No. 108, 111 U.S. 701, 708-709 [4 S.Ct. 663, 667, 28 L.Ed. 569]. '*"[D]ue process," unlike some legal rules is not a technical conception with a fixed content unrelated to time, place and circumstances.'*" 367 U.S. at 894-895, 81 S.Ct. at 1748 (Emphasis supplied.)

We find no decision of the Supreme Court or of any of the Courts of Appeals holding that where, as here, the propriety of the discharge is sustained after plenary administrative and judicial hearings, the public authority—here a school board—must nevertheless pay the discharged employees their wages until such hearings shall have been concluded, however long delayed. The rule that appellants ask us to announce would require that, however wrong the admitted conduct of a school teacher, a school board must refrain from discharging her or him until a full dress hearing upon whether such conduct warranted discharge can be arranged and concluded. We decline to so hold.

We come finally to the question of whether the termination of the appellants without a *prior* hearing denied them due process of law. Since this case was heard in the District Court, and thereafter submitted

to us on appeal, the Supreme Court opinion in Arnett v. Kennedy, 416 U.S. 134, 94 S.Ct. 1633, 40 L.Ed.2d 15 (1974), has come down. We consider that its majority opinion sets at rest the question of whether, no matter what the cause, a hearing must as a matter of obedience to the Constitution, *precede* the termination of a teacher or any public employee. We read the opinion as holding that such a *prior* hearing is not in all cases constitutionally essential. There, a civil service employee was terminated in conformity with an Act of Congress —5 U.S.C. § 7501—which, after setting out certain procedures that had to precede termination of a civil service employee, concluded:

"Examination of witnesses, trial, or hearing is not required but may be provided in the discretion of the individual directing the removal or suspension without pay."

The Act required notice of the charges upon which termination was made and also provided for an appeal that could be taken after the termination to test the validity of the discharge. Without resort to such departmental procedures, the involved employee began an action in the United States District Court attacking his discharge and asserting, as set out in Arnett v. Kennedy, *supra,*

"that the charges were unlawful because he had a right to a trial-type hearing before an impartial hearing officer *before* he could be removed from his employment . . . ." 94 S.Ct. at 1637. (Emphasis supplied.)

He further asserted that statements made by him which caused his termination "were protected by the First Amendment to the United States Constitution." It was his position that his discharge *prior* to a hearing denied him "procedural due process of law."

A three-judge District Court, convened pursuant to 28 U.S.C. §§ 2282 and 2284, held that the discharge procedures authorized by the Act and attendant Civil Service and OEO Regulations denied appellee due process of law. By summary order it directed that appellee be reinstated in his former position with back pay, and that he be accorded a hearing *prior* to removal in any future removal proceedings. The District Court decision, reported as Kennedy v. Sanchez, 349 F.Supp. 863 (N.D.Ill.1972), sets out the claim which it sustained and its dispositive ruling as follows:

"[T]he procedure by which Kennedy's employment was terminated deprives him and his class (which has not been determined) of due process under the Fifth Amendment by its failure to provide a full evidentiary hearing *prior* to termination, with the right to be heard by an impartial hearing officer; the right to present witnesses; the right to confront and cross-examine adverse witnesses; and the right to a written decision indicating the reasons for discharge or suspension and the evidence relied upon. This Court agrees." 349 F.Supp. at 864.

As we read it, the majority opinion of the Supreme Court in reversing the District Court held that a plenary hearing before a termination is not a constitutional essential of due process. There the Court was specifically dealing with a relevant Act of Congress wherein it was provided that in terminating a civil service employee it was not required that a hearing must be had *prior* to discharge. The thrust of the Court's holding can best be gleaned from its statement as to the issue involved. The Court said:

"We must first decide whether these procedures established [by the Congress] for the purpose of determining whether there is 'cause' under the Lloyd-LaFollette Act for the dismissal of a federal employee *comport with procedural due process,* and then decide whether that standard of 'cause' for federal employee dismissals *was within the constitutional power of Congress to adopt.*" 94 S.Ct. at 1641. (Emphasis supplied.)

Its controlling opinion concluded that such procedures did comport with due process and that they were within the constitutional power of Congress to adopt. The opinion from which we quote above was written by Mr. Justice Rehnquist, with concurrence by the Chief Justice and Mr. Justice Stewart. A separate opinion was written by Mr. Justice Powell with the concurrence of Mr. Justice Blackman. Justice Powell's opinion emphasized the post-termination procedures provided in the relevant Act of Congress. It began with the observation, *inter alia,* that,

"I also agree that appellee's discharge did not contravene the Fifth Amendment guarantee of procedural due process." 94 S.Ct. at 1649.

and concluded that:

"On balance, I would conclude that *a prior evidentiary hearing is not required* and that the present statute and regulations comport with due process by providing a reasonable accommodation of the competing interests." 94 S.Ct. at 1653. (Emphasis supplied.)

We are aware that Justice Powell appears to have been motivated in part by the post-termination procedures available to, but not employed by, the discharged employee. As to the reach of the discussed opinion, we observe that it is the law that the Congress may not by its legislation override the Constitution any more than other public employers may do so. Applicable to the case at bar there did not exist any Illinois statute spelling out procedures to be followed in termination of a school teacher. In all events, the *Kennedy* decision sets at rest and denies appellants' contention that absent a *prior* hearing the school board must pay back wages to the appellants. The appellants have now had a plenary hearing, the disclosures of which sustain the validity of the school board's action. The fact that a hearing was initially refused and was had only when ordered by the District Court does not impair the rightness of what was originally done. We repeat that at the time of appellants' termination there was no clear rule of law or constitutional command that a hearing required. It is relevant too that appellants waited for nearly a year before invoking judicial help. At no time have appellants denied the doing of that which prompted the school board's action. Their defense is, and was, that they had the right to do what they did. It should be mentioned that their initial demand for a hearing neither denied that factual recitals of the notice of termination, nor relied upon a claim ultimately made that what they did was merely an exercise of academic freedom.

Evidence at the hearing disclosed that complaints by the parents of appellants' students activated the investigation which led to the board's action. It was right for school authorities to take cognizance of such parental concern. The board did not act without providing appellants with opportunity to explain or offer justification for what they had done. Appellants did neither, and their first response was to employ a lawyer.

Upon consideration of the record before us, we decline to award back wages to appellants.

2) Attorney fees.

Allowance of attorney fees is an "inherent equitable power" of the court, utilized wherever " 'overriding considerations indicate the need for such a recovery.' " Hall v. Cole, 412 U.S. 1, 5, 93 S.Ct. 1943, 1946, 36 L.Ed.2d 702 (1973). The Court in *Hall* stated the following principles for awarding attorney fees:

"Thus, it is unquestioned that a federal court may award counsel fees to a successful party when his opponent has acted 'in bad faith, vexatiously, wantonly, or for oppressive reasons.' 6 J. Moore, Federal Practice ¶54.77 [2], p. 1709 (2d ed. 1972); see, e. g., Newman v. Piggie Park Enterprises, Inc., 390 U.S. 400, 402 n. 4 [88 S.Ct. 964, 966, 19 L.Ed.2d 1263] (1968); Vaughan v. Atkinson, 369 U.S. 527 [82 S.Ct. 997, 8 L.Ed.2d 88] (1962); Bell v. School Bd. of Powhatan County, 321 F.2d 494 (CA 4 1963); Rolax

v. Atlantic Coast Line R. Co., 186 F.2d 473 (CA 4 1951). In this class of cases, the underlying rationale of 'fee-shifting' is, of course, punitive, and the essential element in triggering the award of fees is therefore the existence of 'bad faith' on the part of the unsuccessful litigant.

"Another established exception involves cases in which the plaintiff's successful litigation confers 'a substantial benefit on the members of an ascertainable class, and where the court's jurisdiction over the subject matter of the suit makes possible an award that will operate to spread the costs proportionately among them.' " 412 U.S. at 5, 93 S.Ct. at 1946.

This Court has long held that it is within the discretion of the District Court to allow or refuse the award of attorney fees, and that we will interfere only where that discretion has been abused. Gordon v. Illinois Bell Telephone Co., 330 F.2d 103, 107 (7th Cir.), cert. denied, 379 U.S. 909, 85 S.Ct. 197, 13 L.Ed.2d 182 (1964); Milwaukee Towne Corp. v. Loew's, Inc., 190 F.2d 561, 571 (7th Cir. 1951), cert. denied, 342 U.S. 909, 72 S.Ct. 303, 96 L.Ed. 680 (1952); Official Aviation Guide Co. v. American Aviation Associates, Inc., 162 F.2d 541, 543 (7th Cir. 1947).

We find no such abuse in the present case. Our review convinces us that the board acted at all times in good faith; it did not intend to be oppressive as to the rights of appellants. We similarly find no benefit being conferred on "other members of an ascertainable class," *Hall, supra.*

III. *Defamation.*

In count III of their complaint, appellants alleged that:

"The statements made by defendant members of the BOARD OF EDUCATION . . . *were false and were known by said defendants to be false* when made, recorded and published by them. Said statements were made by defendant members of the BOARD OF EDUCATION with the purpose of injuring plaintiffs."

As a result of such statements, appellants claim to have suffered irreparable harm to their reputations. This claim was dismissed by Judge Bauer on defendants' motion for summary judgment.[5]

We first observe that the only relevant *falsity* resides in appellants' above charge that the statements made by the Board "were false." The truth of the facts upon which the terminations were made was admitted by appellants. We, however, discuss the subject this much further. Appellants' brief alleges that "the matter" was discussed in "executive session" held on April 30, 1970, and an agreement as to dismissing appellants

was reached on May 1, 1970. They allege further, however, that the resolution to dismiss, as set out at length herein, "was adopted in open session." Statements made at such meetings have been held by the Illinois Courts to be absolutely privileged. McLaughlin v. Tilendis, 115 Ill.App.2d 148, 253 N.E.2d 85, 88 (1969); Larson v. Doner, 32 Ill.App.2d 471, 178 N.E.2d 399 (1961).

Because the question of whether an absolute privilege exists is a matter for the court to decide, Larson v. Doner, *supra,* 32 Ill.App.2d at 472, 178 N.E.2d at 400, and because there were no issues of material fact, the District Judge properly dismissed appellants' defamation claim.

The decision of the District Court is affirmed.

FAIRCHILD, Circuit Judge (dissenting).

I do not believe that the Woodstock brochure was either so irrelevant to educational goals or patently offensive that the plaintiffs were precluded from exercising their judgment as teachers and electing to employ it in their classes. Accordingly, I respectfully dissent from the majority's conclusion that the district court correctly held these discharges did not violate first amendment rights. I concur regarding the failure to award attorneys' fees or back pay pending the Roth-type hearing, and dismissal of the defamation action.

Freedom to discuss controversial or unpopular ideas in the schools is "a special concern of the First Amendment, which does not tolerate laws that cast a pall of orthodoxy over the classroom." Keyishian v. Board of Regents, 385 U.S. 589, 603, 87 S.Ct. 675, 683, 17 L.Ed.2d 629 (1966). See also Tinker v. Des Moines School Dist., 393 U.S. 503, 506-507, 89 S.Ct. 733, 21 L.Ed.2d 31 (1969). Academic freedom "does not grant teachers a license to say or write in class whatever they may feel like." Mailloux v. Kiley, 448 F.2d 1242, 1243 (1st Cir., 1971). See Clark v. Holmes, 474 F.2d 928, 931 (7th Cir., 1972), cert. denied 411 U.S. 972, 93 S.Ct. 2148, 36 L.Ed.2d 695 (1973). However, particularly where the school board has not formulated standards to guide him, academic freedom affords a teacher a certain latitude in judging whether material is suitable and relevant to his instruction. "First Amendment freedoms need breathing space to survive. . . ." N.A.A.C.P. v. Button, 371 U.S. 415, 433, 83 S.Ct. 328, 338, 9 L.Ed.2d 405 (1963).

These instructors did not exceed the bounds which germaneness places on protected classroom speech. The discussion and distribution of the Woodstock brochure consumed no significant amount of school time. Compare State ex rel. Wasilewski v. Bd. of School Directors, 14 Wis.2d 243, 260-261, 111 N.W.2d 198, 208-209 (1961), appeal dismissed, 370 U.S. 720, 82 S.Ct. 1574, 8 L.Ed.2d 802 (1962). Further, it was arguably relevant to the course of instruction. Sievert's class had just completed study of the history of rock music; Brubaker's was considering construction of musical instruments. The 1969 rock music festival at Woodstock, New York had at least some significance to these subjects, significance which was perhaps more evident in April, 1970 than it is today. More importantly, however, the appropriateness of a particular classroom discussion topic cannot be gauged solely by its logical nexus to the subject matter of instruction. A teacher may be more successful with his students if he is able to relate to them in philosophy of life, and, conversely, students may profit by learning something of a teacher's views on general subjects.[1] Academic freedom entails the exchange of ideas which promote education in its broadest sense.

The Woodstock brochure was not so offensive that its classroom use was obviously improper. The school board had not promulgated any standards against which plaintiffs could measure this type of literature to determine whether board policy forbade its use.[2] The board points out that certain conduct patently exceeds "the bounds of the recognized standards of propriety" and a particular rule giving advance notice that it is forbidden is unnecessary. *Wasilewski, supra,* 14 Wis.2d at 257, 111 N.W.2d at 206. See also Shirck v. Thomas, 447 F.2d 1025, 1027 (7th Cir., 1971), vacated on other grounds, 408 U.S. 940, 92 S.Ct. 2848, 33 L.Ed.2d 764 (1972). However, the material in question does not fall into this category.

First, plaintiff's experts in the field of education characterized the Woodstock pamphlet as suitable, even admirable, teaching material for eighth grade students. Whether or not this opinion be accepted, the classroom use of this work can hardly be considered "conduct, generally condemned by responsible men." In re Ruffalo, 390 U.S. 544, 88 S.Ct. 1222, 20 L.Ed.2d 117 (1968), reh. denied 391 U.S. 961, 88 S.Ct. 1833, 20 L.Ed.2d 874 (concurring opinion). Second, the brochure is not obscene in the legal sense. The use of profanity does not transform the controversial into obscene. See Cohen v. California 403 U.S. 15, 20, 91 S.Ct. 1780, 29 L.Ed.2d 284 (1971); Fujishima v. Board of Education, *supra* note 2, 460 F.2d at 1359 n.7. Miller v. California, 413 U.S. 15, 24 93 S.Ct. 2607, 2615, 37 L.Ed.2d 419 (1973) described obscenity as limited to "works which, taken as a whole, appeal to the prurient interest in sex, which portray sexual conduct in a patently offensive way, and which, taken as a whole, do not have serious literary, artistic, political or scientific value." The bulk of the pamphlet consists of inoffensive factual accounts of the Woodstock festival. Even assuming the continuing validity of the variable obscenity doctrine,[3] and making the widest allowances for the age of plaintiffs' students, neither the brochure as a whole nor the poem "Getting Together" begin to satisfy

the *Miller* criteria. See *Jacobs, supra* note 2, 490 F.2d at 610.

Whether the board could constitutionally have promulgated specific rules which would have prohibited the classroom use of this literature by eighth grade students is not the issue presented. I cannot conclude that these materials are so clearly improper as to justify the mid-term discharge of an instructor who elected to use them in his teaching.

I would reverse the district court's summary judgment for defendants and remand for determination of the amount of back pay due to plaintiffs as a result of their unlawful discharge.

Appendix to follow.

NOTES

1. Acid and Grass are words popularly employed to identify LSD and marijuana, respectively.
2. The school board's Policy 3547 reads:

   "No material of any kind, whether or not bearing the imprint of a profit making organization, may be distributed by such organization, or any agent thereof, or any district employee, to students of the public school of this district, within the school, on school property, or at any district sponsored operation or function.
   "No material of any kind, supplied by any non-profit organization may be distributed by such organization, or any agent thereof, or any district employee, until the Superintendent of Schools has approved such distribution. The Superintendent's decision shall be based on his judgment of the educational interests served in each individual case. Such decision will be reported to the Board of Education as informational items in its agenda."

   Appellants Brubaker and Sievert testified that they were not aware of such policy. The Board was unable to prove the contrary.
3. The conclusion of their brief to this Court asks that:

   "the case [be] remanded to the district court for entry of a judgment in favor of plaintiffs with respect to the violation of their constitutional rights and for the granting of a trial with respect to their claim of defamation of character."

4. Appellees present a preliminary procedural question asserting that the appeal by Clara Brubaker is not before us. The notice of appeal lists Clara S. Brubaker, John W. Brubaker and Ronald K. Sievert in their individual capacities as parties in this appeal. Relying on Rule 3(c), Federal Rules of Appellate Procedure, appellees argue that because Clara died over one year before the appeal was taken, the notice should have stated that the appeal was being taken in the name of "John Brubaker, individually, and as representative of Clara Brubaker," or words of like import.
   It may well be that given a narrow construction of

Rule 3(c), we would have no jurisdiction to entertain Clara's appeal. This view was adopted by the Ninth Circuit in Penwell v. Newland, 180 F.2d 551 (9th Cir. 1950). In that case, however, only one party was named in the notice of appeal, whereas in the present case, John Brubaker who is Clara's personal representative by appointment of the Cook County, Illinois, Probate Court, is also a party. Her name is included in the notice of appeal. We believe that the estate of Clara Brubaker is a party to the appeal before us.

5. One of appellants' arguments is that Judge Bauer's August 21, 1972 dismissal of their claim on a motion for summary judgment was improper because Judge Will, on September 16, 1971, had refused to grant appellees' motion for summary judgment. In Bowles v. Wilke, 175 F.2d 35, 37 (7th Cir.), cert. denied, 338 U.S. 861, 70 S.Ct. 104, 94 L.Ed. 528 (1949), this Court stated:

> "We think it beyond question that as to interlocutory orders entered in the District Court, the trial judge himself or any judge succeeding him in the disposition of a pending cause may vacate any such prior order. The only restraint upon a second judge in passing upon an interlocutory issue decided by another judge in the same case is one of comity only, which in no way infringes upon the power of the second judge to act."

Under the circumstances of this case, Judge Bauer did not act improperly in granting appellees' renewed motion to dismiss. A period of almost one year had elapsed between Judge Will's and Judge Bauer's rulings. It was during this period that the facts of the case were developed and the issues narrowed.

DISSENTING OPINION NOTES

1. The Supreme Court recently noted, in the context of prisoner correspondence rights, the reciprocal nature of first amendment speech rights in Procunier v. Martinez, 416 U.S. 396, 94 S.Ct. 1800, 40 L.Ed.2d 224 (1974). Similarly, academic freedom includes both the freedom of the student to hear as well as that of the teacher to speak.

2. The board relies in part on a provision in Ill.Rev.Stat. ch. 122, § 27-10 (1969) repealed effective Oct. 1, 1973 by P.A. 78-334, § 2:

> "The nature of alcoholic drinks and other narcotics and their effects on the human system shall be taught in connection with the various divisions of physiology and hygiene, as thoroughly as are other branches, in all schools under State control. . . . "

I fail to see how this statute afforded an instructor any guidance whatsoever in determining whether a particular work which alludes to the use of alcohol and narcotics is suitable educational material.

The board also refers to its policy no. 3547 which in effect prohibits the distribution of printed matter without its prior approval. This court has invalidated similar regulations for overbreadth. Jacobs v. Board of School Commissioners, 490 F.2d 601, 604-609 (7th Cir., 1973), cert. granted, 417 U.S. 929, 94 S.Ct. 2638, 41 L.Ed.2d 232. See also Fujishima v. Board Education, 460 F.2d 1355 (7th Cir., 1972).

3. See. e. g., Ginsberg v. New York, 390 U.S. 629, 88 S.Ct. 1274, 20 L.Ed.2d 195 (1968).

A California Court of Appeal, First District, decides against students and parents who had argued, on religious grounds, that the implementation of a family life and sex education program in their schools violated their constitutional rights. The Court cites from the memorandum opinion of the trial court: "If on the other hand, the plaintiffs contend that the curriculum and material being taught in the challenged courses are contrary to their particular religious beliefs and even though their children are not required to attend such courses, they still have a constitutional right to have such material conform to their religious beliefs, then clearly there is no such constitutional right. If such were not the case, it is obvious that every citizen could seek to control the curriculum and material being taught in our public school system by simply asserting that such material was contrary to their particular religious beliefs. Thus various complainants could actually use the judicial process to in fact 'establish a religion,' in our public school system by using the courts to so control curriculum to ensure that the same would conform to the particular religious concepts of the complainants."

Citizens for Parental Rights v. *San Mateo Co. Bd. of Ed.,* 124 Cal.Rptr. 68 (1975)

TAYLOR, Presiding Justice.

This is an appeal by Citizens for Parental Rights, et al. (an unincorporated association of parents and as individual parents, hereafter parents), from a judgment of dismissal entered to their seventh amended class action complaint for declaratory and injunctive relief. The basic substantive question is whether the implementation of family life and sex education programs by the five respondent school districts in the jurisdiction of respondent, San Mateo County[1] violates the constitutional rights of the individual parents and their children under the First, Ninth, Tenth and Fourteenth Amendments of the U.S. Constitution, and the parallel provisions of the California Constitution.[2] The case also presents a question of first impression as to the constitutionality of Education Code, sections 8506 and 8701.[3] We have concluded that the family life and sex education programs, adoption of the resource guides, and the statutes are constitutional for the reasons set forth below, and that therefore the judgment of dismissal based on the failure of the amended complaint to state a cause of action must be affirmed.[4]

Before turning to the issues involved, a brief summary of the salient aspects of the program in issue is warranted.

The record indicates that in the San Bruno Park School District, one of the four phases of the program has to do with biological aspects of family living, as outlined in the Teachers' Resources Guide. Family life education is taught in various schools and in various grades but the program varies in each grade and school. Family life education at the time here pertinent was being taught to classes containing 3,106 students; 128 of these asked to be excluded.

The Millbrae School District had a sex education program for grades 5, 6, 7 and 8 during the 1970-1971 school year. Of the 1,550 students enrolled, 158 asked to be excluded.

The Hillsborough City School District taught family life education in grades 6, 7 and 8. Of the 181 sixth grade students enrolled in the program in 1969-1970, 20 asked for a course on conservation as an alternative to the unit on human reproduction.

The San Carlos School District has a biological unit taught as a supplement to the health and science course of study in grades 3 through 8. Of the 2,179 students enrolled in the district in grades 3 through 8 at the time here pertinent, 2,015 were in the program; 104 asked to be excluded.

In the South San Francisco Unified School District, family life education is taught from kindergarten through grade 12 with certain phases emphasized in certain grades. Of the 13,000 students taking the course in 1970-1971, 15 asked to be excluded.

In each district, the respective programs were taught by specially selected teachers who had received special training.

The exhibits filed by each of the districts consist of the Teachers' Program Guides. The guides are substantially similar in content but the level of the program, discussion tapes and reading materials increase in detail and complexity for the upper grades. Each guide is divided into three categories: 1) concepts and understandings; 2) learning experiences and examples of content; and 3) resource materials, including publications and films to be used. For example, the guide for grades 7 through 8 in one of the districts relates to problems solving techniques learned in the family that become part of one's personality. The learning experience and example of content suggested the inclusion of role-playing family discussion to solve the problem of division of family chores and suggests a series of readings that include Neff, *Ethics for Everyday Living;* Seashore, *How to Solve Your Problems;* Randolph, *Self-Enhancing Education;* and Ginott, *Between Parent and Child.*

Under the concept of training and guidance of children, the program also suggests for discussion a debate on "Spare the Rod and Spoil the Child" and "Children Should be Seen and not Heard." Also included are topics such as citizenship, financial responsibility, and the roles and responsibilities of children in the family. Among the suggested learning experiences and examples of content under financial responsibilities are a list of items to be included in a family budget and the role-playing of a situation in which the parents have to weigh alternatives in making the family income stretch to meet the needs of various family members. As to roles and responsibilities, it is suggested that students write a story: "My parents expect too much of me" or "My parents don't expect enough of me." Among the concepts and understandings included is that most teenagers have problems with parents and most parents have problems with teenagers. The guide suggests that the absence of problems indicate that no growth is occurring past pre-adolescence.

On the unit relating to normal sexual development from infancy to adulthood, the guide indicates that the teachers should not indicate that certain kinds of a behavior are good or bad, right or wrong, but indicates simply various kinds of normal behavior patterns. As to an area entitled "Unusual Behavior" which includes such topics as child molestation, exhibitionism, homosexuality and prostitution, the guide indicates that this unit is to be withheld until the background material written by the consultants is prepared. Under the concept of the family and home as the basic unit in American life, suggested for brainstorming, are topics such as what changes are taking place in family units, and include such readings as the *History of the American Family* by Kenney.

In the version used at all of the grade levels, the program clearly indicates that there are many kinds of families and that family composition may change from time to time. Among the suggested experiences are: a story describing the family and all of the significant changes that occurred in the family since the student was born; and a family scrapbook.

In the unit under economic factors, it is suggested that the students write a story describing how the work of the parents affects the family's ways of living and how the family decides how to share and expend its resources.

In the unit on human reproduction, the concepts and understandings to be reviewed are the male and female reproductive systems. As to sexual intercourse, there is a special note to the teachers indicating that it should be explained as a natural sequence of studying the reproductive process, and that the physiological facts should be dealt with within the framework of human love of husband and wife and the means of producing new life.[5] As to sexual behavior, the concepts and understandings cover a broad range of behavior and emphasize that curiosity and interest about one's own body are normal and acceptable, including infantile masturbation. The teacher is told to answer questions honestly and sincerely and not to interpret the material and when covering topics, such as masturbation, contraception, abortion and divorce, to indicate that there are many different points of view concerning them, that it is important that each person live within the framework of his religion or moral code of behavior. The section on learning experiences, expressly states: "*Maturbation:* Excessive or prolonged masturbation is thought by psychologists to be a symptom of other emotional problems. Some religions regard masturbation (when it is consciously performed as a substitute for sexual intercourse) as an immoral act to be discouraged.

"The teacher should not say that it is 'bad' or 'good' or 'right' or 'wrong' but should give the above as facts."

Under the concept heading of value of sex within the marriage are covered the legal consequences of sexual intercourse outside of marriage. The learning experience section suggests a discussion of the legal, emotional, social and spiritual consequences of sexual intercourse outside of marriage.[6] In the concept entitled family planning, the outline lists the various factors relating to family planning, including degree of mutual adjustment, economic factors, religious viewpoints, effect on other children, and the number of children and capacity of the parents to care for them, the health of the father and mother and mutual agreement. Under means of planning for pregnancy, it is suggested that medical care is indicated if parents are unable to have children. The means of limiting family size include abstinence, rhythm and contraceptives. The remaining experiences section contains the following note to the teachers: "If questions arise, pupils may be told that there are contraceptives, but that there are varying viewpoints concerning their use. Married couples should seek the advice of their physician and/ or religious counselor.

"Teacher background information related to contraceptives is being prepared by the sub-committee from the Medical Society and the sub-committee on Moral & Ethical Values and will be distributed as soon as completed and approved by the Family Life Education Committee."

In a unit entitled "Self-Understanding—Emotional Development," the learning goals are: to contribute to a student's developing concept of himself as a person; to stimulate growth and self-understanding and personal responsibilities; to increase competence in developing and maintaining mutually satisfactory interpersonal relationships; and to suggest methods of seeking solutions to personal and family problems through increased insight into the needs and behavior of individuals.

Under emotional maturity, some of the suggested learning experiences and examples of content are "How do you act when you are angry?" "Does everyone feel angry at times?" and "What are some good ways to handle this feeling?"

The allegations of the many pleadings comprising the amended complaint and the attached exhibits (a class action on behalf of all similarly situated parents, as well as on behalf of their children who are students in the public schools of the county) may be summarized as follows: 1) the county's Family Life Education Program (hereafter program) interfered with the parents' and the students' free exercise of religion; 2) the program was not neutral but, in fact, established a new and different religion; 3) the excusal system, pursuant to Education Code sections 8506 and 8701[7] did not, in fact, exist and even if an excusal system were in force, it is unconstitutional as it is discriminatory and deprives the parents and students of equal protection and due process; 4) the excusal system of Education Code sections 8506 and 8701 had elements of coercion that violate the Free Establishment Clause; 5) as the program interfered with the right of parental control, it deprived the parents and students of life, liberty and the pursuit of happiness;[8] 6) as to the right of privacy, the program deprived the parents of their right of privacy, the program deprived the parents of their right to control the education of their children in matters relating to marriage, the family, marriage and sex, and also deprived the students of privacy of mind as they were forced to reveal their innermost personal and private feelings and the intimate details of family life to teachers and fellow students; and 7) the program also deprived both the parents and students of equal protection, as well as procedural and substantive due process.

As indicated above, the instant complaint sought declaratory relief as to the unconstitutionality of the program and Education Code section 8506, as well as injunctive relief prohibiting the continuation of the program. The major thrust of each of the parents' contentions on appeal is that they have alleged sufficient facts or raised factual question as to the constitutional issues raised, so that they were at least entitled to a trial on the merits and entitled to prove the allegedly disputed questions of fact raised by their lengthy seventh amended complaint. Contrary to the parents' repeated assertions, the mere pleading of the unconstitutionality of the program and statutes in issue is not sufficient to overcome the dismissal of their complaint based on its failure to raise any substantial constitutional questions as a matter of law.

I—*Contentions Relating to Freedom of Religion*

The parents and amicus curiae first assert that since they have alleged violations of the Free Exercise and Establishment of Religion Clauses, they have stated several causes of action. However, not all infringements of religious beliefs are constitutionally impermissible. A state may require vaccinations against disease of those who object on grounds of transgression of religious beliefs (*Jacobson v. Massachusetts,* 197 U.S. 11, 25 S.Ct. 358, 49 L. Ed. 643), prohibit polygamy (*Reynolds v. United States,* 98 U.S. 145, 25 L.Ed. 244), or require the observance of child labor laws (*Prince v. Massachusetts,* 321 U.S. 158, 64 S.Ct. 438, 88 L.Ed. 645). The issue, properly framed, therefore, is not whether the parents' objections to the program are a matter of religious belief, but whether the program violates the Free Exercise and Establishment Clauses of the First Amendment, as construed by the United States Supreme Court. While we recognize that the individual rights guaranteed by the Free Exercise and Establishment Clauses of the First Amendment (and the state Constitution)[9] interface and overlap, we think a separate discussion of these two clauses is more helpful here to clarify the complex issues presented in this "extraordinarily sensitive area of constitutional law" (*Lemon v. Kurtzman,* 403 U.S. 602, 612, 91 S.Ct. 2105, 2111, 29 L.Ed.2d 745).

A—*The Free Exercise Clause*

The Supreme Court of Hawaii in *Medeiros v. Kiyosaki* (1970) 52 Haw. 436, 478 P.2d 314, faced an identical question with an excusal system substantially like that provided by Education Code sections 8506 and 8701.[10] The court said at page 317: "It has been argued that *requiring* attendance at sex education courses would burden the free exercise of religion of those who honestly believe that exposure to certain subjects covered within those courses is sinful or that sex education must be accompanied by moral instruction." In *Medeiros,* as here, the parties based their "free exercise" argument on *Abington v. Schempp,* 374 U.S. 203, 83 S.Ct. 1560, 10 L.Ed.2d 844. As the Supreme Court of Hawaii pointed out, *Schempp* concerned two state laws: one requiring that at least ten verses from the Holy Bible should be read; the other, the recitation of the Lord's Prayer, without comment, at the opening of each public school day. These statutes also provided that any child shall be excused from the Bible reading or prayer, or attending such Bible reading or prayer, upon the written request of parent or guardian. Justice Clark, in delivering the opinion of the court, held that the reading from the Holy Bible and the recitation of the Lord's Prayer were religious in character and were, therefore, ipso facto, violative of the Establishment Clause.[11] As the court pointed out at page 223, 83 S.Ct. at page 1572: "The distinction between the two clauses is apparent—*a violation of the Free Exercise Clause is predicated on coercion* while the Establishment Clause violation need not be so attended." (Emphasis supplied.)

The *Medeiros* court then continued, 478 P.2d at 318-319:

"Equally pertinent to our discussion is the Supreme Court's holding in *Epperson v. Arkansas,* 393 U.S. 97, 89 S.Ct. 266, 21 L.Ed.2d 228, in which an Arkansas statute prohibiting the teaching of the Darwinian theory of evolution because such theory was contrary to the religious views of some of its citizens was held unconstitutional. At page 104, 89 S.Ct. [266] at 270, the Court stated: . . . 'Our courts, however, have not failed to apply the First Amendment's mandate in our educational system where essential to safeguard the fundamental values of freedom of speech and inquiry and of belief.' . . . And at 106, 89 S.Ct. [266] at 271: 'There is and can be no doubt that the First Amendment does not permit the State to require that teaching and learning must be tailored to the principles or prohibitions of any religious sect or dogma.'

"If we were to hold that the 'family life and sex education' program adopted by the State is contrary to certain religious beliefs of some of our citizens and therefore unconstitutional on the grounds that it prevents the free exercise of their religion, we would come

dangerously close to approving that which is prohibited by *Epperson.* We must be equally protective of the freedoms of speech, inquiry and belief as we are of the freedom of religion." The Hawaiian court then concluded that there was no violation of the Free Exercise Clause. An identical conclusion on the same grounds was reached by the court in *Cornwell v. State Board of Education* (D.C.Md.1969) 314 F.Supp. 340 (cert. den. 400 U.S. 942, 91 S.Ct. 240, 27 L.Ed.2d 246),[12] in granting motions to dismiss for failure to present a substantial federal question. The court said at page 344: " . . . the purpose and primary effect of the bylaw here is not to establish any particular religious dogma or precept, and that the bylaw does not directly or substantially involve the state in religious exercises or in the favoring of religion or any particular religion. The bylaw may be considered quite simply as a public health measure. As the Supreme Court indicated in *Prince v. Massachusetts,* 321 U.S. 158, 64 S.Ct. 438, 88 L.Ed. 645 (1944), the State's interest in the health of its children outweighs claims based upon religious freedom and the right of parental control."

The parents and amicus curiae both rely on *Wisconsin v. Yoder,* 406 U.S. 205, 92 S.Ct. 1526, 32 L.Ed.2d 15, for their Free Exercise contentions. In *Yoder,* the U.S. Supreme Court sustained the rights of Amish parents to keep their children out of the last two years of compulsory education required by state law, on ground that their children would be placed in "an environment hostile to Amish beliefs."[13] Contrary to the contentions of the parents and amicus curiae the issues presented in *Yoder* did not necessarily require a trial on the merits and the case is not good authority for the contention that their amended complaint has alleged any cause of action. While it is repeatedly asserted that the program in issue here provides an interference with the free exercise of religion similar to that of *Yoder,* no part of the lengthy complaint specifically so alleges. There are only the general allegations of interference with First Amendment freedoms. Nor are there any specific allegations indicating what portions of the program are hostile to the beliefs of the parents.

Assuming, for the sake of argument therefore, that the above items constitute an infringement, we note that the Free Exercise Clause has often been invoked by religious groups to gain exemption from laws of general applicability.[14] In *Sherbert v. Verner,* 374 U.S. 398, 83 S.Ct. 1790, 10 L.Ed.2d 965, a Seventh Day Adventist refused on religious grounds, to accept available employment; the South Carolina unemployment compensation statute provided that benefits could be withheld from any applicant who refused to accept available employment. In holding that the Free Exercise Clause required the state to carve out an exemption for the petitioner, the Supreme Court reiterated the distinction between freedom to believe and freedom to act, first enunciated in *Cantwell v. Connecticut*, 310 U.S. 296, 60 S.Ct. 900, 84 L.Ed. 1213. The court in *Sherbert* established (374 U.S. at 403-406, 83 S.Ct. 1790) a three-pronged analysis for determining when a restriction or regulation of conduct, based on religious belief, will be upheld without further inquiry: 1) where there is a substantial and direct threat to the public safety, peace or order (cf. *Chaplinsky v. New Hampshire*, 315 U.S. 568, 62 S.Ct. 766, 86 L.Ed. 1031); 2) in the absence of such threat, if disqualification from receipt of benefits did not impose any burden on the free exercise of the petitioner's religion; or 3) if any incidental burden on that free exercise was justified by a compelling state interest in the regulation of a subject within the state's constitutional power to regulate (*NAACP v. Bulton*, 371 U.S. 415, 438, 83 S.Ct. 328, 9 L.Ed.2d 405).

Therefore, without conceding an infringement here, we proceed to apply the three-step analysis of *Sherbert v. Verner*, to the instant program. It is readily apparent that the parents' refusal to send their children to the program does not directly threaten the public safety, peace or order. We turn next to the contention that the program and excusal system burden the free exercise of the parents' and the students' religion.

The parents and amicus curiae also urge that since Education Code sections 8506 and 8701 (set forth in full below)[15] require the affirmative election of an exemption from the program or any of its parts, an informal pressure is exerted on the students to forego the exercise of their religious beliefs. Thus, they urge that, in effect, the students are required to participate in the program or parts of it, and there is, therefore, an interference with the free exercise of their religion. They urge that the only remedy to prevent this infringement is total prohibition of the program in the public schools of the county.[16]

While we recognize that the U.S. Supreme Court has held in cases arising under the Establishment Clause that informal social pressures can constitute compulsion (*Abington School Dist. v. Schempp*, 374 U.S. 203, 83 S.Ct. 1560, 10 L.Ed. 2d 844; *Engel v. Vitale*, 370 U.S. 421, 82 S.Ct. 1261, 8 L.Ed.2d 601), the court has never applied that reasoning to the Free Exercise Clause: for example, an express dictum in *Abington* (374 U.S. at 233, 83 S.Ct. 1560) indicating that indirect social pressures are not sufficient to cause a violation of the Free Exercise Clause. Further, in *West Virginia State Board of Education v. Barnette*, 319 U.S. 624, 63 S.Ct. 1178, 87 L.Ed.1628, the court did not require the exclusion from the classroom of the students who objected on religious grounds to the flag salute and were excused from it. Nor did the court require that the flag salute ceremony be abolished simply because it interfered with the religious beliefs of some students.

Neither *Engel* nor *Abington*, supra, support the parents' contention that the instant excusal statutes subject the students to sufficient pressure to amount to compulsion. In both Engel and Abington, the students had the option of either leaving the classroom or remaining during the religious exercises. The court's finding of compulsion was based on the fact that the students, by exercising either option, were in direct and immediate contact with their peers when they exercised their beliefs. There is simply not the same degree of pressure[17] where, as here, pursuant to Education Code sections 8506 and 8701, the parents and the students can choose not to enroll in the program or any part of it that is objectionable. We suggest that if, in accordance with the request for an injunctive relief, the trial court had enjoined the program because it incidentally offended the religious beliefs of certain parents and students, the court would have acted in violation of the Establishment Clause. *In Epperson v. Arkansas*, 393 U.S. 97 at 106, 89 S.Ct. 266, at 271, the court said, that there "can be no doubt that the First Amendment does not permit the State to require that teaching and learning must be tailored to the principles or prohibitions of any religious sect or dogma." Thus, under *Epperson*, the state is required to plan its curriculum on the basis of educational considerations and without reference to religious considerations. This was clearly the case here, as indicated by the exhibits attached to the pleadings.

As so well stated by the court below in its excellent and well reasoned memorandum opinion: "Absent some serious contention of harm to the mental or physical health of the children of this state or to the public safety, peace, order or welfare, a mere personal difference of opinion as to the curriculum which is taught in our public school system does not give rise to a constitutional right in the private citizen to control exposure to knowledge."[18]

The final and third prong of *Sherbert v. Verner*, supra, is a Free Exercise Clause balancing test that measures three elements of the competing governmental interest: first, the importance of the secular value underlying the governmental regulations; second, the degree of proximity that the chosen regulation bears to the underlying value; and third the impact that an exemption for religious reasons has on the overall regulatory program. This assessment of the state's interest then has to be balanced against the claim for religious liberty that, in turn, requires an evaluation of two subfactors: first, the sincerity and importance of the religious practice for which special protection is claimed; and second, the degree to which governmental regulation interferes with that practice

(Giannella, Religious Liberty, Nonestablishment, and Doctrinal Development, Part 1. The Religious Liberty Guarantee, 80 Harv.L.Rev. 1381, 1390). Applying each of these factors, we conclude that the compelling state interest in education provides a proper basis here.

Spence v. Bailey (6 Cir. 1972) 465 F.2d 797, cited at oral argument, is distinguishable. In *Spence,* the court held that a compulsory high school ROTC course required of male students for graduation transgressed on the student's free exercise of his religious beliefs as a conscientious objector since there was no compelling state interest in the military training course. In sum then, the direct answer to the parents' contentions concerning free exercise is that the program against which the parents seek a permanent injunction is not compulsory[19] as Education Code sections 8506 and 8701 provide that the student may be excused from any part that conflicts with the parents' religious beliefs or that uses materials to which the parents object. However, even assuming an infringement for the sake of argument, the incidental burden is justified by the compelling state interest in education.[20] (*Medeiros v. Kiyosaki,* supra, 478 P.2d at 318; cf. *Hopkins v. Hamden Board of Education,* 29 Conn.Sup. 397, 289 A.2d 914).

B—*The Establishment of Religion Clause.*

In *Everson v. Board of Education,* 330 U.S. 1, at 15, 67 S.Ct. 504, at 511, 91 L.Ed. 711, the U.S. Supreme Court said that the Establishment Clause meant that: "Neither a state nor the Federal Government can set up a church. Neither can pass laws which aid one religion, aid all religions, or prefer one religion over another." Further, it is also clear from the cases that the First Amendment does not mean that in every and all respects there shall be a "wall" and complete separation of church and state (*Zorach v. Clauson,* 343 U.S. 306, 312, 72 S.Ct. 679, 96 L.Ed. 954).[21]

As stated in *Epperson v. Arkansas,* 393 U.S. 97, 104, 89 S.Ct. 266, 270: "Judicial interposition in the operation of the public school system of the Nation raises problems requiring care and restraint.... By and large, public education in our Nation is committed to the control of state and local authorities. Courts do not and cannot intervene in the resolution of conflicts which arise in the daily operation of school systems and which do not directly and sharply implicate basic constitutional values." The court in the *Epperson* case pointed out that the state may neither prefer any religion nor prohibit any theory just because it be deemed antagonistic to the principles or prohibitions of any religious sect or dogma.

The three main evils, against which the Establishment Clause was intended to afford protection, are sponsorship, financial support and active involvement of the sovereign in religious liberty (*Walz v. Tax Com-*

mission, 397 U.S. 664, 668, 90 S.Ct. 1409, 25 L.Ed.2d 697). The applicable tests developed with respect to the Establishment Clause, as summarized by the U.S. Supreme Court in *Lemon v. Kurtzman,* 403 U.S. 602, 91 S.Ct. 2105, are: "Every analysis in this area must begin with consideration of the cumulative criteria developed by the Court over many years. Three such tests may be gleaned from our cases. First, the statute must have a secular legislative purpose; second, its principal or primary effect must be one that neither advances nor inhibits religion, *Board of Education v. Allen,* 392 U.S. 236, 243, 88 S.Ct. 1923, 1926, 20 L.Ed.2d 1060 (1968); finally, the statute must not foster 'an excessive government entanglement with religion.' *Walz,* supra [397 U.S.], at 674, 90 S.Ct. [1409] at 1414." (Pp. 612-613, 91 S.Ct. p. 2111.)

In the instant case, the primary focus is on the second test as the parents alleged that the program "establishes new or different religious and spiritual practices and beliefs," as the program treats matters of morality, family life and reproduction in a manner that is hostile to their theistic religion.[22] Although the pleadings are lacking in specificity, we glean from the exhibits and the briefs that the parents' complaint refers to the fact that, among others, the program deals with subjects such as abortion, birth control, divorce and masturbation. Our examination of these documents indicates that most of these sensitive areas are carefully delineated with cautionary instructions to the teachers to indicate that a variety of beliefs and practices exist. The teachers are also instructed to refer their students to their parents and religious counselors for guidance and information as to specifics. For example, under the subject of birth control, all present day methods are listed. Thus, there is evidence of neutrality in the religious sphere and ample support as a matter of law for the trial court's finding that the subjects are not covered from a religious point of view, but simply as public health matters.

A similar conclusion was reached with respect to a mandatory health education course in *Hopkins v. Hamden Board of Education,*[23] 289 A.2d 914, where the court denied a temporary injunction and upheld a compulsory health and physical education course that included family life and sex education.

In *Hopkins,* supra, the court said at 923, in language equally apt here: "In *Tilton v. Richardson,* 403 U.S. 672, 91 S.Ct. 2091, 29 L.Ed.2d 790; the United States Supreme Court held that the religious clauses of the first amendment were not violated by public grants to certain Connecticut church-related colleges and universities for construction of buildings and facilities to be used exclusively for secular educational purposes. The court found that the purposes of the use of public funds were religiously neutral and that there was no violation of the plaintiffs' rights under establishment or free exercise clauses of the first amendment. . . . [the] plaintiffs were unable to identify any coercion directed at the practice or exercise of their religious beliefs which would relieve them from the duty to pay taxes. Under our democratic system, citizens of every religious conviction are required to pay taxes. *Walz v. Tax Commission,* supra. . . .

"Judicial concern that the legitimate secular objectives of the state education laws might possibly be violated by conscious design of one or more school teachers or school administrators does not warrant striking down the constitutional legislative authority of the course as unconstitutional. There is no evidence of any such affirmative acts.[24] There is evidence of neutrality in the religious sphere and only a fear that instruction in the health curriculum could possibly conflict with individual beliefs. The court cannot assume that any religious activities seep into or permeate the secular purposes of the curriculum. Since the plaintiffs are unable satisfactorily to identify any coercion directed at the practice or exercise of religious beliefs, there can be no violation of the free exercise clause of the first amendment. There is evidence only that secular teaching might conflict with individual religious beliefs. See *Board of Education v. Allen,* 392 U.S. 236, 88 S.Ct. 1923, 20 L.Ed.2d 1060.

"The governmental and public interests of the state in its educational system are of a kind and weight sufficient to relieve it from claims of violations of the first amendment solely on the ground that its wholly secular purposes could possibly clash with a religious belief of the plaintiffs in one or more areas of the curriculum. Unfair or unreasonable burdens do not appear which would or could violate the plaintiffs' religious guarantees."

The court then continued at 924: "It must be made clear that it is not the function of this court to evaluate a religious belief for ecclesiastical purposes. *School District v. Schempp,* 374 U.S. 203, 83 S.Ct. 1560, 10 L.Ed.2d 844; *State v. Yoder,* 49 Wis.2d 430, 182 N.W. 2d 539. Also irrelevant is this court's opinion of the validity, reasonableness or merits of one's religious beliefs. *State v. Yoder,* supra.

"This case primarily questions the right of the parents to regulate the education of their children in public schools as the parents' religious beliefs dictate, as against the justification of the state for regulating public education in a manner which might in some respects conflict with those beliefs. To permit such interference in the public school system by parents under the circumstances of this case could, unjustifiably, only tend to render a well-regulated public school system vulnerable to fragmentation whenever sincere, conscientious religious conflict is claimed. *Cantwell v. Connecticut,* 310 U.S. 296, 303, 60 S.Ct. 900, 84 L.Ed. 1213, indicates quite clearly that this was not the

intent of the guarantees under the first amendment, and that the state's interests must also be weighed and the public protected.

"The courts have repeatedly held that unconstitutionality based on alleged violations of the religious clauses of the first amendment must be decided on the facts as they appear in each particular case. A study of the cases offers no clear and specific guidelines or rules of law for assistance to the court. In the present case, the curriculum offered is primarily one of a public health nature. It has not been established that serious constitutional questions are involved, even though the parents claim that their rights of control of the child in religious scruples indicate to the contrary. Claims and questions similar to those raised in this count have been held by the federal courts to be inadequate to raise constitutional questions based on the first amendment. See *Murdock v. Pennsylvania,* 319 U.S. 105, 109, 63 S.Ct. 870, 87 L.Ed. 1292; *Cornwell v. State Board of Education,* D.C., 314 F.Supp. 340, 342, aff'd, 4 Cir., 428 F.2d 471[25] [cert. den. 400 U.S. 942, 91 S.Ct. 240]. The *Murdock* case concerned the balancing of the interests of the individual against the interests of the state. See *Prince v. Massachusetts,* 321 U.S. 158, 64 S.Ct. 438, 88 L.Ed. 645."

Nor can we find any indication in the guidelines that the program affirmatively espouses the view that religious beliefs are irrelevant to matters of family life and sex. To the contrary, the program encompasses a wide variety of family life styles and in careful recognition of the diversity of religions and points of view that enhance and enrich the diverse culture and population of the country and the Bay Area, directs the instructors to refer students to their parents or religious advisors for specific instruction.

We agree with the trial court's conclusion of law that the portions of the program challenged simply do not relate to, or seek to establish any religious concept, dogma, idea and precept; nor does the program involve the county school system directly, indirectly or substantially in any way in the establishment of a "religion," or the exercise thereof, or in favoring one religion over another, or for that matter, any particular religion. The program areas that the parents challenge are simply not religious in nature but primarily involve education and public health. The fact that the parents possess certain ideas or views concerning family life relationships and sex which are based on moral standards that are the outgrowth of their religious principles does not make the teaching of sex education and family life religious in nature, nor does it constitute the establishment of a religion in the public schools. Thus, the trial court properly concluded that the complaint alleged no triable factual issues as to these matters.

The parents' contention here overlooks the fact that while in *Abington School Dist. v. Schempp,* supra, 374

U.S. 231, 83 S.Ct. 1560, the court held that the reading of the Bible and Prayer at the beginning of each school day without comment violated the Establishment Clause because of the independent religious significance of the reading (at 223), the majority (at 225) and two of the three concurring opinions (at 300 and 306) explicitly distinguished those practices that have an essentially religious character because of attendant ritual and history, and seemingly identical practices that in a different context are intended to implement secular educational purposes. The majority opinion said at 225, 83 S.Ct. at 1573: "We agree of course that the State may not establish a 'religion of secularism' in the sense of affirmatively opposing or showing hostility to religion, thus 'preferring those who believe in no religion over those who do believe.' Zorach v. Clauson, supra, 343 U.S. at 314, 72 S.Ct. [679] at 684, 96 L.Ed. 954. We do not agree, however, that this decision in any sense has that effect. In addition, it might well be said that one's education is not complete without a study of comparative religion or the history of religion and its relationship to the advancement of civilization. It certainly may be said that the Bible is worthy study for its literary and historic qualities. Nothing we have said here indicates that such study of the Bible or of religion, when presented objectively as part of a secular program of education, may not be effected consistently with the First Amendment."[26] Any other approach would permit any group of parents or students to create chaos in the school system by attempting to enjoin any portion of a school curriculum that allegedly did violence to or interfered with any religious belief. Thus, parents and students whose religious beliefs prohibited the consumption of certain kinds of (or any) meat could interfere with and negate those aspects of a curriculum in nutrition that suggested meat as a good source of protein. Thus, there is no basis for the argument that the program in effect establishes a "religion of secularism" in the schools (cf. Abington School Dist. v. Schempp, 374 U.S. 203, at 225, 83 S.Ct. 1560).

As so well stated by the trial court in its succinct and well-written memorandum opinion: "If on the other hand, the plaintiffs contend that the curriculum and material being taught in the challenged courses are contrary to their particular religious beliefs and even though their children are not required to attend such courses, they still have a constitutional right to have such material conform to their religious beliefs, then clearly there is no such constitutional right. If such were not the case, it is obvious that every citizen could seek to control the curriculum and material being taught in our public school system by simply asserting that such material was contrary to their particular religious beliefs. Thus various complainants could actually use the judicial process to in fact 'establish a religion,' in our public school system by using the courts to so control curriculum to ensure that the same would conform to the particular religious concepts of the complainants. It is simply not for the courts in the constitutional sense to order conformity or limit nonconformity and thereby ensure that the limits of the curriculum subject matter will coincide with a particular religious point of view."

As stated in Prince v. Massachusetts, 321 U.S. 158, 64 S.Ct. 438 the state's interest in the health of its children outweighs claims based upon religious freedom and the right of parental control. The court stated "A democratic society rests . . . upon the healthy, well-rounded growth of young people into full maturity as citizens. . . . It is too late now to doubt that legislation appropriately designed to reach such evils is within the state's police power, whether against the parent's claim to control of the child or one that religious scruples dictate contrary action." (Pp. 168-169, 64 S.Ct. p.443.)

In sum, the program does not violate the Free Establishment Clause.[27]

II—Equal Protection and Substantive Due Process

We turn next to the contention that the program deprives them of equal protection and due process under the U.S. Constitution. As the program on its face applies to all students equally and is taught to all students of mixed religious beliefs without discrimination, there is no denial of equal protection (cf. Cornwell v. State Board of Education, 314 F.Supp. 340, at 342; Medeiros v. Kiyosaki, 478 P.2d 314 at 319; Hopkins v. Hamden Board of Education, 289 A.2d 914, at 919). Nor is there any merit to the contention that the "separation" that results from the operation of the statutory excusal system is an unreasonable and discriminatory classification that deprives the affected students of equal protection.[28] There are no allegations or indications in the record that the county, in approving the program, acted either arbitrarily or unreasonably (Hopkins v. Hamden Board of Education, supra 922).

We turn briefly to the contention that the parents are denied equal protection of the law because a burden is placed upon them to make a choice pursuant to Education Code sections 8506 and 8701. They also urge that the choice, in turn, burdens the students, who are not to participate in the program, or any part of it, by separating them from their regular classes. They contend that these several burdens result in discrimination between similarly situated parents or guardians and between similarly situated students. As indicated above, these contentions are without merit because the decision as to whether or not the students will participate and associate rests solely with the individual parents and students. As the court below indicated, there is thus *no improper state action in the con-*

stitutional sense that discriminates or precludes the students from participating in the program. Accordingly, there is no improper discrimination or denial of equal protection.

As to substantive due process, we find persuasive the following from *Cornwell v. State Board of Education,* supra, 314 F.Supp. 342: *"There is first no denial of substantive due process to the plaintiffs.* Under Section 6 of Article 77 of the Maryland Code (as amended and re-codified by Chapter 405 of the Acts of 1969), the State Board is directed to determine the educational policies of the state and to enact bylaws for the administration of the public school system, which when enacted and published shall have the force of law. Assuredly *it cannot be said that the bylaw here is an arbitrary or unreasonable exercise of the authority vested* in the State Board to determine a teaching curriculum, nor *that there is no basis in fact for the legislative policy expressed in the bylaw."* (Emphasis added; cf. *Medeiros v. Kiyosaki,* 478 P.2d 314, at 319-320.)

We conclude, therefore, that the trial court properly concluded that no cause of action was stated under the Fourteenth Amendment of the U.S. Constitution or the parallel provisions of the state Constitution.

III—Privacy, "Parental Authority" and the Asserted Exclusive Constitutional Right to Teach Family Life and Sex Education Only At Home.

As to privacy, identical contentions were considered by the court in *Medeiros v. Kiyosaki,* supra, at page 316, with respect to an excusal system substantially similar to that of Education Code sections 8506 and 8701. "[A]lthough the right of privacy *is not specifically* afforded in the First Amendment of the United States Constitution, the Supreme Court of the United States has held that the Amendment ' . . . has a penumbra where privacy is protected from governmental instrusion.' *Griswold v. Connecticut,* 381 U.S. 479, 483, 85 S.Ct. 1678, 1681, 14 L.Ed.2d 510 (1968).

" . . . As stated by Justice Douglas in delivering the opinion of the Court at pages 485-486, 85 S.Ct. at page 1682:

" 'The present case, then, concerns a relationship lying within the zone of privacy created by several fundamental constitutional guarantees. And it concerns a law which, in forbidding the *use* of contraceptives rather than regulating their manufacture or sale, seeks to achieve its goals by means having a maximum destructive impact upon that relationship. Such a law cannot stand in light of the familiar principle, so often applied by this Court, that a "governmental purpose to control or prevent activities constitutionally subject to state regulation may not be achieved by means which sweep unnecessarily broadly and thereby invade the area of protected freedoms." *NAACP v. Alabama,* 377

U.S. 288, 307, 84 S.Ct. 1302, 1314, 12 L.Ed.2d 325. Would we allow the police to search the sacred precincts of marital bedrooms for tell-tale signs of the use of contraceptives? The very idea is repulsive to the notions of privacy surrounding the marriage relationship.'

"Thus, the Supreme Court held where the *zone of privacy is invaded by the state by unnecessarily broad* means, its action is in contravention of the First Amendment. Connecticut had forbidden the *use* of contraceptives rather than merely regulating their manufacture or sale. This interdiction, the Court held, was unnecessarily broad." (Emphasis partially added.)

The question we now face is this: Can the county through its proper agencies adopt and initiate a curriculum of family life and sex education for use in its districts without invading its citizens' constitutional right to privacy? We must not look to see if there has been a possible or technical invasion of privacy but instead whether the government has by "unnecessarily broad means" contravened the parents' right of privacy.

The county in formulating policies for the adoption of the program anticipated possible objections by parents and guardians to the program. The Legislature, pursuant to Education Code sections 8506 and 8701, therefore, *established an "excusal system" whereby parents and guardians had the option of withholding or withdrawing their children from the program by submitting a written excuse to the school.* Furthermore, in order to allow the parents and guardians an opportunity to review the audio-visual educational materials used, Education Code section 8506, set forth the elaborate and detailed procedures for giving parents notice of and opportunity to review these materials to enable the parents to consider the content of the program and then submit a written excuse if they found it objectionable. In addition, section 8701 permits excusal at the written request of the parents on the broader ground of "any part of the program" that is objectionable to their religious beliefs.

We view the dual statutory "excusal system" as an effort by the county and state to allow those parents or guardians who might object to the program or any part of it on moral or religious grounds to have their children excused. *The program was in no way compulsory,* and, therefore, we cannot see how the state by "unnecessarily broad means" contravened the parents' right of privacy.

In support of their invasion of privacy theory, the parents cite two other cases: *Meyer v. Nebraska,* 262 U.S. 390, 43 S.Ct. 625, which upheld the rights of parents to have their children learn a foreign language, and *Pierce v. Society of Sisters,* 268 U.S. 510, 45 S.Ct. 571, which upheld the rights of parents to have their children educated in private elementary schools. *Meyer* and *Pierce* are supportive of the *explicit freedoms of speech and press rather than the penumbral right of privacy.* Citing these two cases, the Supreme Court drew the following conclusion in *Griswold v. Connecticut*, 381 U.S. 479, at 482, 85 S.Ct. 1678, at 1680: "In other words, the State may not, consistently with the spirit of the First Amendment, contract the spectrum of available knowledge." Yet, this is the very thing that the plaintiffs would have this court do. *They seek to "contract the spectrum of available knowledge" by enjoining the county from continuing with its family life and sex education program.* (Emphasis supplied.)

The parents and amicus curiae also contend that the program invades the students' right of privacy by requiring them to reveal their innermost thoughts, conversations and facts relating to the personal and intimate lives of their families[29] and invade the privacy of mind of the parents and students. We cannot agree that the subject matter discussed by the program compels the disclosures mentioned by the parents. The same applies to the asserted right of exclusive parental control and authority.

It follows that the trial court properly concluded that Education Code section 8506 is constitutional. The parents' contention that the excusal system of section 8506 is too narrow in scope is vitiated by the broader exclusion provision of Education Code section 8701, which by its terms permits the excusal of the students from the entire program. We hold that the sections, construed together, are constitutional and do not infringe on any rights of the parents under the First, Ninth and Fourteenth Amendments of the U.S. Constitution and the parallel provisions of the state Constitution.

As to "parental control," we adopt, with minor stylistic changes, the excellent discussion of the court below. The parents further assert that, contrary to the First Amendment of the U.S. Constitution,[30] the activities of the county deprive them and their students of their rights to liberty and the pursuit of happiness and that such conduct usurps parental authority. These contentions are without merit, since they presuppose that the Legislature and the county may not make available various courses of studies to all students upon an elective or withdrawal basis. As previously pointed out, the students are not compelled to attend any part of the program and if there is parental objection, may summarily withdraw from any part or the entire program. The Constitution of the United States does not vest in objectors the right to preclude other students who may voluntarily desire to participate in a course of study under the guise that the objector's liberty, personal happiness or parental authority is somehow jeopardized or impaired. To adhere to such a concept would use judicial constitutional authority to limit inquiry to conformity, and to limit knowledge to the known.

We note that as stated in *Wisconsin v. Yoder*, 406 U.S. 205, at 234-235, 92 S.Ct. 1526, at 1542: "Our disposition of this case, however, in no way alters our recognition of the obvious facts that courts are not school boards or legislatures, and are ill-equipped to determine the 'necessity' of discrete aspects of a State's program of compulsory education. *This should suggest* that courts must move with great circumspection in performing the sensitive and delicate task of weighing a State's legitimate social concern when faced with religious claims for exemption from generally applicable educational requirements." (Emphasis added.) We think this is still the applicable principle to be followed by courts. We do not consider pertinent to the instant case some of the recent cases of "interference" cited at oral argument.[31]

Finally, the parents and amicus curiae contend that they have an exclusive constitutional right to teach their children about family life and *sexual matters in their own homes, and that such exclusive right would prohibit the teaching of these matters in the schools.* No authority is cited in support of this novel proposition, and this court knows of no such constitutional right (cf. *Cornwell v. State Board of Education*, 314 F.Supp. 340, 342). We also note that recently a federal court dismissed an action by parents who sought to teach their children entirely at home instead of sending them to school (*Scoma v. The Chicago Board of Education*, et al. D.C., 391 F.Supp. 452 (1974).[32]

We conclude, therefore that the trial court properly concluded that, accepting the various allegations of the complaint to be true, the parents have failed to raise any substantial constitutional issues[33] or any factual issues that would entitle them to the declaratory or injunctive relief sought. Accordingly, the county's motion to dismiss the entire complaint was properly granted and the judgment appealed from is affirmed.

ROUSE, J., concurs.

KANE, Associate Justice (dissenting).

I dissent. Notwithstanding the fact that the fundamental question in this appeal is a procedural one, the proper resolution of which renders any discussion of the substantive constitutional issues premature, the majority reaches the latter by a cavalier disposal of the former in a footnote.

In doing so, the majority has reached a conclusion which is contrary to both the spirit and the law of pleading in this state and, in my opinion, has countenanced the unsavory practice of "judge-shopping" which is specifically prohibited by Code of Civil Procedure, section 1008.

The results of the court's holding are (1) an unnecessary treatise on constitutional principles which are discussed in the abstract for the simple reason that the issues raised by the pleadings have not been filled in with evidentiary support and amplification, and (2) a denial of the right of the plaintiffs to attempt to factually prove their bases for relief.

A brief summary of the pleading and procedural history in the court below will demonstrate why plaintiffs are entitled to go to trial and why, therefore, the granting of the motion to dismiss was erroneous.

Having traveled a very tortuous route of demurrers, motions for judgment on the pleadings and summary judgment, followed by a detailed pretrial conference, plaintiffs finally reached the threshold of trial only to be frustrated by a "motion to dismiss"—the legal equivalent of a general demurrer (*McKay v. County of Riverside* (1959) 175 Cal.App.2d 247, 345 P.2d 949).

Except for the first demurrer to the original complaint, defendants' repetitive attack on plaintiffs' pleadings was the single contention that the complaint failed to state a cause of action. In their first demurrer defendants included a special demurrer that "the Complaint is uncertain and unintelligible for the following reasons:

"A.   The content of the course mentioned in paragraph IV of the Complaint is not pleaded in sufficient particularity for the Court to make any ruling relating to it.

"B.   That the Complaint *does not set forth the parts of the proposed course that are alleged to be objectionable and the reasons why said parts are alleged to be objectionable.*" (Emphasis added.)

It is apparent that plaintiffs conceded the soundness of the special demurrer since the parties stipulated that a first amended complaint be filed which, for the first time included as exhibits excerpts from the teaching material of the Family Life Education course which plaintiffs allege violated various of their constitutional rights.

It is significant to note that once the exhibits were included in the complaint, defendants asserted no further objection as to uncertainty or lack of particularity in the complaint, choosing rather to assert a bare, general demurrer. The demurrer to the first amended complaint was heard by Judge Reisch, who sustained it without leave to amend as to 12 counts contained in two causes of action and overruled it as to eight other counts.

Following that ruling, the defendants answered the first amended complaint. In doing so, no affirmative defenses whatever were set forth.

Next, defendants moved for summary judgment "on the ground that the action has no merit, and that *there is no triable* issue of fact" (and at the same time moved for judgment on the pleadings "on the ground

that the Complaint herein *failed to state facts sufficient* to constitute a cause of action.") (Emphasis added.)

The motion for summary judgment was denied by Judge Scott. The record does not reveal any action on the motion for judgment on the pleadings.

Next, pursuant to stipulation, plaintiffs filed amendments to their first amended complaint to which defendants both answered and demurred generally. The general demurrer was overruled by Judge Blum.

Next, a second motion for judgment on the pleadings "on the ground that the Complaint . . . fails to state facts sufficient to constitute a cause of action" was filed, heard, and denied by Judge Branson.

Thus, four different superior court judges concluded that plaintiffs' complaint did indeed state a cause of action on which they were entitled to go to trial.

Code of Civil Procedure, section 426,[1] which was in effect at the time of the proceedings in the trial court, provided in subdivision 2 that the complaint must contain "A statement of the facts constituting the cause of action, in ordinary and concise language."

The cases interpreting this provision have made it clear that evidentiary facts or argumentative facts are improper; that only ultimate facts should be pleaded (*Green v. Palmer* (1860) 15 Cal. 411, 414; 3 Witkin, Cal.Procedure, Pleading, § 268, p. 1939).

While the line between conclusions of law, evidentiary matters and ultimate facts is very elusive and its distinction "is one of degree only" (Witkin, supra, p. 1940), the rule of liberal construction is firmly settled in Code of Civil Procedure, section 452. Emphasis is placed on an examination of the pleading to determine whether it gives fair notice of the cause of action (*Leet v. Union Pac. R. R. Co.* (1944) 25 Cal.2d 605, 619, 155 P.2d 42).

In ruling upon a general demurrer (or a motion to dismiss) the allegations of the complaint must be regarded as true. It is assumed that plaintiffs can prove all facts as alleged; defects in the complaint which do not affect the substantial rights of the parties are disregarded.

"Neither trial nor appellate courts should be distracted from the main issue, or rather, the only issue involved in a demurrer hearing, namely, whether the complaint, as it stands, unconnected with extraneous matters, states a cause of action" (*Griffith v. Department of Public Works* (1956) 141 Cal.App.2d 376, 381, 296 P.2d 838, 842).

One of the best statements of the policy behind the rule of liberal construction is set forth in *Terry Trading Corp. v. Barsky* (1930) 210 Cal. 428, 292 P. 474, as follows: "It is sometimes a difficult task for the pleader to state enough facts to establish his cause of action or defense, and also to avoid the inclusion of confusing evidentiary matter. The Code has provided adequate means for the correction of an error *in either direction;* the adverse party may move to strike out the evidentiary matter or demur specially to an inadequate statement of the facts on the ground of uncertainty or ambiguity. *But to deny the party his right to a trial, there must be an obvious failure of the pleadings to state a cause of action or defense.''* (Emphasis added.)

In the case at bench, even a cursory reading of plaintiffs' final complaint, as amended and including the exhibits, demonstrates that a cause of action has been alleged. For example, in paragraph II of Count Eleven of the First Amended Complaint, it is alleged that "Portions of the content and subject matter of the Family Life Education course of study and subject matter interfere with and are contradictory to certain of plaintiffs' personal religious beliefs, and therefore are an infringement of, in contradiction to, and in violation of Amendment 1 of the Constitution of the United States, in that they are designed to question, affect, prohibit and interfere with the free exercise of existing religious and spiritual practices and beliefs, and to establish new or different religious and spiritual practices and beliefs that are promulgated by the State through its public school system, as illustrated by items contained in Exhibit 'E', which exhibit is attached hereto and is incorporated herein by this reference.''[2]

Conceding arguendo that such allegations might be subject to a special demurrer for uncertainty, the fact is that defendants raised no such objection and thereby have waived the same.

The rule of liberal construction of pleadings has also been enhanced by the adoption of the rules for discovery whereby any uncertainty as to the factual basis of plaintiffs' cause of action can be efficiently discovered. Such was the holding in *Dahlquist v. State of California* (1966) 243 Cal.App.2d 208, 52 Cal.Rptr. 324.

The body of discovery law has now developed to the point where, for example, it is perfectly proper for a party to submit an interrogatory requiring his adversary to specify, under oath, the facts on which he relies in support of a particular contention or allegation made in a pleading (*Singer v. Superior Court* (1960) 54 Cal.2d 318, 321, 5 Cal.Rptr. 697, 353 P.2d 305). Thus, in the case at bench if defendants were truly in doubt or uncertain as to how or in what manner plaintiffs' constitutional rights were claimed to be violated by the Family Life Education course, a simple interrogatory would have resolved any such doubt. But the record discloses that defendants engaged in no discovery whatever. It is therefore apparent that after the original demurrer defendants' one and only objection to plaintiffs' pleadings was that they failed to state a

cause of action, an objection consistently rejected by four different superior court judges.

This background brings us, then, to the next logical inquiry: How, and by what authority, was a fifth judge empowered to render a decision completely contrary to his predecessors on precisely the same issue? The short answer is that he was not so empowered and that the granting of the motion to dismiss was an abuse of discretion for noncompliance with Code of Civil Procedure, section 1008, which provides: "When an application for an order has been made to a judge, or to the court, and refused in whole or in part, or granted conditionally, or on terms, and subsequent application for the same order, upon an alleged different state of facts, shall be made, it shall be shown by affidavit what application was before made, when and to what judge, what order or decision was made thereon and what new facts are claimed to be shown. For a failure to comply with this requirement, any order made on such subsequent application may be revoked or set aside on ex parte motion.

"A violation of this section may be punished as a contempt; and an order made contrary thereto may be revoked by the judge or commissioner who made it, or vacated by a judge of the court in which the action or proceeding is pending.''

The motion to dismiss is, as we have noted, the legal equivalent of a general demurrer (*McKay v. County of Riverside,* supra). On review of an order and judgment of dismissal pursuant to the granting of a motion to dismiss, the appellate court must consider the matter "in the same light as a judgment upon sustaining of a demurrer without leave to amend'' (*McKay v. County of Riverside,* supra, 175 Cal.App.2d at 249, 345 P.2d at 950).

Consequently, as a matter of true substance the motion to dismiss was a "subsequent application'' for the same orders previously made to each of the preceding four judges. In fact the motion expressly recites (as did the prior general demurrers and motions for summary judgment and judgment on the pleadings) that it was being made *"on the ground that the complaint herein fails to state a cause of action."* (Emphasis added.)

The fact that defendants at pretrial received the right to file a motion to dismiss is of no significance whatever. Likewise, the fact that after the filing of the first amended complaint on September 11, 1968 the Legislature enacted Education Code, section 8506, is of no moment, either, insofar as the argument is made that this was a "new matter'' raised by the motion to dismiss. First of all, section 8506 was enacted in 1969. The ruling by Judge Blum, overruling the general demurrer to the first amended complaint and amendments thereto, was filed on April 15, 1971. The record is silent as to whether Education Code, section 8506, was presented to the court. The same is not true, however, in the case of the later ruling by Judge Branson, denying defendants' motion for judgment on the pleadings. There, the points and authorities filed by defendants specifically address the issue of the constitutionality of section 8506. Judge Branson's ruling was filed February 24, 1972.

Thus, it is manifestly clear that the motion to dismiss was and is nothing more than another general demurrer presented to a different judge. Code of Civil Procedure, section 1008, is a sound and essential mandate for efficient judicial administration. The fact that the sanction of contempt for a violation of the statute is expressly provided is strong evidence of its importance and the need for maintaining its integrity.

Respondents do not contend that they attempted to comply with section 1008 at all. Their argument is simply that the motion to dismiss was a new motion unrelated to the prior demurrers and motions. As we have shown, however, this contention is totally groundless since each and every prior motion or demurrer—save and except the very first demurrer—raised but one issue: Did the complaint state a cause of action? Having received the rulings of four judges that the complaint did state a cause of action, it was incumbent upon defendants in presenting their motion to dismiss to show "by affidavit what application was before made, when and to what judge, what order or decision was made thereon and *what new facts are claimed to be shown.*" (Code Civ.Proc., § 1008; emphasis added.)

The record shows that plaintiffs promptly brought the provisions of section 1008 to the attention of the court by seeking to have the order granting the motion to dismiss vacated.

The pleadings filed by the plaintiffs are technically sufficient. The issues between the parties have been framed and the pretrial order provides an excellent framework in which the case can be tried on its merits. Having arduously and successfully taken their case over nearly every procedural obstacle in the civil advocates' arsenal, plaintiffs should not be denied that right. I would reverse the judgment.

NOTES

1. Also named as respondents were the members of the County Board of Education who had adopted the Family Life Education Teachers' Resource Guides for all grades and encouraged their use by the districts, and the County Superintendent of Schools. The resource guides were "curriculum and instructional materials" pursuant to Education Code section 886, but were not required "courses of study" as then defined by Education Code section 8851 (repealed by Stats.1968, ch. 182, § 30, p. 460). The county, however, has no power or authority to require the course or use of the materials by the districts.

2. The pertinent provisions are: Article I, section 1: "All people are by nature free and independent, and have certain inalienable rights, among which are those of enjoying and defending life and liberty; acquiring, possessing, and protecting property; and pursuing and obtaining safety, happiness, and privacy." Privacy was added as an inalienable right by a specific amendment by the voters of this state in November 1972 and construed for the first time by our Supreme Court in *White v. Davis* (1975) 13 Cal.3d 757, 120 Cal.Rptr. 94, 533 P.2d 222.

   Article I, section 4: "The free exercise and enjoyment of religious profession and worship, without discrimination of preference, shall forever be guaranteed in this State; and no person shall be rendered incompetent to be a witness or juror on account of his opinions on matters of religious belief; but the liberty of conscience hereby secured shall not be so construed as to excuse acts of licentiousness, or justify practices inconsistent with the peace or safety of this State."

3. Education Code section 8506 in substance provides that no governing board of a public elementary or secondary school in this state may require pupils to attend any class that involves family life or sex education. If such classes are in fact to be offered in the public elementary and secondary schools, the parent or guardian of each pupil enrolled in such class shall first be notified in writing of the class. The notice is to be sent through the regular United States mail to all parents. Each parent is to be provided the opportunity to request in writing that his child shall not attend the class and further no child may attend such a class if a request that he not attend the class has been received by the school. The statute further provides that any written or audio-visual material to be used in such a class shall be made available for inspection by the parent or guardian of such child at reasonable times and places prior to the holding of such a class and the parent or guardian shall further be notified in writing of his opportunity to inspect and review the materials. Each of the five respondent school districts has complied with the requirements of section 8506. Education Code section 8701, initially overlooked by the parties, provides in substance that whenever any part of the instruction in health, family life or sex education conflicts with the religious training and beliefs of the parent or guardian, that student shall be excused from that part.

4. We have decided to dispose of the parents' procedural contentions by this footnote. The record indicates that the original complaint was filed on September 6, 1968, and immediately amended on September 11, 1968. The county promptly filed an answer and demurrer but by stipulation, the demurrer was not heard and a first amended complaint filed. The county's demurrer to the first amended complaint was subsequently sustained as to counts V through X of the first and second causes of action and an answer filed as to the remaining counts (I-IV of the first and second causes of action). Subsequently, on July 9, 1969, the county filed a motion for summary judgment that was denied. Immediately thereafter, on September 2, 1969, the county filed an "at

issue" memorandum. In December 1970, by stipulation, the parents were once again allowed to amend their first amended complaint to add additional defendants, counts XI and XII to the first cause of action, and 12 new and supplemental causes of action. The county's general demurrer filed to the re-amended first amended complaint was overruled on April 15, 1971. On January 13, 1972, the county filed a motion for judgment on the pleadings; this motion was denied on February 24, 1972. A pretrial order setting trial for January 1973 was filed on November 16, 1972, and specifically indicating that all law and motion was complete, with the exception of the county's motion to dismiss. On December 13, 1972, the county moved to dismiss the seventh amended complaint on grounds of failure to state a cause of action as a matter of law. In January 1973, this motion was granted and this appeal ensued.

The parents initially contend that by the ruling sustaining the demurrer and the granting of the county's motion to dismiss, they were deprived of a fair hearing and therefore deprived of due process. As their contention that all pretrial terminations of actions are unconstitutional is so patently without merit that it does not warrant further discussion. We simply note that the parents did not attempt to file a jurisdictional writ to test their strange theory (1 Witkin, Cal.Procedure (2d ed.) Jurisdiction, § 194). The contention that the motion to dismiss was a speaking motion is equally without merit. A speaking motion to dismiss or strike is one that is supported by facts outside the pleading, set forth by affidavit or declaration (*Vesely v. Sager,* 5 Cal. 3d 153, 167, 95 Cal.Rptr. 623, 486 P.2d 151). Here, the motion was made for dismissal, immediately before trial and without any submission of new matter and the sole question was whether or not a cause of action had been stated by the seventh amended complaint (cf. *McKay v. County of Riverside,* 175 Cal.App.2d 247, 248-249, 345 P.2d 949).

The parents further contend that the instant motion to dismiss must be considered as a renewed motion for summary judgment and, therefore, subject to the sanctions of Code of Civil Procedure section 1008. They also urge that since the county's 1969 motion for a summary judgment was denied by a different court than the one that dismissed the complaint in 1973, the last court's dismissal was improper and in excess of its jurisdiction, as a successor judge cannot review, modify or reverse final orders of his predecessor. The parents' contention here is entirely without merit. The motion to dismiss was not a review, modification or reversal of any final judgment made by a prior court in the instant action. After the summary denial without opinion of the county's motion for judgment on the pleadings on February 24, 1972, the matter was set for trial. As indicated above, the pretrial conference order specifically indicated that all law and motion was complete with the exception of the county's motion to dismiss. We do not think Code of Civil Procedure section 1008 has any application to the instant case. Furthermore, as clearly spelled out in the lower court's excellent memorandum opinion, the county's final motion to dismiss was

granted on the basis of the failure of the seventh amended complaint to raise any substantial question of law. In reaching its conclusion, the court below properly considered the pleadings in the light most favorable to the parents and ruled on the constitutionality of Education Code section 8506. Thus, there was no resubmission of any previously determined final matters, but a determination that the complaint failed to state a cause of action for either declaratory or injunctive relief. The court below did not abuse its discretion and properly acted within its jurisdiction in dismissing the action.

5. Arguably, this could be contrary to one traditional Roman Catholic view, but also is consistent with Pius XI encyclical on Christian Marriage. (See St. John-Stevas, A Roman Catholic View of Population Control, 25 Law and Contemporary Problems, 445, at 446-447.)

6. Thus, the exhibits provide no basis for the parents' contentions that the program encourages and promotes premarital sexual intercourse.

7. As indicated above at footnote 3, the parties apparently were not aware of Education Code section 8701 until the oral argument on this appeal.

8. As subsequently indicated, although this argument is based on the parents' and students' First Amendment rights, we have chosen to discuss it under the heading of privacy. Our view that "happiness" fits more logically with privacy is consistent with article I, section 1 of the state Constitution, quoted above in footnote 2. (White v. Davis, 13 Cal.3d 757, 120 Cal.Rptr. 94, 533 P.2d 222.)

9. Our present decision is grounded in both the federal and state Constitutions. Although some recent decisions of the California Supreme Court have established that comparable federal and state constitutional provisions are not necessarily co-extensive (see, e. g., *People v. Krivda,* 8 Cal.3d 623, 624, 105 Cal.Rptr. 521, 504 P.2d 457; *Rios v. Cozens,* 9 Cal.3d 454, 455, 107 Cal.Rptr. 784, 509 P.2d 696), we need not explore potential variations in application here, for we believe the same conclusion is mandated by each fundamental document. For convenience, this opinion utilizes "Free Exercise" and "Establishment" clauses based on the specific clauses of the First Amendment of the federal Constitution to refer to the relevant freedom of religion guarantees of both the federal and state Constitutions (cf. *White v. Davis,* supra).

10. We have elected to discuss the contentions pertaining to the constitutionality of the instant excusal system in a subsequent portion of this opinion. The parents here also attempt to argue that *Medeiros* is not controlling as the constitutionality of the excusal system was not in issue. We do not agree with his limited reading of *Medeiros. Medeiros,* although decided after a trial on the merits, does not in any way support the parents' contentions as to the sufficiency of their seventh amended complaint.

11. The essential element of the decision was that the prayer was intended to have and was perceived as having independent religious significance.

12. The parents and amicus curiae here attempt to argue that *Cornwell* is distinguishable as it did not raise any

constitutional issues concerning the subject matter and content of the course there in issue. While admittedly all of the issues here raised were not raised in *Cornwell*, we think the case is pertinent. In *Cornwell*, the taxpayers brought a civil action seeking to prevent the implementation of a program of sex education in the Baltimore County schools, pursuant to a by-law adopted by the Maryland State Board of Education on grounds that the by-law violated the Free Exercise and Establishment clauses of the First Amendment of the U.S. Constitution, the Equal Protection and Due Process clauses of the Fourteenth Amendment and an asserted, exclusive right to teach their children about sexual matters in their own home.

13. "As the record so strongly shows, the values and programs of the modern secondary school are in sharp conflict with the fundamental mode of life mandated by the Amish religion; modern laws requiring compulsory secondary education have accordingly engendered great concern and conflict. The conclusion is inescapable that secondary schooling, by exposing Amish children to worldly influences in terms of attitudes, goals, and values contrary to beliefs, and by substantially interfering with the religious development of the Amish child and his integration into the way of life of the Amish faith community at the crucial adolescent stage of development, contravenes the basic religious tenets and practice of the Amish faith, both as to the parent and the child.

"The impact of the compulsory-attendance law on respondents' practice of the Amish religion is not only severe, but inescapable, for the Wisconsin law affirmatively compels them, under threat of criminal sanction, to perform acts undeniably at odds with fundamental tenets of their religious beliefs. See *Braunfeld v. Brown*, 366 U.S. 599, 605, 81 S.Ct. 1144, 1147, 6 L.Ed.2d 563 (1961). Nor is the impact of the compulsory-attendance law confined to grave interference with important Amish religious tenets from a subjective point of view. It carries with it precisely the kind of objective danger to the free exercise of religion that the First Amendment was designed to prevent. As the record shows, compulsory school attendance to age 16 for Amish children carries with it a very real threat of undermining the Amish community and religious practice as they exist today; they must either abandon belief and be assimilated into society at large, or be forced to migrate to some other and more tolerant region." (Pp. 217-218, 92 S.Ct. p. 1534.)

14. For this refinement of the issues here presented, we are indebted to "The Constitutionality Under the Religion Clauses of the First Amendment of Compulsory Sex Education in Public Schools," 68 Michigan Law Review 1050-1061, April 1970.

15. Education Code section 8506 (added by Stats.1969, ch. 977, § 1) provides: "No governing board of a public elementary or secondary school may require pupils to attend any class in which human reproductive organs and their functions and processes are described, illustrated or discussed, whether such class be part of a course designated 'sex education' or 'family life educa-

tion' or by some similar term, or part of any other course which pupils are required to attend.

"If classes are offered in public elementary and secondary schools in which human reproductive organs and their functions and processes are described, illustrated or discussed, the parent or guardian of each pupil enrolled in such class shall first be notified in writing of the class. Sending the required notice through the regular United States mail, or any other method which such local school district commonly uses to communicate individually in writing to all parents, meets the notification requirements of this paragraph.

"Opportunity shall be provided to each parent or guardian to request in writing that his child not attend the class. Such requests shall be valid for the school year in which they are submitted but may be withdrawn by the parent or guardian at any time. No child may attend a class if a request that he not attend the class has been received by the school.

"Any written or audiovisual material to be used in a class in which human reproductive organs and their functions and processes are described, illustrated, or discussed shall be available for inspection by the parent or guardian at reasonable times and places prior to the holding of a course which includes such classes. The parent or guardian shall be notified in writing of his opportunity to inspect and review such materials.

"This section shall not apply to description or illustration of human reproductive organs which may appear in a textbook, adopted pursuant to law, on physiology, biology, zoology, general science, personal hygiene, or health.

"Nothing in this section shall be construed as encouraging the description, illustration, or discussion of human reproductive organs and their functions and processes in the public elementary and secondary schools.

"The certification document of any person charged with the responsibility of making any instructional material available for inspection under this section or who is charged with the responsibility of notifying a parent or guardian of any class conducted within the purview of this section, and who knowingly and willfully fails to make such instructional material available for inspection or to notify such parent or guardian, may be revoked or suspended because of such act. The certification document of any person who knowingly and willfully requires a pupil to attend a class within the purview of this section when a request that the pupil not attend has been received from the parent or guardian may be revoked or suspended because of such act."

Education Code section 8701 (as amended by Stats. 1969, ch. 1307, § 1) provides: "Whenever any part of the instruction in health, family life education, and sex education conflicts with the religious training and beliefs of the parent or guardian of any pupil, the pupil, on written request of the parent or guardian, shall be excused from the part of the training which conflicts with such religious training and beliefs.

"As used in this section, 'religious training and beliefs' includes personal moral convictions."

In its prior version (Stats.1968, ch. 182, § 31), the

statute read as follows: "Whenever any part of the instruction in 'health' conflicts with the religious beliefs of the parent or guardian of any pupil, the pupil, on written request of the parent or guardian, may be excused from the part of the training which conflicts with such religious beliefs."

16. While this argument is not explicit in the briefs, it is the basis of the request for injunctive relief. The argument was made orally in response to questions from this court at the hearing on February 11, 1975.

17. We recognize differing degrees of pressure as to the lower grades where all or most of the instruction takes place in one location with one teacher than in the junior and senior high school grades where usually each subject is taught by a different teacher in a different location.

18. The parents and amicus curiae also cite *Meyer v. Nebraska,* 262 U.S. 390, 43 S.Ct. 625, 67 L.Ed. 1042, and *Pierce v. Society of Sisters,* 268 U.S. 510, 45 S.Ct. 571, 69 L.Ed. 1070. In *Meyer,* the court held unconstitutional a statute that prohibited teaching any foreign language beyond the eighth grade to postpone the learning of "foreign ideas" until "American ideas" had been thoroughly incalcated (*id* 262 U.S. at 401, 43 S.Ct. 625). *Pierce* held that requiring public school attendance to the exclusion of private schools unreasonably interfered with parental prerogatives in the upbringing of their children. As noted, however, in 43 Southern California Law Review, 548, 566-567, *Pierce* does not grant parents a monopoly over the thoughts of their own children or any one else's. The granting of such a complete monopoly, even in the parent-child context, is inimical to the First Amendment premise that only unfettered exchange can guarantee the informed citizenry essential to a democratic society (*Edwards v. South Carolina,* 372 U.S. 229, 83 S.Ct. 680, 9 L.Ed.2d 697; *Kingsley Pictures Corp.* L.Ed.2d 1512; *Joseph Burstyn, Inc. v. Wilson,* 343 U.S. 495, 72 S.Ct. 777, 96 L.Ed. 1098).

19. The best brief statement of this view is the concurring opinion of Justice Douglas in *Abington School Dist. v. Schempp,* supra, 374 U.S. at 227, 83 S.Ct. 1560, i. e., since the Free Exercise Clause is written in terms of what the state may not require of the individual, the lack of any compulsion by the school district effectively disposes of any issue relating to the "free exercise" of religion.

20. Similarly, in *Hardwick v. Board of School Trustees,* 54 Cal.App. 696, 205 P. 49, there was no compelling state interest in the compulsory social dancing program that was held to violate the Free Exercise and Establishment Clauses, as it was contrary to the religious and moral beliefs of the parent. However, courts have upheld a valid prescribed part of the curriculum courses in music, rhetoric, debating, composition, as well as participation in commencement exercises (see Sex Education: The Constitutional Limits of State Compulsion, 43 So. Cal.L.Rev. 548, 556-557).

21. Thomas Jefferson's metaphor of a wall, as distinct from a fine line easily overstepped (see *McCollum v. Board of Education,* 333 U.S. 203, 245, 68 S.Ct. 461, 92 L.Ed. 649), has been the subject of much discussion and debate (Katz, Freedom of Religion and State Neut-

rality, 20 Univ. of Chicago L.Rev. 426, at 438-439), and it has been said that: "A rule of law should not be drawn from figure of speech," since Jefferson did not exclude religious education from the University of Virginia, which he founded (*McCollum,* supra, 247, 68 S.Ct. 482, dissenting opinion of Reed, J.).

22. The U. S. Supreme Court, however, in *Torcaso v. Watkins,* 367 U.S. 488, 81 S.Ct. 1680, 6 L.Ed.2d 982, struck down a provision of the Maryland Constitution requiring specified state officials, as part of their oath of office, to declare a belief in God. The court held that religious liberty is not limited to theistic beliefs and at 495, 81 S.Ct. 1680, footnote 11, recognized secular humanism as a religion in this country. A similar conclusion was earlier reached by this court (Division One) in *Fellowship of Humanity v. County of Alameda,* 153 Cal. App.2d 673, 315 P.2d 394.

23. The parents attempt to distinguish Hopkins as no claim of violation of individual rights was made and the matter was not a class action but only an application for a temporary injunction by the affected students and their parents. The significant distinguishing factor of Hopkins is that the program there was a compulsory one. Thus, we have found the case helpful in discussing the parents' contentions that some aspects of the statutory refusal system here in issue have elements of coercion and compulsion.

24. In the instant case, likewise no facts relating to affirmative acts have been alleged. We also note that although the parents indicated at oral argument that the statutory excusal system was not working, no such allegations were made in the seventh amended complaint.

25. Similarly in *Cornwell,* supra, the court reviewed the cases pertinent to the Establishment Clause (314 F. Supp. at 343-344): *Engel v. Vitale,* 370 U.S. 421, 82 S.Ct. 1261, wherein official prayers to be recited in the classroom were held unconstitutional; *Chamberlin v. Public Instruction Bd.,* 377 U.S. 402, 84 S.Ct. 1272, 12 L.Ed.2d 407, and *Schempp,* supra, where devotional Bible reading and recitation of the Lord's Prayer were held to be in violation of the First Amendment; and *McCollum v. Board of Education,* 333 U.S. 203, 68 S.Ct. 461, where the *employment of teachers by private religious groups to give religious instruction* in the schools to those children whose parents desired it was held to be proscribed. The *Cornwell* court then continued 314 F.Supp. at 343: "On the other hand, where *such overt religious activities have been absent,* the Supreme Court has upheld governmental programs *even though they had some religious connection. . . . Everson* case, *supra,* where the *reimbursement of parents for transportation expenses to parochial schools* was upheld, *Zorach v. Clauson, supra,* where a *released-time program* allowing students to attend religious instruction centers off school grounds during the school day was upheld, and *Board of Education v. Allen,* 392 U.S. 236, 88 S.Ct. 1923, 20 L.Ed.2d 1060 (1968), *where the loan by the state of textbooks to students in parochial schools was also upheld."* (Emphasis added.)

26. Section 4, article I of the state Constitution provides, in

pertinent part: "The free exercise and enjoyment of religious profession and worship, without discrimination or preference, shall forever be guaranteed in this State; . . . " (quoted in full at fn. 2 above) is a guarantee of religious equality. As stated in 25 Attorney General Opinions, 316 at 319: "Moreover, nothing in the history of this provision suggests that the constitutional draftsmen held any mental reservations concerning the broad and emphatic language which they used. Section 4 of article I is based on the Constitution of New York and goes back to the New York Constitutional Convention of 1777. The principal religious controversy at that convention centered around a proposal (which was defeated) that Catholics be required to take a loyalty oath. A proposal that the state encourage religion was also rejected. Early drafts of the section guaranteeing religious freedom show that careful consideration was given to language, and that the New York framers progressed from such words as 'toleration' to broader terms like 'enjoyment'. At first it was proposed to list certain religious groups which would be accorded the benefits of the section, but it was ultimately decided to mention no particular religion by name and thus, in effect, to extend the principle of religious impartiality to all (see 1 Charles Z. Lincoln, The Constitutional History of New York, p. 541 et seq.). In the California Convention of 1849, the New York section was chosen after a debate in which the language of the Virginia Constitution was urged as a substitute. The Virginia Constitution referred to the duty owed the 'Creator' and admonished all men to display 'Christian' forbearance, love and charity (Report of the Proceedings of the California Convention of 1849, pp. 38-39). The Constitutional Convention of 1879 put section 4 of article I in its present form by changing the word 'allowed' to 'guaranteed'— a further indication of the emphatic character of this constitutional principle."

Thus, the state constitutional guarantee, like the federal one, forbids "any type of discrimination or preference" in "the enjoyment of religious profession," and, as with the federal Constitution, "Religious guarantees in our constitutions stem not from opposition to religion but from respect for it—and for the right of each person to determine for himself his fundamental faith. Children, as they become aware of the religious differences of our people, should be made to understand the true character of the public school's religious neutrality; the omission of religious services from the public school curriculum should never be allowed to assume the appearance of state hostility to religion.

"Although direct instruction in religious principles may not be given in the public schools, it does not follow that every reference to anything religious is prohibited. A course in the history of California which did not describe the early Catholic missions is unthinkable; Father Junipero Serra is justly regarded as one of the great figures in our history and in fact his statue is one of two representing California in the Hall of Fame at the nation's capitol. A high school course in European history could not properly omit reference to the great religious controversies of the middle ages, such as the struggle over lay investiture; and such a course would also devote substantial time to a study of the Protestant Reformation. Instruction concerning the Constitution would similarly involve study of the history of the struggle for religious freedom in colonial times. Religious subjects have many times been used in art and music; Da Vinci's 'Last Supper,' Michelangelo's 'Moses,' the 'Winged Victory' of Samothrace, an Indian totem pole—all have religious significance, and yet all are appropriate for study in a public school class on art. The playing of passages from Beethoven's 'Missa Solemnis' in a music class would not violate constitutional restrictions any more than the playing of Wagner's 'The Valkyrie'.

"Even the Bible itself need not be excluded. It has exerted, and still exerts, a great influence upon English and American literature. Not only may it be discussed in a general way in an appropriate literature class but specific passages, because of their eloquence or poetic beauty, may be used for special study, such as the Song of Ruth or Paul's great tribute to Charity.

"No doubt the indirect use of religious subjects in classes in art, music, literature, and history could be carried to extremes which would offend constitutional guarantees. Properly presented, however, such materials need not involve the promotion of religion. Use of the Bible in the public schools may be proper even though public school use of the Bible *for religious purposes* is prohibited by our constitutions." (Supra, at 325.)

27. On February 18, 1975, the United States Supreme Court noted jurisdiction in *Roemer v. Maryland Board of Public Works,* 420 U.S. 922, 95 S.Ct. 1115, 43 L.Ed.2d 391 which raises the question of whether a statute providing public aid in the form of non-categorical grants to private colleges and universities accredited by the state violates the Establishment Clause. Although the contention concerns excessive government entanglement with religion, the case appears to be factually remote from the instant one.

28. The theoretical basis of this contention, elegantly and eloquently set forth in Kurland, *Of Church and State and the Supreme Court,* 29 University of Chicago Law Review 1, at 96, is that the Freedom and Separation Clauses must be read together so that there can be no classification based on religion either to confer a benefit or impose a burden. Therefore, any statutory excusal system, like that of Education Code sections 8506 and 8701, based on religious grounds, is unconstitutional. The U. S. Supreme Court so intimated in *Abington School Dist. v. Schempp,* supra, 374 U.S. at 224 and 225, 83 S.Ct. 1560, citing *Engel v. Vitale,* supra. Further support for this theory is found in the concurring opinion of Justice Brennan in Abington, at 288, 83 S.Ct. 1560, which reasoned that the evils of the excusal opinion are equally present under both the Establishment and Free Exercise Clauses. This view, however, was not shared by the other members of the court, and has never been accepted as the controlling test by any court.

29. In this connection, we note that the objection is also taken to those portions of the program that relate to family finance management. The proper understanding

and allocation of family resources (also known as Consumer Education) is a proper and well recognized part of the curriculum of the schools of this state and many others. In fact, the establishment of a Consumer Program at the state level in California predated that of most other states (see Stats.1959, ch. 467, relating to the Consumer Counsel, now Bus. & Prof.Code, § 300 et seq.).

30. Although the allegations as to "parental authority" are purportedly based on the First Amendment, we think the concept fits better in the context of privacy and have, therefore, discussed it here.

31. These cases included *Glaser v. Marietta* (Pa.D.C.1972) 351 F.Supp. 555, 561, and *Ingraham v. Wright* (5 Cir. 1974) 498 F.2d 248, both pertaining to corporal punishment of students and, therefore, involving personal rights and due process considerations that are not analogous to those here in issue.

32. In *Scoma*, the court found insubstantial the parents' claim that they had a constitutional right to direct the education of their children as they saw fit and in accordance with their determination of what best serves the family's interest and welfare. The court held that this consideration did not rise above a personal or philosophical choice and cannot claim to be within the bounds of Constitutional protection. In addressing the equal protection argument, the court, citing Rodriguez, applied the "rational relationship" test and found no constitutional violation.

33. (Cf. *Hobolth v. Greenway* (1974) 52 Mich. App. 682, 218 N.W.2d 98.)

DISSENTING OPINION NOTES

1. Although section 426 was repealed in 1971, subdivision 2 is incorporated verbatim in Code of Civil Procedure, section 425.10, subdivision (a).

2. Other examples could be set forth since it is clear that plaintiffs followed a pattern of alleging a particular invasion of their rights by utilization of certain material contained in a particular exhibit.

A United States District Court in West Virginia decides against parents who had brought action to restrain the school board in Kanawha County, West Virginia, from using textbooks and materials the parents claimed were a violation of their First Amendment religious freedoms inasmuch as the textbooks and materials contained "both religious and anti-religious materials, matter offensive to Christian morals, matter which invades personal and familial morals, matter which defames the nation and which attacks civic virtue, and matter which suggests and encourages the use of bad English." The Court declares: "Careful consideration, evaluation and analysis of plaintiffs' complaint and testimony compel the conclusion that materials in some of the controversial textbooks and supplemental materials are offensive to plaintiffs' beliefs, choices of language, and code of conduct. However, the Court cannot find in the defendant's actions in placing the textbooks and supplemental materials in the Kanawha County schools any establishment of religion." The First Amendment, said the Court, "does not guarantee that nothing about religion will be taught in the schools nor that nothing offensive to any religion will be taught in the schools."

Williams v. *Bd. of Education of County of Kanawha,* 388 F. Supp. 93 (1975)

K. K. HALL, District Judge.

This action arises from the public school textbook controversy in Kanawha County, West Virginia—a controversy which developed at the commencement of the 1974-1975 school term following adoption of a series of textbooks and supplemental materials for the county's public school system by the Board of Education, defendant herein. In their complaint plaintiffs state that they are citizens, residents and taxpayers of Kanawha County, that they are parents of two infant school age children, and that their religion requires them to place their children in private schools at added expense since the controversial textbooks and supplemental materials used in the public school system impair and undermine their religious beliefs and invade their personal and familial privacy. Paragraph 6 of the complaint is in the following language:

6. The children of the plaintiffs are entitled, in the public schools, to an education of intellectual and moral excellence and they are, therefore, also entitled to receive instructions and textbooks which are free from religious value inculcations, matters offensive to Christian morals and good citizenship,

matters which invade the personal privacy of their children or familial privacy, and matters which suggest or encourage the use of bad English or mediocrity of mind.

Paragraph 10 in part and paragraph 11 of the complaint are as follow:

10. . . . Plaintiffs allege that textbooks adopted for use by the defendant contain, both religious and anti-religious materials, matter offensive to Christian morals, matter which invades personal and familial morals, matter which defames the Nation and which attacks civic virtue, and matter which suggests and encourages the use of bad English. The textbooks so adopted contain within them articles and stories promoting and encouraging a disbelief in a Supreme Being, and encouragement to use vile and abusive language and encouragement to violate the Ten Commandments as given by the Almighty to Moses, and an encouragement to violate not only Christian beliefs but the civil law.

11. Plaintiffs allege that the defendant by and through the use of said textbooks, has violated the

position of neutrality in religious matters as required by the Supreme Court of the United States and inhibited the exercise of rights of the Plaintiffs in the free exercise of their religion as guaranteed by the First Amendment to the Constitution of the United States.

Paragraph 13 of the complaint states the bases of plaintiffs' action in the following language:

13. Plaintiffs allege that they and their said children will suffer irreparable harm unless this Court enjoin the defendant from violating their constitutional rights of freedom of religion, of privacy and to have their children furnished a public school education which encourages excellence and civic virtue, which rights are guaranteed to them, by the First, Ninth and Fourteenth Amendments to the Constitution of the United States.

Plaintiffs seek injunctive relief restraining defendant from using the challenged textbooks and supplemental materials, as identified in the complaint, in violation of their constitutional rights, particularly their rights of religious freedom and privacy as detailed in paragraph 6 of their complaint.

Defendant is a public statutory corporation, created under the laws of the State of West Virginia, whose membership is composed of five citizens of the county elected by the voters on a non-partisan ballot, each for a term of six years. West Virginia Code, § 18-5-1.

Paragraph 9 of the complaint states:

Jurisdiction of this Court is invoked under Title 28 USC, Section 1343 and Title 28 USC, Section 2281 and 2284.

Jurisdiction is recognized under 28 U.S.C., Section 1343, but 28 U.S.C., Sections 2281-2284, relating to district courts of three judges, may not be a basis of jurisdiction herein. The pleadings present no case for convention of a district court of three judges.

The action is before the Court at this time on defendant's motion to dismiss plaintiffs' amended complaint or, in the alternative, for summary judgment. Rule 12 and Rule 56, Federal Rules of Civil Procedure. Defendant's motion is supported by an affidavit and a supplemental affidavit. At an evidentiary hearing on the motion, the parties were accorded the opportunity to present additional pertinent materials. One of the plaintiffs was called as a witness but defendant supplied no additional materials. Rule 12(b)(6).

Defendant's motion challenges plaintiffs' standing to maintain the action. This issue and position need

not be considered at length. See West Virginia Highlands Conservancy v. Island Creek Coal Co., 441 F.2d 232 (4th Cir. 1971), and Annotation, 11 A.L.R., Federal, 549 (1972).

Plaintiffs' action is based on constitutional rights claimed to be guaranteed under the First, Ninth and Fourteenth Amendments to the Constitution of the United States. The First Amendment, in pertinent part, reads as follows:

Congress shall make no law respecting an establishment of religion, or prohibiting the free exercise thereof;

*   *   *

The Ninth Amendment provides:

The enumeration in the Constitution, of certain rights, shall not be construed to deny or disparage others retained by the people.

The Fourteenth Amendment is construed to make the First Amendment provisions relating to religion applicable to the states and to the subdivisions thereof, including a county board of education. Torcaso v. Watkins, 367 U.S. 488, 81 S.Ct. 1680, 6 L.Ed.2d 982 (1961); Cruz v. Beto, 405 U.S. 319, 92 S.Ct. 1079, 31 L.Ed.2d 263 (1972); West Virginia Board of Education v. Barnette, 319 U.S. 624, 3 S.Ct. 1178, 87 L.Ed. 1628 (1943). While the Constitution does not explicitly mention the right of privacy, a right claimed in paragraph 6 of plaintiffs' complaint, the right is recognized sometimes under the Ninth Amendment and sometimes under the Fourteenth Amendment as a fundamental right or rights implicit in the concept of ordered liberty. Roe v. Wade, 410 U.S. 113, 93 S.Ct. 705, 726-727, 35 L.Ed.2d 147 (1973).

Careful consideration, evaluation and analysis of plaintiffs' complaint and testimony compel the conclusion that materials in some of the controversial textbooks and supplemental materials are offensive to plaintiffs' beliefs, choices of language, and code of conduct. However, the Court cannot find in the defendant's actions in placing the textbooks and supplemental materials in the Kanawha County schools any establishment of religion. A complete loosening of imagination is necessary to find that placing the books and materials in the schools constitutes an establishment of religion contrary to the rights contained in the Constitution. Further, the Court finds nothing in defendant's conduct or acts which constitutes an inhibition on or prohibition of the free exercise of religion. These rights are guaranteed by the First Amendment, but the Amendment does not guarantee that nothing about religion will be taught in the schools nor that nothing offensive to any religion will be taught in the schools. The Court finds nothing in defendant's procedures, actions or conduct incident to placing the books and materials in the schools violative of any rights accorded to plaintiffs and their children under the Ninth Amendment, particularly the right of privacy, as claimed in the complaint.

In the absence of bases for relief in the courts, where no violation of constitutional rights is found, plaintiffs and parties similarly situated, with reference to books and materials found offensive to and objectionable by them, may find administrative remedies through board of education proceedings or ultimately at the polls on election day.

Upon careful review and consideration of the entire record in the action, the Court finds and concludes:

1. The Court has jurisdiction of the action.
2. Plaintiffs have adequate standing for commencement and prosecution of the action.
3. The action is properly considered on defendant's motion for summary judgment.
4. Plaintiffs' complaint, together with the evidence adduced by plaintiffs, considered in the light most favorable to them and with the allegations of the complaint taken as true, fails to state a claim upon which relief can be granted. Rule 12(b)(6). Wright and Miller, Federal Practice and Procedure, § 1357 (1969). Moreover, upon consideration of the entire record, no genuine issue as to any material fact remains for determination or adjudication. Defendant is entitled to judgment as a matter of law. Rule 56(c). Wright and Miller, Federal Practice and Procedure, § 2727 (1973).

Fundamental principles greatly determinative of this action have been clearly stated by the Supreme Court of the United States in Epperson v. Arkansas, 393 U.S. 97, 89 S.Ct. 266, 270-271, 21 L.Ed.2d 228 (1968), in the following language:

The antecedents of today's decision are many and unmistakable. They are rooted in the foundation soil of our Nation. They are fundamental to freedom.

Government in our democracy, state and national, must be neutral in matters of religious theory, doctrine, and practice. It may not be hostile to any religion or to the advocacy of no-religion; and it may not aid, foster, or promote one religion or religious theory against another or even against the militant opposite. The First Amendment mandates governmental neutrality between religion and religion, and between religion and nonreligion.

*   *   *

Judicial interposition in the operation of the public school system of the Nation raises problems requiring care and restraint. Our courts, however, have not failed to apply the First Amendment's mandate in our educational system where essential to safeguard the fundamental values of freedom of speech and inquiry and of belief. By and large, public education in our Nation is committed to the control of state and local authorities. Courts do not and cannot intervene in the resolution of conflicts which arise in the daily operation of school systems and which do not directly and sharply implicate basic constitutional values. On the other hand, "[t]he vigilant protection of constitutional freedoms is nowhere more vital than in the community of American schools," Shelton v. Tucker, 364 U.S. 479, 487, 81 S.Ct. 247, 251, 5 L.Ed.2d 231 (1960).

*   *   *

Upon consideration of the record in the action, the memoranda of counsel and the arguments of counsel theron, it is

Ordered and adjudged that defendant's motion, considered as a motion for summary judgment, be, and it is hereby, granted. Proceedings in this action are concluded and the action is dismissed.

A United States District Court in Oregon decides against a school board that had prohibited a high school political science teacher from inviting to his class a Communist speaker after his class had heard from speakers representing the views of Democrats, Republicans, and the John Birch Society; the school board subsequently banned all political speakers. In deciding against the school board, the District Court concluded that the order banning the speakers was unreasonable and violated the First Amendment; further, "the order, by granting school officials discretion to bar political speakers before those persons speak, creates a system of prior restraint." The Court's opinion concludes: "Finally, I am firmly convinced that a course designed to teach students that a free and democratic society is superior to those in which freedoms are sharply curtailed will fail entirely if it fails to teach one important lesson: that the power of the state is never so great that it can silence a man or woman simply because there are those who disagree."

Wilson v. *Chancellor,* 418 F.Supp. 1358 (1976)

BURNS, District Judge.

Plaintiffs Wilson and Logue seek declaratory and injunctive relief from a school board order banning "all political speakers" from Molalla Union High School (MHS). They contend that the order violates the First Amendment and the equal protection clause of the Fourteenth Amendment, and is unconstitutionally vague and overbroad. Jurisdiction is based on 28 U.S.C. § 1343(3,4).

Wilson teaches the political science class at MHS in which Logue was a student. This dispute arose when Wilson invited a Communist, Anton Kchmareck, to speak to that class. Wilson already and without objection had presented a Democrat, a Republican, and a member of the John Birch Society. The Communist was to be the last of this quadrumvirate through which Wilson hoped to present, in the words of the adherent, each of four points of view.

Wilson followed customary procedure and reported this invitation to the principal. The principal approved. Defendant school board discussed the invitation at its November 1975 meeting and also approved. This procedure was neither unprecedented nor customary.

The board's approval inspired mixed reviews. Two severe critics called a community meeting on December 4 where they circulated a petition asking the board to reverse the decision; approximately 800 persons eventually signed it. Several townsfolk, in letters to the local newspaper, mentioned the possibility of voting down all school budgets and voting out the members of the board.

Faced with this petition and many outraged residents, the board on December 11 reversed its decision and issued orally an order banning "all political speakers" from the high school.

The case came on for hearing on plaintiffs' motion for preliminary injunction. The parties submitted written statements and offered testimony and exhibits. The parties then agreed that the court could regard the hearing as a full trial on the merits because all necessary evidence was in.

I. FIRST AMENDMENT CLAIMS:
A. *Plaintiff Logue: Right to Hear*

Miss Logue contends the order violates her First Amendment right to hear the speech of others.

The right to hear customarily is invoked by prisoners denied access to periodicals, *e. g., Johnson v. Anderson,* 370 F.Supp. 1373, 1391 (D.Del.1974), members of a potential audience for a speaker prohibited from speaking, *e. g., Brooks v. Auburn University,* 296 F.Supp. 188 (M.D.Ala.1969), *aff'd* 412 F.2d 1171 (5th Cir. 1969), or persons asserting either the public's "right to know," *e. g., Red Lion Broadcasting Co. v. F.C.C.*, 395 U.S. 367, 390, 89 S.Ct. 1794, 23 L.Ed.2d 371 (1969) or the emerging right of privacy, *e. g., Stanley v. Georgia*, 394 U.S. 557, 560-64, 89 S.Ct. 1243, 22 L.Ed.2d 542 (1969).

Of these cases, only the potential audience cases are applicable here: *Brooks, supra, Vail v. Board of Education of Portsmouth School Dist.*, 354 F.Supp. 592 (D.N.H. 1973), and *Smith v. University of Tennessee*, 300 F.Supp. 777 (E.D.Tenn.1969). These cases[1] and my recognition that the First Amendment exists to protect a broad range of interests persuade me that Logue suffered an infringement of her First Amendment rights. Whether the infringement was justifiable is discussed *infra* (C (2) Reasonableness of the Order).

B. *Plaintiff Wilson: Right of Academic Freedom*[2]

Few courts have considered whether and to what extent the First Amendment protects academic freedom. Honored in Germanic tradition and prominent in academic debates, the theory rarely surfaces in legal opinions. Moreover, even its most enthusiastic advocates usually distinguish between the freedom to be accorded university professors and that to be accorded elementary and secondary school teachers. It seems to be assumed that the former engage in the search for knowledge and therefore should have far greater freedom than the latter, who merely disseminate knowledge.[3]

The Supreme Court of the United States has discussed academic freedom in "eloquent and isolated statements."[4] See, *e.g., Keyishian v. Board of Regents*, 385 U.S. 589, 87 S.Ct. 675, 17 L.Ed.2d 629 (1967); *Shelton v. Tucker*, 364 U.S. 479, 81 S.Ct. 247, 5 L.Ed.2d 231 (1960); *Barenblatt v. United States*, 360 U.S. 109, 79 S.Ct. 1081, 3 L.Ed.2d 1115 (1959). Lower courts have spoken more frequently, but none has clearly defined the theory's legal contours. Nor will I. This case can be decided by using purely conventional freedom of expression analysis.

C. *Plaintiff Wilson: Freedom of Expression*

A teacher's teaching is expression to which the First Amendment applies. The right to freedom of expression is not absolute; it may be restricted, and restrictions on a teacher's expression should be judged in light of the "special characteristics of the school environment." *Tinker v. Des Moines Independent School Dist.*, 393 U.S. 503, 506, 89 S.Ct. 733, 736, 21 L.Ed.2d 731 (1969).

In imposing restrictions and making other decisions, school boards should be allowed great discretion. No court should intervene merely because a board's decision seems unwise. But if school boards, in exercising their discretion, act so as to interfere impermissibly with the constitutional rights of students or teachers,

or both, courts must and will intervene if their jurisdiction is properly invoked.

These considerations in mind, I address two pivotal questions: First, is a teaching method or vehicle a form of expression protected by the First Amendment? Second, if so, is the restriction at issue here reasonable?

(1) *Teaching methods as forms of expression*

Three cases have treated teaching methods as protected forms of expression: *Keefe v. Geanakos*, 418 F.2d 359 (1st Cir. 1969), *Parducci v. Rutland*, 316 F.Supp. 352 (M.D.Ala.1970), and *Sterzing v. Fort Bend Independent School Dist.*, 376 F.Supp. 657 (S.D. Tex.1972).

The teacher in *Keefe* assigned his class an Atlantic Monthly article containing a word which "admittedly highly offensive, is a vulgar term for an incestuous son."[5]

A school committee summoned Keefe to defend his conduct. When he was asked to agree not to use the word again, he declined. He subsequently was suspended, and sought a temporary injunction against the committee's dismissal hearing.

The district court denied an interlocutory injunction pending a decision on the merits. The court of appeals reversed, holding that plaintiff had demonstrated he probably would succeed on his lack of notice and academic freedom claims.

In *Parducci*, the teacher assigned her eleventh grade English class a Kurt Vonnegut, Jr. short story, "Welcome to the Monkey House." Several parents complained. School officials admonished the teacher not to use the story in any of her classes, and threatened to dismiss her if she refused. The teacher resigned. In her suit for injunctive relief she contended that the school's action violated her First Amendment rights.

The court recognized such a right, but concluded that it must be balanced against competing societal interests, most prominently the "state's vital interest in protecting its young people from any form of extreme propagandism in the classroom." 316 F.Supp. at 355. The court also recognized that *Tinker*, supra, requires the state to demonstrate that

"[T]he forbidden conduct would 'materially and substantially interfere with the requirements of appropriate discipline in the operation of the school.'" 393 U.S. at 509, 89 S.Ct. at 738.

The court then held that because the assignment was appropriate and presented no threat of disruption, the teacher's dismissal for assigning the short story violated her First Amendment rights.

In *Sterzing* a teacher disclosed to his civics class his lack of opposition to interracial marriage. After several parents complained, school officials urged Sterzing to confine his teaching to the assigned textbook. He ignored this request and several times departed from the text during the ensuing five months. Shortly after Sterzing administered an allegedly propagandistic test on race relations, the school board voted to discharge him for insubordination.

The district court ordered that Sterzing be reinstated. It held that a teacher has a substantive right to choose teaching methods which serve a demonstrated educational purpose. "A responsible teacher," wrote the court, "must have freedom to use the tools of his profession as he sees fit." 376 F.Supp. at 662.

Although these three cases involved actual or threatened dismissal, a teacher's freedom of expression can be impermissibly restricted even if dismissal is not threatened; prohibitions against certain teaching practices impliedly carry a threat of sanction and thereby restrict a teacher's freedom of expression.

These cases also recognize the validity of a popular maxim, "the medium is the message." The expresser's medium can affect the persuasiveness of his message, the duration of its influence, and the size and type of audience which it reaches. The act of teaching is a form of expression, and the methods used in teaching are media. Wilson's use of political speakers was his medium for teaching; similarly, the short story was Parducci's medium, the pamphlets were Sterzing's media, and the article containing the controversial words was Keefe's medium. The various school boards which restricted the media employed by Wilson here, and by Keefe, Parducci, and Sterzing in the cases cited, suppressed expression which the First Amendment protects.

But school boards may restrict teachers' expression if the restrictions are reasonable in light of the special circumstances of the school environment. Thus, question two: was this order reasonable?

(2) *Reasonableness of the Order*

I conclude that the order was not reasonable and therefore violated the First Amendment.

The order barred political speakers absolutely, yet no disruptions had occurred in Wilson's classes, or at other school gatherings where political subjects were discussed. Further, none were expected in the future.

The defendants have not shown that outside speakers impair high school education. If they did, the board still would lack justification for banning only outside *political* speakers. Moreover, the evidence demonstrated that the use of outside speakers is widely recommended, widely practiced, and professionally accepted.

The boards cannot justify the ban by contending that political subjects are inappropriate in a high school curriculum. Political subjects frequently are discussed at Molalla High School and other schools

throughout the country, as required by law.[6] Nor does the board have a valid interest in suppressing, as it did, political expression occurring in the course of recognized extracurricular activities.

The board cannot contend it was acting within its discretionary power to exclude incompetent speakers. It acted under pressure from those who feared, rather than doubted, the speaker's competence by banning all speakers without regard to competence.

The board's only apparent reason for issuing the order which suppressed protected speech was to placate angry residents and taxpayers. The First Amendment forbids this; neither fear of voter reaction nor personal disagreement with views to be expressed justifies a suppression of free expression, at least in the absence of any reasonable fear of material and substantial interference with the educational process.

D. *Prior Restraint*

The order, by granting school officials discretion to bar political speakers before those persons speak, creates a system of prior restraint.[7]

Prior restraints are not unconstitutional per se, but their invalidity is heavily presumed. *Bantam Books v. Sullivan*, 372 U.S. 58, 70, 83 S.Ct. 631, 9 L.Ed.2d 584 (1963). They are valid only if they include criteria to be followed by school authorities in determining whether to allow or forbid the expression, and procedural safeguards in the form of an expeditious review procedure. *Baughman v. Freienmuth*, 478 F.2d 1345 (4th Cir. 1973); *Quarterman v. Byrd*, 453 F.2d 54, 58-59 (4th Cir. 1971).[8]

The Molalla board order was completely bare; it failed to include either criteria by which to define "political speakers" or procedural safeguards in any form.

The order therefore constitutes an invalid prior restraint. Although our language contains many words and phrases which require no further definition, the phrase "political speakers" is not among them. *See also Brooks v. Auburn University*, 412 F.2d 1171 (5th Cir. 1969) (University president's prohibition against speech by antiwar activist invalid prior restraint; no criteria for determining speaker eligibility); *Ginsberg v. City of Miami*, 307 F.Supp. 675 (S.D.Fla.1969) (municipal stadium manager's interruption of allegedly obscene poetry reading invalid prior restraint); *Reilly v. Noel*, 384 F.Supp. 741 (D.R.I.1974) (governor's directive forbidding state building's use in a manner involving "singing or boisterous conduct," or involving praying or singing above a "subdued tone" invalid prior restraint).

E. *Vagueness[9] and Overbreadth*

The void-for-vagueness doctrine usually is invoked to invalidate criminal statutes so vague that they deter people from exercising their constitutional rights for fear they will be punished. Harsh administrative sanctions also can produce this "chilling effect," however, see *Soglin* v. *Kauffman*, 418 F.2d 163 (7th Cir. 1969), but courts rarely invalidate non-criminal statutes for that reason. Writing in 1960, a noted commentator could find only one case in which a vagueness challenge to a non-criminal statute succeeded: *A.B. Small Co.* v. *American Sugar Ref. Co.*, 267 U.S. 233, 45 S.Ct. 295, 69 L.Ed. 589 (1925). *Note, Void-for-Vagueness Doctrine in the Supreme Court*, 109 U.Pa.L.Rev. 67, 69–70 n. 16 (1960).

In determining whether a statute or regulation will survive a vagueness attack, courts should look to the penalties which may be imposed. In Professor Amsterdam's words, "the seriousness of what is at stake" is an "extremely significant variable." *Note, supra*, at 70 n. 16.

In *Soglin, supra,* much was at stake; the regulation authorized expulsion from the University, which carried with it loss of academic progress, tuition, and the stigmatizing notation "expelled" on the college student's record.

Less is at stake here. The Molalla order usually will be enforced by an order requiring the speaker to cease, a reprimand, or perhaps temporary suspension. This would not cause financial loss, loss of academic progress, or stigma of the magnitude involved in *Soglin.* These sanctions are not sufficiently severe to require the board to promulgate a less ambiguous regulation.[10]

I also hesitate to declare the order either void-for-vagueness or overly broad because I believe plaintiffs lack standing to raise these claims in a declaratory judgment proceeding. This is true even though the order reaches political speech—the very category of speech which the First Amendment was designed to protect.

Article III standing normally is not an obstacle in overbreadth or vagueness cases because a plaintiff's interest in not being punished is sufficiently adverse to constitute a case or controversy. *See* A. Bickel, *The Least Dangerous Branch*, 149–50 (1962). Plaintiffs do not seek relief from punishment, however; they seek declaratory relief, and the standing hurdle is formidable.

None of the major prior restraint cases dealing with the standing issue involved declaratory relief. *See, e.g., Shuttlesworth* v. *Birmingham*, 394 U.S. 147, 89 S.Ct. 935, 22 L.Ed.2d 162 (1969); *Cox* v. *Louisiana*, 379 U.S. 536, 85 S.Ct. 453, 13 L.Ed.2d 471 (1965); *Kunz* v. *New York*, 340 U.S. 290, 71 S.Ct. 312, 95 L.Ed. 280 (1951). Plaintiffs in all three cases had been charged with or convicted of statutory violations.

Plaintiffs claim the regulation will be applied in the future to forbid their constitutionally protected exercise of free speech. Unless and until the regulation actually is applied in that fashion, however, a justiciable case or controversy would seem not to exist. *See United Public Workers* v. *Mitchell*, 330 U.S. 75, 89, 67 S.Ct. 556, 564, 91 L.Ed. 754 (1947) (" . . . but the facts of [plaintiff's] personal interest in their civil rights, of the general threat of interference with those rights . . . if specified things are done by appellants, does not make a justiciable case or controversy.").

I recognize that garden-variety declaratory judgment actions rarely constitute classic Article III "cases or controversies" and that this circuit has entertained declaratory judgments about the legal consequences of future conduct, *e.g., Crowell* v. *Baker Oil Tools*, 143 F.2d 1003 (9th Cir. 1944). This case raises important constitutional questions, however, and the Supreme Court has held that questions on the scope and constitutionality of legislation, particularly on important questions of law, must not be decided in advance of its immediate adverse effect in the context of a concrete case. *Longshoremen's Union* v. *Boyd*, 347 U.S. 222, 224, 74 S.Ct. 447, 98 L.Ed. 650 (1954).

Viewed alone, plaintiffs' overbreadth and vagueness claims involve an abstract, hypothetical case rather than a concrete one. Hence, I do not reach these claims.[11]

II. EQUAL PROTECTION CLAIMS:

A. The Ban Generally and Prospectively

The challenged order discriminates against political speakers by banning only them from the high school. It also discriminates against teachers of politically-oriented subjects by prohibiting only them from using outside speakers in the classroom.[12]

Legislation invariably classifies and discriminates; whenever it grants benefits to some classes it denies them to others. These classifications are inherent in the legislative act, and are unconstitutional only under prescribed circumstances.

Classifications which restrain conduct protected by the First Amendment are unconstitutional unless they suitably further an appropriate governmental interest. *Chicago Police Department* v. *Mosley*, 408 U.S. 92, 92 S.Ct. 2286, 33 L.Ed.2d 212 (1972); *see also Young* v. *American Mini Theatres*,—U.S.—, 96 S.Ct. 2440, 49 L.Ed.2d 310 (1976).[13] Appropriate governmental interests include the desire to promote effective education by preventing material disruptions of classroom work, substantial disorders, or invasions of the rights of others, *Tinker, supra*, or by averting a clear and present danger, *Whitney* v. *California*, 274 U.S. 357, 47 S.Ct. 641, 71 L.Ed. 1095 (1925).

Because I already have concluded that the order did not further any appropriate governmental interests, and therefore violated the First Amendment, I must also conclude that it violated the equal protection clause. The order exists to silence absolutely the expression of an unpopular political view, solely out of fear that some will listen. This the government, acting through the school board, cannot do.

B. *The Ban as Applied*

The board discriminated in a third way. It allowed Wilson to invite a Republican, a Democrat, and a member of the John Birch Society to speak to his class, but it forbade him from inviting a Communist.

The effect was discriminatory. Persons with palatable views could speak; those with less readily digestible views could not.

An order prohibiting Wilson from inviting a Republican to class after a Democrat had spoken there clearly would be discriminatory. That Wilson invited a Communist rather than a champion of the current political orthodoxy has no constitutional significance.

Wilson has standing to raise the speaker's claim, by analogy to the line of cases in which a plaintiff, by complying with a directive, would have denied the constitutional rights of a third party. *See, e.g., Barrows* v. *Jackson*, 346 U.S. 249, 73 S.Ct. 1031, 97 L.Ed. 1586 (1953)(party sued for breach of racially restrictive covenant may assert the equal protection claims of black persons). Standing should be found whenever a plaintiff is faced with a choice of either asserting a constitutional claim or complying with and abetting a discriminatory policy. *See Griswold* v. *Connecticut*, 381 U.S. 479, 481, 85 S.Ct. 1678, 14 L.Ed.2d 510 (1965)(plaintiff doctor allowed to assert privacy rights of patients); *Eisenstadt* v. *Baird*, 405 U.S. 438, 92 S.Ct. 1029, 31 L.Ed.2d 349 (1972) (married plaintiff allowed to assert equal protection claim of single persons to whom the distribution of contraceptive devices was a felony).

III.   CONCLUSION

I do not imply that members of a community now may sue to compel schools to open their doors to particular outside speakers. Such compulsion would restrict a teacher's freedom rather than protect it, contrary to the important policies that I have outlined.

Nor do I suggest that Federal courts stand ready to regulate the regimen and to control the curricula of our public schools. A teacher is not required to have outside speakers contribute to class. I hold only that this regulation, as it applied in this particular set of facts, does not withstand constitutional scrutiny.

And I do not malign the defendant board members. Their position is sensitive, at once both a challenge and an opportunity. They serve a community in which many persons equate Communism with violence, deception, and imperialism. Yet violence, deception, and imperialism have occurred under many flags and in the name of many creeds. School boards could eliminate much of the high schools' curricula by re-stricting them to theories, philosophies, and practices of resolutely pacifistic, honest, nonexpansionist societies.

It seems these same residents fear that young Molallans will become young Marxists and Maoists, virtually overnight. Because Oregon law, ORS 336.057-067, requires the schools to specially emphasize our form of government, respect for the flag, and obedience to our laws, this fear seems ill-founded. Moreover, today's high school students are surprisingly sophisticated, intelligent, and discerning. They are far from easy prey for even the most forcefully expressed, cogent, and persuasive words.

Finally, I am firmly convinced that a course designed to teach students that a free and democratic society is superior to those in which freedoms are sharply curtailed will fail entirely if it fails to teach one important lesson: that the power of the state is never so great that it can silence a man or woman simply because there are those who disagree. Perhaps that carries with it a second lesson: that those who enjoy the blessings of a free society must occasionally bear the burden of listening to others with whom they disagree, even to the point of outrage.

Plaintiffs should prepare a proposed form of order, and, if necessary, a hearing will be scheduled to discuss the terms of the order. Plaintiffs should submit any statement they wish as to the subject of attorney's fees.

The foregoing constitutes findings of fact and conclusions of law pursuant to F.R. Civ.P. 52(a).

NOTES

1. Compare those cases which discuss the public's right *not* to hear, e.g., *Lehman* v. *City of Shaker Heights*, 418 U.S. 298, 94 S.Ct. 2714, 41 L.Ed.2d 770 (1974); *Kovacs* v. *Cooper*, 336 U.S. 77, 69 S.Ct. 448, 93 L.Ed. 513 (1949).
2. For a general discussion, *see* Miller, *Teacher's Freedom of Expression in the Classroom: A Search for Standards*, 8 Ga.L.Rev. 837 (1974); *Developments—Academic Freedom*, 81 Harv.L. Rev. 1045 (1968).
3. Developments, *supra* note 2, at 1053; T. Emerson, The System of Freedom of Expression, ch. XVI, p. 597 (1969).
4. T. Emerson, *supra* note 3, at 616
5. Writing an opinion involving a discussion of this case and that word presents a dilemma. The use of a euphemism tends to obscure the significance of the decision. The use of the word itself tends to insult the unwary reader of judicial opinions. Perhaps such readers are a hardier breed than I suppose, but I have chosen the former alternative. Those who are made of sterner stuff may consult footnote 7 of the *Keefe* case, 418 F2d at 361; *see, also, Hess* v. *Indiana*, 414 U.S. 105, 94 S.Ct. 326, 38 L.Ed.2d 303 (1973).

6. Political subjects invariably will arise during the course of study required in Oregon schools by Oregon law. ORS 336.057 requires public and private schools to give instruction in the constitution of the United States for a minimum of five years. ORS 336.067 requires "special emphasis" on instruction in obedience to law, respect for the flag, and the federal and state constitutions, and "other lessons which tend to promote and develop an upright and desirable citizenry."

7. For a pertinent discussion, *see Note, Prior Restraints in Public High Schools,* 82 Yale L.J. 1325 (1973).

8. *See also Eisner* v. *Stamford Board of Education,* 440 F.2d 803 (2d Cir. 1971). *But see Fujishima* v. *Board of Education,* 460 F.2d 1355 (7th Cir. 1972)(prior restraint invalid, although adequate procedural safeguards provided).

9. The void-for-vagueness doctrine is treated brilliantly by the author of *Note, The Void-for-Vagueness Doctrine in the Supreme Court,* 109 U.Pa.L.Rev. 67 (1960).

10. Plaintiffs do not contend that the order fails to comply with ORS 339.240, which requires that district school boards "attempt to give the widest possible distribution of reasonable written rules regarding pupil conduct, discipline, and rights and procedures pertaining thereto."

11. In *Opinion of Justices,* 362 Mass. 891, 284 N.E.2d 919 (1972) the Supreme Judicial Court of Massachusetts found impermissibly vague a bill which regulated political advertising without defining it. The resulting vagueness, according to the court, "would produce an unnecessarily chilling effect on the publication of any political advertising." 284 N.E.2d at 922.

The school board probably gave too little thought as to whom, other than Kchmareck, the political speakers ban would apply. The word "political" itself connotes different things to different people, not excluding judges and editors of dictionaries. It has been defined as pertaining to the policy or administration of government, *People* v. *Morgan,* 90 Ill. 558, 563, and as pertaining to

the policy as distinguished from the administration of government, Webster's Third New International Dictionary. In one context, the word was construed to imply only the orderly conduct of government rather than revolution, *Wilson* v. *Loew's Inc.,* 142 Cal. App.2d 183, 298 P.2d 152, 157 (1956), a definition defendants in this case certainly did not intend.

Without more, the word political is too vague and its meaning too elusive to tolerate in regulations aimed at protected conduct. I suspect the board members would have learned this if they had attempted to enforce the regulation across the board.

For example, would they have had to forbid a class discussion of possible environmental harm from a nuclear power plant? What if a nuclear regulation measure was on the fall ballot? Would spokesmen of either point of view be "political" speakers?

Would a guest historian discussing in Molalla's American History class the Indian treaties of the 1850's, and the fishing clauses they contained, be a "political" speaker in the year 1976?

What if a science teacher invited a forester to discuss clear cutting? Is this nonpolitical in light of *Monongahela*?

Are "politicians" always political speakers, regardless of their topic? Would Governor Bob Straub and former Governor Tom McCall ever be nonpolitical speakers, regardless of the subject they discussed?

Fortunately I need not answer these questions because the parties agreed that the disinvited speaker was, indeed, a political speaker.

12. It seems clear that reasonable restrictions on the time, place, and manner for outside speakers would withstand an equal protection-First Amendment challenge. *See Police Department* v. *Mosley, supra; Lovell* v. *Griffin,* 303 U.S. 444, 58 S.Ct. 666, 82 L.Ed. 949 (1938).

13. *Williams* v. *Rhodes,* 393 U.S. 23, 89 S.Ct. 5, 21 L.Ed.2d 24 (1968) is yet another First Amendment-equal protection case.

THE Court of Appeals of New York decides for a tenured high school teacher who had been dismissed for teaching *The Catcher in the Rye* in his sophomore English class. Parents' complaints about the explicit "street language" in the book prompted the school superintendent and principal to tell Harris, the English teacher, not to use the book; however, he resumed use of the Salinger novel and the school officials charged him with insubordination. In deciding for the teacher, the Court of Appeals said: "Under the circumstances, dismissal of the tenured teacher is so disproportionate to the offense as to shock the Court's sense of fairness."

Harris v. *Mechanicville Central School District*, 408 N.Y.S.2d 384 (1978)

BREITEL, Chief Judge.

Petitioner, a tenured teacher, in a CPLR article 78 proceeding, seeks to annul a determination of respondent school district dismissing him on two charges of insubordination (see Education Law, § 3020-a, subd. 5). Special Term sustained the first charge, but annulled the second and remanded the matter to the board of education for fixing of a sanction short of dismissal. The Appellate Division modified by reinstating both the second charge and the dismissal, and petitioner appeals.

The preliminary issue is whether the board's determination, apart from the sanction imposed, is supported by substantial evidence. Assuming it is so supported, also at issue is whether for violating a voluntary agreement not to teach a particular work of fiction and abruptly walking out of a meeting with the school principal, dismissal is a sanction so disproportionate to the offense as to "shock the court's sense of fairness."

The order of the Appellate Division should be modified by reversing so much of the order as reinstated the dismissal and otherwise be affirmed. There being substantial, albeit contested, evidence to support each finding of insubordination, to that extent the board's determination is beyond review (*Matter of Pell* v. *Board of Educ.*, 34 N.Y.2d 222, 230, 356 N.Y.S.2d 833, 838, 313 N.E.2d 321, 325). The dismissal, however, even under the court's limited review of administratively imposed sanctions, cannot stand. Petitioner's conduct was isolated, did not involve grave moral turpitude, and worked no grave injury to the school district. The matter should be remitted to Special Term, therefore, with directions to remand to the school dis-

trict for determination of an appropriate sanction, which may be as restrained as a letter of reprimand but in no event more than one year's suspension without pay.

Petitioner, a teacher employed in the Mechanicville High School since 1966 and eventually tenured, had for several years taught J.D. Salinger's "Catcher in the Rye" to his sophomore English class. It is not contradicted that the book had been taught for several years and had not been removed from the school's curriculum. In the fall of 1973 complaints from parents caused the school superintendent to question the methods employed by petitioner in teaching the novel. Particular exception was taken to his use in the classroom of explicit street language appearing in the book. To resolve the problem, the superintendent and the school principal met with the teacher. According to school officials, and evidenced by a memorandum later circulated by the superintendent, once he was advised of the community reaction to his manner of teaching the novel, the teacher voluntarily agreed to drop the book and find an appropriate substitute. In the fall 1974 semester, however, without warning and despite the earlier understanding, the teacher resumed use of the book.

As a result, on November 25, 1974, the teacher was summoned to a conference in the principal's office. The meeting ended unexpectedly, however, when, after five minutes, the teacher abruptly walked out. Although the principal pursued him and, in the presence of others, asked him to return, the teacher refused.

Two charges of insubordination were made. The first arose out of the aborted conference, and the second was grounded on violation of the voluntary agreement.

Probable cause having been found by the board of education on both charges, a three-member hearing panel was convened (see Education Law, § 3020-a). Following two days of hearings, the panel recommended that the first charge be dismissed and the second sustained, in each case by a two-to-one vote. The only panel member to recommend a particular sanction suggested that at most a letter of reprimand be included in the teacher's file.

Despite the panel recommendations, which then were not binding on the board, the board unanimously found petitioner guilty of both charges and resolved that he be dismissed (see former Education Law, § 3020-a, L.1970, ch. 717, § 16; compare L.1977, ch. 82, in effect since April 15, 1977, under which the board is bound by panel recommendations). This proceeding followed.

With respect to the board's findings of insubordination, extended discussion is unnecessary. Petitioner, it is true, denies having reached a definitive agreement with respect to teaching the Salinger novel. He also seeks to justify his conduct at the November, 1974 conference with the principal. That the evidence is conflicting, however, is irrelevant. What does matter is that there is substantial evidence in the record that petitioner had agreed to cease teaching the novel and that, without acceptable excuse, he terminated the conference with the principal (see *Matter of Pell* v. *Board of Educ.*, 34 N.Y.2d 222, 230–231, 356 N.Y.S.2d 833, 838, 313 N.E.2d 321, 325, *supra*). Hence, the board's determination, apart from the sanction imposed, is beyond review.

Petitioner's resort to constitutional limitations to avoid the consequences of the board's findings is of no avail. Petititioner is not charged with teaching an unacceptable work of literature. Nor are his methods the subject of charges. It is not as though petitioner, concerned with academic freedom, firmly stood his ground against community pressure in defense of his classroom activities. Petitioner instead agreed not to teach the Salinger book, and, without notice, reneged on the understanding. Moreover, evidently when about to be called to task for disregarding his prior agreement, he walked out on his superior. The charges are thus simple ones, and attempts to elevate them to constitutional dimensions misperceive their true nature.

The sanction imposed presents another question. Judicial review of administratively imposed sanctions is limited: only when the sanction is, under the circumstances, so disproportionate to the offense as to "shock the conscience of the court" may it be revised (*Matter of Pell v. Board of Educ.*, 34 N.Y.2d 222, 232-235, 356 N.Y. S.2d 833, 843, 313 N.E.2d 321, 331,

supra). But, that the standard against which such sanctions will be tested leaves the administrative body with great latitude does not mean that disciplinary measures can go unchecked by judicial review.

As it was said in the *Pell* case (supra, pp. 234-235, 356 N.Y.S.2d p.842, 313 N.E.2d pp. 327-28): "Of course, terminology like 'shocking to one's sense of fairness' reflects a purely subjective response to the situation presented and is hardly satisfactory. Yet its usage has persisted for many years and through many cases. Obviously, such language reflects difficulty in articulating an objective standard. . . . At this time, it may be ventured that a result is shocking to one's sense of fairness if the sanction imposed is so grave in its impact on the individual subjected to it that it is disproportionate to the misconduct, incompetence, failure or turpitude of the individual, or to the harm or risk of harm to the agency or institution, or to the public generally visited or threatened by the derelictions of the individuals. Additional factors would be the prospect of deterrence of the individual or of others in like situations, and therefore a reasonable prospect of recurrence of derelictions by the individual or persons similarly employed. There is also the element that the sanctions reflect the standards of society to be applied to the offense involved. Thus, for a single illustrative contrast, habitual lateness or carelessness, resulting in substantial monetary loss, by a lesser employee, will not be as seriously treated as an offense as morally grave as larceny, bribery, sabotage, and the like, although only small sums of money may be involved."

To be sure, the teacher's conduct was not a trivial matter. Crediting the administrators' version, the teacher breached an agreement relied upon by school authorities to quiet parental complaints. Even if innocently motivated by a misguided perception of his responsibilities as a teacher, it was not for petitioner, albeit in an isolated incident, to arrogate the sole power of judgment.

In fairness, however, the teacher's conduct in context involved neither cardinal moral delinquency nor predatory motive. There is no suggestion that his actions were part of a pattern, or that his conduct involved the "persistent unwillingness to accept the directives of his superiors" which merited dismissal in *Matter of Short v. Nassau County Civ. Serv. Comm.*, 45 N.Y.2d 728, 408 N.Y.S.2d 471, 380 N.E.2d 298, decided herewith). Nor did the charges indicate a lack of capacity in general as a teacher, or a grave injury to the school district. It is significant too that the only hearing panel member to recommend a sanction concluded that a letter of administrative reprimand should be the severest measure imposed.

Under the circumstances, dismissal of the tenured teacher is so disproportionate to the offense as to shock the court's sense of fairness. An appropriate sanction may be as light as that recommended by the hearing panel member or, at most, as severe as one year's suspension without pay. Since, however, in this case this court will not presume to determine the precise sanction to be imposed, remittal is appropriate (see *Matter of Pell v. Board of Educ.,* 34 N.Y.2d 222, 233-234, 356 N.Y.S.2d 833, 841, 313 N.E.2d 321, 327, supra). Particularly is this so because there is here presented a matter involving both internal discipline and an understandable concern for the reactions of parents in the school district, areas in which the board possesses special sensitivity (see *Matter of Ahsaf v. Nyquist,* 37 N.Y.2d 182, 184-185, 371 N.Y.S2d 705, 707, 332 N.E.2d 880, 882).

Accordingly, the order of the Appellate Division should be modified, without costs, to reverse so much of the order as reinstated the sanction imposed, and otherwise be affirmed, and the matter remitted to Special Term with directions to remand to the school district for determination of an appropriate sanction.

JASEN, GABRIELLI, JONES, WACHTLER, FUCHSBERG and COOKE, JJ., concur.

Order modified, without costs, and the matter remitted to Special Term with directions to remand to the school district for determination of an appropriate sanction in accordance with the opinion herein and, as so modified, affirmed.

In deciding against five high school English teachers who had argued that their rights had been violated when the school board banned ten books out of a list of 1,285 books for use in language arts classes, the United States Court of Appeals, Tenth Circuit, agreed that "censorship or suppression of expression of opinion, even in the classroom, should be tolerated only when there is a legitimate interest of the state which can be said to require priority," but went on to conclude that "the board was acting within its rights in omitting the books, even though the decision was a political one influenced by the personal views of the members." Judge Doyle wrote in his concurring opinion: "I would disapprove of any arbitrary selection of books that can be read and those which cannot be on the reading list. . . . The approach I prefer would be that the exclusion of books for secondary school students is not to be an arbitrary exclusion. Therefore, reasons have to be given so that there can be court review. If they are excluded because the board member disapproves for a subjective reason, I would say that this is an unlawful and unconstitutional invasion of the classroom."

Cary v. *Bd. of Education Arapahoe School Dist.*, 598 F.2d 535 (1979)

LOGAN, Circuit Judge.

This an appeal from summary judgment denying relief in a declaratory judgment action which sought enforcement of claimed rights under the First and Fourteenth Amendments to the United States Constitution. The action was brought by five high school teachers who asserted their rights were violated when the Board of Education for the Adams-Arapahoe School District in Colorado (the board) banned ten books from use in the teachers' language arts classes.

The trial court found the teachers had a First Amendment right to choose these books for use in their high school English courses, but determined their constitutional rights were waived under the terms of a collective bargaining agreement entered into between the Aurora Education Association (AEA), to which they belonged, and the school district. The teachers have appealed from the adverse ruling on the waiver question; the board has cross-appealed on the constitutional law decision. The case has attracted amicus curiae briefs from the American Association of University Professors, the National Education Association, Colorado Education Association and Aurora Education Association, and the Colorado Association of School Boards.

The relevant facts were stipulated; both sides sought summary judgment. All plaintiffs are tenured teachers who teach high school language arts classes in the defendant school district. The classes involved are elective courses for eleventh and twelfth grade students—Contemporary Literature, Contemporary Poetry, and American Masters—which under the board regulations were designed for elective optional reading materials chosen from classroom libraries or personal sources.

The board first adopted a policy on selection of text material in January, 1975. A High School Language Arts Text Evaluation Committee was established to review current and new materials for language arts courses. Membership was composed of representative teachers, administrators, parents and students. The committee reviewed many books which had been used or were recommended for use in these courses. It was instructed to utilize specified criteria: appropriateness to the grade level, value of the material in relation to the course objectives, and fiscal considerations. The guidelines adopted by the board required a written response, including reasons, when suggested materials were rejected.

Only one book was rejected by the majority report of the committee, with apparently 1,285 books approved. A minority report filed by three members listed nine more books they would reject. The recommended texts were on public display for twelve days. Then at a regularly scheduled public meeting of the school board, and following an open discussion, the board voted to approve a list of 1,275 books for use in language arts classes in the high schools. Ten recommended books, all of which had previously been used in those classes, were excluded from the approved list;[1] six of the ten were among those not recommended in the minority report. The majority and minority reports made reference to the specified criteria in discussing titles they rejected, but the board itself set forth no written statement of the reasons for its vote to ban the ten books. Its edict to the teachers issued after the meeting simply referenced the list of books not being approved and made the following declarations:

Books which are not approved for instructional use will not be purchased, nor used for class assignment, nor will an individual be given credit for reading any of these books.
The books should be given to the Department Chairman who is asked to hold the books pending further directions from the Division of Instructional Services.
Also, each teacher should review the lists of approved materials for each class he/she will be teaching second semester. If the teacher anticipates using any materials not listed, those materials must receive prior approval by the Division of Instructional Services. The Department Chairman and the building Principal should submit that recommendation immediately to Jim Hamilton.

An unwritten board policy had permitted substitution of materials for assignments offensive to a student or his or her parents. That policy was formally adopted by the board in written form after the meeting above described.

By stipulation the parties agreed the books were not obscene, no systematic effort had been made to exclude any particular system of thought or philosophy, and a "constitutionally proper decision-maker" could decide these books were proper for high school language arts classes. It was agreed that the plaintiff teachers were subject to dismissal from their positions for insubordination for any of the following acts:

(a) adding any of the subject textbooks to the reading list of their courses;

(b) assigning the reading of any of the subject textbooks;
(c) giving any student any credit in courses for reading any of the subject textbooks;
(d) reading aloud or causing to be read aloud any of the subject textbooks in the classroom during class time; or
(e) discussing with students in the classroom during class time any of these materials at such length so as to amount to a constructive assignment of the materials.

I

We first consider whether the trial court correctly determined the asserted rights were waived by the collective bargaining agreement.

During contract negotiations the teachers' union (AEA) attempted unsuccessfully to obtain provisions in the agreement under an "academic freedom" heading which would require "questioned material," evidently including readings such as those at issue here, to be referred to a Teachers Advisory Council. Other proposals would have exempted from such referral materials, textbooks and practices already being utilized and "new supplementary materials on textbooks by individual teachers where such use is optional and left to the discretion of the individual teacher."

The relevant provisions of the agreement finally adopted are as follows:

Art. 5 § 2 . . . "Board Rights" [reserved to the school board] as used herein includes the right to: . . . (i) Determine the processes, techniques, methods and means of teaching any and all subjects.

* * *

Art. 7 § 2: The Board agrees that it will not directly or indirectly discourage, deprive or coerce any employee in the enjoyment of any rights conferred by any laws of the State of Colorado or the Constitution of the State of Colorado and the United States.

* * *

Art. 46 § 6: Academic freedom—The parties seek to educate young people in the democratic tradition, to foster a recognition of individual freedom and social responsibility, to inspire meaningful awareness of and respect for the Constitution and the Bill of Rights.
Freedom of individual conscience, association, and expression will be encouraged and fairness in procedures will be observed both to safeguard the legitimate interests of the schools and to exhibit by appropriate examples the basic objectives of a demo-

cratic society as set forth in the Constitution of the United States and the State of Colorado.

The final responsibility in the determination of the above rests with the Board.

We also consider relevant a portion of Colo.Rev.Stat. § 22-32-109 which provides: (1) In addition to any other duty required to be performed by law, each board of education shall have and perform the following specific duties:

*   *   *

(t) To determine the educational programs to be carried on in the schools of the district, and to prescribe the textbooks for any course of instruction or study in such programs;

The state statute would appear to give the Board the right to select textbooks, including those used in elective courses, insofar as the state may do so consistent with the federal and state constitutions. The collective bargaining agreement does not purport to surrender that right to the teachers. The board retains control over the "means of teaching any and all subjects," Art. 5 § 2(i), which surely must include the texts used.

At the same time the contract purports to recognize the teachers' constitutional rights. Art. 7 § 2. The only section which might be construed as a waiver of constitutional rights is the sentence at the end of Art. 46 § 6, in a section labeled "academic freedom," stating the "final responsibility in the determination of the above rests with the Board."[2] We do not construe the sentence as a deliberate waiver of teachers' constitutional rights. Rather it seems a cautionary clause, a reminder that the board retains control over the techniques, method means of teaching the courses, as is set forth in Art. 5 § 2(i).

We thus construe the contract as giving control over textual material to the school board insofar as it can be done consistent with the federal and Colorado constitutions. We do not construe it to call for waiver of teachers' individual constitutional rights. It gives the teachers neither more nor less than their constitutional entitlements. Therefore we do not have to consider whether the AEA had the power to surrender constitutional rights of the teachers.

II

We recognize and support the concept that "teachers [do not] shed their constitutional rights to freedom of speech or expression at the schoolhouse gate." *Tinker v. Des Moines Independent Community School Dist.,* 393 U.S. 503, 506, 89 S.Ct. 733, 736, 21 L.Ed.2d 731 (1969). This general commitment has been stated eloquently on occasion:

Our Nation is deeply committed to safeguarding academic freedom, which is of transcendent value to all of us and not merely to the teachers concerned. That freedom is therefore a special concern of the First Amendment, which does not tolerate laws that cast a pall of orthodoxy over the classroom. "The vigilant protection of constitutional freedoms is nowhere more vital than in the community of American schools." *Shelton v. Tucker, supra,* [364 U.S. 479] at 487, [81 S.Ct. 247, at 251, 5 L.Ed.2d 231]. The classroom is peculiarly the "marketplace of ideas." The Nation's future depends upon leaders trained through wide exposure to that robust exchange of ideas which discovers truth "out of a multitude of tongues, [rather] than through any kind of authoritative selection." *United States v. Associated Press,* [D.C.,] 52 F. Supp. 362, 372.

Keyishian v. Board of Regents, 385 U.S. 589, 603, 87 S.Ct. 675, 683, 17 L.Ed.2d 629 (1967).

To regard teachers—in our entire educational system, from the primary grades to the university—as the priests of our democracy is therefore not to indulge in hyperbole. It is the special task of teachers to foster those habits of open-mindedness and critical inquiry which alone make for responsible citizens, who, in turn, make possible an enlightened and effective public opinion. Teachers must fulfill their function by precept and practice, by the very atmosphere which they generate; they must be exemplars of open-mindedness and free inquiry. They cannot carry out their noble task if the conditions for the practice of a responsible and critical mind are denied to them. . . .

Wieman v. Updegraff, 344 U.S. 183, 196, 73 S.Ct. 215, 221, 97 L.Ed. 216 (1952) (Frankfurter, J., concurring).

Most of the cases, however, have arisen at the university level, and outside the area of curricular decisions and teaching-related speech in the classroom.

In only two instances has the United States Supreme Court discussed prohibitions against what might be taught students as part of a school's curriculum. In *Meyer v. Nebraska,* 262 U.S. 390, 43 S.Ct. 625, 67 L.Ed. 1042 (1923), and its companion case, *Bartels v. Iowa,* 262 U.S. 404, 43 S.Ct. 628, 67 L.Ed. 1047 (1923), the Court struck down state laws making it a crime to teach subjects in any language other than English prior to the time the students completed the eighth grade. The decision was based upon due process grounds and contains little reasoning of aid to us in the instant case.[3] It demonstrates, however, the Supreme Court, when it considers it has an appropriate case, will interfere with a curricular decision made by state or local authorities.

Mr. Justice Holmes dissented in *Meyer* and *Bartels* stating that he was not prepared to say it is unreasonable to require a school child in his early years to hear and speak only English at school.

No one would doubt that a teacher might be forbidden to teach many things, and the only criterion of his liberty under the Constitution that I can think of is "whether, considering the end in view, the statute passes the bounds of reason and assumes the character of a merely arbitrary fiat." . . .

262 U.S. at 412, 43 S.Ct. at 630.

Another noted civil libertarian, Mr. Justice Black, has rejected the views expressed in *Meyer* and severely criticized it. See *Tinker v. Des Moines Independent Community School Dist.*, 393 U.S. 503, 519-22, 89 S.Ct. 733, 21 L.Ed.2d 731 (1969) (dissenting opinion).

In the second case, *Epperson v. Arkansas*, 393 U.S. 97, 89 S.Ct. 266, 21 L.Ed.2d 228 (1968), the Court struck down a "monkey" law making it a crime and subjecting a teacher to dismissal for teaching the theory of evolution in state schools. The Court based its decision on the establishment of religion clause in the First Amendment. In keeping with somewhat sweeping language in the opinion, and perhaps Mr. Justice Stewart's statement in his concurring opinion, all parties in the instant case seem to treat *Epperson* as prohibiting the exclusion of an entire system of respected human thought from a course offered by the school. The Court in *Epperson* recognized that public education is committed to the control of state and local authorities, and the courts "do not and cannot intervene in the resolution of conflicts which arise in the daily operation of school systems and which do not directly and sharply implicate basic constitutional values." 393 U.S. at 104, 89 S.Ct. at 270. It cited *Meyer* for the proposition that the Court would strike down "arbitrary" restrictions upon freedom of teachers to teach and of students to learn.

Relevant to our inquiry, Mr. Justice Black, in a concurring opinion, declared:

I am also not ready to hold that a person hired to teach school children takes with him into the classroom a constitutional right to teach sociological, economic, political, or religious subjects that the school's managers do not want discussed. This Court has said that the rights of free speech "while fundamental in our democratic society, still do not mean that everyone with opinions or beliefs to express may address a group at any public place and at

any time." *Cox v. Louisiana*, 379 U.S. 536, 554, 85 S.Ct. 453, 464, 13 L.Ed.2d 471; *Cox v. Louisiana*, 379 U.S. 559, 574, 85 S.Ct. 476, 485-486, 13 L.Ed.2d 487. I question whether it is absolutely certain, as the Court's opinion indicates, that "academic freedom" permits a teacher to breach his contractual agreement to teach only the subjects designated by the school authorities who hired him.

393 U.S. at 113 114, 89 S.Ct. at 275. Mr. Justice Stewart, concurring in result, stated:

The States are most assuredly free "to choose their own curriculums for their own schools." A State is entirely free, for example, to decide that the only foreign language to be taught in its public school system shall be Spanish. But would a State be constitutionally free to punish a teacher for letting his students know that other languages are also spoken in the world? I think not.

It is one thing for a State to determine that "the subject of higher mathematics, or astronomy, or biology" shall or shall not be included in its public school curriculum. It is quite another thing for a State to make it a criminal offense for a public school teacher so much as to mention the very existence of an entire system of respected human thought.

393 U.S. at 115, 116, 89 S.Ct. at 276.

In one other case the Supreme Court affirmed without opinion a three-judge district court decision which upheld a Michigan statute forbidding instruction in public schools on the subject of birth control. *Mercer v. Michigan State Bd. of Educ.*, 379 F.Supp. 580 (E.D.Mich.), *aff'd mem.*, 419 U.S. 1081, 95 S.Ct. 673, 42 L.Ed.2d 678 (1974). The case was fraught with problems, including whether the plaintiff had standing to sue and whether there was a real case or controversy. Nonetheless, the majority opinion treated the constitutional issue and declared:

The State has the power to establish the curriculum or to delegate some of its authority to local agencies for the final shaping of the curriculum. It also has the power to permit the parents to make the final decision as to exactly which courses the child should take. Implicit in such a state of the law is the observation that a teacher does not have a right, Constitutional or otherwise, to teach what he sees fit, or to overrule the parents' decision as to which courses their children will take unless, of course, the State has in some manner delegated this responsibility to the teacher which is not the case here.

379 F.Supp. at 586.

West Virginia State Board of Education v. Barnette, 319 U.S. 624, 63 S.Ct. 1178, 87 L.Ed. 1628 (1943), struck down a law which required students to participate in a daily salute to the American flag. At first blush it might be considered a case of interference with a school curriculum. But the Court appeared to recognize that a state might require instruction in the history, structure and organization of the U. S. government which tend to inspire patriotism and love of country. But it distinguished that situation from the required flag salute which it treated as "a compulsion of students to declare a belief." 319 U.S. at 631, 63 S.Ct. at 1182.

Quite a number of circuit and district court decisions have involved claims of school board or school authorities' interference with teachers' First Amendment rights to conduct their classes as they see fit in exercise of their professional judgment. Most were discharge cases where the teacher was fired, or a contract not renewed, for allegedly offensive behavior, poor teaching techniques and insubordination. Conflicts over the teachers' use of dirty words in class, or assignment of reading materials containing dirty words, seeming approval of free love, drugs or rebellion against authority, were generally part of a charge of inappropriate conduct alleged to constitute good cause for discharge. The cases which held for the teachers and placed emphasis upon teachers' rights to exercise discretion in the classroom, seemed to be situations where school authorities acted in the absence of a general policy, after the fact, and had little to charge against the teacher other than the assignment with which they were unhappy. See *Sterzing v. Fort Bend Independent School Dist.*, 376 F.Supp. 657 (S.D.Tex.1972), *vacated on remedial grounds*, 496 F.2d 92 (5th Cir. 1974); *Mailloux v. Kiley*, 436 F.2d 565 (1st Cir. 1971), *on remand*, 323 F.Supp. 1387 (D.Mass.), *aff'd on other grounds*, 448 F.2d 1242 (1st Cir. 1971); *Keefe v. Geanakos*, 418 F.2d 359 (1st Cir. 1969); *Parducci v. Rutland*, 316 F.Supp. 352 (M.D.Ala.1979). Cf. *Wilson v. Chancellor*, 418 F.Supp. 1358 (D.Or.1976) (ban on speaker). In the cases where the teachers' First Amendment claims were rejected, generally the school authorities had other good grounds supporting their discharge or nonrenewal of the teacher's contract. *Adams v. Campbell County School Dist.*, 511 F.2d 1242 (10th Cir. 1975); *Brubaker v. Board of Educ.*, 502 F.2d 973 (7th Cir. 1974), *cert. denied*, 421 U.S. 965, 95 S.Ct. 1953, 44 L.Ed.2d 451 (1975); *Clark v. Holmes*, 474 F.2d 928 (7th Cir. 1972), *cert. denied*, 411 U.S. 972, 93 S.Ct. 2148, 36 L.Ed.2d 695 (1973); *Ahern v. Board of Educ.*, 456 F.2d 399 (8th Cir. 1972); *Moore v. School Bd. of Gulf County*, 364 F.Supp. 355 (N.D.Fla.1973); *Parker v. Board of Educ.*, 237 F.Supp. 222 (D.Md.), *aff'd per curiam*, 348 F.2d 464 (4th Cir. 1965), *cert. denied*, 382 U.S. 1030, 86 S.Ct. 653, 15 L.Ed.2d 543 (1966).

Closer to the instant situation perhaps are the cases where the school board voted to remove certain volumes from the school library which it found objectionable. *Minarcini v. Strongsville City School Dist.*, 541 F.2d 577 (6th Cir. 1976), held students had a First Amendment right to know which did not permit removal of books based solely on the "social or political tastes of school board members." *Id.* at 582. Considering an order of a school board to remove a book from its junior high library the board found offensive, the Second Circuit saw no substantial constitutional issue at all. *Presidents Council v. Community School Bd.*, No. 25, 457 F.2d 289 (2d Cir.), *cert. denied*, 409 U.S. 998, 93 S.Ct. 308, 34 L.Ed.2d 260 (1972). It said:

> After a careful review of the record before us and the precedents we find no impingement upon any basic constitutional values. Since we are dealing not with the collection of a public book store but with the library of a public junior high school, evidently some authorized person or body has to make determination as to what the library collection will be. It is predictable that no matter what choice of books may be made by whatever segment of academe, some other person or group may well dissent. The ensuing shouts of book burning, witch hunting and violation of academic freedom hardly elevate this intramural strife to first amendment constitutional proportions. If it did, there would be a constant intrusion of the judiciary into the internal affairs of the school. Academic freedom is scarcely fostered by the intrusion of three or even nine federal jurists making curriculum or library choices for the community of scholars. When the court has intervened, the circumstances have been rare and extreme and the issues presented totally distinct from those we have here. See Developments in the Law—Academic Freedom, 81 Harv.L.Rev. 1045, 1051-1054 (1968).

457 F.2d at 291-92.

The instant case, of course, involves prohibiting high school teachers from assigning books which they had used previously and want to use again in classes where "a constitutionally proper decision-maker" could find them appropriate. Thus we are presented with a conflict between the school board's powers over curriculum and the teachers' rights to classroom expression in a context somewhat different and more sharply drawn than any case which has arisen heretofore. We will decide only the case before us, and cannot answer all of the questions raised by the commentators interested in this area.[4]

The parties before us state the proposition for decision somewhat differently one from the other. The teachers acknowledge the right of the school board to prescribe the curriculum and the principal textbooks used in the courses. They agree the school board does not have to offer the three courses at issue here; but they say that once the courses have been approved the teachers' "right of academic freedom includes the right to use non-obscene materials electively in elective courses taught to high school students." They do not ask the board to purchase or endorse certain books; they do not seek to require a student to read materials against the student's will; but they want to be free from restrictions "based upon the personal predilection of members of the school board."

The school board on the other hand states its position as follows:

A teacher is free to comment upon, or to recommend that any student read any of the ten books. Except as indicated below, he may discuss any of the books during class. Outside of class, a teacher may meet with any student anywhere, at anytime, for any length of time, for the purpose of reading or discussing any book. No student is prohibited from reading any book, except in class or otherwise for course credit . . . Classroom discussion of nonselected works is proscribed only when it becomes so protracted as to approximate or exceed the amount of class time spent on selected works or to effectively require that the student read the book in order to understand and benefit from class discussions. In short, the proscription relates only to activities which in substance, if not form, would reinstate the nonselected work on the reading list from which it was deliberately removed.

Reply Brief, p. 10.

The concession by the school board is important. We think teachers do have some rights to freedom of expression in the classroom, teaching high school juniors and seniors. They cannot be made to simply read from a script prepared or approved by the board. As Mr. Justice Stewart noted in *Epperson*, the teacher cannot be punished for letting students know other languages are spoken in the world, or mentioning the existence of a system of respected human thought. Censorship or suppression of expression of opinion, even in the classroom, should be tolerated only when there is a legitimate interest of the state which can be said to require priority. See *West Virginia State Bd. of Educ. v. Barnette*, 319 U.S. 624, 633, 63 S.Ct. 1178, 87 L.Ed. 1628 (1943). Students' speech cannot be stifled for mere "undifferentiated fear or apprehension of disturbance," nor from a desire to avoid controversy "without evidence that it is necessary to avoid material and substantial interference with school work or discipline." *Tinker v. Des Moines Independent Community School Dist.*, 393 U.S. 503, 508, 511, 89 S.Ct. 733, 737, 739, 21 L.Ed.2d 731 (1969). Surely there is some carryover of these principles to teachers' expressions in the context of course work and classroom teaching.

At the same time we must recognize that the Supreme Court has ruled there is no constitutional right to an education. *San Antonio Independent School Dist. v. Rodriguez*, 411 U.S. 1, 35, 93 S.Ct. 1278, 36 L.Ed.2d 16 (1973). Whether there is a public education system is left to the states. Colorado has assumed the responsibility, and its constitution, Art. IX, § 15, provides the local school boards "shall have control of instruction in the public schools of their respective districts." It is recognized that these local decision-makers may determine what subjects are taught, even selecting ones which promote a particular viewpoint. See *West Virginia Bd. of Educ. v. Barnette*, 319 U.S. 624, 631, 63 S.Ct. 1178, 87 L.Ed. 1628 (1943). It is legitimate for the curriculum of the school district to reflect the value system and educational emphasis which are the collective will of those whose children are being educated and who are paying the costs. We recognized this in *Adams v. Campbell City School Dist.*, 511 F.2d 1242, 1247 (10th Cir. 1975), where we said:

Plaintiffs also argue that teachers have a First Amendment right to discuss controversial subjects and use controversial materials in the classroom. Undoubtedly they have some freedom in the techniques to be employed, but this does not say that they have an unlimited liberty as to structure and content of the courses, at least at the secondary level. Thus in a small community like Gillette the Board members and the principal surely have a right to emphasize a more orthodox approach, for example, and it would seem that they may insist that record playing and current events do interfere with this program. We have found no law which allows a high school teacher to have the broad latitude which appellants seek.

If the board may decide that Contemporary Poetry may not be offered; if it may select the major text of the course; why may it not go further and exclude certain books from being assigned for instruction in the course? As we understand these language arts courses there is no basic text, or if there is one it is utilized only for a portion of the class study. A large part of the instructional time is review and discussion of items selected by students, with consent of the teacher, from the reading list. As adopted by the board the list contained altogether 1,275 titles approved for the three courses. Thus it can be said with some justification the texts adopted by the school board for these courses is the reading list. That, we believe, is the proper view of the situation before us; and the board was acting within its rights in omitting the books, even though the decision was a political one influenced by the personal views of the members.

We agree with the board characterization of the stipulation that it does not prohibit mention of these books in class, nor treatment by the teacher of the books as examples of contemporary poetry, literature or American masters. The ban is upon such extended reference or use in class as to constitute class assignments which in effect evade the exercise of discretion made by the board in its determination of the parameters of the courses.

Since the board gave no reasons for its refusal to approve these books we considered a remand to ascertain that the reasons were constitutionally permissible. It is at least clear the board could not structure its text designation to promote a particular religious viewpoint. *Epperson v. Arkansas, supra.* We also considered remand because the board adopted criteria for the approval of books by the committee charged with the duty to review, yet the board itself gave no reasons for its decision with respect to the ten books rejected. But the stipulation declares that no systemic effort was made "to exclude any particular type of thinking or book." And no objection was made that the board was not following its own standards in rejecting the books. The approved list is broad, containing 1,275 books for the three courses. No objection is made by the teachers that the exclusions prevent them from studying an entire representative group of writers. Rather the teachers want to be freed from the "personal predilections" of the board. We do not see a basis in the constitution to grant their wish.

The trial court entered judgment in favor of the defendant board and its members. Although we place our holding upon a different basis, we affirm that judgment.

WILLIAM E. DOYLE, Circuit Judge, concurring.

I concur in the result and in most of what appears in the opinion. I would, however, approach it somewhat differently. I would disapprove of any arbitrary selection of books that can be read and those which cannot be on the reading list. One can read the majority as, in effect, making such a ruling.

However, the court does not say it. It recognizes that the School Board has a broad right to select texts and to exclude textbooks. The approach which I prefer would be that the exclusion of books for secondary school students is not to be an arbitrary exclusion. Therefore, reasons have to be given so that there can be court review. If they are excluded because the Board member disapproves for a subjective reason, I would say that this is an unlawful and unconstitutional invasion of the classroom.

So, with the above exceptions, I concur in the submitted opinion.

NOTES

1. The banned volumes were:
   a. Contemporary Literature:
      (1) *A Clockwork Orange* by Anthony Burgess;
      (2) *The Exorcist* by William P. Blatty;
      (3) *The Reincarnation of Peter Proud* by Max Ehrlich.
   b. Contemporary Poetry:
      (1) *New American Poetry* by Donald Allen;
      (2) *Starting from San Francisco* by Lawrence Ferlinghetti;
      (3) *The Yage Letters* by William Burroughs and Allen Ginsberg;
      (4) *Coney Island of the Mind* by Lawrence Ferlinghetti;
      (5) *Kaddish and Other Poems* by Allen Ginsberg;
      (6) *Lunch Poems* by Frank O'Hara.
   c. American Masters:
      Rosemary's Baby by Ira Levin.
2. The term "academic freedom," of course, encompasses much more than teaching-related speech rights of teachers. *See Developments in the Law—Academic Freedom,* 81 Harv.L.Rev. 1045 (1968).
3. The decision might well have been supportable on other grounds. See Goldstein, *The Asserted Constitutional Right of Public School Teachers to Determine What They Teach,* 124 U.Pa.L.Rev. 1293, 1306 n.42 (1976). *Meyer* has survived generally to be viewed as a parental rights case standing as authority that parents have some constitutional rights to raise their children as they see fit. *Id.* at 1307-1308.
4. See, e. g., Goldstein, *supra,* note 3: Miller, *Teachers' Freedom of Expression Within the Classroom: A Search for Standards,* 8 Ga.L.Rev. 837 (1974); Van Alstyne, *The Constitutional Rights of Teachers and Professors,* 1970 Duke L.J. 841.

A United States District Court in Mississippi decides for several students, teachers, and authors who had challenged the manner and procedure used by the state "rating committee" in rejecting a history textbook which contained "perspectives on history at odds with those traditionally acceptable in Mississippi." The plaintiffs argued that the motivation behind the rejection of the textbook was based on race and the Court stated in its opinion that "several factors lead this Court to conclude that the plaintiffs have sustained their burden. First, the reasons given by some committee members for rejecting the textbook indicate that race was a motivating factor. These statements . . . indicate without question that some members were influenced by the racial issues." Further, the Court declared that "it is persuaded to intervene in this conflict precisely because this is a case which 'directly and sharply' implicates constitutional values. It does so because the defendants have provided no method by which the plaintiffs may safeguard their First Amendment freedoms. All interested parties, whether they be textbook editors, teachers, parents, or students, have a fundamental interest in maintaining a free and open educational system that provides for the acquisition of useful knowledge."

Loewen v. *Turnipseed*, 488 F.Supp. 1138 (1980)

ORMA R. SMITH, District Judge.

The action sub judice is before the court after an eight-day nonjury trial for decision on the merits. The court has received and given consideration to the post-trial memoranda and proposed findings of fact and conclusions of law submitted by the parties as well as all pretrial submissions. Based upon the pleadings, the evidence, exhibits and memoranda and proposed findings of fact and the conclusions of law submitted by the parties, this Memorandum of Decision is released and contains the findings of fact and conclusions of law for which provision is made in Rule 52 (a), Fed. R.Civ.P.

I. *Findings of fact.*
   A. *The Parties.*
The plaintiffs named in the complaint, as amended, (hereinafter "complaint") are: James W. Loewen and Charles Sallis, the editors and two of the eight co-authors of *Mississippi: Conflict and Change,* a ninth grade textbook in Mississippi History; Monseigneur Paul v. Canonici, Director of Educational Services of the Diocese of Natchez-Jackson, and, as such, the chief

administrative officer of Roman Catholic parochial schools within the diocese, which schools are alleged to be qualified to participate in the Mississippi free textbook program; Father Luke Mikschl, Principal of the Holy Child Jesus Elementary and High School, Canton, Mississippi, a Roman Catholic parochial school; Sister Maureen Sullivan, a teacher of Mississippi History at Holy Child Jesus School; Gregory C. Coleman, Stephen G. Lloyd, Theon E. Lloyd, and Hailicia D. Lloyd, black students enrolled in grades nine, seven, five, and kindergarten, respectively, at Holy Child Jesus School who join in this action through their mother and next friend, Mrs. Alease C. Lloyd; Jacquelyn Ann Chinn, Marie Theresa Chinn, and Madelin Chinn, black students enrolled in grades nine, eight, and four, respectively, at the Holy Child Jesus Elementary School, who join in this action through their mother and next friend, Mrs. Mamie Chinn; the County Board of Education of Jefferson County, Mississippi, together with its president and individual members; the Superintendent and Assistant Superintendent of Education of the Jefferson County, Mississippi School District, a Mississippi public school district; Willie R. Harding and Hennie B. Taylor, teachers of Mississippi History and related subjects in the Jefferson County School District; Nancy Humphrey and Tara Humphrey, black students enrolled in grades nine and eight, respectively, in the Jefferson County School District, who join in this action through their father and mother and next friends, Charles and Dorothy Humphrey; and Catherine Gilmer Gray, a white student enrolled in grade eight at the St. Andrew Episcopal Day School, Jackson, Mississippi, who joins in this action through her father and next friend, the Right Reverend Duncan M. Gray, Jr.

The defendants named in the complaint are John Turnipseed, Howard Riales, Ben Burney, Evelyn Wilder, Mary Kyle, Virginia McElhaney, and James Wash, individually and in their official capacities and collectively as the full membership of the "rating committee" appointed by Mississippi's Governor and State Superintendent of Education to appraise, and, in the exercise of their judgment, recommend textbooks submitted by publishers for use in a required high school course of study, Mississippi History, as provided by § 37-43-21 of the Mississippi Code of 1972, Annotated; the Mississippi State Textbook Purchasing Board, its members The Governor of the State of Mississippi, the Superintendent of Education of the State of Mississippi, Larry Tynes, L. L. Morrison, Sr., and Jean McCool, and its Executive Secretary, W. A. Matthews, in their individual and official capacities.[1]

B.   Nature of Action.

This suit arises from the actions of the "rating committee" defendants in refusing to recommend for adoption as a textbook in the course of Mississippi History, the book *Mississippi: Conflict and Change* edited by the plaintiffs, Dr. Loewen and Dr. Sallis, who are also two of the authors of the book, and in recommending for adopting in the course of Mississippi History the book *Your Mississippi*, by Dr. John K. Bettersworth. Plaintiffs claim that said actions of the "rating committee" defendants, and of the Mississippi State Textbook Purchasing Board, and its members, in ratifying the actions of the "rating committee" defendants, deprived them of their rights guaranteed and secured by the First, Thirteenth and Fourteenth Amendments to the Constitution of the United States, 42 U.S.C. § 1981 and § 1983. Jurisdiction is vested in this court pursuant to 28 U.S.C. § 1343(3) and (4).

C.   The Nature of Relief Sought.

Plaintiffs request the court to grant the following relief:

(1) An order enjoining defendants to forthwith promulgate and implement procedures, consistent with due process, for hearings on textbooks submitted to state authorities for adoption;

(2) An order enjoining defendants from limiting the submission and appraisal of textbooks to intervals longer than one year;[2]

(3) An order enjoining defendants to forthwith approve for use in eligible schools of the state, at state expense, the textbook *Mississippi: Conflict and Change;*

(4) An order enjoining defendants from engaging in policies or practices which discriminate against textbooks containing perspectives on history at odds with those traditionally acceptable in Mississippi;

(5) A judgment declaring § 37-43-21 of the Mississippi Code of 1972 unconstitutional;[3]

(6) An injunction enjoining defendants from denying approval to any submitted textbook which meets minimum standards of scholarship, satisfies fundamental and reasonable curriculum requirements and which obtains the endorsement of a local school district board of education and its rating committee;[4]

(7) An order awarding plaintiffs costs and reasonable attorneys' fees;

(8) An order granting such additional or alternative relief as the court deems just and equitable.

D.   The Applicable State Law.

The pertinent laws of the State of Mississippi governing the process of recommending and adopting books for use as textbooks in the eligible schools of the State of Mississippi are found in Chapter 43, Title 37 (§§ 37-43-1, et seq.) Mississippi Code of 1972, Annotated. This chapter is entitled "Textbooks". The sections pertinent to the action sub judice are set forth verbatim in Appendix "A" to this Memorandum.

E.   The Evidence.

In the fall of 1974, the Mississippi State Textbook Purchasing Board, pursuant to rules and regulations adopted by it based on the authority delegated to it by § 37-43-19, caused notices to be sent to the representatives of publishers advising that qualified publishers might submit proposals for the sale of books for use as textbooks, in various courses of study, including the subject of Mississippi History, to be taught at the ninth grade level. In response to the Board's notice, the following books were submitted by publishers for rating and adopting as textbooks in the course of Mississippi History: Steck-Vaughn Company submitted the book *Your Mississippi* by Dr. John K. Bettersworth; and Pantheon Books, a Division of Random House, submitted *Mississippi: Conflict and Change* edited by the plaintiffs, Dr. James W. Loewen and Dr. Charles Sallis.

As mandated by the provisions of § 37-43-21 of the Mississippi Code, and in accord with the practices and procedures of the Board, these two books were submitted to a rating committee for appraisal and recommendation. In accordance with the statute, the Governor of the State of Mississippi, then Honorable William L. Waller, and the Superintendent of Education of the State of Mississippi, then Dr. Garvin L. Johnston, appointed as members of said rating committee the defendants Burney, Kyle, McElhaney, Riales, Turnipseed, Wash, and Wilder. Based on its statutory authority to promulgate rules and regulations relating to the rating and adoption of textbooks, the State Textbook Purchasing Board had established certain criteria for use by rating committees in rating proposed textbooks in Mississippi History. These criteria were furnished by the Board to the defendant members of the rating committee and consisted of (1) the Board's memorandum to rating committee members, Ex., P-6; (2) the Board's pamphlet, "Suggested Criteria for Textbook Selection," Ex., P-7; and (3) the State curriculum for Mississippi History contained in Mississippi School Bulletin, "Social Studies in the Junior High School," (April, 1967), Ex., P-8.

The defendant rating committee members in due course appraised and rated the two books submitted to them in the course of Mississippi History. The ratings given by each defendant on each book are as follows:

Benjamin B. Burney, Jr., gave the textbook *Your Mississippi* a rating of "2", and the textbook *Mississippi: Conflict and Change* a rating of "1."

Mary Kyle gave the textbook *Your Mississippi* a rating of "2", and the textbook *Mississippi: Conflict and Change* "no rating."

Virginia Wilkins McElhaney gave the textbook *Your Mississippi* a rating of "1", and the textbook *Mississippi: Conflict and Change* "no rating."

Howard E. Riales gave the textbook *Your Mississippi* a rating of "1", and the textbook *Mississippi: Conflict and Change* "no rating."

John Marion Turnipseed gave the textbook *Your Mississippi* a rating of "1", and the textbook *Mississippi: Conflict and Change* "no rating."

James E. Wash gave the textbook *Your Mississippi* a rating of "1", and the textbook *Mississippi: Conflict and Change* a rating of "2".

Evelyn Harvey Wilder gave the textbook *Your Mississippi* a rating of "1", and the textbook *Mississippi: Conflict and Change* "no rating."

The defendant rating committee members Kyle, McElhaney, Riales, Turnipseed, and Wilder are members of the White race; the defendant rating committee members Burney and Wash are Negroes.

The rating committee members returned their appraisals of the two books to the Office of the State Textbook Purchasing Board. Because of the procedures established by § 37-43-21 of the Mississippi Code, the State Textbook Purchasing Board had no authority to adopt the book *Mississippi: Conflict and Change* for use as a textbook in the course of Mississippi History.

Said § 37-43-21 provides, in pertinent part, that "in no case shall the board adopt any book not recommended by the rating committees." Said § 37-43-21 also stipulates "no book shall be recommended which does not receive a majority vote of the members of each committee." Only two of the seven members of the rating committee, defendants Burney and Wash, gave a rating to *Mississippi: Conflict and Change;* a rating by a minimum of four of said rating committee members was necessary to recommend said book to the State Textbook Purchasing Board for adoption.

The book *Your Mississippi* received a rating from all seven members of the rating committee and was eligible to be adopted by the State Textbook Purchasing Board as a textbook in the course of Mississippi History. The State Textbook Purchasing Board did adopt *Your Mississippi* for use as a Mississippi History textbook for a period of four years, to be extended for an additional two years.

The procedures followed by the Mississippi State Textbook Purchasing Board and the members of the rating committee during the adoption process were those generally followed in accordance with the applicable statutes of the State of Mississippi and the rules and regulations of the Textbook Purchasing Board. For the purpose of evaluating and rating books for adoption as textbooks for the 1974 textbook adoption proceedings, the defendant members of the rating committee were appointed, according to statute, by the Governor of Mississippi and the Superintendent of Education of the State of Mississippi, for the general area of the curriculum designated as "Social Studies, Career, Humanities, 7-9." There were 10 courses of study embraced within this area of the curriculum, including the course of Mississippi History to be taught at the ninth grade level. There were 106 books submitted by publishers for adoption in this area of the curriculum, which were evaluated and rated by the defendant members of the rating committee.

After receiving notice of their appointment as members of the rating committee, the rating committee members were requested by the Textbook Purchasing Board to attend, and did attend, a meeting held in the auditorium of the Woolfolk State Office Building in Jackson, Mississippi, on August 28, 1974. Members of all rating committees appointed for the 1974 adoption proceedings were present at this meeting, as well as the Governor, the Superintendent of Education, officials of the Textbook Purchasing Board, and certified publisher's representatives. At this meeting, the defendant members of the rating committee received copies of a number of documents, including the *Suggested Criteria* (Ex., P-7), "Mississippi Textbook Adoption," (Ex., D-13), summary evaluation forms for each book to be considered for adoption, and a list of all certified publisher's representatives who were the only persons authorized to present books to the rating committee members during the rating process.

Under the schedule established by the Textbook Purchasing Board, the rating committee reports, otherwise known as the "ballots," and the accompanying summary evaluation forms were due to be received at the Office of the Textbook Purchasing Board from the rating committee members no later than October 23, 1974. During the interim between the meeting of August 28 and the deadline of October 23, the rating committee members received copies of the books to be evaluated and rated, either through mail or by personal delivery from a publisher's representative. At various times during this interim period while the work of the rating committee members was being accomplished, publisher's representatives were making appointments with, and presentation to, the individual members of the rating committee for the purposes of relating pertinent facts about the book being presented and of answering any questions about the book which the rating committee member might have. During this period, the raitng committee members rated and reviewed the books under consideration for adoption, including *Mississippi: Conflict and Change.*

Approximately two weeks prior to the October 23 deadline for receipt of the "ballots" and summary evaluation forms, the Office of the Textbook Purchasing Board mailed to each member of the rating committee a "ballot" for each course of study for which books were to be rated and recommended for adoption, along with a Memorandum of Instructions for rating books (Ex., P-6). In evaluating and rating the books for adoption, including the books submitted for the course of Mississippi History, the members of the rating committee were guided by the documents previously mentioned furnished them by the Textbook Purchasing Board, especially the *Suggested Criteria for Textbook Selection* (Ex., P-7). The members of the rating committee completed their work, filled out their rating committee report and summary evaluation forms, and mailed them to the Textbook Purchasing Board in Jackson, Mississippi, for arrival on or before October 23, 1974. The staff of the Textbook Purchasing Board tabulated the results of the "ballots" mailed in by the rating committee members, and the Mississippi State Textbook Purchasing Board held a meeting on November 4, 1974, and adopted the recommendations of the rating committtee by placing on the adopted list for the course of Mississippi History the book *Your Mississippi* by Dr. John K. Bettersworth. The Textbook Purchasing Board was precluded by provisions of state law from considering *Mississippi: Conflict and Change* for adoption, because that book failed to receive a recommendation from a majority of the rating committee members.

One salient fact should be noted with regard to the rating process as to the books submitted for consideration in the course of Mississippi History. Each rating committee member was visited by a representative from Steck-Vaughn Company, publisher of *Your Mississippi*, for the purpose of presenting that book. This publisher's representative made a positive presentation of that book, and answered questions that the members of the rating committee had about it. The Steck-Vaughn representative left with each rating committee member, in manuscript form, a copy of a Teacher's Edition to accompany *Your Mississippi*. The Teacher's Edition which accompanies *Your Mississippi* was introduced into evidence in printed form by the defendants in this case (Ex., D-17). The Teacher's Edition of *Your Mississippi* is the same as the edition for use by students, except that the first 60 pages contain material to aid the teacher in teaching the course. The representative from Pantheon Books, a Division of Random House, also visited each member of the rating committee. This representative did not make a positive presentation of the book *Mississippi: Conflict and Change.* He stated to the rating committee members, Mrs. McElhaney, Miss Kyle, Mrs. Kennington, and Mr. Turnipseed that no Teacher's Edition would be available to accompany *Mississippi: Conflict and Change.* He stated to the rating committee member, Mr. Riales, that a Teacher's Edition was not then presently available, but would be available in the future.

The plaintiffs, Dr. James Loewen and Dr. Charles Sallis, testified at the trial that a Teacher's Edition of *Mississippi: Conflict and Change* was available in manuscript form during the 1974 adoption period, but that it was not furnished to the publisher's representative who presented that book to the rating committee members.

The statutes of the State of Mississippi, the rules and regulations of the Textbook Purchasing Board, and the testimony of Mr. W. A. Matthews, Executive Secretary of the Mississippi State Textbook Purchasing Board, make it clear that the only parties to a textbook adoption proceeding in Mississippi are: (1) the members of the various rating committees; (2) the certified publisher's representatives, who are the only persons authorized to make presentations of books to members of the rating committee; and (3) the Mississippi State Textbook Purchasing Board, the members thereof, its executive secretary, and staff.

The *Suggested Criteria for Textbook Selection*, (Ex., P-7), which guided the members of the rating committee in their work, contains 16 general criteria and five specific criteria. Criterion No. 5 of the specific criteria states that each book proposed for adoption should be accompanied by a teacher's edition, one copy to be furnished free for each 25 copies to be used by the students. Criterion No. 6 of the general criteria provides that each text should either contain appropriate suggestions for teachers or be accompanied by a separate teacher's manual.

As has been noted, the two black members of the rating committee, Burney and Wash, rated and recommended the Loewen and Sallis text, *Mississippi: Conflict and Change* (1974). The five white members of the committee, Kyle, McElhaney, Riales, Turnipseed and Wilder, rated and recommended the Bettersworth text, *Your Mississippi* (1975) but failed to recommend the Loewen and Sallis text, *Mississippi: Conflict and Change*. The Textbook Purchasing Board had the statutory power to reject the recommendations of the rating committee and call for further recommendations, but was not empowered to adopt the Loewen and Sallis text, *Mississippi: Conflict and Change* (1974) because the book had not been recommended by the rating committee.

Each rating board member was charged with the duty of making known to the purchasing board the basis of his or her acceptance or rejection of a textbook. The five members of the board who rejected the Loewen and Sallis text, *Mississippi: Conflict and Change,* had an obligation to state in writing his or her reasons for the rejection.

The Textbook Purchasing Board furnished each rating committee member with a Summary Evaluation Form to be completed on each textbook submitted and to be returned to the board with the completed ballot representing such member's vote.

The ballot and the summary evaluation forms on *Your Mississippi* and *Mississippi: Conflict and Change* by committeeman John M. Turnipseed, were introduced in evidence as Plaintiffs' Exhibit 14. A copy of this exhibit is attached as Appendix B and made a part of this Memorandum by reference.

Each committee member was required to submit similar documents.

Mr. Turnipseed's reason, as reflected by the summary evaluation form, for rejecting *Mississippi: Conflict and Change* was "It is my professional opinion that this book is 'unsuitable' for classroom use, therefore, I cannot recommend it in any manner".

Mr. Turnipseed's evaluation of the Bettersworth book *Your Mississippi*, was "average".

Mr. Riales rated *Your Mississippi* as "high". In regard to *Mississippi: Conflict and Change*, Riales rejected the book. He identified the content of the book considered objectionable to him as "page 96–Last Paragraph; page 178–Picture at the bottom of the page". In explaining the effect the objectionable content he assumed to have on the learner, he stated

This is only two examples of many in the book. Continuous coverage of isolated incidents of the mistreatment (sic) of slaves and blacks by whites could easily lead the readers to believe that all slaves and

blacks were treated in the same manner. I feel that this book is too racially oriented and does not concentrate sufficiently on the areas as suggested in the criteria.

Ms. Kyle did not give any reason on the summary evaluation form for *Mississippi: Conflict and Change* for her rejection of the book.

Ms. Wilder's only comment on her summary evaluation form for *Mississippi: Conflict and Change* was given in responding to the request that she identify the content considered objectionable. There she entered on the form "none applicable at this grade level".

Stating her reasons for rejecting *Mississippi: Conflict and Change,* Mrs. McElhaney, when requested to describe the effect that the objectionable content is assumed to have on the learner, stated:

I do not feel that the ideas concentrated on this text are expressed in terms of the junior high student. Perhaps for college level and mature adult. It also does not meet requirement as a textbook. Readability level too high. I do not feel that the overall content presents a true picture of the history of Miss. in terms of the prescribed course pre-requisite.

At trial, rating committee members advanced other reasons for rejecting *Mississippi: Conflict and Change*. As the trier of the facts, however, the court views the testimony of each member of the rating committee wherein reasons for rejection were given other than those reflected on the summary evaluation form, as an after-the-fact judgment.

The court feels that if the reasons given at trial to support the ballots of the five rating committee members in rejecting *Mississippi: Conflict and Change* other than those reflected by the summary evaluation forms, had been substantial and played an important role in the rejection, such reasons would have been inserted in the summary evaluation forms.

One reason for rejecting *Mississippi: Conflict and Change* given at trial was that the publisher did not furnish each rating member a teacher's edition, as required by the rules governing the submissions of textbooks.

The pretrial order provides:

"(7) *Mississippi: Conflict and Change* was submitted in accordance with all standards—procedural and technical—established by regulations promulgated by the State Textbook Purchasing Board." Pre-Trial Order, p. 4b.

The suggested criteria for Textbook Selection (Ex. P-7, p. 6) provides:

"5. Special Instructions: Teacher's manual should be available free—one for each 25 student books sold. These will be supplied from the depository. Hard back required."

This criterion does not require submission of a teacher's edition with the textbook submission. General Criterion 6 (Ex. P-7, p. 1) provides:

"6. Each text should either contain appropriate suggestions for teachers or be accompanied by a separate teacher's manual."

No notice is given that this requirement is mandatory; it is stated under the heading "*Suggested* Criteria for Textbook Selection" (emphasis added). Dr. Loewen testified that a draft teacher's edition was available at the time of the submission, that the publisher's representative, Mr. Herb Stanley, told him that he had informed rating committee members that a teacher's edition would be available if the book was adopted. Dr. Loewen also testified that a teacher's edition in final form (Ex. P-33) is available now. Mr. Turnipseed testified that Mr. Stanley told him that a teacher's edition would be available if the book was adopted.

Further, General Criterion 6 is phrased in the disjunctive; no teacher's manual is even necessary if the text contains "appropriate suggestions for teachers." The evidence in this case is clear that the textbook, *Mississippi: Conflict and Change,* contains numerous "appropriate suggestions for teachers." The book is filled with questions for class discussions (e.g., pp. 8, 13, 18, 21, 29, 61, 67, etc.), maps and other illustrations, definitions of terms used, special projects, suggestions for field trips, and, at the end of each chapter, an annotated bibliography. The rating committee members were unanimous in their testimony that the attitude of the publisher's representation in no way influenced their decision to reject the book.

The court finds that the failure of the publisher of *Mississippi: Conflict and Change* to furnish each rating committee member with a teacher's edition in final form, under the existing circumstances, did not contribute in a substantial way to its rejection.

The defendants introduced evidence questioning the value of *Mississippi: Conflict and Change* on several grounds, that is (1) the lack of proper emphasis in certain subjects; (2) readability and vocabulary; (3) organization of the text; and (4) pictures and captions. The court finds that the evidence does not sustain defendants' position with regard to any of these issues.

Admittedly there were some errors in the captions given to some of the pictures portrayed in the book. This was admitted by the editors. The errors are easily correctible and were not such as to justify the rejection of the book.

The court concludes that the textbook *Mississippi: Conflict and Change* was not rejected for any justifiable reason. The textbook was submitted in accordance with all standards—procedural and technical—established by the regulations and promulgated by the Mississippi State Textbook Purchasing Board.

The Mississippi Statute, Section 37-43-21 expressly provides that:

"[i]t shall be the duty of said rating committees to appraise the books offered for adoption in each field in which textbooks are offered for adoption and recommend five books for each adoption to be made by the board and giving reasons for or basis of such recommendations".

Here the only textbooks in the course of Mississippi History for grade nine students submitted for approval to the committee were the Bettersworth textbook *Your Mississippi* and the Loewen-Sallis textbook *Mississippi: Conflict and Change.* Yet, the majority of the committee recommended only the one—*Your Mississippi.*

The rating committee's action deprived the Mississippi Public Grade schools and such private schools as may qualify for free textbooks, and the teachers and students in those schools, of having available as a course of study in Mississippi history the Loewen-Sallis textbook *Mississippi: Conflict and Change.*

The record reflects that from July 1, 1975 to July 1, 1978, the Mississippi State Textbook Purchasing Board had purchased and loaned to eligible pupils in the schools of the state a total of 33,605 of Bettersworth's *Your Mississippi,* and since July 1, 1978 an estimated number of additional copies of this book have been purchased and loaned by Mississippi Textbook Purchasing Board to eligible pupils.

On November 8, 1974, having learned through unofficial news reports that the constituent rating committee had rejected *Mississippi: Conflict and Change,* Dr. Loewen wrote a letter to defendant Matthews, Executive Secretary of the Purchasing Board, requesting information as to the reasons for the rejection. Mr. Matthews replied on November 15, 1974, expressing surprise in regard to the letter, stating that all the Textbook Board's official communications are made to publishing companies, and the first publication had been made to the publishers on November 4, 1974. Dr. Loewen was referred to his publishing company for further information.

Dr. Sallis and Miss Jean Middleton attended a meeting of the purchasing board on February 11, 1975 to plead the cause of *Mississippi: Conflict and Change.*

Their presentation is reflected in plaintiffs' exhibit P-35. After the meeting adjourned, Mr. Mathews wrote them a letter in which he stated,

"Since the Board has no authority to conduct a formal hearing, no power to redirect committees to re-evaluate their ratings of textbooks, and no power to receive petitions relating thereto, the Board is returning all materials submitted by you at the meeting."

The State of Mississippi has foreclosed every avenue of approach for plaintiffs and the members of the class represented by them in the action sub judice to a hearing of any kind in which the merits of *Mississippi: Conflict and Change* can be presented. The matter is forever foreclosed—the decision of the rating committee stands without any avenue of challenge. The authors and editors of the book and the teachers, parents and pupils making up the plaintiffs' class have no way open to them to challenge the rating committee's action except by recourse to the courts of this country for redress of their grievances.

The evidence submitted by plaintiffs sustains the holding that such was the intention of the state legislature in the enactment of the Textbook Chapter of the Code, Chapter 43, of Title 37, Miss.Code 1972. The Mississippi legislature does not record the legislative history of the enactment of its laws.

The only recorded evidence of the legislative intent capable of production are news items carried in the newspapers contemporaneously with the deliberations of the legislative bodies. These items are trustworthy and can be accepted as correct accounts of events occurring in the legislative halls. Documentary evidence of this type was introduced at trial and convinced the court that the legislative intent was to create a statutory procedure which would vest in the hands of the Governor and Superintendent of Education of the State the power to control the destiny of any textbook offered for adoption by the State Purchasing Board. The intended purpose was accomplished in the case of *Mississippi: Conflict and Change.*

The context in which this statutory procedure was created, as evidenced by the newspaper clippings introduced at trial, clearly reveals an intent on the part of the legislature to eliminate allegedly controversial material from the schools' curriculum, and to insure that only the views of those in authority would be communicated to school children. In 1960, for example, when the present statutory mechanism for the selection of rating committee members was adopted, the Governor of the state supported the bill with these words:

Failure of the House to act favorable upon this bill will, I very much fear, hamper our efforts to clean up our public school textbooks and give our children the instruction material they must have if they are to be properly informed of the Southern and true American way of life.

Ex. P-61. Earlier legislative history of the passage of the first free textbook law reveals an even more adamant intent on the part of the legislature to insure that textbook selection reflected the predominant racial attitudes of the day. *See,* Ex. P-61. The court finds that the statutory procedure regarding textbook approval was established so that the Governor and Superintendent of Education could control, without responsibility to a higher authority, the textbooks selected for use in Mississippi schools, and thereby influence the schools' curriculum. This purpose was insured success by the lack of recourse given to those adversely affected by a rating committee's decision.

The court has previously found that the textbook *Mississippi: Conflict and Change,* was not rejected for any justifiable reason. Further analysis of the evidence presented reveals that the rejection of this textbook was motivated and influenced by racial issues. The evidence shows that Mr. Riales considered the book to be "too racially oriented." Mrs. McElhaney stated that "the overall content" of the book did not present "a true picture of the history of Mississippi." Of course, these views are only those of two committee members. The other members either did not elaborate on their reasons for rejection, or gave no reasons at all. The court finds, however, that the evidence is sufficient to conclude that the treatment which the book gave to controversial racial issues was a factor which led to its rejection. Based upon the suggested criteria for textbook selection, the court finds that this controversial treatment of racial issues was not a justifiable reason for rejection by the committee.

The evidence also reveals that the textbook *Mississippi: Conflict and Change,* received a number of favorable reviews and comments in scholarly publications related to educational issues. One study compared the two textbooks considered by the rating committee and concluded that "By any reasonable criteria, including those used by the Mississippi review committee, *Conflict and Change* is not only eligible for adoption, but is far superior in format and content to all history textbooks we have seen". Ex. P-52. In addition, correspondence to the editors from faculty members at several prominent universities reveals that the book was favorably received in academic circles. Ex. P-26. While this evidence does not indicate that the criteria used by the textbook committee were necessarily incorrect, it does indicate that the textbook met certain other criteria in the academic community. This leads the court to find that other, nonjustifiable factors influenced the committee's rejection of the textbook.

II. *Conclusions of Law.*

A. *Standing to Sue.*

Before proceeding to the merits of this action, the court must first address itself to the defendants' contention that plaintiffs lack standing to pursue this action, in that they have failed to show the deprivation of a "legally cognizable right". The court notes that this preliminary objection is usually raised in cases which present novel constitutional issues, perhaps because the question of standing "is founded in concern about the proper—and properly limited—role of the courts in a democratic society." *Warth* v. *Seldin*, 422 U.S. 490, 498, 95 S.Ct. 2197, 45 L.Ed.2d 343, 354 (1975). The court is not convinced, however, that the issues in this case are particularly novel ones, or that the action extends beyond the court's proper societal role. To put it as simply as possible, the plaintiffs allege that the defendants' conduct deprived them of certain fundamental rights which are constitutionally guaranteed. On that basis, they assert that they have a direct interest in the outcome of this litigation, an interest which entitled them "to have the court decide the merits of the dispute . . . " *Warth* v. *Seldin*, 422 U.S. at 498, 95 S.Ct. at 2205, 45 L.Ed.2d at 354.

The requisite standing to maintain an action can only be "demonstrated by a plaintiff who has a personal interest in the outcome of the controversy, . . . " *Finch* v. *Mississippi State Medical Ass'n. Inc.*, 585 F.2d 765, 771 (5th Cir. 1978). This question of "personal interest" or "personal stake" in the outcome is generally determined through the analysis of two separate requirements: (1) whether or not there has been an "injury in fact"; and (2) whether or not "the interest sought to be protected is arguably within the zone of interests to be protected or regulated by the statute or constitutional guarantee in question." *United States* v. *Gurney*, 558 F.2d 1202, 1206 (5th Cir.), *rehearing denied*, 562 F.2d 1257 (1977), *cert. denied sub. nom.*, 435 U.S. 968, 98 S.Ct. 1606, 56 L.Ed.2d 59 (1978). The first requirement or criterion relates directly to whether or not the plaintiff's interest is sufficient to meet the jurisdictional requirement that the action be a "case of controversy." *See Singleton* v. *Wulff*, 428 U.S. 106, 112–113, 96 S.Ct. 2868, 2873, 49 L.Ed.2d 826, 832 (1976). The second requirement as interpreted most recently by the Supreme Court, is actually a question of causation. In other words, there must be "a 'fairly traceable' causal connection between the claimed injury and the challenged conduct." *Duke Power Co.* v. *Carolina Environmental Study Group, Inc.*, 438 U.S. 59, 72, 98 S.Ct. 2620, 2630, 57 L.Ed.2d

595, 610 (1978). *See also, Village of Arlington Heights* v. *Metropolitan Housing Development Corporation*, 429 U.S. 252, 97 S.Ct. 555, 50 L.Ed.2d 450 (1977). This court must determine, therefore, whether the plaintiffs have alleged sufficient "injury in fact", and whether there is some "causal connection" between the injury and the regulatory procedure which plaintiffs challenge.

In making this analysis, however, the court notes that it does not pass on the merits of the action at this point. Bearing in mind the distinction between standing and the merits of a particular cause of action, *Davis* v. *Passman*, 442 U.S. 228, 99 S.Ct. 2264, 60 L.Ed.2d 846, 859 n.18 (1979), the court finds that the plaintiffs have alleged a sufficient injury or personal stake "that is likely to be redressed by a favorable decision." *Simon* v. *Eastern Kentucky Welfare Rights Organization*, 426 U.S. 26, 38, 96 S.Ct. 1917, 1924, 48 L.Ed.2d 450, 460 (1976). It is arguable that the plaintiffs have suffered an injury as the result of the impairment of their constitutional rights to freedom of speech and freedom of the press. As for the plaintiffs Loewen and Sallis, the editors of the textbook, the committee's action has effectively prevented the distribution of the book within Mississippi. A finding that the state's regulation impairs sales or distribution is sufficient to confer standing on those adversely affected. *Bantam Books* v. *Sullivan*, 372 U.S. 58, 64 n.6, 83 S.Ct. 631, 636 n.6, 9 L.Ed.2d 584, 589 (1963). Similarly, to the extent that the state's authority to regulate local curricula may be subject to constitutional restraints, the plaintiff school district, school superintendents and teachers may assert their first amendment rights to protect academic freedom. Any restraint on that freedom is a palpable injury for which they may seek redress. *See Parducci* v. *Rutland*, 316, F.Supp. 352 (M.D.Ala.1970), *citing Sweezy* v. *New Hampshire*, 354 U.S. 234, 77 S.Ct. 1203, 1 L.Ed.2d 1311 (1957). The plaintiff students and parents also have protected rights under the first amendment to receive useful information and to have a voice in the direction of a student's education. *Pierce* v. *Society of Sisters*, 268 U.S. 510, 45 S.Ct. 571, 69 L.Ed. 1070 (1924); *Meyer* v. *Nebraska*, 262 U.S. 390, 43 S.Ct. 625, 67 L.Ed. 1042 (1923); *Right to Read Defense Committee of Chelsea* v. *School Committee*, 454 F.Supp. 703 (D.Mass.1978).

As to the second prong of the standing issue, the plaintiffs have also alleged a sufficiently "traceable" causal connection between the purported injury to their protected rights, and the defendants' conduct. To borrow a phrase from the law of torts, the defendants' conduct is the *sine qua non* of the alleged injury; but for the rejection of the Loewen and Sallis textbook, the plaintiffs would not be "proper proponents of the particular legal rights on which they base their suit." *Singleton* v. *Wulff*, 428 U.S. 106, at 112–113, 96 S.Ct.

2868, at 2873, 49 L.Ed.2d 826, at 832 (1976). The court concludes, therefore, that the plaintiffs have alleged a sufficient personal stake in the outcome of the controversy, and that they are entitled to have this court decide the merits of their dispute.

B. *Plaintiffs' Cause of Action: 42 U.S.C. §§ 1981, 1983.*

The plaintiffs claim that the action of the rating committee in refusing to recommend *Mississippi: Conflict and Change,* and the action of the Board in ratifying that decision, deprived the plaintiffs of their rights secured by the First, Thirteenth, and Fourteenth Amendments to the Constitution. For such violations of these guaranteed rights, a cause of action has been created in 42 U.S.C. § 1983, and this court has jurisdiction to hear such a claim pursuant to 28 U.S.C. § 1343(3) & (4). Of course, not every action by state officials which adversely affects a person's interests will give rise to a cause of action under § 1983. The "state action" required by the section must rise to the level of a violation of *specific* constitutional guarantees. *Wood* v. *Strickland,* 420 U.S. 308, 95 S.Ct. 992, 43 L.Ed.2d 214, *rehearing denied,* 421 U.S. 921, 95 S.Ct. 1589, 43 L.Ed.2d 790 (1975). The prerequisites to liability under § 1983 are twofold: (1) The plaintiff must prove that the defendant deprived him of his rights secured by either the Constitution or the laws of the United States; and (2) the plaintiff must prove that the defendant acted under color of state law. *Adickes* v. *S.H. Kress & Co.,* 398 U.S. 144, 90 S.Ct. 1598, 26 L.Ed.2d 142 (1970); *Downing* v. *Arnold,* 461 F.Supp. 54 (D.N.H.1978); *Reilly* v. *Leonard,* 459 F.Supp. 291 (D.Conn.1978). It is not necessary that the plaintiff prove that the defendant acted with the specific intent to deprive plaintiff of his rights, for as the Supreme Court has stated, § 1983 "should be read against the background of tort liability that makes a man responsible for the natural consequences of his actions." *Monroe* v. *Pape,* 365 U.S. 167, 187, 81 S.Ct. 473, 484, 5 L.Ed.2d 492, 505 (1961). Of course, in alleging under § 1983 that the defendant deprived the plaintiff of equal protection of the laws through racially discriminatory practices, the plaintiff must prove "discriminatory intent" on the part of the defendant. *Village of Arlington Heights* v. *Metropolitan Housing Development Corp.,* 429 U.S. 252, 97 S.Ct. 555, 50 L.Ed.2d 450 (1977); *Washington* v. *Davis,* 426 U.S. 229, 96 S.Ct. 2040, 48 L.Ed.2d 597 (1976). The Fifth Circuit, however, has reconciled these two cases with *Monroe* and has found that the two principles are not inconsistent:

[W]e do not read *Washington* v. *Davis* and *Arlington Heights* as banishing from the law of racial and ethnic discrimination that venerable common law tort principle that a person intends the natural and foreseeable consequences of his actions. When the official actions challenged as discriminatory include acts and decisions that do not have a firm basis in well accepted and historically sound nondiscriminatory social policy, discriminatory intent may be inferred from the fact that those acts had foreseeable discriminatory consequences.

United States v. *Texas Education Agency,* 564 F.2d 162, 168 (5th Cir. 1977).

An action brought under § 1981 is essentially one for the redress of a tort, although the relief available under that section is somewhat more limited than that available under § 1983. *Campbell* v. *Gadsen County District School Board,* 534 F.2d 650, 654 n.8 (5th Cir. 1976). Section 1981 provides, in pertinent part, that "All persons . . . shall have the same right in every State . . . to make and enforce contracts . . . and to the full and equal benefit of all laws and proceedings for the security of persons and property as is enjoyed by white citizens . . . ." It is clear that the section provides relief for racial discrimination, and discriminatory intent under the standard of *Arlington Heights* is a necessary element.

The proper defendant under the Civil Rights statutes is one who acts under color of state law, although an action for damages does not extend to the state itself. In *Edelman* v. *Jordan,* 415 U.S. 651, 94 S.Ct. 1347, 39 L.Ed.2d 662 (1974), the Supreme Court "reaffirmed the rule that had evolved in . . . earlier cases that a suit in federal court by private parties seeking to impose a liability which must be paid from public funds in the state treasury is barred by the Eleventh Amendment." *Quern* v. *Jordan,* 440 U.S. 332, 337, 99 S.Ct. 1139, 1145, 59 L.Ed.2d 358, 364 (1979). The defendants in the action sub judice submit that the State Textbook Purchasing Board, as an agency of the state, comes within the general rule and should therefore be dismissed. It is true that a suit against the state and its agencies is barred unless the state waives its sovereign immunity, *Alabama* v. *Pugh,* 438 U.S. 781, 98 S.Ct. 3057, 57 L.Ed.2d 1114 (1978), but it is also true that "a federal court, consistent with the Eleventh Amendment may enjoin state officials to conform their future conduct to the requirements of federal law, even though an injunction may have an ancillary effect on the state treasury." *Quern* v. *Jordan,* 440 U.S. at 337, 99 S.Ct. at 1143, 59 L.Ed.2d at 364, *citing Ex parte Young,* 209 U.S. 123, 28 S.Ct. 441, 52 L.Ed. 714 (1908). The members of the Board, therefore, may be sued in their individual and official capacities; merely "[s]triking the state's name from the list of parties will have no impact on the effectiveness of [the] relief." *Alabama* v. *Pugh,* 438 U.S. at 783, 98 S.Ct. at 3058, 57

L.Ed.2d at 1117 (Stevens, J., dissenting). The court notes that plaintiffs do not seek damages in this cause; they ask for prospective injunctive and declaratory relief only. Even though such relief "may have an ancillary effect on the state treasury", the court concludes that the plaintiffs' action against the individual defendants is not barred by the Eleventh Amendment.

C. *Denial of First Amendment Rights and Due Process.*

The field of education is one which needs particular constitutional protection. This is so because educational issues such as academic freedom are fundamentally linked with First Amendment guarantees. In this case, the plaintiffs' First Amendment rights are affected not only in the educational area, but also in the area of circulation and distribution of published material. For the following reasons, the court concludes that the defendants have impermissibly abridged the plaintiffs' rights under the First Amendment.

The primary issue here is whether or not, given the accepted principle that curriculum choice is a matter of local educational concern, state officials may have unfettered authority to decide which books children may read in school, without providing for a method by which those affected by such decisions may oppose them. This court concludes that such authority does not and cannot exist. As the Supreme Court concluded in *Bantam Books* v. *Sullivan,* 372 U.S. 58, 70, 83 S.Ct. 631, 639, 9 L.Ed.2d 584, 593 (1963), "[a]ny system of prior restraints of expression comes to this Court bearing a heavy presumption against its constitutional validity." This court must apply the same standard here.

A comparison of the facts in *Bantam Books* with the facts in this case, shows a striking similarity. In *Bantam Books,* the state legislature created the Rhode Island Commission to Encourage Morality in Youth, and charged the commission members "to educate the public concerning any book . . . containing obscene, indecent or impure language . . . ." *Id.* at 59, 83 S.Ct. at 633, 9 L.Ed.2d at 587. In the case at bar, the state legislature created a statutory scheme for the appointment of textbook approval committees, and the court has found that the avowed purpose of such a scheme was to insure that no unauthorized ideas crept into the classroom. In *Bantam Books,* the State commission would notify book distributors within the state that certain books were determined to be obscene and therefore objectionable for sale to minors. The notice would also remind the distributor of the commission's duty to recommend prosecution to the state attorney general. The statutory scheme in this action is not quite as harsh: the committee merely approves those books to be purchased with state funds, and those not approved

may not be so purchased. As a result, they are not used in the schools. The Supreme Court concluded in *Bantam Books* that the acts and practices of the state commission effectively foreclosed the circulation and distribution of the offensive books throughout the state. The same may be said in this case, where the state formally places its seal of approval upon a particular book and denies its approval to another book, without providing for a method of review. The commission's practice in *Bantam Books* was struck down because it provided "no safeguards whatever against the suppression of non-obscene, and therefore constitutionally protected, matter." 372 U.S. at 70, 83 S.Ct. at 639, 9 L.Ed.2d at 593. This court has found that the regulatory scheme in this case forecloses the committee's decision from further review, without giving those adversely affected by it a voice in the matter. This procedure is objectionable, not because it regulates, but because it regulates *unreasonably.*

The Supreme Court has stated previously that state and local control over public education may not be completely unfettered:

> Our courts . . . have not failed to apply the First Amendment's mandate in our educational system where essential to safeguard the fundamental values of freedom of speech and inquiry and of belief. By and large, public education in our Nation is committed to the control of state and local authorities. Courts do not and cannot intervene in the resolution of conflicts which arise in the daily operation of school systems and which do not directly and sharply implicate constitutional values. On the other hand . . . the First Amendment "does not tolerate laws that cast a pall of orthodoxy over the classroom."

Epperson v. *Arkansas,* 393 U.S. 97, 104-05, 89 S.Ct. 266, 270, 21 L.Ed.2d 228, 234 (1968), *quoting Keyishian* v. *Board of Regents,* 385 U.S. 589, 603, 87 S.Ct. 675, 683, 17 L.Ed.2d 629, 640 (1967). The court is persuaded to intervene in this conflict precisely because this is a case which "directly and sharply" implicates constitutional values. It does so because the defendants have provided no method by which the plaintiffs may safeguard their First Amendment freedoms. All interested parties, whether they be textbook editors, teachers, parents, or students, have a fundamental interest in maintaining a free and open educational system that provides for the acquisition of useful knowledge. *See Meyer* v. *Nebraska,* 262 U.S. 390, 43 S.Ct. 625, 67 L.Ed. 1042 (1923).

Obviously, there is no specific language in the First Amendment which creates a freedom to teach any subject at all. As one court observed, however,

The First Amendment references to freedom of speech and of the press are designed to assure the free exchange in the general marketplace of ideas. Academic freedom, it can be argued, is the adaptation of those specific constitutional rights to protect communication in the classroom as a special market place of ideas.

Cary v. *Board of Education,* 427 F. Supp. 945, 949 (D.Colo.1977). To the extent that the decisions of the textbook committee impinge upon a teacher's free choice of curriculum, or upon an editor's right to distribute his book, or upon a student's right to obtain an education, there must be some method by which uninhibited governmental control over "the free exchange" of ideas can be checked. There is no such method here. In *Sterzing* v. *Fort Bend Independent School District,* 376 F.Supp. 657, 661 (S.D.Tex.1972), the court held that the "freedom of speech of a teacher . . . must not be so lightly regarded that he stands in jeopardy of dismissal for raising controversial issues in an eager but disciplined classroom." By the same token, the First Amendment freedoms of all interested parties should not be completely disregarded by those persons, acting under color of state law, who make curriculum decisions from which there is no appeal. It is "the binding duty of an administrative body to act with full information, with reason and deliberation, and with full benefit of the views of supervisors, principals and others familiar with the curriculum and teaching techniques in the schools . . . ." 376 F.Supp. at 661. No less should be required here, where the defendants' actions have the potential for denying to the plaintiffs valuable governmental benefits. Procedures must be instituted which insure that these benefits are not denied on a basis which infringes constitutionally protected interests. *Perry* v. *Sindermann,* 408 U.S. 593, 92 S.Ct. 2694, 33 L.Ed.2d 570 (1972).

The court concludes, therefore, that the defendants have deprived the plaintiffs, under color of state law, of their constitutionally protected rights of freedom of speech and of the press, and of their rights to due process of law under the Fourteenth Amendment. 42 U.S.C. § 1983.

D. *Racially Discriminatory Rejection and Intent to Dismiss.*

It has been held by this court and by the Fifth Circuit Court of Appeals that those acting under color of state law may not act to censor a publication simply because it contains controversial viewpoints. *Bazaar* v. *Fortune,* 476 F.2d 570 (5th Cir. 1973); *Burnside* v. *Byars,* 363 F.2d 744 (5th Cir. 1966). The court has concluded that the committee's rejection of *Mississippi: Conflict and Change,* while not constituting censorship *per se,* was certainly an impermissible rejection because the procedure violated the plaintiffs' con-

stitutional rights. The court concludes that the rejection of the book for the reasons given evidences a racially discriminatory purpose on the part of the defendants.

The court has found that the textbook was not rejected for any justifiable reason. The lack of a justifiable reason is not in and of itself a constitutional violation. However, the court has also found that the racial issues substantially influenced the committee in its decision. That finding, coupled with the finding that the legislative history suggests an intent to perpetuate ideas of segregation and discrimination, leads this court to conclude that the requisite "discriminatory intent" has been demonstrated. *Village of Arlington Heights* v. *Metropolitan Housing Development Corp.,* 429 U.S. 252, 97 S.Ct. 555, 50 L.Ed.2d 450 (1977).

Under the standard of *Arlington Heights,* it is only necessary for the plaintiffs to prove "that a discriminatory purpose has been a motivating factor in the decision" to reject the textbook. Id. at 265-66, 97 S.Ct. at 563, 50 L.Ed.2d at 465. The court also suggested several "evidentiary sources" from which such proof may be drawn. Several factors lead this court to conclude that the plaintiffs have sustained their burden. First, the reasons given by some committee members for rejecting the textbook indicate that race was a motivating factor. These statements, set forth in the court's findings of fact, need not be repeated here, but they indicate without question that some members were influenced by racial issues. Secondly, those members who did not indicate that race influenced them in their decision, also did not indicate any other reason. This appears to be a violation of the committee's statutory duty to state the reasons for its recommendation. Miss.Code Ann. § 37-43-21 (1972). A failure to do so is clearly a departure from the "normal procedural sequence", a factor "which might afford evidence that improper purposes are playing a role." 429 U.S. at 267, 97 S.Ct. at 564, 50 L.Ed.2d at 466. Thirdly, as the court has previously indicated, the legislative history and background of the textbook statutes also demonstrates racially discriminatory policies as a motivating factor. Because this legislation does not have "a firm basis in well accepted and historically sound non-discriminatory social policy," the court concludes that those charged with carrying out this legislation may be determined to have foreseen the discriminatory consequences of their actions. *United States* v. *Texas Education Agency,* 564 F.2d 162, 168 (5th Cir. 1977). The plaintiffs have therefore demonstrated the requisite discriminatory intent necessary for a cause of action under the Civil Rights statutes.

E. *Conclusion: Appropriate Remedy.*

Plaintiffs would have this court find that the textbook which was approved is a "symbol of resistance to integration in Mississippi schools," and that its approval over the Loewen and Sallis text was an unlawful perpetuation of racial discrimination. The court will not make any such finding. Having concluded that the principles of free speech embodied in the concept of academic freedom warrant protection, the court cannot now place the judicial seal of approval on the ideas found in one book, and denigrate the ideas found in another. To do so would violate the same constitutional principles which the court now seeks to protect.

The court concludes that the manner in which *Mississippi: Conflict and Change* was rejected by the defendants violated the plaintiffs' rights guaranteed by the First and Fourteenth Amendments. The court also concludes that the rejection of *Mississippi: Conflict and Change* was unjustified and motivated by reasons which the defendants should have known would have racially discriminatory consequences.

The only method by which the court can assure that these plaintiffs' constitutional interests are protected in this action is to enjoin the defendants to approve *Mississippi: Conflict and Change,* placing it on the state-approved list for purchase and distribution to students in eligible schools. The defendants and their successors will be requried to approve the textbook, after the plaintiffs have had a reasonable time period within which to submit proposed revisions and corrections to the book. Any objections which the defendants may have to the proposed revisions must be based upon objective criteria contained in the Board's *Suggested Criteria for Textbook Selection.*

Plaintiffs also request this court to enjoin the defendants to implement procedures consistent with the requirements of due process, in the approval or rejection of textbooks. It must be kept in mind that the plaintiffs do not submit, and this court does not hold, that the statute relating to textbook approval committees is unconstitutional. The question here is whether the court may properly order the defendants to implement broad changes in the procedure for approval of textbooks without requiring the defendants, in effect, to violate the statute. It is not clear from the language of the statute, for example, whether or not all committee members are required to state the reasons for their individual decisions. Nor is it clear under the existing statutory scheme that the Purchasing Board would have the power or authority to conduct *de novo* hearings in a review of the committee's actions. Given the language of the statute, the court could not possibly require the promulgation of far reaching regulations without also giving the legislature the opportunity to correct the statute. The court declines to institute such a practice.

Given the accepted principle that the equitable power of this court to remedy past wrongs is quite broad, it is also true that the "nature of the violation determines the scope of the remedy." *Swann* v. *Charlotte-Mecklenburg Board of Education,* 402 U.S. 1, 16, 91 S.Ct. 1267, 1276, 28 L.Ed.2d 554, 567 (1971). Even though the violations in the instant case are those involving due process, which under most circumstances would require procedural changes, the violations have occurred at the state level. In addressing the scope of a district court's equitable power, the Supreme Court has stated that the court should keep in mind "important considerations of federalism." *Rizzo* v. *Goode,* 423 U.S. 362, 378, 96 S.Ct. 598, 607, 46 L.Ed.2d 561, 573 (1976). In situations where "the exercise of authority by state officials is attacked, federal courts must be constantly mindful of the 'special delicacy of the adjustment to be preserved between federal equitable power and State administration of its own law.' " 423 U.S. at 378, 96 S.Ct. at 607, 46 L.Ed.2d at 573, *quoting Stefanelli v. Minard,* 342 U.S. 117, 120, 72 S.Ct. 118, 120, 96 L.Ed. 138, 142 (1951).

If the court were to mandate the revision of textbook approval procedures, it would not be giving due consideration to the principles of federalism in this particular case. The plaintiffs have challenged the rejection of one book only; the defendants consider literally hundreds of books, utilizing the existing procedure. The remedial relief which the plaintiffs will be granted will make them whole, and the particular violation in this case does not necessitate a broader remedy. The court should not undertake to dictate to the defendants a plan of textbook approval. Underlying notions of federalism do not allow the court to supervise state administrative proceedings. Having placed these particular plaintiffs in a position which will remedy the particular violations of due process committed against them, the court will not extend its equitable powers further.

The court concludes that the plaintiffs, in addition to the injunctive relief, are entitled to recover their costs of the action from the defendants. Additionally, the plaintiffs, as prevailing parties in this litigation, are entitled to an award of reasonable attorney's fees as part of the costs. 42 U.S.C. § 1988. The plaintiffs shall, within 30 days of this decision, submit an itemization of fees and expenses, supported by appropriate affidavits of counsel. The defendants shall have 20 days thereafter to submit any objections to plaintiffs' itemization.

[Ed. note: appendices A and B deleted here.]

NOTES

1. At the time of the institution of this action, Honorable William L. Waller was governor and Garvin H. Johnson was Superintendent of Education of the State of Mississippi. Honorable William Winter is now Governor and

Charles E. Holladay is Superintendent of Education of the State of Mississippi.

2. Plaintiffs have modified the request to provide for biennial submission and approval of textbooks.

3. Plaintiffs have abandoned their request for this relief.

4. Plaintiffs have abandoned the following provision of this requested remedy: "And which obtains the endorsement of a local school district board of education and its rating committee", and ask that education criteria be promulgated.

In deciding that a school superintendent's decision to cancel the high school production of the musical play "Pippin" because of its sexual content did not violate the students' First Amendment rights, the United States Court of Appeals, Third Circuit, stated: "The court [district court] found that no student was prohibited from expressing his views on any subject; no student was prohibited from reading the script, an unedited version of which remains in the school library; and no one was punished or reprimanded for any expression of ideas. In light of these facts, the court could find no reasonable threat of a chilling effect on the free exchange of ideas within the school community. . . . We agree with the district court that the conflict here does not 'directly and sharply implicate' the First Amendment rights of the students."

Seyfried v. *Walton,* 668 F.2d 214 (1981)

ALDISERT, Circuit Judge.

The question presented is whether a public school superintendent's decision to cancel a high school dramatic production because of its sexual theme violated the students' first amendment right of expression. Plaintiffs, parents of three students in the play, sued the school district, the school board, and the district superintendent, seeking compensatory and equitable relief under 42 U.S.C. § 1983. The district court, sitting without a jury, held that the school superintendent's decision to cancel the production as inappropriate for school sponsorship was no different from other administrative decisions involving allocation of educational resources and that the cancellation did not offend the students' first amendment rights. We accept the reasoning given by the district court and we will affirm for the reasons set forth in Judge Stapleton's opinion. *Seyfried* v. *Walton,* 512 F.Supp. 235 (D.Del. 1981).

I.

Because the facts underlying this controversy were set out in detail by the district court, our recitation will be abbreviated. Caesar Rodney High School, located in Dover, Delaware, sponsors autumn and spring theatrical productions each year. In December 1980, the director of the spring production, an English teacher at the school, selected the musical "Pippin" for presentation the following spring. Because the play contained certain sexually explicit scenes, the director consulted the assistant principal before reaching a final decision.

After the director edited the script, she and the assistant principal agreed that the revised scenes, although still sexually suggestive, were appropriate for a high school production.

In March 1981, shortly after rehearsals for the spring production had begun, the father of a "Pippin" cast member complained to his brother, the president of the school board, that the play mocked religion. The board president directed the district superintendent to look into the matter. After reviewing the edited script, the superintendent determined that the play did not mock religion, but that it was inappropriate for a public high school because of its sexual content. He directed the principal to stop production of the play. After hearing the views of interested parents, the school board refused to overturn the superintendent's decision. As a result, the school did not present a spring play in 1981.

Parents of three members of the "Pippin" cast and crew then filed a civil rights action under 42 U.S.C. § 1983, claiming that the students' first amendment rights of expression had been unconstitutionally abridged. After a two-day trial, the district court entered judgment in favor of the defendants. Plaintiffs appeal.

II.

Appellants' principal contention is that the students of the "Pippin" cast and crew had a first amendment right to produce the play. Although we agree that, in general, dramatic expression is "speech" for purposes of the first amendment, see *Southeastern Promotions, Ltd. v. Conrad,* 420 U.S. 546, 557-58, 95 S.Ct. 1239, 1245-46, 43 L.Ed.2d 448 (1975), we also agree with the district court that the decision to cancel the production of "Pippin" in these circumstances did not infringe on the students' constitutional rights.

In his well reasoned opinion, Judge Stapleton noted that a school community "exists for a specialized purpose—the education of young people," including the communication of both knowledge and social values. 512 F.Supp. at 237. The first amendment, he concluded, must therefore be "applied in light of the special characteristics of the school environment...." Id. (quoting *Tinker v. Des Moines School District,* 393 U.S. 503, 506, 89 S.Ct. 733, 736, 21 L.Ed.2d 731 (1969)).

We believe that the district court properly distinguished student newspapers and other "non-program related expressions of student opinion" from school-sponsored theatrical productions. 512 F.Supp. at 238-39. The critical factor in this case is the relationship of the play to the school curriculum. As found by the district court, both the staff and the administration view the spring production at Caesar Rodney as "an integral part of the school's educational program." Participation in the play, though voluntary, was considered a part of the curriculum in the theater arts. 512 F.Supp. at 238 & n.5. On review of the record we conclude that this finding is not clearly erroneous. *Krasnov v. Dinan,* 465 F.2d 1298, 1302-03 (3d Cir. 1972). Viewed in this light,

the selection of the artistic work to be given as the spring production does not differ in principle from the selection of course curriculum, a process which courts have traditionally left to the expertise of educators. Just as a student has no First Amendment right to study a particular aspect or period of history in his or her senior history course, he or she has no First Amendment right to participate in the production of a particular dramatic work or version thereof.

Id. at 238-39.

The district court also noted the likelihood that the school's sponsorship of a play would be viewed as an endorsement of the ideas it contained. A school has an important interest in avoiding the impression that it has endorsed a viewpoint at variance with its educational program. The district court cautioned that administrators may not so chill the school's atmosphere for student and teacher expression that they cast "a pall of orthodoxy" over the school community, *Keyishian v. Board of Regents,* 385 U.S. 589, 603, 87 S.Ct. 675, 683-84, 17 L.Ed.2d 629 (1967), but it found no such danger here. 512 F.Supp. at 239. The court

found that no student was prohibited from expressing his views on any subject; no student was prohibited from reading the script, an unedited version of which remains in the school library; and no one was punished or reprimanded for any expression of ideas. In light of these facts, the court could find no reasonable threat of a chilling effect on the free exchange of ideas within the school community. These findings are amply supported by the record.

We agree with the district court that those responsible for directing a school's educational program must be allowed to decide how its limited resources can be best used to achieve the goals of educating and socializing its students. "Limitations of time and resources... dictate that choices be made.... [S]ince the objective of the process is the 'inculcation of both knowledge and social values' in young people, these decisions as to what will be taught will necessarily involve an acceptance or preference of some values over others." 512 F.Supp. at 237 (quoting *Pico v. Board of Education,* 638 F.2d 404, 432 (2d Cir. 1980) (Newman, J., concurring), *cert. granted,*—U.S.—, 102 S.Ct. 385, 70 L.Ed.2d 205 (1981)).

Because of the burden of responsibility given to school administrators, courts are reluctant to interfere with the operation of our school systems. As the Supreme Court has observed:

By and large, public education in our Nation is committed to the control of state and local authorities. Courts do not and cannot intervene in the resolution of conflicts which arise in the daily operation of school systems and which do not directly and sharply implicate basic constitutional values.

Epperson v. Arkansas, 393 U.S. 97, 104, 89 S.Ct. 266, 270, 21 L.Ed.2d 228 (1968). We agree with the district court that the conflict here does not "directly and sharply implicate" the first amendment rights of the students. We hold, therefore, that the court properly entered judgment for the defendants.

III.

The judgment of the district court will be affirmed.[1]

ROSENN, Circuit Judge, concurring.

The issues raised in this appeal are complex, for they implicate the thorny tangle which results from the confrontation between the right of local school administrators to determine the content of their pupils' education and the first amendment rights of those very students in the secondary school setting Although I agree with the majority that school authorities enjoy broad discretion in the making of decisions in curricular matters, I write separately to emphasize that their discretion is not unfettered and that courts have a duty to vindicate the complementary constitutional rights of students to express and to hear more than one point of view.

It is important at the outset to make clear the nature of the present challenge. Although the students assert that their right to free expression has been abridged, their challenge at its roots is directed not merely to a restriction of their freedom of expression but also to the school's right to bar their participation in a school-sponsored production of the play.[1] It is not contended that the students subscribe to the *weltanschauung* embodied in "Pippin" and wish to stage the play to give voice to their views. Thus, the instant dispute concerns the breadth of discretion enjoyed by school authorities to limit the exposure of their students to certain curricular material which the authorities believe to be unsuitable to their charges, and the proper role of the courts in superintending that exercise of discretion.[2]

Local control of a school system's curriculum by school boards organized at a community level characterizes the traditional allocation of responsibility for the education of our youth in the United States. Accepting the wisdom of deferring to local school authorities regarding quotidian educational matters, "the courts have traditionally been reluctant to intrude upon the domain of educational affairs, not only in recognition of their lack of educational competence in such matters, but also out of respect for the autonomy of educational institutions." *Developments in the Law—Academic Freedom*, 81 Harv.L.Rev. 1045, 1050 (1968); see Comment, *Challenging Ideological Exclusion of Curriculum Material: Rights of Students and Parents*, 14 Harv.C.R.—C.L.L.Rev. 485, 487-88 (1979) (hereinafter *Comment*). The Supreme Court has repeatedly given voice to this need for judicial deference "to the comprehensive authority of the States and of school officials, consistent with fundamental constitutional safeguards," concerning educational matters. See, e.g., *Tinker v. Des Moines Independent Community School District*, 393 U.S. 503, 507, 89 S.Ct. 733, 737, 21 L.Ed.2d 731 (1969); *accord, Epperson v. Arkansas*, 393 U.S. 97, 104, 89 S.Ct. 266, 270, 21 L.Ed.2d 228 (1968).

Other courts have also proved reluctant to interfere with the educational decisions of school officials. See, e.g., *Zykan v. Warsaw Community School Corp.*, 631 F.2d 1300 (7th Cir. 1980); *Cary v. Board of Education*, 598 F.2d 535 (10th Cir. 1979); *President's Council, District 25, v. Community School Board No. 25*, 457 F.2d 289 (2d Cir.), *cert. denied*, 409 U.S. 998, 93 S.Ct. 308, 34 L.Ed.2d 260 (1972). The simple fact that those decisions are usually governed by school administrators' social, political, and moral tastes is fully con-

sistent with local control over primary and secondary education. *Zykan v. Warsaw Community School Corp., supra*, 631 F.2d at 1305-06.

At the same time, however, '[o]ur courts . . . have not failed to apply the First Amendment's mandate in our educational system where essential to safeguard the fundamental values of freedom of speech and inquiry and of belief." *Epperson v. Arkansas*, 393 U.S. 97, 104, 89 S.Ct. 266, 270, 21 L.Ed.2d 228 (1968); see, e.g., *Tinker v. Des Moines Independent Community School District*, 393 U.S. 503, 89 S.Ct. 733, 21 L.Ed.2d 731 (1969); *West Virginia State Board of Education v. Barnette*, 319 U.S. 624, 63 S.Ct. 1178, 87 L.Ed. 1628 (1943); *Meyer v. Nebraska*, 262 U.S. 390, 43 S.Ct. 625, 67 L.Ed. 1042 (1923). And nowhere is " '[t]he vigilant protection of constitutional freedoms . . . more vital than in the community of American schools.' " *Epperson v. Arkansas, supra*, 393 U.S. at 104, 89 S.Ct. at 270 (quoting *Shelton v. Tucker*, 364 U.S. 479, 487, 81 S.Ct. 247, 251, 5 L.Ed.2d 231 (1960)). These and other judicial decisions which were willing to intrude into the operation of school systems emphasize the essential role played by education in the intellectual and moral development of our youth,[3] and the concomitant need to expose our youngsters "to that robust exchange of ideas which discovers truth 'out of a multitude of tongues, [rather] than through any kind of authoritative selection.' " *Keyishian v. Board of Regents*, 385 U.S. 589, 603, 87 S.Ct. 675, 683, 17 L.Ed.2d 629 (1967).

Although many of the decisions regarding first amendment guarantees in the schoolhouse are concerned with the rights of students and teachers to express their views, see, e.g., *Tinker v. Des Moines Independent Community School District, supra*; *James v. Board of Education*, 461 F.2d 566 (2d Cir.), *cert. denied*, 409 U.S. 1042, 93 S.Ct. 529, 34 L.Ed.2d 491 (1972), there has also emerged a corresponding right of students to challenge on first amendment grounds actions of school officials which circumscribe the range of ideas to which students are exposed.[4] In addition to its foundation in basic first amendment expressive values, the right of students to object to overly narrow or ideological curriculum-related decisions finds support in the concept of "freedom to hear" recently clarified by the Supreme Court in *Virginia State Board of Pharmacy v. Virginia Consumer Council, Inc.*, 425 U.S. 748, 96 S.Ct. 1817, 48 L.Ed.2d 346 (1976); see *President's Council, District 25 v. Community School Board No. 25*, 409 U.S. 998, 999, 93 S.Ct. 308, 309, 34 L.Ed.2d 260 (1972) (Douglas, J., dissenting from denial of certiorari), *Zykan v. Warsaw Community School Corp., supra*, 631 F.2d at 1304; *Minarcini v. Strongsville City School District, supra*, 541 F.2d at 583; *Comment, supra*, at 513-17.

It is the inherent tension between these two essential functions, on the one hand exposing young minds to the clash of ideologies in the free marketplace of ideas, and on the other hand the need to provide our youth with a solid foundation of basic, moral values, that gives rise to the present dispute. Striking a balance between them is difficult; and not all distortions will require judicial intervention. The Supreme Court has acknowledged this tension:

> Judicial interposition in the operation of the public school system of the Nation raises problems requiring care and restraint.... By and large, public education in our Nation is committed to the control of state and local authorities. Courts do not and cannot intervene in the resolution of conflicts which arise in the daily operation of school systems and which do not directly and sharply implicate constitutional values. On the other hand, ... [a]s this Court said in *Keyishian v. Board of Regents,* the First Amendment "does not tolerate laws that cast a pall of orthodoxy over the classroom." 385 U.S. 589, 603, 87 S.Ct. 675, 683, 17 L.Ed.2d 629 (1967) (footnote omitted).

Epperson v. Arkansas, 393 U.S. 97, 104-05, 89 S.Ct. 266, 270, 21 L.Ed.2d 228 (1968). It remains for this and other courts to evolve criteria for determining when constitutional values are so sharply implicated that judicial intervention is necessry.

In attempting to reconcile these goals in a particular case, several observations can be made. First, the court can take judicial notice of the progressively higher levels of intellectual and emotional development of students in the later grades of secondary school. As a result, more deference should be shown school authorities' curricular decisions regarding grade school, and perhaps junior high school students, in the face of a challenge that a particular point of view has been excluded.[5] High school students, in contrast, are at an age approaching both adulthood and franchise. As the Second Circuit has noted in a related context, "It would be foolhardy to shield our children from political debate and issues until the eve of their first venture into the voting booth. Schools must play an essential role in preparing their students to think and analyze and to recognize the demagogue." *James v. Board of Education,* 461 F.2d 566, 574 (2d Cir.), *cert. denied,* 409 U.S. 1042, 93 S.Ct. 529, 34 L.Ed.2d 491 (1972).

A second consideration to be evaluated is the nature of the material, access to which the school authorities are attempting to restrict, and the basis for the restriction. Great deference should be accorded when material is deemed unsuited for youths, for example, because of its overt sexual references or because it is otherwise deemed vulgar and unsuited for youngsters. Local authorities have always enjoyed wide latitude in proscribing material which, although not obscene, because of its sexual content is deemed inappropriate for minors. See *Ginsberg v. New York,* 390 U.S. 629, 88 S.Ct. 1274, 20 L.Ed.2d 195 (1968). In contrast, a court should have much less tolerance for any attempt to exclude a particular point of view from open consideration in the school. See *Epperson v. Arkansas,* 393 U.S. 97, 89 S.Ct. 266, 21 L.Ed.2d 228 (1968). The evil to be avoided is the ideological indoctrination which would result from attempting to attain the laudable goal of instilling our youth with a set of moral values by barring their exposure to ideas inconsistent with those values.[6] Again, the age of the students will be significant. A decision to limit the exposure of young adolescents, who have less developed critical skills, to works such as *Mein Kampf,* which express an ideology that school administrators find abhorrent, should normally remain undisturbed. See *Comment, supra,* at 524. The same would not be true if the students in question were high school seniors.

Weighing the pertinent considerations, the instant claim does not command the intervention of the courts. The school superintendent objected to production of "Pippin" not because of its ideas—a youth's search for the meaning of existence—but because of its explicit sexual overtones. School authorities should have more latitude in limiting the performance by their students in a school forum of a play which the authorities find vulgar and inappropriate because of sharp sexual overtones. Their acquiescence in such a performance might be construed as tacit approval of not only the performance but also the play's content.

No attempt has been made to restrict access to the play: two copies of the unedited script remain available in the school library. Nor is it alleged that discussion of the play or its subject matter has been restricted. In sum, the decision of the school authorities to prohibit production of "Pippin" in a high school forum because of its sexual overtones does not threaten to stifle the free exchange of ideas so as to warrant judicial interference with the decision of the school authorities.

I therefore agree that the judgment of the district court should be affirmed.

NOTE

1. We have considered the remaining arguments raised by appellants and we conclude that they are without merit. Because of our disposition of this case we need not consider the parties' contentions on the issue of immunity from damages.

CONCURRING OPINION NOTES

1. The district court found that participation in the school play "does not differ in principle from the selection of

course curriculum," 512 F.Supp. at 238, a finding I accept as not clearly erroneous.

2. In the present case a school superintendent overrode the decision of a dramatic arts teacher to produce "Pippin." The teacher has not challenged that action, and has not been in any way reprimanded for her decision. Thus neither the statutory and constitutional rights of teachers, acting at variance with the views of school administrators, to expose their students to certain views, nor a teacher's own constitutional right of free expression are before the court.

3. Public education . . . "fulfills a most fundamental obligation of government to its constituency." *Foley v. Connelie,* 435 U.S. 291, 297, 98 S.Ct. 1067, 1071, 55 L.Ed.2d 287 (1978). The importance of public schools in the preparation of individuals for participation as citizens, and in the preservation of values on which our society rests, has long been recognized by our decisions. . . . *Ambach v. Norwick,* 441 U.S. 68, 76, 99 S.Ct. 1589, 1594, 60 L.Ed.2d 49 (1979).

4. Most of the decisions involve the right of school authorities to exclude or remove certain books from the school library. In general, those actions have been upheld when they related only to the inclusion of the books in the school library and when discussion of the subject matter covered by the books was not also proscribed. *Compare Cary v. Board of Education,* 598 F.2d 535, 544 (10th Cir. 1979) (teachers not prohibited from treating books in class "as examples of contemporary poetry, literature, or American masters") and *President's Council, District 25 v. Community School Board No. 25,* 457 F.2d 289, 292 (2d Cir.), *cert. denied,* 409 U.S. 998, 93 S.Ct. 308, 34 L.Ed.2d 260 (1972) (removal of book to restricted shelf in library did not preclude discussion of subject covered by book in class) with *Pico v. Board of Education,* 638 F.2d 404, 436 (2d Cir. 1981), *cert. granted,*—U.S.—,102 S.Ct. 385, 70 L.Ed.2d 205 (1981) (Newman, J., concurring) (allegation that removal of books "was designed to suppress ideas"), and *Minarcini v. Strongsville City School District,* 541 F.2d 577, 579 (6th Cir. 1976) (school board prohibited teacher and student discussion in class of books not approved by board).

A recent district court decision from the Northern District of Mississippi addressed a more direct challenge to school officials' control of curriculum decisions. In *Loewen v. Turnipseed,* 488 F.Supp. 1138 (N.D.Miss. 1980), students, their parents, and their teachers successfully challenged a decision of the Mississippi "textbook rating committee" not to purchase a particular textbook designed for a ninth grade course in Mississippi history. The plaintiffs argued that the excluded textbook presented a more complete view of the role of blacks in Mississippi. The court concluded, *inter alia,* that the students' first amendment rights to a free and open educational system had been abridged. Id. at 1152-54.

5. A school board's decision may be so blatantly aimed at curtailing a particular viewpoint that even a decision regarding the curriculum for young adolescents warrants judicial intervention. See *Loewen v. Turnipseed,* 488 F.Supp. 1138 (N.D.Miss.1980); note 4 supra.

6. Of course it may sometimes be difficult to ascertain whether school officials have acted to suppress "politically unpopular ideas," *Pico v. Board of Education,* 646 F.2d 205, 714 (2d Cir. 1981), *cert. granted,*—U.S.—, 102 S.Ct. 385, 70 L.Ed.2d 205 (1981) (Newman, J., concurring in the denial of rehearing *en banc*) or whether they sought merely to prevent students from encountering "obviously indecent and vulgar material." Id. at 716 (Mansfield, J., dissenting from denial of *en banc* consideration).

The Arkansas "Balanced treatment for Creation-Science and Evolution-Science Act" is declared unconstitutional by a United States District Court in Arkansas. In deciding the act violated the First Amendment prohibition against the establishment of religion, Judge Overton declared: "No doubt a sizeable majority of Americans believe in the concept of a Creator or, at least, are not opposed to the concept and see nothing wrong with teaching school children about the ideas. The application and content of First Amendment principles are not determined by public opinion polls or by a majority vote. Whether the proponents of Act 590 constitute the majority or the minority is quite irrelevant under a constitutional system of government. No group, no matter how large or small, may use the organs of government, of which the public schools are the most conspicuous and influential, to foist its religious beliefs on others."

McLean v. *Arkansas Bd. of Education*, 529 F.Supp. 1255 (1982)

OVERTON, District Judge.

Introduction

On March 19, 1981, the Governor of Arkansas signed into law Act 590 of 1981, entitled the "Balanced Treatment for Creation-Science and Evolution-Science Act." The Act is codified as Ark.Stat.Ann. § 80-1663, *et seq.* (1981 Supp.). Its essential mandate is stated in its first sentence: "Public schools within this State shall give balanced treatment to creation-science and to evolution-science." On May 27, 1981, this suit was filed[1] challenging the constitutional validity of Act 590 on three distinct grounds.

First, it is contended that Act 590 constitutes an establishment of religion prohibited by the First Amendment to the Constitution, which is made applicable to the states by the Fourteenth Amendment. Second, the plaintiffs argue the Act violates a right to academic freedom which they say is guaranteed to students and teachers by the Free Speech Clause of the First Amendment. Third, plaintiffs allege the Act is impermissibly vague and thereby violates the Due Process Clause of the Fourteenth Amendment.

The individual plaintiffs include the resident Arkansas Bishops of the United Methodist, Episcopal, Roman Catholic and African Methodist Episcopal Churches, the principal official of the Presbyterian Churches in Arkansas, other United Methodist, Southern Baptist and Presbyterian clergy, as well as several persons who sue as parents and next friends of minor children attending Arkansas public schools. One plaintiff is a high school biology teacher. All are also Arkansas taxpayers. Among the organizational plaintiffs are the American Jewish Congress, the Union of American Hebrew Congregations, the American Jewish Committee, the Arkansas Education Association, the National Association of Biology Teachers and the National Coalition for Public Education and Religious Liberty, all of which sue on behalf of members living in Arkansas.[2]

The defendants include the Arkansas Board of Education and its members, the Director of the Department of Education, and the State Textbooks and Instructional Materials Selecting Committee.[3] The Pulaski County Special School District and its Directors and Superintendent were voluntarily dismissed by the plaintiffs at the pre-trial conference held October 1, 1981.

The trial commenced December 7, 1981, and continued through December 17, 1981. This Memorandum Opinion constitutes the Court's findings of fact and conclusions of law. Further orders and judgment will be in conformity with this opinion.

I.

There is no controversy over the legal standards under which the Establishment Clause portion of this case must be judged. The Supreme Court has on a number of occasions expounded on the meaning of the clause, and the pronouncements are clear. Often the issue has arisen in the context of public education, as it has here. In *Everson v. Board of Education*, 330 U.S. 1, 15-16, 67 S.Ct. 504, 511, 91 L.Ed. 711 (1947), Justice Black stated:

"The 'establishment of religion' clause of the First Amendment means at least this: Neither a state nor the Federal Government can set up a church. Neither can pass laws which aid one religion, aid all religions, or prefer one religion over another. Neither can force nor influence a person to go to or to remain away from church against his will or force him to profess a belief or disbelief in any religion. No person can be punished for entertaining or professing religious beliefs or disbeliefs, for church-attendance or non-attendance. No tax, large or small, can be levied to support any religious activities or institutions, whatever they may be called, or whatever form they may adopt to teach or practice religion. Neither a state nor the Federal Government can, openly or secretly, participate in the affairs of any religious organizations or groups and *vice versa*. In the words of Jefferson, the clause . . . was intended to erect 'a wall of separation between church and State.' "

The Establishment Clause thus enshrines two central values: voluntarism and pluralism. And it is in the area of the public schools that these values must be guarded most vigilantly.

"Designed to serve as perhaps the most powerful agency for promoting cohesion among a heterogeneous democratic people, the public school must keep scrupulously free from entanglement in the strife of sects. The preservation of the community from divisive conflicts, of Government from irreconcilable pressures by religious groups, of religion from censorship and coercion however subtly exercised, requires strict confinement of the State to instruction other than religious, leaving to the individual's church and home, indoctrination in the faith of his choice."

McCollum v. Board of Education, 333 U.S. 203, 216-217, 68 S.Ct. 461, 468, 92 L.Ed. 649 (1948), (Opinion of Frankfurter, J., joined by Jackson, Burton and Rutledge, JJ.).

The specific formulation of the establishment prohibition has been refined over the years, but its meaning has not varied from the principles articulated by Justice Black in *Everson*. In *Abington School District v. Schempp*, 374 U.S. 203, 222, 83 S.Ct. 1560, 1571, 10 L.Ed.2d 844 (1963), Justice Clark stated that "to withstand the strictures of the Establishment Clause there must be a secular legislative purpose and a primary effect that neither advances nor inhibits religion." The Court found it quite clear that the First Amendment does not permit a state to require the daily reading of the Bible in public schools, for "[s]urely the place of the Bible as an instrument of religion cannot be gainsaid." Id. at 224, 83 S.Ct. at 1572. Similarly, in *Engel v. Vitale*, 370 U.S. 421, 82 S.Ct. 1261, 8 L.Ed.2d 601 (1962), the Court held that the First Amendment prohibited the New York Board of Regents from requiring the daily recitation of a certain prayer in the schools. With characteristic succinctness, Justice Black wrote, "Under [the First] Amendment's prohibition against governmental establishment of religion, as reinforced by the provisions of the Fourteenth Amendment, government in this country, be it state or federal, is without power to prescribe by law any particular form of prayer which is to be used as an official prayer in carrying on any program of governmentally sponsored religious activity." Id. at 430, 82 S.Ct. at 1266. Black also identified the objective at which the Establishment Clause was aimed: "Its first and most immediate purpose rested on the belief that a union of government and religion tends to destroy government and to degrade religion." Id. at 431, 82 S.Ct. at 1267.

Most recently, the Supreme Court has held that the clause prohibits a state from requiring the posting of the Ten Commandments in public school classrooms for the same reasons that officially imposed daily Bible reading is prohibited. *Stone v. Graham*, 449 U.S. 39, 101 S.Ct. 192, 66 L.Ed.2d 199 (1980). The opinion in *Stone* relies on the most recent formulation of the Establishment Clause test, that of *Lemon v. Kurtzman*, 403 U.S. 602, 612-613, 91 S.Ct. 2105, 2111, 29 L.Ed.2d 745 (1971):

"First, the statute must have a secular legislative purpose; second, its principal or primary effect must be one that neither advances nor inhibits religion . . . ; finally, the statute must not foster 'an excessive government entanglement with religion.' "

Stone v. Graham, 449 U.S. at 40, 101 S.Ct. at 193.

It is under this three part test that the evidence in this case must be judged. Failure on any of these grounds is fatal to the enactment.

II.

The religious movement known as Fundamentalism began in nineteenth century America as part of evangelical Protestantism's response to social changes, new religious thought and Darwinism. Fundamentalists viewed these developments as attacks on the Bible and as responsible for a decline in traditional values.

The various manifestations of Fundamentalism have had a number of common characteristics,[4] but a central premise has alway been a literal interpretation of the Bible and a belief in the inerrancy of the Scriptures. Following World War I, there was again a perceived decline in traditional morality, and Fundamentalism focused on evolution as responsible for the decline. One aspect of their efforts, particularly in the South, was the promotion of statutes prohibiting the teaching of evolution in public schools. In Arkansas, this resulted in the adoption of Initiated Act 1 of 1929.[5]

Between the 1920's and early 1960's, anti-evolutionary sentiment had a subtle but pervasive influence on the teaching of biology in public schools. Generally, textbooks avoided the topic of evolution and did not mention the name of Darwin. Following the launch of the Sputnik satellite by the Soviet Union in 1957, the National Science Foundation funded several programs designed to modernize the teaching of science in the nation's schools. The Biological Sciences Curriculum Study (BSCS), a nonprofit organization, was among those receiving grants for curriculum study and revision. Working with scientists and teachers, BSCS developed a series of biology texts which, although emphasizing different aspects of biology, incorporated the theory of evolution as a major theme. The success of the BSCS effort is shown by the fact that fifty percent of American school children currently use BSCS books directly and the curriculum is incorporated indirectly in virtually all biology texts. (Testimony of Mayer; Nelkin, Px 1)[6]

In the early 1960's, there was again a resurgence of concern among Fundamentalists about the loss of traditional values and a fear of growing secularism in society. The Fundamentalist movement became more active and has steadily grown in numbers and political influence. There is an emphasis among current Fundamentalists on the literal interpretation of the Bible and the Book of Genesis as the sole source of knowledge about origins.

The term "scientific creationism" first gained currency around 1965 following publication of the The Genesis Flood in 1961 by Whitcomb and Morris. There is undoubtedly some connection between the appearance of the BSCS texts emphasizing evolutionary thought and efforts by Fundamentalists to attack the theory. (Mayer)

In the 1960's and early 1970's, several Fundamentalist organizations were formed to promote the idea that the Book of Genesis was supported by scientific data. The terms "creation science" and "scientific creationism" have been adopted by these Fundamentalists as descriptive of their study of creation and the origins of man. Perhaps the leading creationist organization is the Institute for Creation Research (ICR), which is affiliated with the Christian Heritage College and supported by the Scott Memorial Baptist Church in San Diego, California. The ICR, through the Creation-Life Publishing Company, is the leading publisher of creation science material. Other creation science organizations include the Creation Science Research Center (CSRC) of San Diego and the Bible Science Association of Minneapolis, Minnesota. In 1963, the Creation Research Society (CRS) was formed from a schism in the American Scientific Affiliation (ASA). It is an organization of literal Fundamentalists[7] who have the equivalent of a master's degree in some recognized area of science. A purpose of the organization is "to reach all people with the vital message of the scientific and historic truth about creation." Nelkin, *The Science Textbook Controversies and the Politics of Equal Time*, 66. Similarly, the CSRC was formed in 1970 from a split in the CRS. Its aim has been "to reach the 63 million children of the United States with the scientific teaching of Biblical creationism." *Id.* at 69.

Among creationist writers who are recognized as authorities in the field by other creationists are Henry M. Morris, Duane Gish, G. E. Parker, Harold S. Slusher, Richard B. Bliss, John W. Moore, Martin E. Clark, W. L. Wysong, Robert E. Kofahl and Kelly L. Segraves. Morris is Director of ICR, Gish is Associate Director and Segraves is associated with CSRC.

Creationists view evolution as a source of society's ills, and the writings of Morris and Clark are typical expressions of that view.

"Evolution is thus not only anti-Biblical and anti-Christian, but it is utterly unscientific and impossible as well. But it has served effectively as the pseudo-scientific basis of atheism, agnosticism, socialism, fascism, and numerous other false and dangerous philosophies over the past century."

Morris and Clark, *The Bible Has the Answer*, (Px 31 and Pretrial Px 89).[8]

Creationists have adopted the view of Fundamentalists generally that there are only two positions with respect to the origins of the earth and life: belief in the inerrancy of the Genesis story of creation and of a worldwide flood as fact, or belief in what they call evolution.

Henry Morris has stated, "It is impossible to devise a legitimate means of harmonizing the Bible with evolution." Morris, "Evolution and the Bible," *ICR Impact Series* Number 5 (undated, unpaged), quoted in Mayer, Px 8, at 3. This dualistic approach to the subject of origins permeates the creationist literature.

The creationist organizations consider the introduction of creation science into the public schools part of their ministry. The ICR has published at least two pamphlets[9] containing suggested methods for convincing school boards, administrators and teachers that creationism should be taught in public schools. The ICR has urged its proponents to encourage school officials to voluntarily add creationism to the curriculum.[10]

Citizens For Fairness In Education is an organization based in Anderson, South Carolina, formed by Paul Ellwanger, a respiratory therapist who is trained in neither law nor science. Mr. Ellwanger is of the opinion that evolution is the forerunner of many social ills, including Nazism, racism and abortion. (Ellwanger Depo. at 32–34). About 1977, Ellwanger collected several proposed legislative acts with the idea of preparing a model state act requiring the teaching of creationism as science in opposition to evolution. One of the proposals he collected was prepared by Wendell Bird, who is now a staff attorney for ICR.[11] From these various proposals, Ellwanger prepared a "model act" which calls for "balanced treatment" of "scientific creationism" and "evolution" in public schools. He circulated the proposed act to various people and organizations around the country.

Mr. Ellwanger's views on the nature of creation science are entitled to some weight since he personally drafted the model act which became Act 590. His evidentiary deposition with exhibits and unnumbered attachments (produced in response to a subpoena *duces tecum*) speaks to both the intent of the Act and the scientific merits of creation science. Mr. Ellwanger does not believe creation science is a science. In a letter to Pastor Robert E. Hays he states, "While neither evolution nor creation can qualify as a scientific theory, and since it is virtually impossible at this point to educate the whole world that evolution is not a true scientific theory, we have freely used these terms—the evolution theory and the theory of scientific creationism—in the bill's text." (Unnumbered attachment to Ellwanger Depo., at 2.) He further states in a letter to Mr. Tom Bethell, "As we examine evolution (remember, we're not making any scientific claims for creation, but we are challenging evolution's claim to be scientific) . . . " (Unnumbered attachment to Ellwanger Depo. at 1.)

Ellwanger's correspondence on the subject shows an awareness that Act 590 is a religious crusade, coupled with a desire to conceal this fact. In a letter to State Senator Bill Keith of Louisiana, he says, "I view this whole battle as one between God and anti-God forces, though I know there are a large number of evolutionists who believe in God." And further, " . . . it behooves Satan to do all he can to thwart our efforts and confuse the issue at every turn." Yet Ellwanger suggests to Senator Keith, "If you have a clear choice between having grassroots leaders of this statewide bill promotion effort to be ministerial or non-ministerial, be sure to opt for the non-ministerial. It does the bill effort no good to have ministers out there in the public forum and the adversary will surely pick at this point . . . Ministerial persons can accomplish a tremendous amount of work from behind the scenes, encouraging their congregations to take the organizational and P.R. initiatives. And they can lead their churches in storming Heaven with prayers for help against so tenacious an adversary." (Unnumbered attachment to Ellwanger Depo. at 1.)

Ellwanger shows a remarkable degree of political candor, if not finesse, in a letter to State Senator Joseph Carlucci of Florida:

"2. It would be very wise, if not actually essential, that all of us who are engaged in this legislative effort be careful not to present our position and our work in a religious framework. For example, in written communications that might somehow be shared with those other persons whom we may be trying to convince, it would be well to exclude our own personal testimony and/or witness for Christ, but rather, if we are so moved, to give that testimony on a separate attached note." (Unnumbered attachment to Ellwanger Depo. at 1.)

The same tenor is reflected in a letter by Ellwanger to Mary Ann Miller, a member of FLAG (Family, Life, America under God) who lobbied the Arkansas Legislature in favor of Act 590:

" . . . we'd like to suggest that you and your co-workers be very cautious about mixing creation-science with creation-religion . . . Please urge your co-workers not to allow themselves to get sucked into the 'religion' trap of mixing the two together, for such mixing does incalculable harm to the legislative thrust. It could even bring public opinion to bear adversely upon the higher courts that will eventually have to pass judgment on the constitutionality of this new law." (Ex. 1 to Miller Depo.)

Perhaps most interesting, however, is Mr. Ellwanger's testimony in his deposition as to his strategy for having the model act implemented:

Q. You're trying to play on other people's religious motives.
A. I'm trying to play on their emotions, love, hate, their likes, dislikes, because I don't know any other way to involve, to get humans to become

involved in human endeavors. I see emotions as being a healthy and legitimate means of getting people's feelings into action, and . . . I believe that the predominance of population in America that represents the greatest potential for taking some kind of action in this area is a Christian community. I see the Jewish community as far less potential in taking action . . . but I've seen a lot of interest among Christians and I feel, why not exploit that to get the bill going if that's what it takes. (Ellwanger Depo. at 146–147.)

Mr. Ellwanger's ultimate purpose is revealed in the closing of his letter to Mr. Tom Bethell: "Perhaps all this is old hat to you, Tom, and if so, I'd appreciate your telling me so and perhaps where you've heard it before—the idea of killing evolution instead of playing these debating games that we've been playing for nigh over a decade already." (Unnumbered attachment to Ellwanger Depo. at 3.)

It was out of this milieu that Act 590 emerged. The Reverend W. A. Blount, a Biblical literalist who is pastor of a church in the Little Rock area and was, in February, 1981, chairman of the Greater Little Rock Evangelical Fellowship, was among those who received a copy of the model act from Ellwanger.[12]

At Reverend Blount's request, the Evangelical Fellowship unanimously adopted a resolution to seek introduction of Ellwanger's act in the Arkansas Legislature. A committee composed of two ministers, Curtis Thomas and W. A. Young, was appointed to implement the resolution. Thomas obtained from Ellwanger a revised copy of the model act which he transmitted to Carl Hunt, a business associate of Senator James L. Holsted, with the request that Hunt prevail upon Holsted to introduce the act.

Holsted, a self-described "born again" Christian Fundamentalist, introduced the act in the Arkansas Senate. He did not consult the State Department of Education, scientists, science educators or the Arkansas Attorney General.[13] The Act was not referred to any Senate committee for hearing and was passed after only a few minutes' discussion on the Senate floor. In the House of Representatives, the bill was referred to the Education Committee which conducted a perfunctory fifteen minute hearing. No scientist testified at the hearing, nor was any representative from the State Department of Education called to testify.

Ellwanger's model act was enacted into law in Arkansas as Act 590 without amendment or modification other than minor typographical changes. The legislative "findings of fact" in Ellwanger's act and Act 590 are identical, although no meaningful fact-finding process was employed by the General Assembly.

Ellwanger's efforts in preparation of the model act and campaign for its adoption in the states were motivated by his opposition to the theory of evolution and his desire to see the Biblical version of creation taught in the public schools. There is no evidence that the pastors, Blount, Thomas, Young or The Greater Little Rock Evangelical Fellowship were motivated by anything other than their religious convictions when proposing its adoption or during their lobbying efforts in its behalf. Senator Holsted's sponsorship and lobbying efforts in behalf of the Act were motivated solely by his religious beliefs and desire to see the Biblical version of creation taught in the public schools.[14]

The State of Arkansas, like a number of states whose citizens have relatively homogeneous religious beliefs, has a long history of official opposition to evolution which is motivated by adherence to Fundamentalist beliefs in the inerrancy of the Book of Genesis. This history is documented in Justice Fortas' opinion in *Epperson v. Arkansas*, 393 U.S. 97, 89 S.Ct.266,21 L.Ed.2d 228 (1968), which struck down Initiated Act 1 of 1929, Ark.Stat.Ann. §§ 80-1627-1628, prohibiting the teaching of the theory of evolution. To this same tradition may be attributed Initiated Act 1 of 1930, Ark.Stat.Ann. § 80-1606 (Repl.1980), requiring "the reverent daily reading of a portion of the English Bible" in every public school classroom in the State.[15]

It is true, as defendants argue, that courts should look to legislative statements of a statute's purpose in Establishment Clause cases and accord such pronouncements great deference. See, e.g., *Committee for Public Education & Religious Liberty v. Nyquist*, 413 U.S. 756, 773, 93 S.Ct. 2955, 2965, 37 L.Ed.2d 948 (1973) and *McGowan v. Maryland*, 366 U.S. 420, 445, 81 S.Ct. 1101, 1115, 6 L.Ed.2d 393 (1961). Defendants also correctly state the principle that remarks by the sponsor or author of a bill are not considered controlling in analyzing legislative intent. See, e.g., *United States v. Emmons*, 410 U.S. 396, 93 S.Ct. 1007, 35 L.Ed.2d 379 (1973) and *Chrysler Corp. v. Brown*, 441 U.S. 281, 99 S.Ct. 1705, 60 L.Ed.2d 208 (1979).

Courts are not bound, however, by legislative statements of purpose or legislative disclaimers. *Stone v. Graham*, 449 U.S. 39, 101 S.Ct. 192, 66 L.Ed.2d 199 (1980); *Abington School Dist. v. Schempp*, 374 U.S. 203, 83 S.Ct. 1560, 10 L.Ed.2d 844 (1963). In determining the legislative purpose of a statute, courts may consider evidence of the historical context of the Act, *Epperson v. Arkansas*, 393 U.S. 97, 89 S.Ct. 266, 21 L.Ed.2d 228 (1968), the specific sequence of events leading up to passage of the Act, departures from normal procedural sequences, substantive departures from the normal, *Village of Arlington Heights v. Metropolitan Housing Corp.*, 429 U.S. 252, 97 S.Ct. 555, 50 L.Ed.2d 450 (1977), and contemporaneous statements of the legislative sponsor, *Fed. Energy Admin. v. Algonquin SNG, Inc.*, 426 U.S. 548, 564, 96 S.Ct. 2295, 2304, 49 L.Ed.2d 49 (1976).

The unusual circumstances surrounding the passage of Act 590, as well as the substantive law of the First Amendment, warrant an inquiry into the stated legislative purposes. The author of the Act had publicly proclaimed the sectarian purpose of the proposal. The Arkansas residents who sought legislative sponsorship of the bill did so for a purely sectarian purpose. These circumstances alone may not be particularly persuasive, but when considered with the publicly announced motives of the legislative sponsor made contemporaneously with the legislative process; the lack of any legislative investigation, debate or consultation with any educators or scientists; the unprecedented intrusion in school curriculum;[16] and official history of the State of Arkansas on the subject, it is obvious that the statement of purposes has little, if any, support in fact. The State failed to produce any evidence which would warrant an inference or conclusion that at any point in the process anyone considered the legitimate educational value of the Act. It was simply and purely an effort to introduce the Biblical version of creation into the public school curricula. The only inference which can be drawn from these circumstances is that the Act was passed with the specific purpose by the General Assembly of advancing religion. The Act therefore fails the first prong of the three-pronged test, that of secular legislative purpose, as articulated in *Lemon* v. *Kurtzman, supra,* and *Stone* v. *Graham, supra.*

III

If the defendants are correct and the Court is limited to an examination of the language of the Act, the evidence is overwhelming that both the purpose and effect of Act 590 is the advancement of religion in the public schools.

Section 4 of the Act provides:
Definitions. As used in this Act:
(a) "Creation-science" means the scientific evidences for creation and inferences from those scientific evidences. Creation-science includes the scientific evidences and related inferences that indicate: (1) Sudden creation of the universe, energy, and life from nothing; (2) The insufficiency of mutation and natural selection in bringing about development of all living kinds from a single organism; (3) Changes only within fixed limits of originally created kinds of plants and animals; (4) Separate ancestry for man and apes; (5) Explanation of the earth's geology by catastrophism, including the occurrence of a worldwide flood; and (6) A relatively recent inception of the earth and living kinds.
(b) "Evolution-science" means the scientific evi-

dences for evolution and inferences from those scientific evidences. Evolution-science includes the scientific evidences and related inferences that indicate: (1) Emergence by naturalistic processes of the universe from disordered matter and emergence of life from nonlife; (2) The sufficiency of mutation and natural selection in bringing about development of present living kinds from simple earlier kinds; (3) Emergence by mutation and natural selection of present living kinds from simple earlier kinds; (4) Emergence of man from a common ancestor with apes; (5) Explanation of the earth's geology and the evolutionary sequence by uniformitarianism; and (6) An inception several billion years ago of the earth and somewhat later of life.
(c) "Public schools" mean public secondary and elementary schools.

The evidence establishes that the definition of "creation science" contained in 4(a) has as its unmentioned reference the first 11 chapters of the Book of Genesis. Among the many creation epics in human history, the account of sudden creation from nothing, or *creatio ex nihilo,* and subsequent destruction of the world by flood is unique to Genesis. The concepts of 4(a) are the literal Fundamentalists' view of Genesis. Section 4(a) is unquestionably a statement of religion, with the exception of 4(a)(2) which is a negative thrust aimed at what the creationists understand to be the theory of evolution.[17]

Both the concepts and wording of Section 4(a) convey an inescapable religiosity. Section 4(a)(1) describes "sudden creation of the universe, energy and life from nothing." Every theologian who testified, including defense witnesses, expressed the opinion that the statement referred to a supernatural creation which was performed by God.

Defendants argue that: (1) the fact that 4(a) conveys ideas similar to the literal interpretation of Genesis does not make it conclusively a statement of religion; (2) that reference to a creation from nothing is not necessarily a religious concept since the Act only suggests a creator who has power, intelligence and a sense of design and not necessarily the attributes of love, compassion and justice;[18] and (3) that simply teaching about the concept of a creator is not a religious exercise unless the student is required to make a commitment to the concept of a creator.

The evidence fully answers these arguments. The ideas of 4(a)(1) are not merely similar to the literal interpretation of Genesis; they are identical and parallel to no other story of creation.[19]

The argument that creation from nothing in 4(a)(1) does not involve a supernatural deity has no evidentiary or rational support. To the contrary, "creation out of nothing" is a concept unique to Western religions. In traditional Western religious thought, the conception of a creator of the world is a conception of God. Indeed, creation of the world "out of nothing" is the ultimate religious statement because God is the only actor. As Dr. Langdon Gilkey noted, the Act refers to one who has the power to bring all the universe into existence from nothing. The only "one" who has this power is God.[20]

The leading creationist writers, Morris and Gish, acknowledge that the idea of creation described in 4(a)(1) is the concept of creation by God and make no pretense to the contrary.[21] The idea of sudden creation from nothing, or *creatio ex nihilo,* is an inherently religious concept. (Vawter, Gilkey, Geisler, Ayala, Blount, Hicks.)

The argument advanced by defendants' witness, Dr. Norman Geisler, that teaching the existence of God is not religious unless the teaching seeks a commitment, is contrary to common understanding and contradicts settled case law. *Stone v. Graham,* 449 U.S. 39, 101 S.Ct. 192, 66 L.Ed.2d 199 (1980); *Abington School District v. Schempp,* 374 U.S. 203, 83 S.Ct. 1560, 10 L.Ed.2d 844 (1963).

The facts that creation science is inspired by the Book of Genesis and that Section 4(a) is consistent with a literal interpretation of Genesis leave no doubt that a major effect of the Act is the advancement of particular religious beliefs. The legal impact of this conclusion will be discussed further at the conclusion of the Court's evaluation of the scientific merit of creation science.

IV. (A)

The approach to teaching "creation science" and "evolution science" found in Act 590 is identical to the two-model approach espoused by the Institute for Creation Research and is taken almost verbatim from ICR writings. It is an extension of Fundamentalists' view that one must either accept the literal interpretation of Genesis or else believe in the godless system of evolution.

The two model approach of the creationists is simply a contrived dualism[22] which has no scientific factual basis or legitimate educational purpose. It assumes only two explanations for the origins of life and existence of man, plants and animals: It was either the work of a creator or it was not. Application of these two models, according to creationists, and the defendants, dictates that all scientific evidence which fails to support the theory of evolution is necessarily scientific evidence in support of creationism and is, therefore, creation science "evidence" in support of Section 4(a).

IV. (B)

The emphasis on origins as an aspect of the theory of evolution is peculiar to creationist literature. Although the subject of origins of life is within the province of biology, the scientific community does not consider origins of life a part of evolutionary theory. The theory of evolution assumes the existence of life and is directed to an explanation of *how* life evolved. Evolution does not presuppose the absence of a creator or God and the plain inference conveyed by Section 4 is erroneous.[23]

As a statement of the theory of evolution, Section 4(b) is simply a hodgepodge of limited assertions, many of which are factually inaccurate.

For example, although 4(b)(2) asserts, as a tenet of evolutionary theory, "the sufficiency of mutation and natural selection in bringing about the existence of present living kinds from simple earlier kinds," Drs. Ayala and Gould both stated that biologists know that these two processes do not account for all significant evolutionary change. They testified to such phenomena as recombination, the founder effect, genetic drift and the theory of punctuated equilibrium, which are believed to play important evolutionary roles. Section 4(b) omits any reference to these. Moreover, 4(b) utilizes the term "kinds" which all scientists said is not a word of science and has no fixed meaning. Additionally, the Act presents both evolution and creation science as "package deals." Thus, evidence critical of some aspect of what the creationists define as evolution is taken as support for a theory which includes a worldwide flood and a relatively young earth.[24]

IV. (C)

In addition to the fallacious pedagogy of the two model approach, Section 4(a) lacks legitimate educational value because "creation science" as defined in that section is simply not science. Several witnesses suggested definitions of science. A descriptive definition was said to be that science is what is "accepted by the scientific community" and is "what scientists do." The obvious implication of this description is that, in a free society, knowledge does not require the imprimatur of legislation in order to become science.

More precisely, the essential characteristics of science are:
(1) It is guided by natural law;
(2) It has to be explanatory by reference to natural law;
(3) It is testable against the empirical world;
(4) Its conclusions are tentative, i.e., are not necessarily the final word; and

(5)   It is falsifiable. (Ruse and other science witnesses).

Creation science as described in Section 4(a) fails to meet these essential characteristics. First, the section revolves around 4(a)(1) which asserts a sudden creation "from nothing." Such a concept is not science because it depends upon a supernatural intervention which is not guided by natural law. It is not explanatory by reference to natural law, is not testable and is not falsifiable.[25]

If the unifying idea of supernatural creation by God is removed from Section 4, the remaining parts of the section explain nothing and are meaningless assertions.

Section 4(a)(2), relating to the "insufficiency of mutation and natural selection in bringing about development of all living kinds from a single organism," is an incomplete negative generalization directed at the theory of evolution.

Section 4(a)(3) which describes "changes only within fixed limits of originally created kinds of plants and animals" fails to conform to the essential characteristics of science for several reasons. First, there is no scientific definition of "kinds" and none of the witnesses was able to point to any scientific authority which recognized the term or knew how many "kinds" existed. One defense witness suggested there may be 100 to 10,000 different "kinds." Another believes there were "about 10,000, give or take a few thousand." Second, the assertion appears to be an effort to establish outer limits of changes within species. There is no scientific explanation for these limits which is guided by natural law and the limitations, whatever they are, cannot be explained by natural law.

The statement in 4(a)(4) of "separate ancestry of man and apes" is a bald assertion. It explains nothing and refers to no scientific fact or theory.[26]

Section 4(a)(5) refers to "explanation of the earth's geology by catastrophism, including the occurrence of a worldwide flood." This assertion completely fails as science. The Act is referring to the Noachian flood described in the Book of Genesis.[27] The creationist writers concede that *any* kind of Genesis Flood depends upon supernatural intervention. A worldwide flood as an explanation of the world's geology is not the product of natural law, nor can its occurrence be explained by natural law.

Section 4(a)(6) equally fails to meet the standards of science. "Relatively recent inception" has no scientific meaning. It can only be given meaning by reference to creationist writings which place the age at between 6,000 and 20,000 years because of the genealogy of the Old Testament. See, e.g. Px 78, Gish (6,000 to 10,000); Px 87, Segraves (6,000 to 20,000). Such a reasoning process is not the product of natural law; not explainable by natural law; nor is it tentative.

Creation science, as defined in Section 4(a), not only fails to follow the canons defining scientific theory, it also fails to fit the more general descriptions of "what scientists think" and "what scientists do." The scientific community consists of individuals and groups, nationally and internationally, who work independently in such varied fields as biology, paleontology, geology and astronomy. Their work is published and subject to review and testing by their peers. The journals for publication are both numerous and varied. There is, however, not one recognized scientific journal which has published an article espousing the creation science theory described in Section 4(a). Some of the State's witnesses suggested that the scientific community was "close-minded" on the subject of creationism and that explained the lack of acceptance of the creation science arguments. Yet no witness produced a scientific article for which publication had been refused. Perhaps some members of the scientific community are resistant to new ideas. It is, however, inconceivable that such a loose knit group of independent thinkers in all the varied fields of science could, or would, so effectively censor new scientific thought.

The creationists have difficulty maintaining among their ranks consistency in the claim that creationism is science. The author of Act 590, Ellwanger, said that neither evolution nor creationism was science. He thinks both are religion. Duane Gish recently responded to an article in *Discover* critical of creationism by stating:

"Stephen Jay Gould states that creationists claim creation is a scientific theory. This is a false accusation. Creationists have repeatedly stated that neither creation nor evolution is a scientific theory (and each is equally religious)." Gish, letter to editor of *Discover*, July, 1981, App. 30 to Plaintiffs' Pretrial Brief.

The methodology employed by creationists is another factor which is indicative that their work is not science. A scientific theory must be tentative and always subject to revision or abandonment in light of facts that are inconsistent with, or falsify, the theory. A theory that is by its own terms dogmatic, absolutist and never subject to revision is not a scientific theory.

The creationists' methods do not take data, weigh it against the opposing scientific data, and thereafter reach the conclusions stated in Section 4(a). Instead, they take the literal wording of the Book of Genesis and attempt to find scientific support for it. The method is best explained in the language of Morris in his book (Px 31) *Studies in The Bible and Science* at page 114:

" . . . it is . . . quite impossible to determine anything about Creation through a study of present processes, because present processes are not creative in character. If man wishes to know anything about Creation (the time of Creation, the duration of Creation, the order of Creation, the methods of Creation, or anything else) his sole source of true information is that of divine revelation. God was there when it happened. We were not there . . . Therefore, we are completely limited to what God has seen fit to tell us, and this information is in His written Word. This is our textbook on the science of Creation!"

The Creation Research Society employs the same unscientific approach to the issue of creationism. Its applicants for membership must subscribe to the belief that the Book of Genesis is "historically and scientifically true in all of the original autographs."[28] The Court would never criticize or discredit any person's testimony based on his or her religious beliefs. While anybody is free to approach a scientific inquiry in any fashion they choose, they cannot properly describe the methodology used as scientific, if they start with a conclusion and refuse to change it regardless of the evidence developed during the course of the investigation.

IV. (D)

In efforts to establish "evidence" in support of creation science, the defendants relied upon the same false premise as the two model approach contained in Section 4, i.e., all evidence which criticized evolutionary theory was proof in support of creation science. For example, the defendants established that the mathematical probability of a chance chemical combination resulting in life from non-life is so remote that such an occurrence is almost beyond imagination. Those mathematical facts, the defendants argue, are scientific evidences that life was the product of a creator. While the statistical figures may be impressive evidence against the theory of chance chemical combinations as an explanation of origins, it requires a leap of faith to interpret those figures so as to support a complex doctrine which includes a sudden creation from nothing, a worldwide flood, separate ancestry of man and apes, and a young earth.

The defendants' argument would be more persuasive if, in fact, there were only two theories or ideas about the origins of life and the world. That there are a number of theories was acknowledged by the State's

witnesses, Dr. Wickramasinghe and Dr. Geisler. Dr. Wickramasinghe testified at length in support of a theory that life on earth was "seeded" by comets which delivered genetic material and perhaps organisms to the earth's surface from interstellar dust far outside the solar system. The "seeding" theory further hypothesizes that the earth remains under the continuing influence of genetic material from space which continues to affect life. While Wickramasinghe's theory[29] about the origins of life on earth has not received general acceptance within the scientific community, he has, at least, used scientific methodology to produce a theory of origins which meets the essential characteristics of science.

Perhaps Dr. Wickramasinghe was called as a witness because he was generally critical of the theory of evolution and the scientific community, a tactic consistent with the strategy of the defense. Unfortunately for the defense, he demonstrated that the simplistic approach of the two model analysis of the origins of life is false. Furthermore, he corroborated the plaintiffs' witnesses by concluding that "no rational scientist" would believe the earth's geology could be explained by reference to a worldwide flood or that the earth was less than one million years old.

The proof in support of creation science consisted almost entirely of efforts to discredit the theory of evolution through a rehash of data and theories which have been before the scientific community for decades. The arguments asserted by creationists are not based upon new scientific evidence or laboratory data which has been ignored by the scientific community.

Robert Gentry's discovery of radioactive polonium haloes in granite and coalified woods is, perhaps, the most recent scientific work which the creationists use as argument for a "relatively recent inception" of the earth and a "worldwide flood." The existence of polonium haloes in granite and coalified wood is thought to be inconsistent with radiometric dating methods based upon constant radioactive decay rates. Mr. Gentry's findings were published almost ten years ago and have been the subject of some discussion in the scientific community. The discoveries have not, however, led to the formulation of any scientific hypothesis or theory which would explain a relatively recent inception of the earth or a worldwide flood. Gentry's discovery has been treated as a minor mystery which will eventually be explained. It may deserve further investigation, but the National Science Foundation has not deemed it to be of sufficient import to support further funding.

The testimony of Marianne Wilson was persuasive evidence that creation science is not science. Ms. Wilson is in charge of the science curriculum for

Pulaski County Special School District, the largest school district in the State of Arkansas. Prior to the passage of Act 590, Larry Fisher, a science teacher in the District, using materials from the ICR, convinced the School Board that it should voluntarily adopt creation science as part of its science curriculum. The District Superintendent assigned Ms. Wilson the job of producing a creation science curriculum guide. Ms. Wilson's testimony about the project was particularly convincing because she obviously approached the assignment with an open mind and no preconceived notions about the subject. She had not heard of creation science until about a year ago and did not know its meaning before she began her research.

Ms. Wilson worked with a committee of science teachers appointed from the District. They reviewed practically all of the creationist literature. Ms. Wilson and the committee members reached the unanimous conclusion that creationism is not science; it is religion. They so reported to the Board. The Board ignored the recommendation and insisted that a curriculum guide be prepared.

In researching the subject, Ms. Wilson sought the assistance of Mr. Fisher who initiated the Board action and asked professors in the science departments of the University of Arkansas at Little Rock and the University of Central Arkansas[30] for reference material and assistance, and attended a workshop conducted at Central Baptist College by Dr. Richard Bliss of the ICR staff. Act 590 became law during the course of her work so she used Section 4(a) as a format for her curriculum guide.

Ms. Wilson found all available creationists' materials unacceptable because they were permeated with religious references and reliance upon religious beliefs.

It is easy to understand why Ms. Wilson and other educators find the creationists' textbook material and teaching guides unacceptable. The materials misstate the theory of evolution in the same fashion as Section 4(b) of the Act, with emphasis on the alternative mutually exclusive nature of creationism and evolution. Students are constantly encouraged to compare and make a choice between the two models, and the material is not presented in an accurate manner.

A typical example is *Origins* (Px 76) by Richard B. Bliss, Director of Curriculum Development of the ICR. The presentation begins with a chart describing "preconceived ideas about origins" which suggests that some people believe that evolution is atheistic. Concepts of evolution, such as "adaptive radiation," are erroneously presented. At page 11, figure 1.6, of the text, a chart purports to illustrate this "very important" part of the evolution model. The chart conveys the idea that such diverse mammals as a whale, bear, bat and monkey all evolved from a shrew through the

process of adaptive radiation. Such a suggestion is, of course, a totally erroneous and misleading application of the theory. Even more objectionable, especially when viewed in light of the emphasis on asking the student to elect one of the models, is the chart presentation at page 17, figure 1.6. That chart purports to illustrate the evolutionists' belief that man evolved from bacteria to fish to reptile to mammals and, thereafter, into man. The illustration indicates, however, that the mammal from which man evolved was a *rat*.

Biology, A Search For Order in Complexity[31] is a high school biology text typical of creationists' materials. The following quotations are illustrative:

"Flowers and roots do not have a mind to have purpose of their own; therefore, this planning must have been done for them by the Creator."
—at page 12.
"The exquisite beauty of color and shape in flowers exceeds the skill of poet, artist, and king. Jesus said (from Matthew's gospel), 'Consider the lilies of the field, how they grow; they toil not, neither do they spin . . . ' "
Px 129 at page 363.

The "public school edition" texts written by creationists simply omit Biblical references but the content and message remain the same. For example, *Evolution—The Fossils Say No!*,[32] contains the following:

Creation. By creation we mean the bringing into being by a supernatural Creator of the basic kinds of plants and animals by the process of sudden, or fiat, creation.

We do not know how the Creator created, what processes He used, *for He used processes which are not now operating anywhere in the natural universe.* This is why we refer to creation as Special Creation. We cannot discover by scientific investigation anything about the creative processes used by the Creator."
—page 40

Gish's book also portrays the large majority of evolutionists as "materialistic atheists or agnostics."

Scientific Creationism (Public School Edition) by Morris is another text reviewed by Ms. Wilson's committee and rejected as unacceptable. The following quotes illustrate the purpose and theme of the text:

Forword
"Parents and youth leaders today, and even many scientists and educators, have become concerned about the prevalence and influence of evolutionary philosophy in modern curriculum. Not only is this

system inimical to orthodox Christianity and Judaism, but also, as many are convinced, to a healthy society and true science as well."
at page iii.

* * *

"The rationalist of course finds the concept of special creation insufferably naive, even 'incredible'. Such a judgment, however, is warranted only if one categorically dismisses the existence of an omnipotent God."
at page 17.

Without using creationist literature, Ms. Wilson was unable to locate one genuinely scientific article or work which supported Section 4(a). In order to comply with the mandate of the Board she used such materials as an article from *Readers Digest* about "atomic clocks" which inferentially suggested that the earth was less than 4 1/2 billion years old. She was unable to locate any substantive teaching material for some parts of Section 4 such as the worldwide flood. The curriculum guide which she prepared cannot be taught and has no educational value as science. The defendants did not produce any text or writing in response to this evidence which they claimed was usable in the public school classroom.[33]

The conclusion that creation science has no scientific merit or educational value as science has legal significance in light of the Court's previous conclusion that creation science has, as one major effect, the advancement of religion. The second part of the three-pronged test for establishment reaches only those statutes having as their *primary* effect the advancement of religion. Secondary effects which advance religion are not constitutionally fatal. Since creation science is not science, the conclusion is inescapable that the *only* real effect of Act 590 is the advancement of religion. The Act therefore fails both the first and second portions of the test in *Lemon v. Kurtzman,* 403 U.S. 602, 91 S.Ct. 2105, 29 L.Ed.2d 745 (1971).

IV. (E)

Act 590 mandates "balanced treatment" for creation science and evolution science. The Act prohibits instruction in any religious doctrine or references to religious writings. The Act is self-contradictory and compliance is impossible unless the public schools elect to forego significant portions of subjects such as biology, world history, geology, zoology, botany, psychology, anthropology, sociology, philosophy, physics and chemistry. Presently, the concepts of evolutionary theory as described in 4(b) permeate the public school textbooks. There is no way teachers can teach the Genesis account of creation in a secular manner.

The State Department of Education, through its textbook selection committtee, school boards and school administrators will be required to constantly monitor materials to avoid using religious references. The school boards, administrators and teachers face an impossible task. How is the teacher to respond to questions about a creation suddenly and out of nothing? How will a teacher explain the occurrence of a worldwide flood? How will a teacher explain the concept of a relatively recent age of the earth? The answer is obvious because the only source of this information is ultimately contained in the Book of Genesis.

References to the pervasive nature of religious concepts in creation science texts amply demonstrate why State entanglement with religion is inevitable under Act 590. Involvement of the State in screening texts for impermissible religious references will require State officials to make delicate religious judgments. The need to monitor classroom discussion in order to uphold the Act's prohibition against religious instruction will necessarily involve administrators in questions concerning religion. These continuing involvements of State officials in questions and issues of religion create an excessive and prohibited entanglement with religion. *Brandon v. Board of Education,* 487 F.Supp. 1219, 1230 (N.D.N.Y.), *aff'd.,* 635 F.2d 971 (2nd Cir. 1980).

V.

These conclusions are dispositive of the case and there is no need to reach legal conclusions with respect to the remaining issues. The plaintiffs raised two other issues questioning the constitutionality of the Act and, insofar as the factual findings relevant to these issues are not covered in the preceding discussion, the Court will address these issues. Additionally, the defendants raised two other issues which warrant discussion.

V. (A)

First, plaintiff teachers argue the Act is unconstitutionally vague to the extent that they cannot comply with its mandate of "balanced" treatment without jeopardizing their employment. The argument centers around the lack of a precise definition in the Act for the word "balanced." Several witnesses expressed opinions that the word has such meanings as equal time, equal weight, or equal legitimacy. Although the Act could have been more explicit, "balanced" is a word subject to ordinary understanding. The proof is not convincing that a teacher using a reasonably acceptable understanding of the word and making a good faith effort to comply with the Act will be in jeopardy of termination. Other portions of the Act are arguably vague, such as the "relatively recent" inception of the earth and life.

The evidence establishes, however, that relatively recent means from 6,000 to 20,000 years, as commonly understood in creation science literature. The meaning of this phrase, like Section 4(a) generally, is, for purposes of the Establishment Clause, all too clear.

V. (B)

The plaintiffs' other argument revolves around the alleged infringement by the defendants upon the academic freedom of teachers and students. It is contended this unprecedented intrusion in the curriculum by the State prohibits teachers from teaching what they believe should be taught or requires them to teach that which they do not believe is proper. The evidence reflects that traditionally the State Department of Education, local school boards and administration officials exercise little, if any, influence upon the subject matter taught by classroom teachers. Teachers have been given freedom to teach and emphasize those portions of subjects the individual teacher considered important. The limits to this discretion have generally been derived from the approval of textbooks by the State Department and preparation of curriculum guides by the school districts.

Several witnesses testified that academic freedom for the teacher means, in substance, that the individual teacher should be permitted unlimited discretion subject only to the bounds of professional ethics. The Court is not prepared to adopt such a broad view of academic freedom in the public schools.

In any event, if Act 590 is implemented, many teachers will be required to teach material in support of creation science which they do not consider academically sound. Many teachers will simply forego teaching subjects which might trigger the "balanced treatment" aspects of Act 590 even though they think the subjects are important to a proper presentation of a course.

Implementation of Act 590 will have serious and untoward consequences for students, particularly those planning to attend college. Evolution is the cornerstone of modern biology, and many courses in public schools contain subject matter relating to such varied topics as the age of the earth, geology and relationships among living things. Any student who is deprived of instruction as to the prevailing scientific thought on these topics will be denied a significant part of science education. Such a deprivation through the high school level would undoubtedly have an impact upon the quality of education in the State's colleges and universities, especially including the pre-professional and professional programs in the health sciences.

V. (C)

The defendants argue in their brief that evolution is, in effect, a religion, and that by teaching a religion which is contrary to some students' religious views, the State is infringing upon the student's free exercise rights under the First Amendment. Mr. Ellwanger's legislative findings, which were adopted as a finding of fact by the Arkansas Legislature in Act 590, provides:

"Evolution-science is contrary to the religious convictions or moral values or philosophical beliefs of many students and parents, including individuals of many different religious faiths and with diverse moral and philosophical beliefs." Act 590, § 7(d).

The defendants argue that the teaching of evolution alone presents both a free exercise problem and an establishment problem which can only be redressed by giving balanced treatment to creation science, which is admittedly consistent with some religious beliefs. This argument appears to have its genesis in a student note written by Mr. Wendell Bird, "Freedom of Religion and Science Instruction in Public Schools," 87 Yale L.J. 515 (1978). The argument has no legal merit.

If creation science is, in fact, science and not religion, as the defendants claim, it is difficult to see how the teaching of such a science could "neutralize" the religious nature of evolution.

Assuming for the purposes of argument, however, that evolution is a religion or religious tenet, the remedy is to stop the teaching of evolution; not establish another religion in opposition to it. Yet it is clearly established in the case law, and perhaps also in common sense, that evolution is not a religion and that teaching evolution does not violate the Establishment Clause, *Epperson v. Arkansas, supra; Willoughby v. Stever*, No. 15574-75 (D.D.C. May 18, 1973), *aff'd.* 504 F.2d 271 (D.C.Cir.1974), *cert. denied*, 420 U.S. 927, 95 S.Ct. 1124, 43 L.Ed.2d 397 (1975); *Wright v. Houston Indep. School Dist.*, 366 F.Supp. 1208 (S.D.Tex.1978), *aff'd.* 486 F.2d 137 (5th Cir. 1973), cert. denied 417 U.S. 969, 94 S.Ct. 3173, 41 L.Ed.2d 1140 (1974).

V. (D)

The defendants presented Dr. Larry Parker, a specialist in devising curricula for public schools. He testified that the public school's curriculum should reflect the subjects the public wants taught in schools. The witness said that polls indicated a significant majority of the American public thought creation science should be taught if evolution was taught. The point of this testimony was never placed in a legal context. No doubt a sizeable majority of Americans believe in the concept of a Creator or, at least, are not opposed to the concept and see nothing wrong with teaching school children about the idea.

The application and content of First Amendment principles are not determined by public opinion polls or by a majority vote. Whether the proponents of Act 590 constitute the majority or the minority is quite irrelevant under a constitutional system of government. No group, no matter how large or small, may use the organs of government, of which the public schools are the most conspicuous and influential, to foist its religious beliefs on others.

The Court closes this opinion with a thought expressed eloquently by the great Justice Frankfurter:

"We renew our conviction that 'we have staked the very existence of our country on the faith that complete separation between the state and religion is best for the state and best for religion.' *Everson v. Board of Education,* 330 U.S. at 59 [67 S.Ct. at 532]. If nowhere else, in the relation between Church and State, 'good fences make good neighbors.' " *McCollum v. Board of Education,* 333 U.S. 203, 232, 68 S.Ct. 461, 475, 92 L.Ed. 649 (1948).

An injunction will be entered permanently prohibiting enforcement of Act 590.

NOTES

1. The complaint is based on 42 U.S.C. § 1983, which provides a remedy against any person who, acting under color of state law, deprives another of any right, privilege or immunity guaranteed by the United States Constitution or federal law.

    This Court's jurisdiction arises under 28 U.S.C. §§ 1331, 1343(3) and 1343(4). The power to issue declaratory judgments is expressed in 28 U.S.C. §§ 2201 and 2202.

2. The facts necessary to establish the plaintiffs' standing to sue are contained in the joint stipulation of facts, which is hereby adopted and incorporated herein by reference.

    There is no doubt that the case is ripe for adjudication.

3. The State of Arkansas was dismissed as a defendant because of its immunity from suit under the Eleventh Amendment. *Hans v. Louisiana,* 134 U.S. 1, 10 S.Ct. 504, 33 L.Ed. 842 (1890).

4. The authorities differ as to generalizations which may be made about Fundamentalism. For example, Dr. Geisler testified to the widely held view that there are five beliefs characteristic of all Fundamentalist movements, in addition, of course, to the inerrancy of Scripture: (1) belief in the virgin birth of Christ, (2) belief in the deity of Christ, (3) belief in the substitutional atonement of Christ, (4) belief in the second coming of Christ, and (5) belief in the physical resurrection of all departed souls. Dr. Marsden, however, testified that this generalization, which has been common in religious scholarship, is now thought to be historical error. There is no doubt, however, that all Fundamentalists take the Scriptures as inerrant and probably most take them as literally true.

5. Initiated Act 1 of 1929, Ark.Stat.Ann. § 80-1627 *et seq.,* which prohibited the teaching of evolution in Arkansas schools, is discussed *infra* at text accompanying note 15.

6. Subsequent references to the testimony will be made by the last name of the witness only. References to documentary exhibits will be by the name of author and the exhibit number.

7. Applicants for membership in the CRS must subscribe to the following statement of belief: "(1) The Bible is the written Word of God, and because we believe it to be inspired thruout (sic), all of its assertions are historically and scientifically true in all of the original autographs. To the student of nature, this means that the account of origins in Genesis is a factual presentation of simple historical truths. (2) All basic types of living things, including man, were made by direct creative acts of God during Creation Week as described in Genesis. Whatever biological changes have occurred since Creation have accomplished only changes within the original created kinds. (3) The great Flood described in Genesis, commonly referred to as the Noachian Deluge, was an historical event, world-wide in its extent and effect. (4) Finally, we are an organization of Christian men of science, who accept Jesus Christ as our Lord and Savior. The account of the special creation of Adam and Eve as one man and one woman, and their subsequent Fall into sin, is the basis for our belief in the necessity of a Savior for all mankind. Therefore, salvation can come only thru (sic) accepting Jesus Christ as our Savior." (Px 115)

8. Because of the voluminous nature of the documentary exhibits, the parties were directed by pre-trial order to submit their proposed exhibits for the Court's convenience prior to trial. The numbers assigned to the pre-trial submissions do not correspond with those assigned to the same documents at trial and, in some instances, the pre-trial submissions are more complete.

9. Px 130, Morris, *Introducing Scientific Creationism Into the Public Schools* (1975), and Bird, "Resolution for Balanced Presentation of Evolution and Scientific Creationism," *ICR Impact Series* No. 71, App. 14 to Plaintiffs' Pretrial Brief.

10. The creationists often show candor in their proselytization. Henry Morris has stated, "Even if a favorable statute or court decision is obtained, it will probably be declared unconstitutional, especially if the legislation or injunction refers to the Bible account of creation." In the same vein he notes, "The only effective way to get creationism taught properly is to have it taught by teachers who are both willing and able to do it. Since most teachers now are neither willing nor able, they must first be both persuaded and instructed themselves." Px 130, Morris, *Introducing Scientific Creationism Into the Public Schools* (1975) (unpaged).

11. Mr. Bird sought to participate in this litigation by representing a number of individuals who wanted to intervene as defendants. The application for intervention was denied by this Court. *McLean v. Arkansas* (E.D. Ark.1981), aff'd. *per curiam,* 663 F.2d 47 (8th Cir. 1981).

12. The model act had been revised to insert "creation

science" in lieu of creationism because Ellwanger had the impression people thought creationism was too religious a term. (Ellwanger Depo. at 79.)

13. The original model act had been introduced in the South Carolina Legislature, but had died without action after the South Carolina Attorney General had opined that the act was unconstitutional.

14. Specifically, Senator Holsted testified that he holds to a literal interpretation of the Bible; that the bill was compatible with his religious beliefs; that the bill does favor the position of literalists; that his religious convictions were a factor in his sponsorship of the bill; and that he stated publicly to the *Arkansas Gazette* (although not on the floor of the Senate) contemporaneously with the legislative debate that the bill does presuppose the existence of a divine creator. There is no doubt that Senator Holsted knew he was sponsoring the teaching of a religious doctrine. His view was that the bill did not violate the First Amendment because, as he saw it, it did not favor one denomination over another.

15. This statute is, of course, clearly unconstitutional under the Supreme Court's decision in *Abington School Dist. v. Schempp,* 374 U.S. 203, 83 S.Ct. 1560, 10 L.Ed.2d 844 (1963).

16. The joint stipulation of facts establishes that the following areas are the only *information* specifically required by statute to be taught in all Arkansas schools: (1) the effects of alcohol and narcotics on the human body, (2) conservation of national resources, (3) Bird Week, (4) Fire Prevention, and (5) Flag etiquette. Additionally, certain specific courses, such as American history and Arkansas history, must be completed by each student before graduation from high school.

17. Paul Ellwanger stated in his deposition that he did not know why Section 4(a)(2) (insufficiency of mutation and natural selection) was included as an evidence supporting creation science. He indicated that he was not a scientist, "but these are the postulates that have been laid down by creation scientists." Ellwanger Depo. at 136.

18. Although defendants must make some effort to cast the concept of creation in non-religious terms, this effort surely causes discomfort to some of the Act's more theologically sophisticated supporters. The concept of a creator God distinct from the God of love and mercy is closely similar to the Marcion and Gnostic heresies, among the deadliest to threaten the early Christian church. These heresies had much to do with development and adoption of the Apostle's Creed as the official creedal statement of the Roman Catholic Church in the West. (Gilkey.)

19. The parallels between Section 4(a) and Genesis are quite specific: (1) "sudden creation from nothing" is taken from Genesis, 1:1-10 (Vawter, Gilkey); (2) destruction of the world by a flood of divine origin is a notion peculiar to Judeo-Christian tradition and is based on Chapters 7 and 8 of Genesis (Vawter); (3) the term "kinds" has no fixed scientific meaning, but appears repeatedly in Genesis (all scientific witnesses); (4) "relatively recent inception" means an age of the

earth from 6,000 to 10,000 years and is based on the genealogy of the Old Testament using the rather astronomical ages assigned to the patriarchs (Gilkey and several of defendants' scientific witnesses); (5) separate ancestry of man and ape focuses on the portion of the theory of evolution which Fundamentalists find most offensive, *Epperson v. Arkansas,* 393 U.S. 97, 89 S.Ct. 266, 21 L.Ed.2d 228 (1968).

20. "[C]oncepts concerning . . . a supreme being of some sort are manifestly religious . . . These concepts do not shed that religiosity merely because they are presented as philosophy or as a science . . . " *Malnak v. Yogi,* 440 F.Supp. 1284, 1322 (D.N.J.1977); *aff'd per curiam,* 592 F.2d 197 (3d Cir. 1979).

21. See, e.g., Px 76, Morris, *et al, Scientific Creationism,* 203 (1980) ("If creation really is a fact, this means there is a *Creator,* and the universe is His creation.") Numerous other examples of such admissions can be found in the many exhibits which represent creationist literature, but no useful purpose would be served here by a potentially endless listing.

22. Morris, the Director of ICR and one who first advocated the two model approach, insists that a true Christian cannot compromise with the theory of evolution and that the Genesis version of creation and the theory of evolution are mutually exclusive. Px 31, Morris, *Studies in the Bible & Science,* 102-103. The two model approach was the subject of Dr. Richard Bliss's doctoral dissertation. (Dx 35). It is presented in Bliss, *Origins: Two Models-Evolution, Creation* (1978). Moreover, the two model approach merely casts in educationalist language the dualism which appears in all creationist literature—creation (i.e. God) and evolution are presented as two alternative and mutually exclusive theories. See, e.g., Px 75, Morris, *Scientific Creationism* (1974) (public school edition); Px 59, Fox, *fossils: Hard Facts from the Earth.* Particularly illustrative is Px 61, Boardman, *et al, Worlds Without End* (1971), a CSRC publication: "One group of scientists, known as creationists, believe that God, in a miraculous manner, created all matter and energy . . .

"Scientists who insist that the universe just grew, by accident, from a mass of hot gases without the direction or help of a Creator are known as evolutionists."

23. The idea that belief in a creator and acceptance of the scientific theory of evolution are mutually exclusive is a false premise and offensive to the religious views of many. (Hicks) Dr. Francisco Ayala, a geneticist of considerable renown and a former Catholic priest who has the equivalent of a Ph.D. in theology, pointed out that many working scientists who subscribed to the theory of evolution are devoutly religious.

24. This is so despite the fact that some of the defense witnesses do not subscribe to the young earth or flood hypotheses. Dr. Geisler stated his belief that the earth is several billion years old. Dr. Wickramasinghe stated that no rational scientist would believe the earth is less than one million years old or that all the world's geology could be explained by a worldwide flood.

25. "We do not know how God created, what processes He

used, for *God used processes which are not now operating anywhere in the natural universe.* This is why we refer to divine creation as Special Creation. We cannot discover by scientific investigation anything about the creative processes used by God." Px 78, Gish, *Evolution? The Fossils Say No!,* 42 (3d ed. 1979) (emphasis in original).

26. The evolutionary notion that man and some modern apes have a common ancestor somewhere in the distant past has consistently been distorted by anti-evolutionists to say that man descended from modern monkeys. As such, this idea has long been most offensive to Fundamentalists. See, *Epperson v. Arkansas,* 393 U.S. 97, 89 S.Ct. 266, 21 L.Ed.2d 228 (1968).

27. Not only was this point acknowledged by virtually all the defense witnesses, it is patent in the creationist literature. See, e.g., Px 89, Kofahl & Segraves, *The Creation Explanation,* 40: "The Flood of Noah brought about vast changes in the earth's surface, including vulcanism, mountain building, and the deposition of the major part of sedimentary strata. This principle is called 'Biblical catastrophism.' "

28. See n. 7, *supra,* for the full text of the CRS creed.

29. The theory is detailed in Wickramasinghe's book with Sir Fred Hoyle, *Evolution From Space* (1981), which is Dx 79.

30. Ms. Wilson stated that some professors she spoke with sympathized with her plight and tried to help her find scientific materials to support Section 4(a). Others simply asked her to leave.

31. Px 129, published by Zonderman Publishing House (1974), states that it was "prepared by the Textbook Committee of the Creation Research Society." It has a disclaimer pasted inside the front cover stating that it is not suitable for use in public schools.

32. Px 77, by Duane Gish.

33. The passage of Act 590 apparently caught a number of its supporters off guard as much as it did the school district. The Act's author, Paul Ellwanger, stated in a letter to "Dick" (apparently Dr. Richard Bliss at ICR): "And finally, if you know of any textbooks at any level and for any subjects that you think are acceptable to you and also constitutionally admissible, these are things that would be of *enormous* to these bewildered folks who may be caught, as Arkansas now has been, by the sudden need to implement a whole new ball game with which they are quite unfamiliar." (sic) (Unnumbered attachment to Ellwanger depo.)

$\mathbf{A}$ United States District Court in Maine decides against the Baileyville School Committee which had the book *365 Days* removed from the
high school library and prohibited students from possessing the book anywhere on school property, including school buses. In deciding that the book
banning was unconstitutional, the Court declared: "The legitimacy of the
Committee action in this case may ultimately depend in part upon
whether it could rationally conclude that exposure to *365 Days* might be
harmful to students. . . . The Committee rationale was neither articulated
nor memorialized. The record discloses no finding that harm might result
to students exposed to the coarse language in *365 Days*. It may be considered implicit in the Committee vote that three of its members found the
language 'objectionable,' but it does not appear that the ban was predicated on a Committee determination that exposure might be *harmful* to
students. . . . There is a strong likelihood that the Committee ban is
unconstitutional by reason of its overbreadth. . . . The entire book has
been banned, not only its 'objectionable' language. The ban applies to
adults as well as students and to mature as well as immature students,
regardless of their age or sophistication. The ban prohibits its peaceable
possession of private copies of the book anywhere on school property,
including buses."

Sheck v. *Baileyville School Committee*, 530 F.Supp. 679 (1982)

CYR, District Judge.

The present civil rights action challenges the constitutionality of the banning of the book *365 Days* from
the Woodland High School library by the Baileyville
School Committee. The plaintiffs, students and parents of students, seek declaratory and injunctive relief
restoring the book to the library shelves. The present
ruling is restricted to a determination of the appropriateness of preliminary injunctive relief pending
further proceedings and a final decision on the
merits.

I.

FACTS

365 Days by Ronald J. Glasser [the book], a com-
pilation of nonfictional Vietnam War accounts by
American combat soldiers, was acquired by the Woodland High School library[1] [library] in 1971. During the
ensuing decade the book was checked out of the library
on thirty-two occasions before being banned by the
Baileyville School Committee [Committee] on April

28, 1981. It was last checked out by the 15-year-old
daughter of the defendant Mrs. Mary Davenport.

A friend informed Mrs. Davenport that her daughter had obtained the book from the library and that it
contained objectionable language.[2] Mr. and Mrs. Davenport promptly secured the book from their daughter
and, on April 23, 1981, showed some of its objectionable
language to defendant Thomas Golden, Committee
chairperson,[3] demanding that the book be removed
from the library. The Davenports then complained to
the librarian and to defendant Raymond Freve, school
superintendent. Freve photocopied Chapter 8 and advised the Davenports that their complaint would be
considered at the next Committee meeting on April 28.
In advance of that meeting, the Davenports informed Committee member Clifford McPhee of their
complaint.

The April 28 meeting agenda, available to Committee members at noon that day, simply noted "Mr. &
Mrs. Davenport," but there is no evidence that any of
the three remaining Committee members, Susan
White, Xavier Romero and Stephen Neale, a defen-

dant, became aware of the subject matter of the "Davenport" agenda item prior to the meeting.

At the April 28 meeting, the Davenports, who had scanned the book for objectionable language, urged that it be banned. Superintendent Freve presented the Committee with a photocopy of the text and title of Chapter 8 in which 'the word' and other objectionable language appears more prominently than in other chapters. Freve related excerpts from uniformly favorable book reviews made available by the librarian, who was invited but chose not to appear before the Committee. The Committee briefly discussed the book and the reviews, then voted 5 to 0 to remove *365 Days* from the library. None of the principal participants in the process, including the Davenports, the superintendent and the Committee members, read the book before it was banned.

Sometime after the April 28 meeting, plaintiff Michael Sheck, then a Woodland High School senior, having previously read the book and being strongly opposed to its removal, brought a copy of *365 Days* to school as a means of protesting and promoting student discussion of the ban. The high school principal informed Sheck that possession of the book on school property would result in its confiscation. The high school principal and the superintendent testified that the Committee ban constituted a prohibition against its possession anywhere on school property, including school buses. No countervailing evidence was offered.

At the May 5 Committee meeting, Sheck and a fellow student presented views in opposition to the ban. No Committee action was taken and the ban remained in effect. On May 14, the Woodland High School Student Council formally requested that the Committee return the book to the library. On May 19, a motion to place *365 Days* on a restricted shelf, enabling student access absent parental objection, failed to carry, with the three Committee defendants, Golden, McPhee and Neale, opposing the motion. On June 17, the Committee voted [3-2] to place *365 Days* on a restricted shelf pending development and adoption of a challenged material policy. The book thereupon became available to students with parental permission, but the record is silent as to whether student access to the school library was possible during the summer recess.

The Committee developed a challenged material policy during the summer. The 'Baileyville School Department Challenged Material Policy'[4] became effective immediately upon its adoption on August 17, 1981 by unanimous Committee vote. The immediately ensuing motion to submit *365 Days* to the Baileyville School Department Challenged Material Policy failed by a vote of 2 to 3, with the Committee defendants McPhee, Golden and Neale in opposition. Superinten-

dent Freve advocated defeat of the motion because of his belief that the earlier Committee ban would place too much pressure on the seven-member review committee charged with considering *365 Days* under the challenged material policy. Defendant Golden candidly stated that 'reconsideration' would serve no purpose, since the Committee had already decided to ban the book.

The Committee action of June 17 required that "... the book *365 Days* [be] placed on a restricted shelf—parental permission necessary prior to withdrawal—this above to be in effect until a 'Challenged Material Policy' is accepted." The August 17 Committee actions, adopting the Baileyville School Department Challenged Material Policy but declining to apply it to *365 Days,* reinstated the total ban adopted April 28, presently in effect.

Three Committee members, the defendant Golden, who supported the ban, and White and Romero, who opposed it, read the book before the August 17 reinstatement of the April 28 ban. The Committee defendants McPhee and Neale, who supported the ban, were aware of some of its objectionable language.

II.

PRELIMINARY LEGAL CONSIDERATIONS

Jurisdiction.

Original jurisdiction of the action[5] is conferred upon the United State district court by title 28 United States Code, section 1343(3). The complaint sufficiently alleges state action subjecting the student plaintiffs to actual deprivations of civil rights guaranteed by the First and Fourteenth Amendments to the Constitution of the United States. A justiciable controversy, ripe for the exercise of article III judicial power, arising under the Civil Rights Act and the first and fourteenth amendments, has been brought by student plaintiffs with standing.

Venue.

Venue lies in the District of Maine where all defendants reside and the action arose. 28 U.S.C. § 1391(b).

Abstention.

There are no unsettled questions of state law requiring clarification by the courts of the State of Maine, *see Railroad Commission of Texas v. Pullman Co.,* 312 U.S. 496, 61 S.Ct. 643, 85 L.Ed. 971 (1941), nor are there pending or contemplated state judicial or administrative proceedings warranting abstention, *see Younger v. Harris,* 401 U.S. 37, 91 S.Ct. 746, 27 L.Ed.2d 669 (1971); *Rizzo v. Goode,* 423 U.S. 362, 96 S.Ct. 598, 46 L.Ed.2d 561 (1976).

III.

PRELIMINARY INJUNCTIVE RELIEF

The court is to determine whether plaintiffs are entitled to preliminary injunctive relief pending further proceedings and a determination on the merits. Preliminary injunctive relief may not be granted unless the plaintiffs demonstrate—

(1) that [they] will suffer *irreparable injury* if the injunction is not granted; (2) that such injury *outweighs* any *harm* which granting injunctive relief would inflict on the defendant[s]; (3) that plaintiff[s] [have] exhibited a *likelihood of success on the merits;* and (4) that the *public interest* will not be adversely affected by the granting of the injunction.

Planned Parenthood League v. Bellotti, 641 F.2d 1006, 1009 (1st Cir. 1981), *quoting Women's Community Health Center, Inc. v. Cohen,* 477 F.Supp. 542, 544 (D.Me.1979) (emphasis added).

(1)

Irreparable Injury

Plaintiffs predicate the pending action on alleged deprivations of their first and fourteenth amendment rights. "It is well established that the loss of first amendment freedoms constitutes irreparable injury." *Maceira v. Pagan,* 649 F.2d 8, 18 (1st Cir. 1981) [plausible "chilling effect" on exercise of right of expression satisfies irreparable-harm requirement]. *See Elrod v. Burns,* 427 U.S. 347, 373, 96 S.Ct. 2673, 2689, 49 L.Ed.2d 547 (1976) [first amendment right of association]; *Keefe v. Geanakos,* 418 F.2d 359, 363 (1st Cir. 1969) ["Academic freedom is not preserved by compulsory retirement, even at full pay."]

Plaintiffs have made a clear showing that irreparable injury is likely to result before a determination can be made on the merits unless preliminary injunctive relief is granted.

(2)

Counterbalancing the Hardship

Whatever injury preliminary injunctive relief might cause the defendants is inconsiderable in comparison with the severe impact upon plaintiffs absent interim relief. Any denial of plaintiffs' rights pending a determination on the merits would work an *irretrievable* loss of constitutionally-guaranteed liberties for which no adequate remedy exists at law. The defendants point to no qualitatively-comparable right of their own which would be adversely affected by restoring *365 Days* to the library pending a decision on the merits.

(3)

Likelihood of Success on the Merits

The probability of success on the merits "has loomed large in cases before [the First] Circuit," *Auburn News Co., Inc. v. Providence Journal Co.,* 659 F.2d 273, 277 (1st Cir. 1981).

First Amendment Rights.

Plaintiffs demand redress of their first amendment "rights of freedom of speech [and] freedom of access."[6] In order to prevail on the merits, plaintiffs must demonstrate that their basic first amendment rights have been "directly and sharply implicated" by the ban, *Epperson v. Arkansas,* 393 U.S. 97, 104, 89 S.Ct. 266, 270, 21 L.Ed.2d 228 (1968), whereupon the defendants must show that encroachment upon first amendment rights was warranted by a sufficient state interest. *Compare Elrod v. Burns,* 427 U.S. 347, 362, 96 S.Ct. 2673, 2684, 49 L.Ed.2d 547 (1976) [patronage dismissals require showing of *paramount* state interest] and *Police Dept. of Chicago v. Mosley,* 408 U.S. 92, 98-99, 92 S.Ct. 2286, 2291-2292, 33 L.Ed.2d 212 (1972) [restrictions on expressive conduct in true public forum require showing of *substantial* state interest] *with Tinker v. Des Moines Indep. School Dist.,* 393 U.S. 503, 506, 89 S.Ct. 733, 736, 21 L.Ed.2d 731 (1969) [less stringent showing of state interest required in "school environment"] *and Ginsberg v. New York,* 390 U.S. 629, 639, 88 S.Ct. 1274, 1280, 20 L.Ed.2d 195 (1968) [variable obscenity standard based on *rational* legislative determination that materials might be harmful to minors held constitutional]. The existence of a sufficient state interest does not end the matter. The burden of persuasion that there has been no *unnecessary* abridgement of first amendment rights rests with the defendants. *Elrod v. Burns,* 427 U.S. at 362-63, 96 S.Ct. at 2684; *Buckley v. Valeo,* 424 U.S. 1, 25, 96 S.Ct. 612, 637, 46 L.Ed.2d 659 (1976).

The banning of *365 Days* could be viewed as not directly and sharply implicating a basic constitutional right under some recent authority. *See Zykan v. Warsaw Community School Corp.,* 631 F.2d 1300, 1308 (7th Cir. 1980) [first amendment not implicated unless removal is part of attempt to purge library materials conflicting with committee orthodoxy or book is otherwise completely unavailable to students]; *Pico v. Bd. of Educ.,* 638 F.2d 404, 414-15 (2d Cir. 1980), *cert. granted,* —U.S.—, 102 S.Ct. 385, 70 L.Ed.2d 205 (Sifton, J., plurality opinion) [ban does not directly and sharply implicate basic constitutional values unless circumstances are so unusual and irregular as to create misunderstanding as to its scope and purpose thereby chilling other forms of expression by teachers, librarians, and students]; *id.* at 432 (Newman, J., concurring) [removal encroaches on first amendment if it tends to suppress ideas]. Other courts disagree. *See Minarcini v. Strongsville City School Dist.*, 541 F.2d 577, 583 (6th Cir. 1976) [right of students to receive information is implicated by book removal]; *Salvail v. Nashua Bd. of Educ.*, 469 F.Supp. 1269, 1274 (D.N.H.1979) [secondary school library magazine protected by first amendment]; *Right to Read Defense Comm. v. School Comm.*, 454 F.Supp. 703, 712-14 (D.Mass.1978) [right to read implicated by banning of book because of its theme and offensive language].

More than a decade ago the Supreme Court handed down its landmark decision in *Tinker v. Des Moines Indep. Community School Dist.*, 393 U.S. 503, 89 S.Ct. 733, 21 L.Ed.2d 731 (1969), recognizing that secondary school students "may not be regarded as closed-circuit recipients of only that which the State chooses to communicate." *Id.* at 511, 89 S.Ct. at 739. The Court struck down a regulation prohibiting secondary students from wearing black armbands in school as a form of silent protest against the Vietnam War, on the ground that the regulation encroached impermissibly upon the students' first amendment right of free expression absent a showing that the regulated conduct would materially disrupt classwork or substantially intrude upon the privacy of others. *Id.* at 513, 89 S.Ct. at 740. The first amendment right of secondary students to be free from governmental restrictions upon nondisruptive, nonintrusive, silent expression in public schools was sustained by the Court in *Tinker* notwithstanding full awareness of the "comprehensive authority" traditionally accorded local officials in the governance of public schools. *Id.* at 507, 89 S.Ct. at 736. *See id.* at 515-26, 89 S.Ct. at 741-46 (Black, J., dissenting).

With but one exception,[7] it does not appear that the banning of *365 Days* deprived these plaintiffs of their first amendment right to *initiate* expression. Book bans do not directly restrict the readers' right to initiate expression but rather their right to receive information and ideas, *the indispensable reciprocal of any meaningful right of expression, Procunier v. Martinez*, 416 U.S. 396, 408, 94 S.Ct. 1800, 1808, 40 L.Ed.2d 224 (1974); *Kleindienst v. Mandel*, 408 U.S. 753, 762-63, 92 S.Ct. 2576, 2581-82, 33 L.Ed.2d 683 (1972); *Lamont v. Postmaster General*, 381 U.S. 301, 308, 85 S.Ct. 1493, 1497, 14 L.Ed.2d 398 (1965) (Brennan, J., concurring).

Although its constitutional contours remain rudimentary, the right to receive information and ideas has been recognized by the United States Supreme Court in a variety of contexts. *E.g. Procunier v. Martinez*, 416 U.S. 396, 408, 94 S.Ct. 1800, 1808, 40 L.Ed.2d 224 (1974) [individual *right to receive uncensored mail* from prisoner]; *Stanley v. Georgia*, 394 U.S. 557, 564, 568, 89 S.Ct. 1243, 1247, 1249, 22 L.Ed.2d 542 (1969)

[individual *right to receive* "information and ideas, regardless of their social worth" and *right to read* obscene material, at least in privacy of home]; *Red Lion Broadcasting Co. v. FCC*, 395 U.S. 367, 390, 89 S.Ct. 1794, 1806, 23 L.Ed.2d 371 (1969) [public *right of access* to social, political, esthetic, moral and other *ideas*]; *Lamont v. Postmaster General*, 381 U.S. 301, 308, 85 S.Ct. 1493, 1497, 14 L.Ed.2d 398 (1965) (Brennan, J., concurring) [individual *right to receive mail publications*]; *Martin v. City of Struthers*, 319 U.S. 141, 143, 149, 63 S.Ct. 862, 863, 866, 87 L.Ed. 1313 (1943) [*right to receive* home delivery of religious *literature*]; see also *Kleindienst v. Mandel*, 408 U.S. 753, 92 S.Ct. 2576, 33 L.Ed.2d 683 (1972); *Thomas v. Collins*, 323 U.S. 516, 65 S.Ct. 315, 89 L.Ed. 430 (1945).

Courts recognizing a constitutional right to receive information emphasize the inherent societal importance of fostering the free dissemination of knowledge and ideas in a democratic society. *E.g. Kleindienst* v. *Mandel*, 408 U.S. at 763, 92 S.Ct. at 2581; *Martin* v. *City of Struthers*, 319 U.S. 141, 145, 63 S.Ct. 862, 864, 87 L.Ed. 1313 (1943). The right to receive information does not depend on the existence of an attempted direct personal communication between the speaker and the recipient, *see Virginia State Bd. of Pharmacy* v. *Virginia Citizens Council*, 425 U.S. 748, 756–57, 96 S.Ct. 1817, 1822–23, 48 L.Ed.2d 346 (1976) [first amendment rights of *potential* recipients violated by statute prohibiting drug-price advertisements], nor upon there being no other way to obtain the information, *id.* at 757 n.15, 96 S.Ct. 1823 n.15.

The full force of the reasoning in these cases is particularly apposite in the *educational* environment of the secondary school library. The public school remains a most important public resource in the training and development of youth for citizenship and individual fulfillment. "The American people have always regarded education and acquisition of knowledge as matters of supreme importance which should be diligently promoted." *Meyer v. Nebraska*, 262 U.S. 390, 400, 43 S.Ct. 625, 627, 67 L.Ed. 1042 (1923).[8] The right to receive information and ideas "is 'nowhere more vital' than in our schools and universities." *Kleindienst* v. *Mandel*, 408 U.S. 753, 763, 92 S.Ct. 2576, 2581, 33 L.Ed.2d 683 (1972); *see also Shelton* v. *Tucker*, 364 U.S. 479, 487, 81 S.Ct. 247, 251, 5 L.Ed.2d 231 (1960). Secondary school libraries are "forum[s] for silent speech," *Minarcini* v. *Strongsville City School Dist.*, 541 F.2d 577, 583 (6th Cir. 1976), and "warehouses of ideas," *Right to Read Defense Comm.* v. *School Comm.*, 454 F.Supp. 703, 710 (D.Mass.1978). "Teachers and students must always remain free to inquire, to study and to evaluate, to gain new maturity and understanding; otherwise our civilization will stagnate and die." *Sweezy* v. *New Hampshire,* 354 U.S. 234, 250, 77 S.Ct. 1203, 1211, 1 L.Ed.2d 1311 (1957) [investigation of university professor]; *cf. Widmar* v. *Vincent,*—U.S.—,—, n.5, 102 S.Ct. 269, 273, n.5, 70 L.Ed.2d 440 [university campus shares characteristics of public forum and is peculiarly the marketplace of ideas].

The robust traditions of public education in our constitutional jurisprudence contradict assertions that the Bill of Rights constrains the abridgement of free expression for the exclusive benefit of the speaker, *cf. Virginia State Bd. of Pharmacy* v. *Virginia Citizens Council,* 425 U.S. 748, 96 S.Ct. 1817, 48 L.Ed.2d 346 (1976) [right of consumers to receive information in drug advertisements], or of adults, *see, e.g., Tinker* v. *Des Moines Indep. School Dist.,* 393 U.S. 503, 89 S.Ct. 733, 21 L.Ed.2d 731 (1969). Public schools are major marketplaces of ideas, and first amendment rights must be accorded all "persons" in the market for ideas, including secondary school students, *id.* at 511, 89 S.Ct. at 739, seeking redress of state action banning a book from the "warehouse of ideas,"*see Right to Read Defense Comm.* v. *School Comm.,* 454 F.Supp. 703, 710 (D.Mass.1978). The way would be open to pare the protections of the first amendment to constitutional insignificance in our public schools were courts to accede to suggestions, *see, e.g., Zykan* v. *Warsaw Community School Corp.,* 631 F.2d 1300, 1308 (7th Cir. 1980); *Pico* v. *Bd. of Educ.,* 474 F.Supp. 387, 397 (E.D.N.Y.1979), *rev'd,* 638 F.2d 404 (2d Cir. 1980), that the banning of a library book, *the least obtrusive conventional communication resource available,* does not at least presumptively implicate the reciprocal first amendment right of secondary students to receive the information and ideas there written.[9]

It stands to reason that the state may have a greater responsibility to protect youth from obscenity than from materials merely deemed objectionable on vocabular grounds. Yet the state may not impede individual expression even on obscenity grounds except in accordance with judicially-supervised standards requiring a showing that the challenged expression, taken as a whole, lacks "serious literary, artistic, political, or scientific value" and "appeal[s] to the prurient interest in sex," *Miller* v. *California,* 413 U.S. 15, 24, 93 S.Ct. 2607, 2614, 37 L.Ed.2d 419 (1973) [adult obscenity]; *cf. Ginsberg* v. *New York,* 390 U.S. 629, 88 S.Ct. 1274, 20 L.Ed.2d 195 (1968) [variable obscenity rule permits less stringent standards for materials directed at minors]; *Keefe* v. *Geanakos,* 418 F.2d 359, 362 (1st Cir. 1969) ["What is to be said or read to students is not to be determined by obscenity standards for adult consumption. At the same time, the issue must be one of degree."] How anomalous and dangerous then to *presume* that state action banning an entire book, where

the social value of its content is roundly praised and stands unchallenged by the state, does not directly and sharply implicate first amendment rights because the ban was not intended to suppress ideas.

The social value of the conceptual and emotive content of censored expression is not to be sacrificed to arbitrary official standards of vocabular taste without constitutional recourse. *See Cohen* v. *California,* 403 U.S. 15, 26, 91 S.Ct. 1780, 1788, 29 L.Ed.2d 284 (1971) [State may not "seize upon the censorship of particular words as a convenient guise for banning the expression of unpopular views."] As long as words convey ideas, federal courts must remain on first-amendment alert in book-banning cases, even those ostensibly based strictly on vocabular considerations. A less vigilant rule would leave the care of the flock to the fox that is only after their feathers.

Countervailing Interests.

The recognition that first amendment rights are directly and sharply implicated does not end the inquiry. An appropriate balance and, if possible, a reasonable accommodation, must be struck among the traditional rights of parents in the rearing of their own children, *see, e.g., Wisconsin* v. *Yoder,* 406 U.S. 205, 213-14, 92 S.Ct. 1526, 1532, 32 L.Ed.2d 15 (1972); *Ginsberg* v. *New York,* 390 U.S. 629, 639, 88 S.Ct. 1274, 1280, 20 L.Ed.2d 195 (1968); *Pierce* v. *Society of Sisters,* 268 U.S. 510, 534-35, 45 S.Ct. 571, 573, 69 L.Ed. 1070 (1925); *Meyer* v. *Nebraska,* 262 U.S. 390, 400, 43 S.Ct. 625, 627, 67 L.Ed. 1042 (1923); *Presidents' Council, Dist. No. 25* v. *Community School Bd. No. 25,* 457 F.2d 289, 292, n.5 (2d Cir. 1972); *Davis* v. *Page,* 385 F.Supp. 395, 405-06 (D.N.H.1974), the power of the state to control public schools, *see, e.g., Wisconsin* v. *Yoder,* 406 U.S. 205, 213, 92 S.Ct. 1526, 1532, 32 L.Ed.2d 15 (1972); *Tinker* v. *Des Moines Indep. Community School Dist.,* 393 U.S. 503, 507, 89 S.Ct. 733, 736, 21 L.Ed.2d 731 (1969); *Epperson* v. *Arkansas,* 393 U.S. 97, 104, 89 S.Ct. 266, 270, 21 L.Ed.2d 228 (1968), and individual rights of free expression. In the context of public school education considerable deference must be accorded parents and local school authorities in determining the effect upon students of exposure to reading material.

Parents do not surrender their right "to control the education of their own [children]," *Meyer* v. *Nebraska,* 262 U.S. 390, 401, 43 S.Ct. 625, 627, 67 L.Ed. 1042 (1923), by enrolling them in public school, except to the extent that the prescribed curriculum serves legitimate educational purposes, *Davis* v. *Page,* 385 F.Supp. 395, 405-06 (D.N.H. 1974) [music "distasteful" to parents for religious reasons insufficient to require that children be excused from music class on parental request].

"[T]he power of the state to control the conduct of children reaches beyond the scope of its authority over adults. . . . " *Prince* v. *Massachusetts*, 321 U.S. 158, 170, 64 S.Ct. 438, 444, 88 L.Ed. 645 (1944); *see also Ginsberg* v. *New York*, 390 U.S. 629, 638, 88 S.Ct. 1274, 1279, 20 L.Ed.2d 195 (1968) [sustaining application of variable obscenity standard]. In fact the independent police power of the state to regulate the public conduct of minors may be paramount to parental power over their own children, *see, e.g., Prince* v. *Massachusetts*, 321 U.S. at 170, 64 S.Ct. at 444 [sustaining conviction of guardian for allowing nine-year-old daughter to sell religious material on street], provided there is a "rational" basis for the state to find that harm might otherwise result to the minor, *see Ginsberg* v. *New York,* 390 U.S. at 639, 88 S.Ct. at 1280.[10]

The parties have given insufficient consideration to the *derivative power* of local school authorities, on parental request, to restrict the vocabular form which the communication of information and ideas may take in the extracurricular environment of the school library. The state may determine that parents in their role as the primary guardians of their children "are entitled to the support of laws designed to aid discharge of that responsibility." *Ginsberg* v. *New York,* 390 U.S. 629, 639, 88 S.Ct. 1274, 1280, 20 L.Ed.2d 195 (1968).[11] The state may see "fit to insure [that] a particularly sensitive subject be left to the wisdom of parents." *Mercer* v. *Michigan State Bd. of Educ.,* 379 F.Supp. 580, 586 (E.D.Mich.1974) (three-judge district court), *aff'd. mem.,* 419 U.S. 1081, 95 S.Ct. 673, 42 L.Ed.2d 678 (1974) [upholding statute prohibiting birth control instruction in public schools, but permitting local school option to offer elective course in sex education.] The court would be loathe on the present record to rule out an appropriate parental role in prescribing standards of taste in the reading materials to which one's *own* children may be exposed in the *extracurricular* environment of the school library.[12] *But cf. Keefe* v. *Geanakos*, 418 F.2d 359, 361-63 (1st Cir. 1969) [reversing denial of preliminary injunction to tenured *teacher* threatened with dismissal for use of 'the word' in *classroom*].

The information and ideas in books placed in a school library by proper authority are protected speech and the first amendment right of students to receive that information and those ideas is entitled to constitutional protection.[13] A book may not be banned from a public school library in disregard of the requirements of the fourteenth amendment.

Fourteenth Amendment.

The Fourteenth Amendment to the Constitution of the United States prohibits the states from depriving "any person of life, liberty, or property, without due process of law . . . ." U.S.Const. amend. 14, § 1. The fourteenth amendment protects first amendment liberties, including freedom of speech, against state infringement. *Baggett* v. *Bullitt,* 377 U.S. 360, 372, 84 S.Ct. 1316, 1322, 12 L.Ed.2d 377 (1964); *Fiske* v. *Kansas,* 274 U.S. 380, 387, 47 S.Ct. 655, 657, 71 L.Ed. 1108 (1927). First Amendment free speech is a fundamental individual liberty which no state may withhold without due process. *Lovell* v. *Griffin,* 303 U.S. 444, 450, 58 S.Ct. 666, 668, 82 L.Ed. 949 (1938); *Gitlow* v. *New York,* 268 U.S. 652, 666, 45 S.Ct. 625, 629, 69 L.Ed. 1138 (1925). The protections of the fourteenth amendment extend to all "persons," including secondary school students. *Tinker* v. *Des Moines Indep. School Dist.,* 393 U.S. 503, 511, 89 S.Ct. 733, 739, 21 L.Ed.2d 731 (1969). The procedural regularity required by the fourteenth amendment constrains all creatures of the state, "[b]oards of [e]ducation not excepted." *West Virginia State Bd. of Educ.* v. *Barnett,* 319 U.S. 624, 637, 63 S.Ct. 1178, 1185, 87 L.Ed. 1628 (1943). The duties of school boards must be exercised "consistently with federal constitutional requirements." *Morgan* v. *McDonough,* 548 F.2d 28, 32 (1st Cir. 1977); *see also Salvail* v. *Nashua Bd. of Educ.,* 469 F.Supp. 1269, 1273 (D.N.H.1979).

Arbitrary official interference with the free flow of information and ideas is unconstitutional. Public officials cannot exercise overbroad discretion to censor speech. *Smith* v. *Goguen,* 415 U.S. 566, 573, 94 S.Ct. 1242, 1247, 39 L.Ed.2d 605 (1974).[14] In order to avoid chilling legitimate speech-related conduct, governmental regulation of free speech must be limited by reasonably precise "ascertainable standards." *Keyishian* v. *Bd. of Regents,* 385 U.S. 589, 603-04, 87 S.Ct. 675, 683-84, 17 L.Ed.2d 629 (1967) ["Precision of regulation must be the touchstone in an area so closely touching our most precious freedoms. . . ."]; *Southeastern Promotions Ltd.* v. *Conrad,* 420 U.S. 546, 553, 95 S.Ct. 1239, 1243, 43 L.Ed.2d 448 (1975); *Shanley* v. *Northeast Indep. School Dist.,* 462 F.2d 960, 977 (5th Cir. 1972).

There is no more appropriate context than the present for the careful delineation and observance of "due process" standards and procedures. The convergence of so many sensitive individual and societal interests poses a constant threat of constitutional collision. The fourteenth amendment has been held to mandate that governmental units adhere to their own rules and regulations. *United States ex rel. Accardi* v. *Shaugnessy,* 347 U.S. 260, 74 S.Ct. 499, 98 L.Ed. 681 (1954) [regulations of Attorney General for processing applications of aliens]; *Service* v. *Dulles,* 354 U.S. 363, 77 S.Ct. 1152, 1 L.Ed.2d 1403 (1959) [State Department procedures for dismissal of employee on loyalty grounds]; *Vitarelli* v. *Seaton,* 359 U.S. 535, 79 S.Ct. 968, 3 L.Ed.2d 1012 (1959) [Interior Department regulations for employee suspension]; *Yellin v. United States,* 374 U.S. 109, 83 S.Ct. 1828, 10 L.Ed.2d 778 (1963) [congressional committee rules for conducting executive session]; *Salvail v. Nashua Bd. of Educ.,* 469 F.Supp. 1269, 1273 (D.N.H.1979) [failure of school board to follow procedures for removal of magazine from school library]. Adherence to established procedures is essential to prevent the kind of arbitrary action that is inherent in the violation by a governmental agency of its own rules. *Associated Builders v. United States Dep't of Energy,* 451 F.Supp. 281, 289 (S.D.Tex.1978).

The Supreme Court has held that there must be adequate procedures by which those affected by state action inhibiting the availability of reading material may safeguard their first amendment rights. *See, e.g., Bantam Books v. Sullivan,* 372 U.S. 58, 59, 66, 83 S.Ct. 631, 633, 637, 9 L.Ed.2d 584 (1963) [practices of state commission charged with educating "the public concerning any book . . . containing obscene, indecent or impure language . . . " held unconstitutional]; *see also Loewen v. Turnipseed,* 488 F.Supp. 1138 (N.D.Miss. 1980) [students and parents must be provided means of vindicating first amendment rights denied by state-created textbook approval committee]. Another court has required a school board to act "with full information, with reason and deliberation, and with the full benefit of the views of supervisors, principals, and others familiar with the curriculum and teaching techniques in the schools . . . " in deciding whether to dismiss a teacher for discussing controversial issues in the classroom. *Sterzing v. Fort Bend Indep. School Dist.,* 376 F.Supp. 657, 661 (S.D.Tex.1972). Nothing that has as yet been brought to the attention of the court would warrant relaxation of these procedural standards in library book-removal cases.[15]

The legitimacy of the *Committee* action in this case may ultimately depend in part upon whether it could *rationally* conclude that exposure to *365 Days* might be harmful to students.[16] *Cf. Ginsberg v. New York,* 390 U.S. 629, 641, 88 S.Ct. 1274, 1281, 20 L.Ed.2d 195 (1968). The *Committee* rationale was neither articulated nor memorialized. The record discloses no finding that harm might result to students exposed to the coarse language in *365 Days.* It may be considered implicit in the Committee vote that three of its members found the language "objectionable," but it does not appear that the ban was predicated on a *Committee* determination that exposure might be *harmful* to students. Two Committee members testified that certain words in *365 Days* were considered *inappropriate* for use by or to students, but no evidence has been presented that even these Committee members believed that *harm* might result to *all* students exposed to such language. Although a rational demonstration that

harm might result to some students may be possible in these circumstances, by reason of their tender age or lack of sophistication or maturity, it is not an acceptable *assumption* that all students, regardless of their age or maturity, might be harmed by exposure to such language. *Cf. Mailloux v. Kiley,* 448 F.2d 1242-43 (1st Cir. 1971) [Restrictions on student access to "objectionable" language must be predicated, *inter alia,* on "the age and sophistication of the students. . . . "]

The identification of criteria considered by the Committee in determining to ban *365 Days* is complicated by the utter absence of procedural ground rules[17] or minutes memorializing the Committee rationale. Until the adoption of the Baileyville School Department Challenged Material Policy, there were no prescribed policies, guidelines or criteria for the consideration of challenged materials by teachers, administrators, parents, students, or the Committee. The Committee appears to have considered the challenge to *365 Days* on the basis of the subjective standards of its individual members.

There is no direct evidence that *365 Days* was banned because of its conceptual or emotive content.[18] There is no suggestion that the Committee acted on obscenity grounds. The direct evidence suggests instead that *365 Days* was banned because three Committee members considered some of its language, although not obscene, inappropriate for use in a library book available to students.[19]

The criteria to be considered in advance of state action restricting student access to "objectionable" language include "the age and sophistication of the students, the closeness of the relation between the specific technique used and some concededly valid educational objective, and the content and manner of presentation." *Mailloux v. Kiley,* 448 F.2d 1242-43 (1st Cir. 1971).[20] There is no evidence that the Committee has accorded appropriate consideration to these criteria. The ban was imposed without regard to the age and sophistication of students. It is difficult to understand how at least two members of the Committee, who have not read the book, could have given fair consideration to its content.

There is a strong likelihood that the Committee ban is unconstitutional by reason of its overbreadth. In nearly every respect the ban appears unnecessarily broad, lacking in the required "narrow specificity," and fashioned without the use of "sensitive tools." *See Pico v. Bd. of Educ.,* 638 F.2d 404, 417 (2d Cir. 1980) (Sifton, J. plurality opinion), *cert. granted,*—U.S.—, 102 S.Ct. 385, 70 L.Ed.2d 205, *citing Keyishian v. Bd. of Regents,* 385 U.S. at 603-04, 87 S.Ct. at 683-84. The ban cannot be considered as "minimally intrusive" an infringement of first amendment rights as could have been devised. *See id.; United States v. O'Brien,* 391

U.S. 367, 377, 88 S.Ct. 1673, 1679, 20 L.Ed.2d 672 (1968). The entire book has been banned, not only its "objectionable" language. The ban applies to adults as well as students and to mature as well as immature students, regardless of their age or sophistication. The ban prohibits peaceable possession of private copies of the book anywhere on school property, including buses.[21]

IV.

Public Interest

The final prerequisite to preliminary injunctive relief implicates the public interest. *See Yakus v. United States,* 321 U.S. 414, 440-41, 64 S.Ct. 660, 674-75, 88 L.Ed. 834 (1944). The public interest carries considerable weight in these matters. *Id.* The court must weigh any hindrance or furtherance of the public interest likely to result from interim injunctive relief. *Id.*

The special sensitivity with which the courts must approach their responsibility for assuring compliance by local authorities with constitutional standards in the governance of public schools leaves little reason to doubt that the public interest is significantly implicated in this case. The United States Supreme Court put it this way in *Epperson v. Arkansas,* 393 U.S. 97, 104-05, 89 S.Ct. 266, 270, 21 L.Ed.2d 228 (1968):

Judicial interposition in the operation of the public school system of the Nation raises problems requiring care and restraint. Our courts, however, have not failed to apply the First Amendment's mandate in our educational system where essential to safeguard the fundamental values of freedom of speech and inquiry and of belief. By and large, public education in our Nation is committed to the control of state and local authorities. Courts do not and cannot intervene in the resolution of conflicts which arise in the daily operation of school systems and which do not directly and sharply implicate basic constitutional values. On the other hand, '[t]he vigilant protection of constitutional freedoms is nowhere more vital than in the community of American schools,' *Shelton v. Tucker,* 364 U.S. 479, 487 81 S.Ct. 247, 251, 5 L.Ed.2d 231 (1960). As this Court said in *Keyishian v. Board of Regents,* the First Amendment 'does not tolerate laws that cast a pall of orthodoxy over the classroom.' 385 U.S. 589, 603 87 S.Ct. 675, 683, 17 L.Ed.2d 629 (1967). (Footnote omitted.)

The court cannot escape the recognition that courts may not entirely avert interposition in local school administration without abdicating their "role of final arbiter of the validity of all laws and protector of the people, young and old, from the governmental exercise of unconstitutional power," *Breen v. Kahl,* 419 F.2d 1034, 1038 (7th Cir. 1969). Yet, in the opinion of this court the preliminary injunctive relief interposed in this case represents the minimum required to enable performance of its constitutional function. The important principles of federalism, soundly approached, do not require that federal courts cede their constitutional role to local school boards.

The interim injunctive relief granted here well serves the public interest in several important respects. It minimizes significant intrusion upon any of the important public policies competing for preeminence in the present controversy. It prevents any irreparable loss of important individual liberties during the interim before the parties can be fully heard on the merits. Traditional parental prerogatives in rearing their own children are accommodated with virtually no significant imposition upon majoritarian rights and interests.

CONCLUSION

The court concludes that plaintiffs have made a strong showing of their entitlement to interim injunctive relief as required in *Planned Parenthood League v. Bellotti,* 641 F.2d 1006, 1009 (1st Cir. 1981).

NOTES

1. The Woodland High School library serves both junior high school and high school students. Elementary school students and Baileyville townspeople may, but seldom do, use the library.

2. The book contains coarse language consisting principally of expletives devoid of prurient connotation. 'The word,' an Anglo Saxon "f" word, immediately became the focal concern in the dirty-word debate over the appropriateness of retaining the book in the school library. A number of "s," "p," and "b" words, as counsel have referred to them, as well as profane uses of "Jesus Christ" and "God," were likewise cited as objectionable.

3. The five-member Committee is an administrative arm of the Town of Baileyville which is responsible for the operation of Woodland High School pursuant to 20 M.R.S.A. § 851. The Committee is the superintending school committee required by 20 M.R.S.A. § 471 in each municipality not included in a school administrative district. The Committee is elected at annual town meetings and is responsible for the management of town schools, the provision of "school books," and the custody and care of all school property. *See* 20 M.R.S.A. §§ 471, 473(1), 856 & 857.

4. *Baileyville School Department Challenged Material Policy.*

I. A review committee of at least seven members, consisting of

(1) Administrator

(2) Student

(2) Lay person

(2) Staff members

shall be appointed each year by the principal, subject to the approval of the superintendent and the school committee. It shall be the duty of this committee to review any book which has its appropriateness challenged and to complete the review within fifteen working days. No selected materials whose appropriateness is challenged shall be removed from the school except upon the written recommendation of this committee with the concurrance [sic] of the principal and superintendent, or by the school committee when a recommendation of a review committee is received. Access to questioned materials can be denied the student, if the parent desires so.

1. All complaints to staff members regarding any book shall be reported to the building principal involved, whether the complaint is by telephone, letter, or in personal conversation.

2. The building principal shall contact the complainant to discuss the complaint and attempt to resolve it informally.

3. If the complaint is not resolved informally, the complainant shall be supplied with a standard printed form which shall be completed and returned before consideration is given to the complaint.

4. If the principal does not receive the formal request consideration within two weeks, the complaint is considered closed.

If the completed form is returned, the reasons for selection of the specific work shall be established by the review committee.

Upon a receipt of a completed objection form, the principal will call a meeting of the review committee to consider the complaint.

The committee shall meet to discuss and evaluate the disputed material and shall prepare a written report on the material containing their recommendation or disposition of the matter.

II. The reconsideration committee shall:

a. Examine the challenged material.

b. Determine professional acceptance by reading critical reviews of the material.

c. Weigh values and faults and form opinions based on the material as a whole rather than on passages and sections taken out of context.

d. Discuss the challenged resource in the context of the educational program.

e. Extend invitation to discuss the challenged item with the individual questioner when appropriate.

f. Prepare a written report to the [sic] submitted to the Superintendent of Schools.

The principal shall notify the complainant of the decision. In answering the complainant, the principal shall explain how and why the book was selected, give the guidelines used in selection, and cite authorities used in reaching decisions. If the committee decides to retain the work that prompted the complaint, the complainant shall be given an explanation. If the complaint is judged valid, the principal will acknowledge it and make recommended changes.

If the complainant is still not satisfied, he/she may appeal to the Baileyville School Committee, through the superintendent, which shall make a final determination of the issue.

Books for oral reports: Each student is presented with a list of books for possible reading. If any student chooses a book containing subject matter which he considers improper, he should bring the material to the attention of his teacher and should choose a different book for his/her report.

The teacher shall supply the student with a request for reconsideration form when he makes his objection.

Books for in-depth class study: If any student or parent has a valid objection to any book discussed in any classroom, he/she should follow the steps to have the book reconsidered. The teacher shall supply the student with an alternate book for equal credit. The above excludes textbooks.

Audio-visual: Each teacher must/will assume responsibility for the quality of any enrichment materials used in his/her classrooms.

5. *See* 42 U.S.C. § 1983.

6. Complaint, at 6.

7. The threatened confiscation of *365 Days* from Michael Sheck on school premises plainly implicates the constitutional right of secondary students to initiate nondisruptive, nonintrusive expression on school premises. *See Tinker v. Des Moines Indep. Community School Dist.*, 393 U.S. 503, 513, 89 S.Ct. 733, 740, 21 L.Ed.2d 731 (1969). *Cf. Cohen v. California*, 403 U.S. 15, 91 S.Ct. 1780, 29 L.Ed.2d 284 (1971) [wearing jacket displaying 'the word' in public]. Defendants do not allege and it does not appear from the present record that the threatened confiscation related in any way to the preservation of school discipline or to the protection of privacy. See 393 U.S. at 513-14, 89 S.Ct. at 740. This kind of symbolic expression by secondary school students was held to involve "direct, primary First Amendment rights akin to 'pure speech,'" *id.* at 508, 89 S.Ct. at 737, protected by the first and fourteenth amendments, *id.* at 513, 89 S.Ct. at 740.

Although Michael Sheck graduated from Woodland High School prior to the commencement of this action and therefore arguably would not benefit from injunctive relief, except perhaps as a resident adult permitted library access, other plaintiffs currently attending Woodland High School and Woodland Junior High School have a direct personal stake in preliminary injunctive relief.

8. Perhaps for these reasons the Supreme Court has said that

'[t]he vigilant protection of constitutional freedoms is nowhere more vital than in the community of American schools,' *Shelton v. Tucker*, 364 U.S. 479, 487, 81 S.Ct. 247, 251, 5 L.Ed.2d 231 1960. As this Court said in *Keyishian v. Board of Regents*, the First Amend-

ment 'does not tolerate laws that cast a pall of orthodoxy over the classroom.' 385 U.S. 589, 603, 87 S.Ct.
675, 683, 17 L.Ed.2d 629 (1967).

Epperson v. Arkansas, 393 U.S. 97, 104-105, 89 S.Ct.
266, 270, 21 L.Ed.2d 228 (1968).

9. Although federal courts are understandably reluctant to
review school library book bans in deference to the
traditional prerogatives of local school authorities and
for fear of inviting a flood of litigation, *see, e.g., Pico v.
Bd. of Educ.,* 638 F.2d 404, 414-15 (2d Cir. 1980) (Sifton,
J., plurality opinion), "the judiciary's role of final
arbiter of the validity of all laws and protector of the
people, young and old, from the exercise of unconstitutional power," *Breen v. Kahl,* 419 F.2d 1034, 1038 (7th
Cir. 1969), *cert. denied,* 398 U.S. 937, 90 S.Ct. 1836, 26
L.Ed.2d 268 (1970) [school regulation regarding student
hair styles], bars their retreat.

The institutional burdens on the judiciary resulting
from the need to sift the circumstances in all library
book-banning challenges could be considerable, but
"[t]he First and Fourteenth Amendments have never
been treated as absolutes. . . . " *Miller v. California,* 413
U.S. 15, 23, 93 S.Ct. 2607, 2614, 37 L.Ed.2d 419
(1973).

> This may not be an easy road, free from difficulty.
> But no amount of 'fatigue' should lead us to adopt a
> convenient 'institutional' rationale—an absolutist,
> 'anything goes' view of the First Amendment—
> because it will lighten our burdens [footnote omit-
> ted]. 'Such an abnegation of judicial supervision in
> this field would be inconsistent with our duty to
> uphold the constitutional guarantees. . . . ' Our duty
> admits of no 'substitute for facing up to the tough
> individual problems of constitutional judgment in-
> volved in every obscenity case.'

Id. at 29-30, 93 S.Ct. at 2617-2618 (Burger, C. J.,
majority opinion).

10. In *Ginsberg,* the Supreme Court felt unable to rule that
a finding by the New York Legislature that certain
"obscene" material would be harmful to minors was
irrational. 390 U.S. at 643, 88 S.Ct. at 1282. Mr. Justice
Brennan, speaking for the Court, demonstrated that the
view that obscenity may precipitate antisocial conduct
or produce harmful effects in youth may be rationally
held:

> . . . But despite the vigor of the ongoing controversy
> whether obscene material will perceptibly create a
> danger of antisocial conduct, or will probably induce
> its recipients to such conduct, a medical practitioner
> recently suggested that the possibility of harmful
> effects to youth cannot be dismissed as frivolous. Dr.
> Gaylin of the Columbia University Psychoanalytic
> Clinic, reporting on the views of some psychiatrists in
> 77 Yale L.J., at 592-593, said:
> 'It is in the period of growth [of youth] when these
> patterns of behavior are laid down, when environ-

> mental stimuli of all sorts must be integrated into a
> workable sense of self, when sensuality is being de-
> fined and fears elaborated, when pleasure confronts
> security and impulse encounters control—it is in this
> period, undramatically and with time, that legalized
> pornography may conceivably be damaging.'
> Dr. Gaylin emphasizes that a child might not be as
> well prepared as an adult to make an intelligent
> choice as to the material he chooses to read:
> '[P]sychiatrists . . . made a distinction between the
> reading of pornography, as unlikely to be per se harm-
> ful, and the permitting of the reading of pornography,
> which was conceived as potentially destructive. The
> child is protected in his reading of pornography by the
> knowledge that it is pornographic, i.e., disapproved.
> It is outside of parental standards and not a part of
> his identification processes. To openly permit implies
> parental approval and even suggests seductive en-
> couragement. If this is so of parental approval, it is
> equally so of societal approval—another potent in-
> fluence on the developing ego.'

Id. at 642 n.10, 88 S.Ct. at 1282 n.10.

11. The Supreme Court in *Ginsberg* quoted the following
language with approval—

> While the supervision of children's reading may
> best be left to their parents, the knowledge that
> parental control or guidance cannot always be pro-
> vided and society's transcendent interest in protect-
> ing the welfare of children justify reasonably regula-
> tion of the sale of material to them. It is, therefore,
> altogether fitting and proper for a state to include in a
> statute designed to regulate the sale of pornography
> to children special standards, broader than those
> embodied in legislation aimed at controlling dis-
> semination of such material to adults.

390 U.S at 640, 88 S.Ct. at 1281.

12. *See* note 20 *infra.*

13. At least one court has said that because a school board
has no obligation to establish a library or to select a particular library book it may not be prevented from
removing a book, *President's Council, Dist. 25 v. Community School Bd. No. 25,* 457 F.2d 289, 293 *(2d Cir.
1972), cert. denied,* 409 U.S. 998, 93 S.Ct. 308, 34
L.Ed.2d 260 (1972), but that reasoning has been refuted
in *Minarcini v. Strongsville City School Dist.,* 541 F.2d
577, 582 (6th Cir. 1976) and in *Right to Read Defense
Comm. v. School Comm.,* 454 F.Supp. 703, 712
(D.Mass.1978).

> We are well beyond the belief that any manner of
> state regulation is permissible simply because it
> involves an activity which is part of the university
> structure and is financed with funds controlled by the
> administration. The state is not necessarily the un-
> restrained master of what it creates and fosters. Thus
> in cases concerning school-supported publications or
> the use of school facilities, the courts have refused to
> recognize as permissible any regulations infringing

free speech when not shown to be necessarily related to the maintenance of order and discipline within the educational process. [Citations omitted.]

Antonelli v. Hammond, 308 F.Supp. 1329, 1337 (D. Mass.1970); *quoted in Bazaar v. Fortune,* 476 F.2d 570, 575 (5th Cir. 1973). Analogous authoritative disapproval of the doctrine in *President's Council* is found in *Widmar v. Vincent,*—U.S.—, at—·—, 102 S.Ct. 269, 273, 70 L.Ed.2d 440 [8-1 decision], where the United States Supreme Court held that a university, though not required to do so, did create a constitutionally-protected forum by making its facilities generally available for student activities.

14. The Supreme Court has frequently condemned, because of their potential for selective suppression of ideas, licensing schemes lodging broad discretion in public officials to restrict particular forms of expression. *See, e.g., Police Dep't of Chicago v. Mosley,* 408 U.S. 92, 97, 92 S.Ct. 2286, 2291, 33 L.Ed.2d 212 (1972). *See also Grayned v. City of Rockford,* 408 U.S. 104, 108-09, 92 S.Ct. 2294, 2298-99, 33 L.Ed.2d 222 (1972), for cases requiring explicit standards for the guidance of those who apply them, particularly where the statute "abuts upon sensitive areas of basic First Amendment freedoms," id. at 109, 92 S.Ct. at 2299.

15. Although the First Circuit has sustained discretionary state action withholding funds from a literary magazine because of a poem which officials considered "an item of filth," the court found it "most troubling" that the denial of support "should be based on a reading of just one poem in a back issue, without consideration of the overall quality of the publication either alone or as compared to competing grant applicants." *Advocates For Arts v. Thomson,* 532 F.2d 792, 797 (1st Cir.), *cert. denied,* 429 U.S. 894, 97 S.Ct. 254, 50 L.Ed.2d 177 (1976). The banning of *365 Days,* for which public funds had already been expended, without first reading or considering the overall quality of the censored expression, may be violative of the principle that discretionary official action regulating expression must be accompanied by "rigorous procedural safeguards," *Southeastern Promotions, Ltd. v. Conrad,* 420 U.S. 546, 561, 95 S.Ct. 1239, 1247, 43 L.Ed.2d 448 (1975), and the requirement that official discretion be hedged by "narrow, objective and definite standards," *Shuttlesworth v. City of Birmingham,* 394 U.S. 147, 151, 89 S.Ct. 935, 938, 22 L.Ed.2d 162 (1969).

A library book ban presupposes reversal of the decision by appropriate school authorities to acquire the book in the first place. Consideration should be given to whether the initial determination to make the book available is entitled to a presumption of procedural regularity *see* Note, *Schoolbooks, School Boards, and the Constitution,* 80 Colum.L.Rev. 1092, 1123-24 (1980), which may only be overcome by adequate findings based on ascertainable standards.

16. Of course, it may be appropriate to require an even more rigorous showing where state action is aimed at restricting access to concededly nonobscene materials deemed objectionable on vocabular grounds only.

17. School personnel simply passed complaints along the "chain of command." The chairperson of the Woodland High School English Department identified a written *complaint* form which can in no sense be considered a challenged materials *policy.* It was not used in this instance and there is no evidence that it has ever been used.

18. The court does not suggest that there is no evidence of a Committee intent to suppress ideas. The arbitrariness of the Committee refusal to submit *365 Days* for consideration under its own new challenged material policy could well be considered evidence of pretextual censorship, as could the overbreadth of the ban itself which neither distinguishes between mature and immature students, nor between students and adults.

19. Measured by the criteria later adopted by the Committee itself, *see* 'Baileyville School Department Challenged Material Policy,' note 4 *supra,* the Committee action banning *365 Days* appears seriously deficient due to its procedural irregularity, arbitrariness, vagueness, and overbreadth.

20. These criteria, requiring case-by-case application, would seem to impose an onerous administrative burden upon the local superintending school committee, which would have little occasion and less time to evaluate, for instance, the sophistication of individual students. Librarians and teachers possess certain expertise not as likely to be found on the local school committee, especially in the area of assessing individual-student intellectual and literary interests and sophistication. On the other hand, as a general rule parents are better suited to the task of evaluating the emotional and intellectual maturity and sophistication of their *own* children. The expertise of parents is based on a more fully informed understanding and concern for the social, educational, cultural, moral and spiritual well-being and development of their own children.

21. *See note 7 supra.*

The United States Court of Appeals, Eighth Circuit, decides for the junior and senior high school students who sought to compel the school board to reinstate the film "The Lottery" which had been eliminated from the school district's curriculum because of parents' objections to the film's alleged violence and impact on the religious and family values of students. The Court states that the school board "cannot constitutionally ban the films because a majority of its members object to the film's religious and ideological content and wish to prevent the ideas contained in the material from being expressed in the school. . . . [the school board] has failed to carry its burden of establishing that a substantial governmental interest existed for interfering with the students' right to receive information. Hence, the board's action violated the First Amendment."

Pratt v. *Ind. Sch. Dist. No. 831, Forest Lake,* 670 F.2d 771 (1982)

HEANEY, Circuit Judge.

I. INTRODUCTION.

"The Lottery" is a short story by American author Shirley Jackson in which the citizens of a small town randomly select one person to be stoned to death each year. Since 1972, the curriculum of Independent School District No. 831, Forest Lake, Minnesota, has included the Encyclopedia Brittanica Educational Corporation's film version of "The Lottery," and its accompanying "trailer" film which discusses the story and its themes.

During the 1977-1978 school year, a group of parents and other citizens became concerned about the use of the films in American literature courses taught in the senior high school, and sought to have them removed from the District's curriculum. The citizens' objections focused on the alleged violence in the films and their purported impact on the religious and family values of students.

After the citizens had pursued their complaints through the appropriate procedures for review and selection of instructional materials, the school board acceded to their demands and voted to remove the films from the District's curriculum. This action was then commenced in United States District Court for the District of Minnesota by three students enrolled in the junior and senior high schools operated by District No. 831. They sought to compel Distrct No. 831 to reinstate the film version of "The Lottery" and its trailer film to the high school curriculum.

After a hearing, the district court found that the board's objections to the films had "religious overtones" and that the films had been banned because of their "ideological content." It held the school board's decision violated the First Amendment and ordered the films reinstated to their prior place in the curriculum. We affirm. Under the circumstances presented here, the First Amendment protects the right of the Forest Lake students not to have these films removed from the high school classrooms. The school board cannot constitutionally ban the films because a majority of its members object to the films' religious and ideological content and wish to prevent the ideas contained in the material from being expressed in the school.

II. FACTS.

Independent School District No. 831 serves the communities of Forest Lake, Linwood and Wyoming, Minnesota, and provides public education to approximately 6,500 students. A seven-member school board is elected by residents of the district to govern the School District.

In the winter of 1977, several parents of students enrolled in the high school became concerned about the use of "The Lottery" and trailer films in American literature courses. After the parents had voiced their concern to the teachers, an informational meeting was held on February 21, 1978, at the high school. Approximately fifty people attended, including several board members and teachers. Both films were shown at the beginning of the meeting. Several teachers discussed how they used the films and their reasons for using them. Essentially, they explained that the films were used to study the interpretation of fiction and "The Lottery" 's place in American literature, and to provoke discussion of the consequences of blind adherence to tradition. Numerous objections to the films were raised by the parents and other members of the public. The objections centered on the films' alleged violence and impact on the religious and family values of students.

Shortly after the informational meeting, three parents filed formal Citizens' Requests for Reconsideration of Instructional Materials, asking that the film version of the "The Lottery" and its trailer be removed from the curriculum.[1] The Citizens' Requests were filed pursuant to Instructional Policy No. 605, which sets forth the District's procedures for selection and review of instructional materials.[2]

A Committee for Challenged Materials (Challenge Committee) conducted a public meeting on March 28, 1978, to review the films and adopt a recommendation with regard to their future use. Notice of the meeting appeared in local newspapers and, once more, approximately fifty people attended. Again, the films were shown to those in attendance and the teachers discussed their reasons for using the material. Persons in attendance were then given an opportunity to express their views. Those opposing the films raised essentially the same objections as those advanced at the February informational meeting and in the Citizens' Requests.

At the conclusion of the meeting, the Challenge Committee recommended that the films not be used at the junior high school level, that the films be included in the curriculum in the high school, and that before the films be shown, an information sheet be sent to the students' parents advising them they could exclude their children from viewing the films.

The Committee's recommendations were appealed to the school board. At a public meeting held on April 17, 1978, the board, by a four-to-three vote, rejected a motion to "accept and confirm" the Challenge Committee's recommendations. The board then passed a resolution, again by a vote of four-to-three, to completely eliminate the film and the trailer from the District's curriculum. The board gave no reasons for its decision.

The plaintiffs then commenced this action. The district court, on cross-motions for summary judgment, found that the material was unconstitutionally excluded because of its "ideological content and its alleged adverse impact upon the students' family, religious, and moral values," and ordered the films to be reinstated to their prior place in the curriculum. The district court, however, gave the board an opportunity to present evidence that its actions were based on reasons that did not offend the First Amendment. Rather than presenting additional evidence, however, the board submitted a resolution which stated in part:

> The motion picture version of "The Lottery" and the trailer film discussing the short story graphically place an exaggerated and undue emphasis on violence and bloodshed which is not appropriate or suitable for showing in a high school classroom and which has the effect of distorting the short story and overshadowing its many otherwise valuable and educationally important themes.[3]

The district court found that this resolution did not constitute "cognizable, credible evidence as to any legitimate reason for excluding" the films from the curriculum. It, therefore, affirmed its earlier order to reinstate the films. This appeal followed.

III. DISCUSSION.

Local authorities are the principal policymakers for the public schools. Thus, school boards are accorded comprehensive powers and substantial discretion to discharge the important tasks entrusted to them. *E.g.*, *Pico v. Board of Education, Island Trees Union Free School District*, 638 F.2d 404, 412 (2d Cir. 1980) (opinion of Sifton, J.);[4] *Zykan v. Warsaw Community School Corp.*, 631 F.2d 1300, 1304-1305 (7th Cir. 1980); *Minarcini v. Strongsville City School District*, 541 F.2d 577, 580 (6th Cir. 1976). As the Supreme Court stated in *Epperson v. Arkansas*, 393 U.S. 97, 104, 89 S.Ct. 266, 270, 21 L.Ed.2d 228 (1968):

> By and large, public education in our Nation is committed to the control of state and local authorities. Courts do not and cannot intervene in the resolution of conflicts which arise in the daily operation of school systems and which do not directly and sharply implicate basic constitutional values. [Footnote omitted.]

Necessarily included within the board's discretion is the authority to determine the curriculum that is most suitable for students and the teaching methods that are to be employed, including the educational tools to be used. *Pico v. Board of Education, Island Trees Union Free School District, supra*, 638 F.2d at 425 (Mansfield, J., dissenting).[5] These decisions may properly reflect local community views and values as to educational content and methodology. *James v. Board of Education of Central District No. 1*, 461 F.2d 566, 573 (2d Cir.), *cert. denied*, 409 U.S. 1042, 93 S.Ct. 529, 34 L.Ed.2d 491 (1972).

Notwithstanding the power and discretion accorded them, school boards do not have an absolute right to remove materials from the curriculum. *E.g., Minarcini v. Strongsville City School District, supra,* 541 F.2d at 581; *Right to Read Defense Committee of Chelsea v. School Committee of City of Chelsea,* 454 F.Supp. 703, 711 (D.Mass.1978). Students do not "shed their constitutional rights to freedom of speech or expression at the schoolhouse gate." *Tinker v. Des Moines Independent School District,* 393 U.S. 503, 506, 89 S.Ct. 733, 736, 21 L.Ed.2d 731 (1969); *Minarcini v. Strongsville City School District, supra,* 541 F.2d at 583. At the very least, the First Amendment precludes local authorities from imposing a "pall of orthodoxy" on classroom instruction which implicates the state in the propagation of a particular religious or ideological viewpoint. *See Keyishian v. Board of Regents,* 385 U.S. 589, 603, 87 S.Ct. 675, 683, 17 L.Ed.2d 629 (1967); *Zykan v. Warsaw Community School Corp., supra,* 631 F.2d at 1306. Thus, the students here had a right to be free from official conduct that was intended to suppress the ideas expressed in these films. *See Pico v. Board of Education, Island Trees Union Free School District, supra,* 638 F.2d at 433 (opinion of Newman, J.).

There has been a flurry of cases recently in which the federal courts have considered First Amendment challenges to the removal of books from school libraries. Those courts have generally concluded that a cognizable First Amendment claim exists if the book was excluded to suppress an ideological or religious viewpoint with which the local authorities disagreed. *Pico v. Board of Education, Island Trees Union Free School District, supra; Bicknell v. Vergennes Union High School Board,* 638 F.2d 438 (2d Cir. 1980) (dicta); *Zykan v. Warsaw Community School Corp., supra* (dicta); *Cary v. Board of Education, Adams-Arapahoe School District,* 598 F.2d 535 (10th Cir. 1979) (dicta); *Minarcini v. Strongsville City School District, supra; Salvail v. Nashua Board of Education,* 469 F.Supp. 1269 (D.N.H.1979); *Right to Read Defense Committee of Chelsea v. School Committee of City of Chelsea, supra.* We believe that this focus provides the proper framework for analysis here.[6]

The district court found that the objections of the board's majority had "religious overtones" and that the films had been eliminated because of their "ideological content." It concluded that the plaintiffs had established a prima facie case that the board's action was unconstitutional. The district court's findings are not clearly erroneous.

Opponents of "The Lottery" focused primarily on the purported religious and ideological impact of the films. They contended that the movies must be removed from the curriculum because they posed a threat to the students' religious beliefs and family values.[7]

In contrast to these value-laden objections, several teachers testified that "The Lottery" is an important American short story, that the film was faithfully adapted from the short story, that the story stimulates students to consider new ideas, and that the films are an effective teaching tool and involve students who might not otherwise read the story. Moreover, an empirical study conducted by two University of Maryland education professors was provided to the board, which concluded that the film version of "The Lottery" produced no negative effects on students in terms of violence and attitudes toward family or religious values.[8] Forest Lake teachers attending the February and March meetings concurred with this assessment of the effect of the films.

After hearing these contrasting points of view, the Challenge Committee set up to evaluate the dispute recommended that the films be retained in the high school curriculum. But the board, obviously in response to the citizens' objections and without offering any reasons for its action, decided to remove the films from all of the District's schools.

On these facts, the district court could properly conclude that the plaintiffs met their burden of establishing that the board banned the films because the majority of its members objected to the ideas expressed in them.[9]

Therefore, to avoid a finding that it acted unconstitutionally, the board must establish that a substantial and reasonable governmental interest exists for interfering with the students' right to receive information. *Pico v. Board of Education, Island Trees Union Free School District, supra,* 638 F.2d at 415-416 (opinion of Sifton, J.); *Minarcini v. Strongsville City School District, supra,* 541 F.2d at 581-582; *Right to Read Defense Committee of Chelsea v. School Committee of City of Chelsea, supra,* 454 F.Supp. at 712-713. Bare allegations that such a basis existed are not sufficient. *Pico v. Board of Education, Island Trees Free Union School District, supra,* 638 F.2d at 415 (opinion of Sifton, J.).

The board's purported rationale for its action, offered in its resolution to the district court, was that

[t]he motion picture version of "The Lottery" and the trailer film discussing the short story graphically place an exaggerated and undue emphasis on violence and bloodshed which is not appropriate or suitable for showing in a high school classroom and which has the effect of distorting the short story and overshadowing its many otherwise valuable and educationally important themes.

The district court concluded that this resolution did not provide a sufficient basis to justify the board's action. The district court found that "the self-serving statements of the school board, made after the fact and not based on the previous record, to the effect that this film is excluded because of the violence it teaches, are untenable in the light of the circumstances under which they were made." It further found that the school board has "failed to produce any cognizable, credible evidence as to any legitimate reason for excluding this film [sic], other than the fact that the School Board and certain elements of populace object to the ideas disseminated therein." Once again, these findings are not clearly erroneous.

First, the contention that the films graphically emphasize violence is simply not supported by the facts. The two films contain but a single scene showing any physical violence—and that scene in the final brief frames of the main film is faithfully adapted from the short story.

Second, no systematic review of violence in the curriculum has been undertaken by the board. Indeed, there is no evidence that the board has ever removed from the high school curriculum any materials other than the films in dispute here because of their violent content.

Third, and most importantly, the sequence of events set forth above supports the district court's findings. Parents and citizens sought to have the films removed largely on the basis of the purported negative impact the material would have on the religious and family values of students. In response to these objections, teachers stated that "The Lottery" and trailer films are valuable pedagogical resources. On this evidence, the Challenge Committee recommended that films be retained in the high school curriculum. Nonetheless, the board voted to ban the showing of the films in the District. The board gave no reasons for its decision. Only after the district court invited the appellant to submit evidence showing that its decision was based on reasons neutral in First Amendment terms did the board attempt to justify its action by stating it was concerned with the violence in the films. Even then, the board did not produce any evidence but, instead, merely submitted its conclusory resolution reciting its purported concern about violence without any support.

The board—not this Court—has the authority to determine that a literary or artistic work's violent content makes it inappropriate for the District's curriculum. But after carefully reviewing the record, we must agree with the district court that the board eliminated the films not because they contain scenes of violence or because they distort the short story, but rather it so acted because the majority of the board

agreed with those citizens who considered the films' ideological and religious themes to be offensive.

Moreover, the First Amendment requires, in a situation such as the instant one, that the school board act so that the reasons for its decisions are apparent to those affected. The rationale for this requirement is summarized in *Keyishian v. Board of Regents, supra,* 385 U.S. at 603-604, 87 S.Ct. at 683-684:

"We emphasize once again that '[p]recision of regulation must be the touchstone in an area so closely touching our most precious freedoms,' . . . When one must guess what conduct or utterance may lose him his position, one necessarily will 'steer far wider of the unlawful zone. . . .' . . . *The danger of that chilling effect upon the exercise of vital First Amendment rights must be guarded against by sensitive tools which clearly inform . . . what is being proscribed.*" [Citations omitted; emphasis added.]

Here, the board, in response to citizens' complaints that centered on their ideological and religious beliefs, banned the films without giving any reasons for its actions. Only after the district court asked for an explanation of the board's action did it offer its violence rationale. Even then, the board failed to specify why the films were too violent or how they distorted the short story. This approach inevitably suggests that the board acted not out of its concern about violence, but rather to express an "official policy with respect to God and country of uncertain and indefinite content which is to be ignored by pupils, librarians and teachers at their peril." *Pico v. Board of Education, Island Trees Union Free School District, supra,* 638 F.2d at 416 (opinion of Sifton, J.). Consequently, the board failed to "clearly inform" students and teachers what it was proscribing as the constitution requires.

The board seeks to justify its action by pointing out that the the short story remains available to teachers and students in the library in printed form and a phonographic recording.[10] This fact is not decisive. Restraint on protected speech generally cannot be justified by the fact that there may be other times, places or circumstances for such expression. *Pico v. Board of Education, Island Trees Union Free School District, supra,* 638 F.2d at 434 (opinion of Newman, J.); *Minarcini v. Strongsville City School District, supra,* 541 F.2d at 582. The symbolic effect of removing the films from the curriculum is more significant than the resulting limitation of access to the story. The board has used its official power to perform an act clearly indicating that the ideas contained in the films are unacceptable and should not be discussed or considered. This message is not lost on students and teachers, and its chilling effect is obvious. *Pico v.*

Board of Education, Island Trees Union Free School District, supra, 638 F.2d at 436 (opinion of Newman, J.).

For these reasons, the appellant has failed to carry its burden of establishing that a substantial governmental interest existed for interfering with the students' right to receive information. Hence, the board's action violated the First Amendment. *Pico v. Board of Education, Island Trees Union Free School District, supra,* 638 F.2d at 418 (opinion of Sifton, J.); *Salvail v. Nashua Board of Education,* 469 F.Supp. 1269, 1276 (D.N.H.1979); *Right to Read Defense Committee of Chelsea v. School Committee of City of Chelsea, supra,* 454 F.Supp. at 713-714. The school board premised its action on the assumption that scenes offensive to the majority of the board and some parents had no place in the Forest Lake school system. This action was impermissible.

"The Lottery" is not a comforting film. But there is more at issue here than the sensibilities of those viewing the films. What is at stake is the right to receive information and to be exposed to controversial ideas—a fundamental First Amendment right. If these films can be banned by those opposed to their ideological theme, then a precedent is set for the removal of any such work.

In sum, while we are mindful that our role in reviewing the decisions of local school authorities is limited, we also have an obligation to uphold the Constitution to protect the fundamental rights of all citizens. As the Supreme Court stated in *Epperson v. Arkansas, supra,* 393 U.S. at 104, 89 S.Ct. at 270:

Judicial interposition in the operation of the public school system of the Nation raises problems requiring care and restraint. Our courts, however, have not failed to apply the First Amendment's mandate in our educational system where essential to safeguard the fundamental values of freedom of speech and inquiry and of belief. . . . "[t]he vigilant protection of constitutional freedoms is nowhere more vital than in the community of American schools," *Shelton v. Tucker,* 364 U.S. 479, 487, 81 S.Ct. 247, 251, 5 L.Ed.2d 231, 236 (1960).

The decision of the district court is therefore affirmed.

NOTES

1. The Citizens' Request to remove the main film from the curriculum stated that the "theme or purpose" of this film was "the breakdown of family values and tradition" and that viewing the films may cause students to "begin to question their own family loyalties." It also

stated that "the matter of fact way in which the ceremony proceeds accentuates its brutality and senselessness in our times."

The Citizens' Request regarding the trailer film stated that the "theme or purpose" of the trailer was a "subtle way of accomplishing destruction of family unit. Causing them [the students] again to question their values, traditions and religious beliefs." This Citizens' Request also objected to the portrayal of a "vengeful God" rather than a "loving God."

2. This procedure provides for three levels of review of a citizen's complaint. First, the objection to the material must be made to the person having control over the questioned material. If the challenge is not resolved with the media specialist or teacher, the citizen has a right to have his objections evaluated by a Committee for Challenged Materials which is set up to review the complaint. The seven-person Challenge Committee—composed of two citizens, two teachers, one media person, one administrator and one student—has the duty to evaluate the material based on the criteria set forth in the policy, and make a recommendation regarding its future use. Finally, if the Challenge Committee's recommendation is unsatisfactory, the challenger has a right to appeal to the school board.

3. The full text of the board's resolution stated:

The motion picture version of "The Lottery" and the trailer film discussing the short story graphically place an exaggerated and undue emphasis on violence and bloodshed which is not appropriate or suitable for showing in a high school classroom and which has the effect of distorting the short story and overshadowing its many otherwise valuable and educationally important themes. Consequently, the two films neither enrich nor met the needs of the curriculum and clearly do not constitute the most suitable medium for the presentation of the short story "The Lottery" in senior high school classes. This action is not, however, intended to limit in any manner the use of "The Lottery" as written literature nor limit classroom discussion of the short story.

4. In *Pico v. Board of Education, Island Trees Union Free School District,* 638 F.2d 404 (2d Cir. 1980), a three-judge panel, with one member dissenting, held that a school board's removal of books from the library gave rise to a cognizable First Amendment claim by students. The two judges in the majority relied on different rationales for their decisions, and each authored a separate opinion.

5. Judge Mansfield summarized the basis of his dissent as follows:

[In *President's Council, District 25 v. Community School Board, No. 25,* 457 F.2d 289 (2d Cir.), *cert. denied,* 409 U.S. 998 [93 S.Ct. 308, 34 L.Ed.2d 260] (1972)], we held that the removal from the school library by school authorities of a book containing vulgar language and explicit sexual allusions did not sharply and directly infringe upon freedom of speech and thought within the meaning of [*Epperson v. Arkansas*, 393 U.S. 97, 89 S.Ct. 266, 21 L.Ed.2d 228 (1968)]. That holding represents the law of this Circuit, by which we are bound.

Pico v. Board of Education, Island Trees Union Free School District, supra, 638 F.2d at 429 (Mansfield, J., dissenting).

6. These cases cannot be distinguished on a principled basis from the instant one even though films rather than books were involved here and even though "The Lottery" remained available to students in forms other than film. That is because the effect of banning the films due to their ideological and religious content is the same as the effect of removing books from a library for the same reasons. In both situations, the action of the school officials clearly indicates that the ideas contained in the banned materials are unacceptable and, hence, the exercise of First Amendment freedoms is inhibited.

   The appellant relies primarily on *President's Council School District No. 25 v. Community School Board, No. 25, supra*, which upheld a school board's removal of a book from the the school library, to argue that the Forest Lake board acted within its discretion and that the removal of materials from the curriculum is not significant enough to rise to the level of a constitutional violation. We disagree. Because the officials in *President's Council* removed the book due to the extensive violence and sex it contained, we do not believe that it is necessarily inconsistent with our decision here. *See Pico v. Board of Education, Island Trees Union Free School District, supra*, 638 F.2d at 435-436 (opinion of Newman, J.); *Right to Read Defense Committee of Chelsea v. School Committee of the City of Chelsea*, 454 F.Supp. 703, 711 (D.Mass.1978).

7. The appellant correctly observes that several opponents of the films at the two meetings objected to the violence contained in the materials. But many of the objections to the films in fact reflected disapproval of the religious and ideological content of the films. For example, one parent asked, "Why is it being used in school, questioning the child's faith in God?" Another stated that "They are questioning tradition of Judeo-Christian God who is

vengeful. Kids will pick up this thinking." Another citizen stated:

> They equated the stoning with the shedding of blood for the atonement for wrongdoing or for the good of society. This is the very basis of Christianity, the shedding of blood, but this slanted view of a God that is blood thirsty is out and out blasphemy. Our God is a God of love that demands nothing of us but pours out his love to us even though man keeps blowing it and he made this all possible not through a violent scene of the town throwing rocks at its members but rather a sacrifice of himself for us. This slanted view of old morality and of that kind of a God will bring about doubts and fears in children that instead need to be reinforced in love. They need to believe in something that is permanent and not in fluctuating morals that are based on your man. This also puts a wedge between parents and children.

Also *see* n.1, *supra*, regarding the ground for removal asserted in the Citizens' Requests.

8. The study, entitled *"The Lottery": An Empirical Analysis of Its Impact*, attempted to measure the impact of the film by examining changes in the attitudes of high school students toward God, tradition, community and violence.

9. No discussion was held at the meeting at which the board voted to remove the films from the curriculum because the board members were familiar with the films and the Citizens' Requests, and had attended the prior meetings or reviewed transcripts of the meetings. Thus, the district court did not commit clear error in deducing the board's reasons for its decision from the transcripts of the two public meetings and the Citizens' Requests.

10. The board also argues that it acted constitutionally because it complied with the procedural requirements of Policy No. 605. This argument is unavailing. Even strict procedural compliance with the board's policy cannot save a decision whose substance violates the Constitution. *See Pico v. Board of Education, Island Trees Union Free School District, supra*, 638 F.2d at 417 (opinion of Sifton, J.); *James v. Board of Education of Central District No. 1*, 461 F.2d 566, 574 (2d Cir.), *cert. denied*, 409 U.S. 1042, 93 S.Ct. 529, 34 L.Ed.2d 491 (1972).

The United States Court of Appeals, Ninth Circuit, decides that students and parents have standing to challenge the constitutionality of an Oregon textbook selection regulation which read in part: "No textbook shall be used in the schools which speaks slightingly of the founders of the republic or of those who preserved the union or which belittles or undervalues their work." In deciding that students and parents, but not teachers, had standing, the Court said: "Our conclusion as to the standing of the students and the ripeness of their claims applies equally to the parents, for they may assert claims of constitutional violation primarily affecting their children's education."

Johnson v. *Stuart*, 702 F.2d 193 (1983)

BROWNING, Chief Judge:

Public School teachers, students, and students' parents brought suit under 42 U.S.C. § 1983 against the Oregon State Board of Education, the Oregon State Textbook Commission, Portland School District No. 1 J, and Gresham Grade School District No. 4,[1] challenging the constitutionality of Oregon's textbook selection statute, Or.Rev.Stat. §§ 337.011-.260 (1981), under the first and fourteenth amendments to the United States Constitution.

On cross motions for summary judgment, the district court held the students and parents lacked standing to sue and the teachers did not present a controversy ripe for decision. We affirm the dimissal of the teachers' claim, but reverse the dismissal of the claims of the students and their parents.

I.

Chapter 337 of the Oregon Revised Statutes establishes a multi-stage scheme for selection of textbooks to be used in Oregon public schools. Section 337.260 of the statute reads:

Every board, commission, committee or officer responsible for the selection of textbooks for use in the public schools shall select textbooks on American history and government which adequately stress the services rendered by those who achieved our national independence, who established our form of constitutional government and who preserved our federal union. *No textbook shall be used in the schools which speaks slightingly of the founders of the republic or of those who preserved the union or which belittles or undervalues their work. Respect for all people, regardless of race, color, creed, national origin, age, sex, or handicap, and their contributions to our history and system of government shall be reflected in the textbooks adopted by the State Board of Education.*

(Emphasis added). Appellants contend the second sentence is unconstitutional.

Under the statute the State Board of Education establishes guidelines and criteria for the review and selection of textbooks, Or.Rev.Stat. § 337.035, and appoints a State Textbook Commission to review and select suggested textbooks for each grade and subject. Or.Rev.Stat. §§ 337.011, .050. In even-numbered years the Superintendent of Public Instruction, under the direction of the State Board, mails a circular to major textbook publishing companies that quotes the statute, including the challenged provision. Or.Rev.Stat. § 337.030. The list of selected textbooks compiled by the Textbook Commission is submitted to the State Board which may ratify or reject any textbook listed. Or. Rev.Stat. § 337.055. Copies of the list are transmitted to district school boards. School boards may adopt and use textbooks in place of or in addition to those listed by the State Board, but the substituted textbooks must meet the requirements of the statute and the criteria established by the State Board. Or.Rev.Stat. § 337. 141.

II.

The teachers, through their representative associations,[2] assert they have sustained "injury-in-fact" because the statutory scheme denies them the opportunity to use books in the classroom that express views inconsistent with the statute.

They point out that although the first sentence of section 337.260 is directed only to those "responsible for the selection of textbooks," the second sentence prohibits, in general terms, the *use* of any textbook "which speaks slightingly of the founders of the republic. . . ." The teachers argue that because their employment contracts require them to obey all Oregon laws, they would breach their contracts and could lose their jobs if they used a forbidden textbook. They concede, however, that no teacher has been charged with violating section 337.260, and no teacher has been denied permission to use any book.

The teachers rely on *Epperson v. Arkansas,* 393 U.S. 97, 89 S.Ct. 266, 21 L.Ed.2d 228 (1968), *Craig v. Boren,* 429 U.S. 190, 97 S.Ct. 451, 50 L.Ed.2d 397 (1976), and *Vorbeck v. McNeal,* 407 F.Supp. 733 (E.D. Mo.1976) (three-judge court), *aff'd* 426 U.S. 943, 96 S.Ct. 3160, 49 L.Ed.2d 1180 (1976), as authority that even though the statute has not been enforced against them and there is no threat of such enforcement, the mere existence of the statute chills their exercise of free speech as teachers and is sufficient to give them standing. But *Epperson, Craig,* and *Vorbeck* involved statutes aimed directly at those asserting standing to challenge them. In *Epperson,* teachers challenged a criminal statute that forbade "any teacher . . . to teach" Darwin's theory of evolution. 393 U.S. at 99 n.3, 89 S.Ct. at 267 n.3. In *Craig* the Court noted "[t]he legal duties created by the statutory sections under challenge are addressed directly to vendors such as appellant." 429 U.S. at 194, 97 S.Ct. at 455. In *Vorbeck,* police officers challenged a police department rule providing that "[a]ll members of the department are forbidden . . . to become members of" any union. 407 F. Supp. at 737.

Section 337.260 was not intended to regulate the conduct of teachers. The language of the second sentence of the section is broad, but it must be read in context. Considered as a whole, chapter 337 of the Oregon Revised Statutes applies only to those empowered to select textbooks for use in the schools. Nothing in the record suggests that section 337.260 limits the teachers' use of supplemental materials or the scope of classroom dialogue, or that teachers face a credible threat of discharge or discipline under the statute. The Attorney General of Oregon has repeatedly disavowed any interpretation of section 337.260 that would make it applicable in any way to teachers, and counsel for the Portland School District has stated his agreement with this position. On this record Oregon teachers have "no fears of [discharge or discipline] except those that are imaginary or speculative. . . ." *Babbitt v. United Farm Workers National Union,* 442 U.S. 289, 298, 99 S.Ct. 2301, 2308, 60 L.Ed.2d 895 (1979) (quoting *Younger v. Harris,* 401 U.S. 37, 42, 91 S.Ct. 746, 749, 27 L.Ed.2d 669 (1971)). They have failed to show that they have "suffered some actual or threatened injury as a result of the putatively illegal conduct of the defendant[s]." *Gladstone, Realtors v. Village of Bellwood,* 441 U.S. 91, 99, 99 S.Ct. 1601, 1607, 60 L.Ed.2d 66 (1979).

III.

The students claim Oregon's school book screening system restricts their first amendment right of free access to information.

To establish actual injury from a restriction of the right to receive information, there must be a speaker who is willing to convey the information. *Virginia State Board of Pharmacy v. Virginia Citizens Consumer Council,* 425 U.S. 748, 756-57, 96 S.Ct. 1817, 1822-1823, 48 L.Ed.2d 346 (1976). "[W]here a speaker exists, . . . the protection afforded is to the communication, to its source and to its recipients both." *Id.* at 756, 96 S.Ct. at 1822.

The district court took judicial notice that textbooks "that belittle the work of the founders of the republic or preservers of the union exist," and that consequently "a 'willing speaker' could be said to be present in this case." Neither party challenges this factual premise. As persons who would have received the information except for its alleged suppression by the state, the students were directly injured if a constitutional violation occurred.[3]

The district court held the students nonetheless lacked standing because textbooks were tested against numerous criteria in addition to those stated in section 337.260 and books that did not conform to section 337.260 may not have been rejected for that reason but rather for non-compliance with any of the other criteria. Therefore the court held the students had failed to show that "but for" the section 337.260 standard, books that did not conform to this standard "would be in their classrooms."

The court erred in requiring the students to meet a "but for" test. The requirement that the injury "fairly can be traced to the challenged action" and "is likely to be redressed by a favorable decision," *Simon v. Eastern Kentucky Welfare Rights Organization,* 426 U.S. 26, 38, 41, 96 S.Ct. 1917, 1924, 1925, 48 L.Ed.2d 450 (1976), requires "no more than a showing that there is a 'substantial likelihood' that the relief requested will redress the injury claimed. . . . " *Duke Power Co. v. Carolina Environmental Study Group, Inc.,* 438 U.S. 59, 75 n. 20, 98 S.Ct. 2620, 2631 n. 20, 57 L.Ed.2d 595 (1978); *Legal Aid Society of Alameda County v. Brennan,* 608 F.2d 1319, 1333 (9th Cir. 1979). This court has approved Professor Davis's suggestion that "when proof of causal relationship between governmental action and injury to a plaintiff is difficult or impossible, the court should make a judgment as to whether the causal relation is probable enough to allow standing." *Boating Industry Associations v. Marshall,* 601 F.2d 1376, 1383 (9th Cir. 1979) (quoting K. Davis, *Administrative Law Treatise* § 22.20 at 196 (Supp.1978)).

The statutory scheme challenged in this case would allow appellees to enforce the statute *sub silentio,* allowing the students no reasonable opportunity to prove particular books either were not submitted or were rejected in compliance with the statute. Every two years the State Board distributes a circular to publishers quoting the statute and stating that any contract with the state for books will require the publisher to agree to abide by the statute. The Textbook Commission states it abides by the law and considers the statute in selecting textbooks. When a book is rejected neither the Board nor the Commission gives reasons. These circumstances, considered with the fact that books that do not conform with section 337.260 exist but are not found in Oregon schools, make it "probable enough" that as a result of Oregon's book screening system, publishers were prevented from submitting non-conforming books to the Textbook Commission or that such books were screened out by the Textbook Commission or the State Board without notice or comment. We conclude it is "substantially likely" that the injunctive relief sought would redress the injury claimed.

The students also satisfy the prudential limitations on standing. Their claim of restricted access to information is not a mere generalized grievance, but an injury "peculiar to . . . a distinct group of which [they are] a part. . . . " *See Gladstone, Realtors,* 441 U.S. at 100, 99 S.Ct. at 1608; *Legal Aid Society of Alameda County,* 608 F.2d at 1336. They assert their own legal rights and not those of third parties. *See Valley Forge Christian College v. Americans United for Separation of Church and State, Inc.,* 454 U.S. 464, 102 S.Ct. 752, 759-60, 70 L.Ed.2d 700 (1982); *Legal Aid Society of Alameda County,* 608 F.2d at 1336. And their claim "fall[s] within 'the zone of interests to be protected or regulated by the . . . constitutional guarantee in question.' " *Valley Forge Christian College,* 102 S.Ct. at 760 (quoting *Association of Data Processing Service Organizations v. Camp,* 397 U.S. 150, 153, 90 S.Ct. 827, 829, 25 L.Ed.2d 184 (1970)).

We also agree with the students' contention that their claim is ripe for decision.

Ripeness has a " 'twofold aspect, . . . the fitness of the issues for judicial decision and the hardship to the parties of withholding court consideration.' " *Pence v. Andrus,* 586 F.2d 733, 737 (9th Cir.1978) (quoting *Abbott Laboratories v. Gardner,* 387 U.S. 136, 149, 87 S.Ct. 1507, 1515, 18 L.Ed.2d 681 (1967)). Since the students have sustained actual injury and this injury would be redressed by the relief sought, the constitutional requirement of ripeness as well as standing is met. *See Duke Power Co.,* 438 U.S. at 81, 98 S.Ct. at 2634.

The prudential aspects of ripeness are also satisfied. Because the statutory scheme permits *sub silentio* enforcement of the challenged statutory provision, the district court in all likelihood "will be in no better position later than [it is] now to confront the validity" of section 337.260, *Regional Rail Reorganization Act Cases,* 419 U.S. 102, 145, 95 S.Ct. 335, 359, 42 L.Ed.2d 320 (1974), *quoted in Pence v. Andrus,* 586 F.2d at 737 n. 12. The challenge is to the statute on its face, rather than as applied. Deferring adjudication would add nothing material to resolution of the legal issues presented, and delay would foreclose relief for those students presently being denied free access to information in the continuing process of their education. Moreover, "[r]estraint on expression may not generally be justified by the fact that there may be other times, places, or circumstances available for such expression." *Minarcini v. Strongsville City School District,* 541 F.2d 577, 582 (6th Cir.1976).

Our conclusion as to the standing of the students and the ripeness of their claims applies equally to the parents, for they may assert claims of constitutional violation primarily affecting their children's education. *See, e.g., Tinker v. Des Moines Independent Community School District,* 393 U.S. 503, 506, 89 S.Ct. 733, 736, 21 L.Ed.2d 731 (1969); *Meyer v. Nebraska,* 262 U.S. 390, 400, 43 S.Ct. 625, 627, 67 L.Ed. 1042 (1923).

AFFIRMED in part, REVERSED in part, and REMANDED.

NOTES

1. Although Gresham School District No. 4 was served with process, it did not file an Answer to the Complaint or make an appeareance before either the district court or this court.

2. An association has standing to sue as a representative of its members if its "members, or any one of them, are suffering immediate or threatened injury as a result of the challenged action of the sort that would make out a justiciable case had the members themselves brought suit." *Warth v. Seldin,* 422 U.S. 490, 511, 95 S.Ct. 2197, 2211, 45 L.Ed.2d 343 (1975). Thus, the teacher associations

have standing if the teachers would have standing in their own right. *See Black Faculty Ass'n of Mesa College v. San Diego Community College Dist.*, 664 F.2d 1153, 1156 (9th Cir.1981).

3. Since the complaint was dismissed for lack of standing and as not presenting a controversy ripe for decision, we express no opinion on the constitutionality of the challenged provision.

A United States District Court in Tennessee decides against school children and their parents who sought an injunction which would have prohibited "Hawkins County from compelling the students to be present in any class or any room where the *Holt Basic Readers* are read from, recited from, or in which their contents are discussed"; the children and parents alleged the books contained objectionable ideas such as teaching witchcraft, teaching that some values are relative, teaching concepts of disrespect to parents, and teaching that humans and apes evolved from a common ancestor. The Court stated: "The First Amendment does not protect the plaintiffs from exposure to morally offensive value systems or from exposure to antithetical religious ideas. Only if the plaintiffs can prove that the books at issue are teaching a particular religious faith as true (rather than as a cultural phenomenon), or teaching that the students must be saved through some religious pathway, or that no salvation is required, can it be said the mere exposure to these books is a violation of free exercise rights."

Mozert v. *Hawkins County Public Schools,* 579 F.Supp. 1051 (1984)

HULL, District Judge.

This is a civil rights action, 42 U.S.C. § 1983, for damages and injunctive relief, alleging violations of the free exercise clause of the First Amendment to the United State Constitution and of the fundamental right of parents to control the education and religious and moral instruction of their children.

The plaintiffs are certain Hawkins County, Tennessee, school children and their parents who object to the fact that all Hawkins County public school children from the first to the eighth grade are taught to read from the *Holt Basic Readings* published by Holt, Rhinehart and Winston. Plaintiffs allege that these books do the following objectionable things:

(1) teach witchcraft and other forms of magic and occult activities;

(2) teach that some values are relative and vary from situation to situation;

(3) teach attitudes, values, and concepts of disrespect and disobedience to parents;

(4) depict prayer to an idol;

(5) teach that one does not need to believe in God in a specific way but that any type of faith in the supernatural is an acceptable method of salvation;

(6) depict a child who is disrespectful of his mother's Bible study;

(7) imply that Jesus was illiterate;

(8) teach that man and apes evolved from a common ancestor; and

(9) teach various humanistic values.

The plaintiffs' position, in essence, is that their First Amendment freedom to believe as they choose is meaningless if the state can force their children to read books that contain ideas and values to which they do not subscribe. They seek, *inter alia,* the right of the student plaintiffs to "opt out" by reading from some other state-approved texts and an injunction which would prohibit Hawkins County from compelling the students to be present in any class or any room where the *Holt Basic Readers* are read from, recited from, or in which their contents are discussed.

The complaint contains no allegation that the defendants are attempting to coerce the school children into performing any symbolic act, subscribing to any particular value, or professing any particular form of belief. The plaintiffs' assertion appears to be that the mere exposure to this broad spectrum of ideas and values which they find offensive amounts to a constitutional violation.

This Court is of the opinion that only claim 5 [that the books teach that one does not need to believe in

God in a specific way but that any type of faith in the supernatural is an acceptable method of salvation], may state a constitutional violation. This would only be the case if the books appear to assert that salvation or some form of religion is necessary at all or that no religion is necessary. The plaintiffs have yet to specify to this Court exactly which parts of which books substantiate this claim.

In this highly diverse nation, it is not uncommon that a group of people will form a sincere and passionate distaste for a particular set of textbooks chosen by an apparently well-meaning board of education. In *Williams v. Board of Education of the County of Kanawha*, 388 F.Supp. 93 (D.W.Va.1975), aff'd 530 F.2d 972 (4th Cir.1975), a group of parents of public school children brought an action challenging the chosen textbooks as containing "both religious and anti-religious materials, matter offensive to Christian morals, matter which invades personal and familial morals, matter which defames the nation and which attacks civic virtue, and matter which suggests and encourages the use of bad English." *Id.* at 95. The Kanawha County plaintiffs, like those in this action, alleged that the use of these textbooks was a violation of their First Amendment right to free exercise of their religion. After an evidentiary hearing, the *Williams* court concluded that the materials were genuinely offensive to the beliefs of the plaintiffs but that, as a matter of law, there was nothing in the defendant's conduct that constituted an inhibition of, or prohibition of, the free exercise of religion. About the plaintiffs' rights of free exercise of religion it wrote:

These rights are guaranteed by the First Amendment, but the Amendment does not guarantee that nothing about religion will be taught in the schools or that nothing offensive to any religion will be taught in the schools . . .

Government in our democracy, state and national, must be neutral in matters of religious theory, doctrine, and practice. It may not be hostile to any religion or to the advocacy of no-religion; and it may not aid, foster, or promote one religion or religious theory against another or even against the militant opposite. The First Amendment mandates governmental neutrality between religion and religion, and between religion and nonreligion . . . By and large, public education in our Nation is committed to the control of state and local authorities. Courts do not and cannot intervene in the resolution of conflicts which arise in the daily operation of school systems and which do not directly and sharply implicate basic constitutional values. *Id.* at 96, 97.

No basic constitutional values are implicated in the allegation that the *Holt Basic Readings* depict witchcraft, the worship of idols, situational ethics, disrespect for parents, the theory of evolution, or the values of humanism. None of these allegations suggest a departure from the constitutionally mandated neutrality between religion and religion and between religion and nonreligion. The First Amendment does not protect the plaintiffs from exposure to morally offensive value systems or from exposure to antithetical religious ideas. Only if the plaintiffs can prove that the books at issue are teaching a particular religious faith as true (rather than as a cultural phenomenon), or teaching that the students must be saved through some religious pathway, or that no salvation is required, can it be said the mere exposure to these books is a violation of free exercise rights.

Accordingly, it is ORDERED that the defendants' motion to dismiss, Rule 12(b)(6), Federal Rules of Civil Procedure, is hereby GRANTED in part and DENIED in part. The plaintiffs' claim is hereby limited to its fifth allegation as indicated above.

The United States Court of Appeals, Ninth Circuit, decides that the use of Gordon Parks' *The Learning Tree* in a high school sophomore English literature class did not violate the Establishment Clause nor the Free Exercise Clause of the First Amendment as had been claimed by a student and her parent who found the book offensive to their religious beliefs. In deciding against the removal of the book, the Court said: "The burden on Grove's free exercise of religion was minimal. Cassie [Grove] was assigned an alternate book as soon as she and her parent objected to *The Learning Tree*. Cassie was given permission to avoid class discussions of *The Learning Tree*. We agree with the district court's finding that no coercion existed." Further, the Court argued: "*The Learning Tree* . . . was included in a group of religiously neutral books in a review of English literature, as a comment on an American subculture. Its use does not constitute establishment of religion or anti-religion."

In his concurring opinion, Judge Canby concludes: "We must remain sensitive to claims that government is either interfering with a religion or is supporting a competing religion . . . neither is the case here. On the contrary, if we were to grant the relief sought by plaintiffs and remove *The Learning Tree* from the curriculum because of plaintiffs' hostility to its ideas, our action would itself threaten First Amendment values. 'Our Constitution does not permit the official suppression of ideas.'"

Grove v. *Mead School Dist. No. 354*, 753 F.2d 1528 (1985)

EUGENE A. WRIGHT, Circuit Judge:

At issue here is a school board's refusal to remove a book from a sophomore English literature curriculum based on plaintiffs' religious objections to the book. Plaintiffs brought this civil rights suit arguing that use of the book violates religion clauses of the First Amendment.

The district court granted summary judgment to defendants, finding no violation of the Constitution. We also must decide whether plaintiffs have standing to bring this suit, whether they were given adequate notice that the district court was considering a grant of summary judgment, and whether attorneys' fees should have been awarded to the defendant intervenor.

FACTS

Cassie Grove was assigned *The Learning Tree*, by Gordon Parks, in her public school sophomore English literature class. She read part of it, found it offensive to her religious beliefs, and showed it to her mother. Her mother read the entire book and agreed.

The Groves informed the teacher of their objections and Cassie was assigned another book. She was given permission to leave during classroom discussion of *The Learning Tree*, but chose to remain.

Mrs. Grove (hereinafter Grove) filed a formal complaint concerning the book with the school district. An evaluation committee concluded that *The Learning Tree* "is an appropriate element of the sophomore English curriculum." Grove and the Riddles, taxpayers, appealed to the Board of Directors of the school district. After a hearing, the Board denied the request to remove the book from the curriculum.

Plaintiffs then brought this civil rights suit under 42 U.S.C. § 1983 against the school district. They contend that use of *The Learning Tree* violated the religion clauses of the First Amendment. They seek damages and injunctive relief. The Mead Education Association, bargaining representative for the district teachers, was allowed to intervene as a defendant.

The defendants filed motions to dismiss in district court. After reading plaintiffs' affidavits and the book and conducting a hearing, the judge granted summary judgment for the defendants and denied their requests for attorneys' fees.

ANALYSIS

I.   STANDING

If the plaintiffs lack standing to bring this suit, the courts lack jurisdiction to consider it. *Allen v. Wright,*—U.S.—, 104 S.Ct. 3315, 3324-3325, 82 L.Ed. 2d 556 (1984). To satisfy constitutional standing requirements, a plaintiff must allege distinct personal injury that is fairly traceable to the challenged conduct and likely to be redressed by requested relief. *Id.* 104 S.Ct. at 3325. Prudential limitations on the exercise of jurisdiction include a general prohibition on a litigant's raising another's rights. *Id.* at 3324-25.

A. *Free Exercise Claims*

Appellants have standing to challenge alleged violations of the free exercise clause of the First Amendment only if they claim infringement of their personal religious freedom. *McGowan v. Maryland,* 366 U.S. 420, 429, 81 S.Ct. 1101, 1107, 6 L.Ed.2d 393 (1961).

One aspect of the religious freedom of parents is the right to control the religious upbringing and training of their minor children. *See Wisconsin v. Yoder,* 406 U.S. 205, 92 S.Ct. 1526, 32 L.Ed.2d 15 (1972). As a parent, Grove has a direct, personal right to direct Cassie's religious training. *Collins v. Chandler Unified School District,* 644 F.2d 759, 764 n. 1 (9th Cir.), *cert. denied,* 454 U.S. 863, 102 S.Ct. 322, 70 L.Ed.2d 163 (1981).

The Riddles present no claim of violation of a personal right of religious freedom. In the complaint, their only interest is identified as their taxpayer status. Appellants assert that the Riddles are the parents of school-age children in the district, but not that the children have attended public school there. The Riddles do not have standing to pursue their free exercise claims.

B. *Establishment Claims*

Appellants have standing to challenge alleged violations of the establishment clause of the First Amendment if they are directly affected by use of *The Learning Tree* in the English curriculum. *Abington School District v. Schempp,* 374 U.S. 203, 224 n. 9, 83 S.Ct. 1560, 1572 n. 9, 10 L.Ed.2d 844 (1963). Grove has standing as a parent whose right to direct the religious training of her child is allegedly affected. *See Wisconsin v. Yoder,* 406 U.S. 205, 92 S.Ct. 1526, 32 L.Ed.2d 15; *Abington School District,* 374 U.S. at 224 n. 9, 83 S.Ct. at 1572 n. 9.

As taxpayers, the Riddles may bring an establishment clause challenge only if they show direct and particular economic detriment resulting from the disputed practice. *Doremus v. Board of Education,* 342 U.S. 429, 433-35, 72 S.Ct. 394, 396-98, 96 L.Ed. 475 (1952). Standing is not established by a citizen's general interest in constitutional governance. *Valley Forge Christian College v. Americans United for Separation of Church and State, Inc.,* 454 U.S. 464, 482-83, 102 S.Ct. 752, 763-64, 70 L.Ed.2d 700 (1982).

Expenditure of public funds in an unconstitutional manner is not an injury conferring standing. *Id.* at 477, 102 S.Ct. at 761. A religious objection to public expenditures will not confer taxpayer standing either. *Id.* at 478, 102 S.Ct. at 761. The Riddles have alleged no more direct and particular injury that would confer standing.

Because the Riddles have not alleged that use of *The Learning Tree* caused them personal detriment, they have no standing to challenge it. We will consider Grove's claims only.

II.   NOTICE OF CONSIDERATION OF MOTION FOR SUMMARY JUDGMENT

Grove contends that the district judge provided insufficient notice of his intent to treat defendants' pretrial motions as motions for summary judgment. She argues that she was denied an adequate opportunity to conduct discovery that would support her claims, in violation of due process.

Whenever a district court looks beyond the pleadings in evaluating a Rule 12(b)(6) motion to dismiss, the motion must be treated as one for summary judgment under Rule 56. Fed.R.Civ.P. 12(b)(6); *Portland Retail Druggists Association v. Kaiser Foundation Health Plan,* 662 F.2d 641, 645 (9th Cir.1981). Before summary judgment may be entered, all parties must be given notice of the motion and an opportunity to respond. *Portland Retail Druggists,* 662 F.2d at 645. The opportunity to respond must include time for discovery necessary to develop facts justifying opposition to the motion. *Id.; Fed.R.Civ.P.* 56.

In this circuit, notice is adequate if the party against whom judgment is entered is "fairly apprised" that the court will look beyond the pleadings, thereby transforming the motion to dismiss into a motion for summary judgment. *Mayer v. Wedgewood Neighborhood Coalition,* 707 F.2d 1020, 1021 (9th Cir.1983) (per curiam) (citing *Portland Retail Druggists,* 662 F.2d at 645). When a party is represented by counsel, formal notice may be unnecessary. *See Garaux v. Pulley,* 739 F.2d 437, 439-40 (9th Cir.1984). Notice occurs when a party has reason to know that the court will consider matters outside the pleadings. *See Townsend v. Columbia Operations,* 667 F.2d 844, 849 (9th Cir. 1982).

A represented party who submits matters outside the pleadings to the judge and invites consideration of them has notice that the judge may use them to decide a motion originally noted as a motion to dismiss, requiring its transformation to a motion for summary judgment. *Id.; see Garaux,* 739 F.2d at 439.

Grove submitted matters outside the pleadings. On August 18 the parties agreed that the judge should then read *The Learning Tree.* On August 30 Grove submitted copies of affidavits of her witnesses. At the September 13 hearing the judge relied on the book and Grove's affidavits in deciding the motion. Grove had adequate notice that he would do so.

III. FIRST AMENDMENT

The grant of summary judgment is reviewable de novo. *National Union Fire Insurance Co. v. Argonaut Insurance Co.,* 701 F.2d 95, 96 (9th Cir.1983). Summary judgment is appropriate if there is no genuine issue of material fact and the moving party is entitled to judgment as a matter of law. Fed.R.Civ.P. 56(c).

Local school boards have broad discretion in the management of schools. *Epperson v. Arkansas,* 393 U.S. 97, 104, 89 S.Ct. 266, 270, 21 L.Ed.2d 228 (1968). Judicial supervision of public education is limited to the resolution of conflicts that clearly involve constitutional values. *Id.; Nicholson v. Board of Education,* 682 F.2d 858, 863 (9th Cir.1982).

Grove contends that the Board's refusal to prohibit use of *The Learning Tree* in high school English courses violated the First Amendment religion clauses. Those clauses provide that "Congress shall make no law respecting an establishment of religion, or prohibiting the free exercise thereof." U.S. Const. amend. I.

A. *Free Exercise of Religion*

The free exercise clause recognizes the right of every person to choose among types of religious training and observance, free of state compulsion. *Abington School District,* 374 U.S. at 222, 83 S.Ct. at 1571. To establish a violation of that clause, a litigant must show that challenged state action has a coercive effect that operates against the litigant's practice of his or her religion. *Id.* at 223, 83 S.Ct. at 1572.

The state action at issue here is a school board policy of academic freedom and refusal to remove from the curriculum a book that offends Grove's religious sensibilities. Three factors are relevant in our analysis: (1) the extent of the burden upon the exercise of religion, (2) the existence of a compelling state interest justifying that burden, and (3) the extent to which accommodation of the complainant would impede the state's objectives. *Callahan v. Woods,* 736 F.2d 1269, 1273 (9th Cir.1984).

The burden on Grove's free exercise of religion was minimal. Cassie was assigned an alternate book as soon as she and Grove objected to *The Learning Tree.* Cassie was given permission to avoid classroom dis-

cussions of *The Learning Tree.* We agree with the district court's finding that no coercion existed.

The state interest in providing well-rounded public education would be critically impeded by accommodation of Grove's wishes.

If we are to eliminate everything that is objectionable to any of [the religious bodies existing in the United States] or inconsistent with any of their doctrines, we will leave public education in shreds.

Florey v. Sioux Falls School District 49-5, 619 F.2d 1311, 1318 (8th Cir.), *cert. denied,* 449 U.S. 987, 101 S.Ct. 409, 66 L.Ed.2d 251 (1980) (quoting *McCollum v. Board of Education,* 333 U.S. 203, 235, 68 S.Ct. 461, 477, 92 L.Ed. 649 (1948) (Jackson, J., concurring)).

In light of the absence of coercion and the critical threat to public education, we conclude that the school board has not violated the free exercise clause. *Id.* at 1318-19.

B. *Establishment of Religion*

The establishment clause of the First Amendment requires government neutrality with respect to religion. *Abington School District,* 374 U.S. at 215, 83 S.Ct. at 1567. It was intended to protect against "sponsorship, financial support, and active involvement of the sovereign in religious activity." *Lemon v. Kurtzman,* 403 U.S. 602, 612, 91 S.Ct. 2105, 2111, 29 L.Ed.2d 745 (1971) (quoting *Walz v. Tax Commission,* 397 U.S. 664, 668, 90 S.Ct. 1409, 1411, 25 L.Ed.2d 697 (1970)).

To pass constitutional muster, challenged state action (1) must have a secular purpose, (2) must have a primary effect that neither advances nor inhibits religion, and (3) must not foster excessive state entanglement with religion. *Lemon,* 403 U.S. at 612-13, 91 S.Ct. at 2111-12. The option of nonparticipation does not save state action from an establishment clause challenge. *Engel v. Vitale,* 370 U.S. 421, 430, 82 S.Ct. 1261, 1266, 8 L.Ed.2d 601 (1962).

Religious activities prohibited in public schools include daily readings from the Bible, *Abington School District,* 374 U.S. 203, 83 S.Ct. 1560, 10 L.Ed.2d 844, recitation of the Lord's Prayer, *id.;* posting the Ten Commandments in every classroom, *Stone v. Graham,* 449 U.S. 39, 101 S.Ct. 192, 66 L.Ed.2d 199 (1980), beginning school assemblies with prayer, *Collins,* 644 F.2d 759, and teaching a Transcendental Meditation course that includes a ceremony involving offerings to a deity, *Malnak v. Yogi,* 592 F.2d 197 (3d Cir.1979). The Supreme Court has stated clearly that literary or historic study of the Bible is *not* a prohibited religious activity. *Stone,* 449 U.S. at 42, 101 S.Ct. at 194; *Abington School District,* 374 U.S. at 225, 83 S.Ct. at 1573. Not all mention of religion is prohibited in public schools.

Appellants contend that use of *The Learning Tree* in an English literature class has a primary effect of inhibiting their religion, fundamentalist Christianity, and advancing the religion of secular humanism. The district court concluded that use of the book was not a religious activity and that it served a secular educational function.

At issue here is not a ritual, but students reading

a novel with autobiographic overtones used in the English literature class . . . for purposes of exposing students to expectations and orientations of Black Americans.

District Court Memorandum Decision at 4. The central theme of the novel is life, especially racism, from the perspective of a teenage boy in a working class black family. Comment on religion is a very minor portion of the book. Its primary effect is secular.

Secular humanism may be a religion. *See Rhode Island Federation of Teachers v. Norberg*, 630 F.2d 850, 854 (1st Cir.1980). *The Learning Tree*, however, was included in a group of religiously neutral books in a review of English literature, as a comment on an American subculture. Its use does not constitute establishment of religion or anti-religion.

IV.   ATTORNEYS' FEES

Defendant-intervenor Mead Education Association moved for an award of attorneys' fees below, under 42 U.S.C. § 1988. Its motion was denied. It cross-appeals that denial of fees and seeks an award of fees on appeal.

A defendant who prevails in a § 1983 action is awarded attorneys' fees "only where the action brought is found to be unreasonable, frivolous, meritless or vexatious." *Mayer v. Wedgewood Neighborhood Coalition*, 707 F.2d 1020, 1021 (9th Cir.1983) (citing *Christiansburg Garment Co. v. EEOC*, 434 U.S. 412, 421, 98 S.Ct. 694, 700, 54 L.Ed.2d 648 (1978)). Awards to intervenors should not be granted unless the intervenor plays a significant role in the litigation. *See Seattle School District No. 1 v. State of Washington*, 633 F.2d 1338, 1349-50 (9th Cir.1980), *aff'd*, 458 U.S. 457, 102 S.Ct. 3187, 73 L.Ed.2d 896 (1982); *see also Donnell v. United States*, 682 F.2d 240, 245-49 (D.C.Cir.1982), *cert. denied*, 459 U.S. 1204, 103 S.Ct. 1190, 75 L.Ed.2d 436 (1983). A district court's denial of fees is reviewed for abuse of discretion. *Seattle School District No. 1*, 633 F.2d at 1349.

The Education Association did not play an exceptional role in this litigation. The district court's denial of attorneys' fees was not an abuse of discretion. Attorneys' fees on appeal are denied also.

AFFIRMED.

CANBY, Circuit Judge (concurring):

I concur in Judge Wright's clear and concise opinion. Because plaintiffs pose a novel problem, however, in the delicate area of church-state relations, I write separately to amplify my views on this matter of first impression.

I.   Establishment Clause

"[O]ne of the mandates of the First Amendment is to promote a viable, pluralistic society and to keep government neutral, not only between sects, but between believers and nonbelievers." *Walz v. Tax Commission*, 397 U.S. 664, 716, 90 S.Ct. 1409, 1436, 25 L.Ed.2d 697 (1970) (Douglas, J., dissenting).[1] Plaintiffs do not dispute this goal. They claim, however, that *The Learning Tree* reflects a set of secular, if not anti-religious values—values which they denominate "secular humanism"—so that inclusion of the book in the public secondary school curriculum violates this salutary principle of neutrality.[2]

The sincerity of plaintiffs' religious objections to *The Learning Tree* is not disputed, nor is the fact that the book deeply offends plaintiffs. Even accepting, however, that the work is antithetical to the particular Christian beliefs espoused by plaintiffs, its inclusion in the high school curriculum does not violate the establishment clause.

The first amendment prohibits the establishment of religion but does not define religion. Plaintiffs insist that *The Learning Tree* embodies the philosophy of secular humanism, and that secular humanism is a religion. There are substantial analytical difficulties with this contention, and with its underlying use of the term "secular humanism."[3]

A.   *Secularism as Religion*

Plaintiffs frequently seem to regard "secular" and "humanist" as synonyms for "anti-religious."[4] The common meaning of those terms does not support the assumption. "Humanism,"[5] for example, is not necessarily incompatible with religion generally or with theistic commitments, including Christianity, in particular.[6] We assume, however, that the thrust of plaintiffs' attack is against nontheistic[7] humanism, which they might label "secular humanism."

The analytical difficulty with plaintiffs' approach is that it tends to divide the universe of value-laden thought into only two categories—the religious and the anti-religious. By adopting this dualistic social outlook, and by denominating the anti-religious half of their universe as "secular," plaintiffs erect an insurmountable barrier to meaningful application of the establishment clause to controversies like this one. Whether the inclusion of *The Learning Tree* in the curriculum violates the establishment clause depends, under *Lemon v. Kurtzman,* 403 U.S. 602, 612-13, 91 S.Ct. 2105, 2111-12, 29 L.Ed.2d 745 (1971), upon whether that inclusion reflects a secular purpose and produces a secular effect. The difficulty is that plaintiffs might well concede that the primary purpose and effect was secular; indeed, that is precisely their point.

It is apparent that so long as plaintiffs deem that which is "secular" in orientation to be anti-religious, they are not dealing in the same linguistic currency as the Supreme Court's establishment decisions. If the establishment clause is to have any meaning, distinctions must be drawn to recognize not simply "religious" and "anti-religious," but "non-religious" governmental activity as well. In the parlance of *Lemon v. Kurtzman,* "secular" must mean "non-religious." Therefore, plaintiffs cannot succeed in demonstrating a violation of the establishment clause by showing that the school authorities are somehow advancing "secular" goals.

Part of plaintiff's argument, however, is that secular humanism is itself a religion. They rely principally upon *Torcaso v. Watkins,* 367 U.S. 488, 81 S.Ct. 1680, 6 L.Ed.2d 982 (1961).[8] In *Torcaso,* the Supreme Court did assume without deciding that certain nontheistic beliefs, including secular humanism, were "religions" for purposes of the first amendment:

Among religions in this country which do not teach what would generally be considered a belief in the existence of God are Buddhism, Taoism, Ethical Culture, Secular Humanism, and others (citations omitted).

Id. at 495 n. 11, 81 S.Ct. at 1684 n. 11 (dictum). The apparent breadth of the reference to "Secular Humanism," however, is entirely dependent upon viewing the term out of context. In context, it is clear that the Court meant

no more than a reference to the group seeking an exemption in *Fellowship of Humanity v. County of Alameda,* 153 Cal.App.2d 673 [315 P.2d 394] (1957) which, although non-Theist in belief, also met weekly on Sundays and functioned much like a church. . . . Thus *Torcaso* does not stand for the proposition that "humanism" is a religion, although an organized group of "Secular Humanists" may be.

Malnak v. Yogi, 592 F.2d 197, 206 & 212 (3d Cir.1979) (Adams, J., concurring).

Even if *The Learning Tree* is viewed as representative of what can fairly be characterized as "secular humanism," it remains an autobiographical novel only tangentially concerned with religion. The work "is still

far removed from a comprehensive belief system laying claim to ultimate truth and supported by a formal group," *id.* at 212, which the Court was prepared to concede in *Torcaso* would constitute a religion. *See also Womens Services, P.C. v. Thone,* 483 F.Supp. 1022, 1034 (D.Neb.1979), *aff'd* 636 F.2d 206 (8th Cir.1980), *vacated on other grounds,* 452 U.S. 911 (1981) (concluding that nontheistic beliefs are "religions" in constitutional terms only if characterized by tenets and organization).

Furthermore, in suggesting that secular humanism may be a religion, neither *Torcaso* nor plaintiffs distinguish between "establishment" and "free exercise."[9] *Torcaso* is a free exercise case. While the Supreme Court has embraced a concept of religion in the free exercise context sufficiently expansive to encompass nontheistic views,[10] there is much to be said for the view that the definition of religion should vary with the clause under review.

While a generous functional (and even idiosyncratic) definition best serves free exercise values, the same expansiveness in interpreting the establishment clause is simply untenable in an age of such pervasive governmental activity:

To borrow the ultimate concern test from the free exercise context and use it with present establishment clause doctrines would be to invite attack on all programs that further the ultimate concerns of individuals or entangle the government with such concerns.

Note, "Toward a Constitutional Definition of Religion," 91 Harv.L.Rev. 1056, 1084 (1978); *see Int'l Soc. for Krishna Consciousness, Inc. v. Barber,* 650 F.2d 430, 439-40 (2d Cir.1981) (Kaufman, J.). Thus, "a less expansive notion of religion [is] required for establishment clause purposes lest all 'humane' programs of government be deemed constitutionally suspect." L. Tribe, *American Constitutional Law* 827-28 (1978).[11]

In any event, it is sufficient here simply to point out that plaintiffs have not alleged facts showing anything remotely resembling an establishment of a religion of secular humanism. At issue is not the wholesale imposition of secular humanist dogma, however defined,[12] but the assignment in the secondary curriculum of a discrete work, *The Learning Tree* by Gordon Parks. In assessing whether inclusion of a work violates the establishment clause, conclusionary characterizations are of little aid in the inquiry. *See Lynch v. Donnelly,*—U.S.—,—104 S.Ct. 1355, 1361-62 (1984). Establishment clause analysis is necessarily fact-dependent. *Id.* We must apply the clause in light of the text of the book itself, and the manner of its use in the curriculum.

B. *Entanglement, Purpose and Effect*

In *Lynch v. Donnelly,*—U.S.—, 104 S.Ct. 1355, 79 L.Ed.2d 604 (1984), the Supreme Court reaffirmed the relevance of what had generally been known as the *Lemon v. Kurtzman,* 403 U.S. 602, 91 S.Ct. 2105, 29 L.Ed.2d 745 (1971), tripartite test.[13] Under *Lemon,* a state action or enactment does not violate the establishment clause if (1) it has a secular purpose; (2) its principal or primary effect is neither to advance nor inhibit religion; and (3) it does not foster excessive governmental entanglement with religion. *Id.* at 612-13, 91 S.Ct. at 2111-12. Although clarity, in the current context, would be aided by substituting "non-religious" for "secular," none of these factors supports a finding of impermissible establishment in this case.

In a somewhat novel twist on the issue of entanglement, plaintiffs claim that

> [t]his is not a case where we must show that the State has been too intertwined with religious agencies. In this case, the State *is* the agency of (anti-)religion. It is hard to become more entangled than that.

Appellants' Brief 44. This conclusion, however, is entirely dependent upon the fallacious dichotomy discounted above. *The Learning Tree* was neither purchased from nor provided by official humanist organizations. Nor does the work carry the imprimatur of these or similar religio-philosophical bodies.[14] There is no entanglement.

Nor was selection and subsequent retention of the work impermissibly sectarian. The Supreme Court

> has invalidated legislation or governmental action on the ground that a secular purpose was lacking ... only when it has concluded that there was *no question* that the statute or activity was motivated *wholly* by religious considerations.

Lynch,——U.S. at——, 104 S.Ct. at 1362 (emphasis added).

Here, there is no question that the book was included within the curriculum for the entirely non-religious (*i.e.,* secular) and commendable purpose of exposing students to different cultural attitudes and outlooks.[15] In marked contrast to the orchestrated prayer, mandatory Bible reading, Decalogue, or creationism cases,[16] the record is devoid of any evidence that *The Learning Tree* was initially selected by Cassie's teacher or subsequently retained by Mead School District officials out of hostility toward Christianity or fealty to any secularist credo. "The purpose prong of the *Lemon* test asks whether government's

actual purpose is to endorse or disapprove of religion." *Lynch,*——U.S. at——, 104 S.Ct. at 1368 (O'Connor, J., concurring). No such purpose has been shown.

The crux of plaintiffs' establishment claim is therefore that inclusion of *The Learning Tree* in the public schools has the primary effect of advancing the "religion" of secular humanism while inhibiting the plaintiffs' own religion of "Biblical Christianity." Plaintiffs insist that "the book ... clearly teaches anti-Christian concepts, values, and beliefs." Appellants' Brief 16. Assuming, *arguendo,* that this characterization is correct, and that such views are consistent with the "religions" of humanism or secularism, "'not every law that confers an "indirect," "remote," or "incidental" benefit upon [religion] is, for that reason alone, constitutionally invalid.'" *Lynch,* 104 S.Ct. at 1364 (*citing Committee for Public Education & Religious Liberty v. Nyquist,* 413 U.S. 756, 771, 93 S.Ct. 2955, 2965, 37 L.Ed.2d 948 (1973)); *see Crowley v. Smithsonian Institution,* 636 F.2d 738, 742–43 (D.C. Cir.1980). Total separation of church and state is simply impossible. *Lynch,* 104 S.Ct. at 1362. The first amendment is not violated merely because particular governmental activity " 'happens to coincide or harmonize with the tenets of some or all religions.' " *Harris v. McRae,* 448 U.S. 297, 319, 100 S.Ct. 2671, 2689, 65 L.Ed.2d 784 (1980) (*citing McGowan v. Maryland,* 366 U.S. 420, 442, 81 S.Ct. 1101, 1113, 6 L.Ed.2d 393 (1961)).

The issue is *not* whether *The Learning Tree* embodies anti-Christian elements; I have assumed, *arguendo,* that it does. Instead, the issue is whether its selection and retention by school officials "communicat[es] a message of government endorsement" of those elements.[17] It is not the purpose of the public schools "to cultivate an official faith or ideology, whether religious or humanistic in character...." Kauper, "Prayer, Public Schools and the Supreme Court," 61 Mich.L.Rev. 1031, 1066 (1963).[18] Yet even the Bible may occupy a place in the classroom, provided education and exposure do not become advocacy or endorsement. *Abington,* 374 U.S. at 225, 83 S.Ct. at 1573.

In assessing whether inclusion of *The Learning Tree* communicates governmental endorsement or approval of its purportedly "anti-Christian" or "secular humanist" elements, we must first examine the work as a whole. *See Lynch,* 104 S.Ct. at 1362. The passages identified by plaintiffs are simply scattered references to religion in a much larger work depicting a poor, black adolescent's painful process of coming of age. Nor are these passages as much theology as anthropology, less commentary on religion than comment prompted by the frustrating confrontation of adolescents with evil, hypocrisy, and suffering. *See* Appendix. Indeed, while that distinction might be lost on third-graders, it is bound to be understood by Cassie Grove's classmates—high school sophomores confronting many of the same questions, and doubtless beginning to appreciate that many of the comforting assumptions and illusions of childhood are not always what they seemed.

Second, we must examine the work as a whole in the context of the entire curriculum.[19] Were the school board in Cassie's district to require local principals to read over their public address systems a resolution, drawn in words from the book, declaring Jesus Christ to be a "poor white trash God" or "a long-legged white son-of-a-bitch," Appendix, *infra* at 1543, there would be little doubt that the effect would be to communicate governmental endorsement of anti-Christian sentiments.

By contrast, *The Learning Tree* bears the sole signature of its author, Gordon Parks. It is a work of fiction, not dogmatic philosophy. It is one book, only tangentially "religious," thematically grouped with others in the sophomore literature curriculum. Its purpose and effect is to expose students to the attitudes and outlooks of an important American subculture.

Plaintiffs may be correct in suggesting that the work "hard[ly] ... constitutes the objective study of Christianity," Appellants' Brief 22, yet objectivity in education need not inhere in each individual item studied; if that were the requirement, precious little would be left to read. Instead, objectivity is to be assessed with reference to the manner in which often highly partisan, subjective material is presented, handled, and "integrated into the school curriculum, where [even] the Bible may constitutionally be used in an appropriate study of history, civilization, ethics, comparative religion, or the like." *Stone*, 449 U.S. at 42, 101 S.Ct. at 194; *see Abington*, 374 U.S. at 225, 83 S.Ct. at 1573.

Luther's "Ninety-five Theses" are hardly balanced or objective, yet their pronounced and even vehement bias does not prevent their study in a history class' exploration of the Protestant Reformation, nor is Protestantism itself "advanced" thereby. The study of Greek mythology does not "advance" pantheism. Teaching about "the divine right of kings" does not endorse a particular dogma, although one is necessarily explored.[20]

Similarly, inclusion of *The Learning Tree* as representative of a particular literary genre neither religiously inhibits nor instills, but simply informs and educates students on a particular social outlook forged in the crucible of black rural life. To include the work no more communicates governmental endorsement of the author's or characters' religious views than to assign *Paradise Lost, Pilgrim's Progress,* or *The Divine Comedy* conveys endorsement or approval of Milton's, Bunyan's, or Dante's Christianity.[21]

Even though *The Learning Tree* does not "advance" secular humanism, it remains to consider whether the work "inhibits" fundamentalist or Biblical Christianity, as plaintiffs contend. There is, at least initially, apparent merit to this claim. When the work does discuss religion, it does so in a fashion which generally denigrates the figure of Jesus and casts doubt upon much fundamentalist doctrine—from the efficacy of prayer to the inerrancy of Scripture and benevolence of God. *See* Appendix. Nevertheless, in the context presented, these passages do not offend the establishment clause.

First, the work's purported hostility to religion may be more apparent than real. It is true that religious hypocrisy is one theme in the work. *See* Appendix. Yet the same might be said of both Jesus and the Old Testament prophets,[22] let alone such secular—and celebrated—authors as Chaucer, Voltaire, Paine, Twain, or Sinclair Lewis.[23] It is also true that the adolescent protagonist in the *The Learning Tree* comes to doubt and question many of the simple pieties he has been taught. In the novel, the good die young while the wicked prosper, prejudice reigns, the innocent suffer; these circumstances lead to searching questions and nagging doubts. *See* Appendix. But they are not new questions; Job asked them as well.[24] Neither do they reflect hostility toward religion.[25]

Of course, plaintiffs may personally espouse and prefer an unwavering acceptance of a number of the traditional religious doctrines doubted by characters in *The Learning Tree*. The issue, however, is not whether the work disapproves of any particular religious vision, including plaintiffs', but whether its inclusion in the public school curriculum indicates, intentionally or not, that the government joins in that disapproval.

It is true that *The Learning Tree* poses questions and ponders doubts with which plaintiffs may be uncomfortable. Yet to pose questions is not to impose answers. Since the first amendment is designed as much to protect the former as prevent the latter, I cannot conclude, on the record presented, that use of *The Learning Tree* inhibits religion.

II. Free Exercise Clause

Plaintiffs allege that they believe that "eternal religious consequences" result to them and their children from exposure to *The Learning Tree* or discussion of it. That allegation[26] would probably be sufficient to present a free exercise question if Cassie Grove had been compelled to read the book or be present while it was discussed in class. She was not.[27]

Plaintiffs' free exercise claims appear to go further, however, and to contest the inclusion of the book in the curriculum whether or not Cassie Grove was excused. The free exercise clause does not go nearly so far. While it protects individuals from governmental interference with their religion in the absence of compelling justification, *see Wilson v. Block,* 708 F.2d 735, 740 (D.C.Cir), *cert. denied,* 104 S.Ct. 371 (1983). *Callahan v. Woods,* 736 F.2d 1269, 1272 (9th Cir.1984), it does not protect the individual from being religiously offended by what the government does.

Plaintiffs' submissions to this court make clear that they regard *The Learning Tree* as but a single symptom of a larger social disease: the wholesale secularization of society. As one prominent theologian has observed,

what is meant when people speak of a "secular" ... world [is that] it seems that ... more or less all the important spheres of human life—learning, economy, politics, law, state, culture, education, medicine, social welfare—have been withdrawn from the influence of the churches, of theology and religion, and placed under the direct responsibility and control of man ...

H. Kung, *On Being a Christian* 26–27 (1974). While plaintiffs are free to decry this secularization, and to resist, insofar as possible, its alleged perniciousness in their private lives, it is inevitable that in such a society, plaintiffs will find much with which they disagree.[28]

The inevitability of this conflict between plaintiffs' religious rejection of "secularism" and the secularization of society suggests why antipathy alone, however sincere, is never enough to sustain a free exercise challenge. Plaintiffs are religiously offended by a particular novel; others previously before us have been religiously offended by Trident submarines or the nuclear arms race.[29] Were the free exercise clause violated whenever governmental activity is offensive to or at variance with sincerely held religious precepts, virtually no governmental program would be constitutionally possible.

When the contention is applied to education, Justice Jackson's admonition is especially appropriate:

Authorities list 256 separate and substantial religious bodies to exist in the ... United States. ... If we are to eliminate everything that is objectionable to any of these warring sects or inconsistent with any of their doctrines, we will leave public education in shreds. Nothing but educational confusion and a discrediting of the public school system can result. ...

McCollum v. Bd. of Educ., 333 U.S. 203, 235, 68 S.Ct. 461, 477, 92 L.Ed. 649 (1948) (Jackson, J., concurring). The lesson is clear: governmental actions that merely offend or cast doubt on religious beliefs do not on that account violate free exercise. An actual burden on the profession or exercise of religion is required. *See Wilson,* 708 F.2d at 741.

In short, distinctions must be drawn between those governmental actions that actually interfere with the exercise of religion, and those that merely require or result in exposure to attitudes and outlooks at odds with perspectives prompted by religion. Plaintiffs allege that they believe that "eternal religious consequences" would result from Cassie Grove's exposure to *The Learning Tree.* Such a belief might well require her being excused from such exposure. *See note 26, supra.* Mere offense, however, would not require her being excused, nor does mere offense at having *The Learning Tree* in the curriculum bring the free exercise clause to the aid of plaintiffs. There has been no violation of free exercise in this case.[30]

III. Conclusion

We must remain sensitive to claims that government is either interfering with a religion or is supporting a competing religion. *See Crowley v. Smithsonian Institution,* 636 F.2d at 743. Neither is the case here. On the contrary, if we were to grant the relief sought by plaintiffs and remove *The Learning Tree* from the curriculum because of plaintiffs' hostility to its ideas, our action would itself threaten first amendment values. "Our Constitution does not permit the official suppression of ideas." *Bd. of Educ. v. Pico,* 457 U.S. 853, 871, 102 S.Ct. 2799, 2810, 73 L.Ed.2d 435 (1982) (Brennan, J.) (plurality opin.). We are bound to respect that command as well.

APPENDIX

To illustrate their objections to *The Learning Tree,* appellants appended fifteen separate passages from the work to their opening brief. Because analysis under the establishment clause is pre-eminently fact-dependent, *see Lynch v. Donnelly,* ——U.S. at——, 104 S.Ct. at 1361–62, I have appended the most relevant portions of those passages.

Passage 1

Jack Winger was a poor man, but the supper he blessed that night was of things Newt liked best—fried chicken, yams, browned clabber gravy and cornbread. Immediately the talk centered around the big storm and its casualties.

"Jim was a fine fella, one of the best round here."

"How long'd you know him, Poppa?"

"Well on to twenty years, ain't it, Sarah?"

"Closer to twenty-three, if mem'ry serves me right—use your fork, Newt! Seems he came about two years after us."

"Funny thing," Newt said, "old Collie was right 'side him and didn't even git scratched. How you figger that, Poppa?"

"The Lord works in funny ways. Just wasn't the dog's time to go—pass the gravy, Prissy—was Jim's time. Simple as that."

"Anybody hear from Uncle Rob?". . . .

Sarah was about to answer when Pastor Broadnap appeared at the screen door. "O-ho," he beamed, "caught you sittin' for supper!"

The rotund minister swept into the room, his long black preacher coat flapping at his knees. Little pods of sweat stood out on his forehead at the point where the hairline receded sharply, as if it were shaved. He scanned the table. "Just in time to share the gifts of the Lord," he said.

"Oh my," Newt mumbled, "there goes my chicken legs."

. . .

"Bless you, Jack. Bless you." He was flooding the cornbread with gravy now. "Well," he continued, chewing, "I attach a very special meanin' to that storm. It's (Newt winced as Broadnap teethed the meat from the bone) a warnin' to the wrongdoin' of all these sinners round here. This place is poppin' with sin—people drinkin', cuttin', fightin' and doin' all sorts of things the Lord don't approve of; nobody comin' to church like they ought'a. Why, I'd say Chappie Logan's place got more drunks in it than we got members on Sunday mornin'."

Sarah Winger looked at the pastor and said, "For some reason it's the good ones who go first."

"Thinkin' 'bout Jim Pullens, huh, sister Winger?" Broadnap said, dipping into the jar of apple butter with his knife. "Well, it's hard to explain—hard to explain. Jim was a fine man. Always come to church and prayer meetin'. Only way I figger it is that the Lord takes the good ones like that so the bad ones'll hafta take more responsibility."

"Old Sam Wong got it too. They ain't found him yet, I hear."

"Naw, and with half that block on top of him they might not find him for a couple of days," Pete said. "And to think he was out safe, then went back for his cat and got killed."

"Well, you find out lots 'bout people in a big wind like that. Some proves weak, some proves strong." Jack Winger wiped his long mustache with his wrist and pulled his pipe from his pocket. "It's a easy time to cut

lamb from sheep. Think God does prob'ly send things like this to test us. Wouldn't be surprised if he didn't get tangled up hisself tryin' to figger out these here folks in Cherokee Flats."

. . .

"Now, Newt, you been studyin' your Sunday school lessons lately?"

Newt gulped, "Yessir, I—"

"Fine. Now if you tell me the name of the weapon Samson slew the Philistines with, the leg's yours." Broadnap grinned smugly.

Newt scratched his head in deep thought (Slingshot . . . naw, that was David . . . spear . . . naw . . .). "I got it!" he blurted out. "The jawbone of a—a—" He looked sideways at his mother.

"A what?" Broadnap snapped.

A wry smile wrinkled Newt's face. "Well, I can't name it right out, but it's the same name as that part left on the platter."

"The ass," Broadnap grunted, dumping the leg on Newt's plate, "the jawbone of an ass."

Everybody laughed.

"Newt," Sarah admonished, "you shouldn't take that leg from Reverend Broadnap. Now—"

"Oh no, sister. The boy won it fair 'n square. I'll take what's left," Broadnap countered, spearing the chicken rump from the platter.

. . .

"You been over to see the little Johnson girl, Reverend?"

"Yes, sister Sarah. That child's lucky to be livin'. Hardly any hair or skin left on her. Doc Cravens says we got to ask for some volunteers in church Sunday."

"Volunteers for what?" Jack asked.

"Well, seems like Doc's gonna try to graft new skin on her. That means somebody's gonna have to give some'a theirs."

Sarah looked up in astonishment. "You mean Doc intends to strip skin off somebody else and put it on her?"

"That's what he's sayin', sister Sarah, if she's gonna live any kind'a normal life again."

"Poor child. It's a awful thing—a awful thing," Sarah said, shaking her head.

"Don't worry, sister Sarah, she'll be helped. Some good souls'll come forward."

"Hot coffee, brother Broadnap?"

"No, Jack. Ain't been sleepin' too well lately. Next time round, maybe. Got some more visitin' to do on my way to the parsonage. Sister Pullens and a few others." He got up. Those about the table started to rise, but he spread his arms above them. "Sit, my dear children, and bless you, sister Sarah, for the wonderful repast." He plucked several toothpicks from a bowl and picked up his black "preacher's" hat from the sideboard. As he passed Newt he patted him on the head. "Keep studyin', boy. Givin' the right answer meant that chicken's leg instead of the part that went over the fence last." He chuckled. Then he plopped the hat on his head and left as suddenly as he had come.

Passage 2

*   *   *

He thought, "What are grasshoppers for anyway, and snakes and mosquitoes and flies and worms, wasps, potato bugs and things? Seems they ain't much good to the world, but God put 'em here. Seems they got as much rights as we have to live. If the grasshoppers didn't eat the crops, they'd starve. No worse'n us killin' hogs and chickens so we don't go hungry. Hogs and chickens and cows and rabbits and squirrels, possums and such must hate us much as we hate mosquitoes and gnats and flies. Dogs and cats and horses are 'bout the luckiest. 'Bout the only ones we don't go round killin' off all the time. The Ten Commandments saw we oughtn's kill, then we come home from church and wring a chicken's neck for dinner—and Reverend Broadnap eats more'n anybody else." Newt stretched. "Too much for me to figger out," he said aloud.

Passage 3

*   *   *

"Momma, can I ask you somethin'?"

"Yes, boy. What you want to ask me?"

Newt pondered briefly, and Sarah slowed her pace. "Well, I don't know offhand, just about people and things like that."

Sarah smiled to herself, for she remembered that for the past year she had wanted to talk with Newt about "people and things" but thought him too young to understand the things she wanted to speak of. She had planned especially for him, her youngest, since the day he was born, but in the trials of living and caring for all the others she found it hard to clarify and formulate these plans. Now she welcomed the breakthrough. "Newt, you just ask me anything you want and I'll try to answer you."

"Well, after the storm, Poppa said that the storm and the people killed and everything was the doin' of God. You care if I ask you why he kills some people and not the others? Poppa said hisself that Mister Pullens was a good man. And why did some of the town git torn up and the rest didn't?"

Sarah Winger came to a complete stop, and Newt was instantly afraid he had offended her. He took a step beyond his mother, his face pointed straight ahead, eyes lowered and cast sideways for the reaction. Her lips parted, but she didn't speak immediately; then she started moving again.

"Newt."

"Yessem."

"You know your poppa and me are religious people, don't you?"

"Yessem."

"Well, it would be real easy for me to say, you don't question the ways of God—and I was tempted to—but I know deep in my heart that there's more to it than that. It's true he guides us. But we cain't depend on him for everything. We gotta do things for ourself. Now, maybe if Jim had built himself a storm cellar or a stronger house, he wouldn't a got killed so easy. And if little Fannie Johnson's momma hadn't been drunk, she'd a held onto that lamp and her daughter wouldn't a got burnt. It's like I say, we got to do some things for ourself. If you got a battle to fight, you cain't rightfully ask the Lord to help you and not the other fella. Now can you?"

"No, ma'am."

"No, son, you got to fight and hope God likes the way you're using your fists. And that goes for the boy you're fightin'. Ain't neither one of you got time for prayin' while you're flingin' fists. Too many people, especially some of ours, boy, sit round waitin' when they should be out doin'. You got to always remember that, boy, always."

"Yessem. Are we gonna live here all our life?"

Sarah looked searchingly at him. "Don't you like it here?"

"I don't know, Momma. I ain't never been no place else."

"I hope you won't have to stay here all your life, Newt. It ain't a all-good place and it ain't a all-bad place. But you can learn just as much here about people and things as you can learn any place else. Cherokee Flats is sorta like a fruit tree. Some of the people are good and some of them are bad—just like the fruit on a tree. You know that, don't you, boy?"

"Yessem."

"Well, if you learn to profit from the good and bad these people do to each other, you'll learn a lot 'bout life. And you'll be a better man for that learnin' someday. Understand?"

"Yessem."

"No matter if you go or stay, think of Cherokee Flats like that till the day you die—let it be your learnin' tree."

"Do we all have to die someday?"

"That's one thing we all have to do, boy. No matter who you are. That's why it's so important to be ready when your time comes."

"You mean to be a Christian, like you and Poppa?"

"In a way—in a way. But it's even more than sayin' you're a Christian. It's a matter of givin' more to this world than you take away from it. So when you die you don't owe it anything. It's bein' able to love when you want'a hate—to forgive them that work against you—to tell the truth even when it hurts—to share your bread, no matter how hungry you are yourself. Dyin' comes easy when you know you've done all these things right."

"I'm gonna hate dyin'."

"Won't none of us like it, boy—none of us."

"I hate dyin' so much I wish sometimes that I wasn't even born."

Sarah blurted,"Why, I'm surprised at you sayin' such a thing." When she saw his face she knew he realized that she was stalling for time.

"Is there anybody who has ever come back from death that saw heaven?"

Sarah sighed (Who's this boy been talkin' to? Where's he gettin' such notions?) "No, boy. Ain't no such thing as that ever happened, to my knowin'."

"Well then, how does anybody know there is such a place?"

Her mind's eye flashed frantically from Matthew to Revelations, criss-crossed ages of praying, of shouting and of preaching. And finally her lips betrayed her teaching, ages of it—made light of the blindness, broke with believers; with the mountains of ever-so-solid faith. "Newt." (And already her expression made him sorry he'd sprung the trap.) "Honestly, I don't know. Maybe there ain't no hell either. Maybe there ain't no gold thrones in the clouds and maybe there ain't no pits of fire tended by a devil with a pitchfork tail. I honestly think God made us and expects us to do some good while we're here on earth. I cain't even say that God's his real name, but it's good as any. It means Almighty."

Confusion disturbed her thoughts. "All my life I've been told there is a better place beyond this one, Newt. And I guess I'll go to my grave believin' it. Such believin' has kept our family goin' when there wasn't much else to go on." She paused for a moment. Swallows, flying low and fast, fluttered the stillness. Then she spoke. "These are the things I was taught. It's awful hard now, this late, not to believe them." They didn't talk after that.

Passage 4

* * *

Wham! The blast came as he fumbled with the other strap (sounded like a double-barreled shotgun . . .). He got to his feet, leaped over the bed, then, ever so cautiously, peeped out the window. It was Clint, on top the overturned chicken house, reloading the gun and hollering, "I'll git the son-of-a-bitch yet! I'll git him!"

Newt started for his mother's room, but she was already rushing to the kitchen door. Newt followed her.

Pete's voice ricocheted against Prissy's. "Who's shootin'? What the matter? Momma! Momma! What's goin' on? Come back here, Newt! Somebody's shootin' out there!"

"It's Clint. He's still drunk!" Newt hollered, slyly enjoying the early excitement. And as he ran out behind his mother, he saw Clint blast away at the sky. Wham! "I'll get the son-of-a-bitch!" Wham!

Sarah Winger didn't stop until she was at the foot of the chicken house. "What you call yourself doin', boy? Who're you shootin' at?" Her tone was in keeping with the Sabbath.

Clint rocked around unsteadily, reloading the gun. "I'm gonna git him! Don't worry. I'm gonna git him!"

"Git who? Who you shootin' at, boy?" she shouted.

Clint wobbled precariously, pushing in the shells. "I'm gonna blow the ass off Jesus Christ, the long-legged white son-of-a-bitch! I burned him a little that last shot. I'll git him for shore this time!"

Passage 5

* * *

"He's a thinkin' boy, Jack. You should'a heard some of the questions he asked me about religion and death. I was hard put for the right answers, I'll tell you."

"Religion and death?"

"That's right, religion and death."

"I declare, he's gittin' crazy notions from someplace."

"His questions wasn't just crazy notions. They made me do a lot of thinkin' afterward. They were about things I used to wonder about when I was a girl, but didn't talk about just because I was scared to, for some reason or another."

"Well, one thing 'bout death, when your time comes, you're goin', and that's that. Ain't very hard to answer that."

"It ain't just dyin' he wonders about. It's what comes after."

"He needs to go to church more, maybe."

"We been goin' to church all our lives, and so has he; still hearin' the same things we been hearin' since we was his age. The answers that used to satisfy us ain't goin' to satisfy Newt and the young ones comin' up now. They want proof. Some kind they can see and feel. And they're goin' to want more out of this world than we're gettin' out of it. Time's changin', Jack."

"This is a white man's world, Sarah. Ain't no time goin' to change that."

"No, maybe time won't, but this new crop of colored boys and girls will. You and me prob'ly won't live to see it, but these kids comin' along today are goin' to find a way to change things."

"The white man's got the money and guns—that spells power."

"There's more'n one way to skin a cat, Jack. Schoolin's more powerful than guns or money in the end. I honestly hope someday Newt'll git out of here and go where chances will be better for him. I pray for that."

Passage 6

*   *   *

"Now, my good children, look at me. Cast your eyes upon the servant of the Lord! Look at me." (Newt feels his mother's eyes upon him—and his shoulders lean back to the time-polished bench, his eyes are stubbornly toward the pulpit.)

Suddenly Broadnap hunches his shoulders, extends his long arms from his coat sleeves, points his index fingers at the congregation. His head, hawklike and fierce, juts forward. His eyes, burning under sweat-drenched brow, search the upturned, hypnotized faces. "Look at me and tell me, my dear children, *what's your life?* . . . think about it in the bright of day and the black of night! . . . *what's your life?* (his fingers recoil into his fists—his arms drop: the tempo breaks and calm begins to return; the choir is singing, "What a friend we have in Jesus") . . . Thank you, dear God who giveth us life through our Lord, Jesus Christ . . . bless you, my children, and lest we forget His kindness to us during this awful tragedy—let us pray." (The congregation, spent and still moaning, bows in silent prayer. Newt slumps forward again and brings his mind to the fried chicken that always comes with the Sabbath.)

Reverend Broadnap raises his arms again, this time for sinners and confessioners. Several are going forward—Fred Jenkins, Clara Brown and Otis Moses. Now everybody's curiosity is up, because Lester Saunders (he's wearing them white spats) is raising his head for confession. "What can God do to make me understand myself?" he asks.

Broadnap, mopping his brow, looks down at him. "What's troublin' you, son?"

"I don't like women." The church is very still.

"You don't like women?"

"No, I don't like women."

"How long have you been like that, brother Saunders?"

"Ever since I was a man."

Broadnap's thumbing his Bible. "Don't worry or be ashamed, brother Saunders. God acts in many ways. It may be your conviction." Now he stops and reads from the Bible—from Romans, 14th Chapter, " 'One man hath faith to eat all things; but he that is weak eateth herbs. Let not him that eateth set at nought him that eateth not; and let not him that eateth not, judge him

that eateth: for God hath received him. Who art thou that judgest the servant of another? To his own Lord he standeth or falleth.' "

Lester is looking the minister straight in the eye. He turns and looks at the congregation. His left eye is damp. Now he is walking very fast, switching-like, down the aisle. Sadness is on his face. He's pushing through the swinging doors at the rear of the church. They swish back and forth—and he is gone. It is still very quiet. Reverend Broadnap raises his arms above the others and begins to bless them into the church—and again the choir is singing, "What a friend we have in Jesus."

Passage 7

*   *   *

"Help him up, boy. Git him to the house. He's so drunk he can hardly stand up, let alone shoot anybody." Newt bent down and helped Clint to his feet, and the three of them went back to the house.

As they entered, Newt saw Rende peeping at the bedroom door. When she heard her husband groan and collapse to the floor, she crept back into the parlor with Busty and Gin-gin in time to see her mother hide the gun behind the china cabinet.

Jack threw some more coal in the fire and spat in the scuttle. "Just look at him" he said in a half growl, "his maw and paw shore wasted a night when they made him."

*   *   *

Rende wept. "What am I goin' to do, Momma? What am I goin' to do?"

Sarah put her arms about Rende's shoulders. "We've just got to pray over him, that's all. We've got to keep prayin'."

Jack blew out a ring of smoke. "I declare, prayin' ain't gonna do that varmint no good, none a'tall."

"Jack, I want you to stop talkin' like that. You know—"

"I'm tellin' you, Sarah—Clint's lost. God and the devil's both quit strugglin' for him, so it ain't much nobody else can do—I don't care how long and how loud they pray." He knocked his pipe on the coal scuttle and some loose ashes fell out. "He's lucky it's you who handles him. If it's ever me who has to take that gun away from him, he ain't gonna find it so easy. Fact is, he's gonna end up with a cracked skull."

Passage 8

Christmas at Spit's School for Boys wasn't much different from any other day . . .

Marcus ate alone in the dimness of his cell.

*   *   *

He had just settled back on the cot when Crapper hollered, "You got some visitors, Savage! Git up and try lookin' happy."

"Screw you." Marcus growled sullenly.

"Fool with me and you don't see nobody," Crapper warned.

"I don't give a goddam. Ain't nobody I want to see nohow."

But by now the visitors were coming down the corridor.

"Right this way, Rev'rend," Crapper said. He spoke with an exaggerated politeness that forced a grunt of disgust from Marcus. The cell door swung open and through it came Reverend Broadnap, Maggie Pullens—carrying a bag of fruit and candy—and Deacon Henry Fuller. Reverend Broadnap stepped over and touched Marcus on the shoulder. Marcus stiffened. He wanted to tell them all to go, but he held his tongue.

"We come to pray for you and to wish you a merry Christmas, son." He didn't answer, and Broadnap turned to the others and said, "Let's pray."

They knelt on the floor. Marcus' fingernails dug into the palms of his hands and his teeth ground together in an angry embarrassment. He kept his eyes low and straight ahead, as if ignoring their presence.

"Oh Almighty God," Broadnap began, "we come to you on bended knee prayin' for the soul of this young sinner." Marcus' muscles flexed and his gaze shot defiantly to the tops of their heads, then to Crapper, who stood in the doorway with an evil grin on his face. "Wash his black sins away in these white snows of your holy Christmas. Lighten the troubles he has brought to his young dark days. Bring peace to his tormented soul and help him to someday leave this place a cleaner and better young man. Oh God, show him the light. Show—"

"Shut up! Shut up!" Marcus shouted, "and git the hell out'a here!" He was on his feet now. "I don't want'a hear none of your Uncle Tom prayin' over me!" The three people rose, shocked beyond belief.

"You don't know what you're sayin', boy," Broadnap half whispered, trying to quiet him down, reaching again toward his shoulder.

"I know much 'bout what I'm sayin' as you do," he shot back, pulling away.

Maggie put the bag of fruit on his bed. Broadnap took out a Sunday school card with the picture of Christ on it and placed it on the table. "Read the scripture here on the back, son," he said, "and pray to the Savior. He'll hear you."

Marcus snatched the card, tore it in half and threw it at the preacher. "You and your white God git the hell out'a here!" he shouted. "I don't want no part of you soul savers—bendin' down, like Paw says you do, kissin' the feet of a poor white trash God." Tears were in his eyes now. "Look at Crapper there! He's white!

Whyn't you git down and start moanin' and groanin' to him, so he can kick the crap out'a you like he does all us 'nigga' boys. Yeh, that's what he calls us—nigga! nigga! nigga! Tell 'em, Crapper. Tell 'em what you gonna do to me when they leave! Tell 'em."

"Son—"

"Don't son me. Just git goin'! So Crapper can tease me 'bout you niggas comin' here to pray over me!"

Broadnap, Maggie and Henry Fuller filed out, their heads shaking. Crapper slammed the door shut and followed them down the corridor. Marcus sat very still awhile, then suddenly he began to feel a deep sense of guilt, deeper than any he had ever felt in his whole life. He was bewildered. These people had come all that way to help him and he had hurt them, said things he didn't realize he could say. But what he'd said was more for Crapper than for them, he realized. If Crapper hadn't stood in the door with that silly grin on his face, things might have been different. But it was too late now. The harm was done. Yet, somehow, he felt he had got a point across to Crapper. He didn't know just what. Maybe he was really defending those people against somebody like Crapper, who had once told him, "All niggas are stupid and crazy." In a way he was telling him that they weren't, that he was on to his kind and their "lily-white God" that his paw damned when he got drunk.

He glanced up. Crapper was back. Marcus said nothing.

"Merry Christmas—nigga," Crapper said disdainfully, and turned back down the corridor.

Marcus was silent. His head fell back in the shadows and he closed his eyes, trying to form the image of a God with black skin, thick lips and coarse hair like his—but he couldn't. The image on the torn card at the foot of his bed had been implanted much too long before. It was difficult to erase that image now, or even substitute another one for it.

Passage 9

"It was awful the way that Savage boy talked to us—simply awful," Maggie Pullens told Sarah as the two of them sat in the Winger front room that night.

Sarah thought for a while before answering, then she spoke what she knew to be the truth. "It ain't really the boy's fault, Maggie."

"Then whose is it, for the good Lord's sake?"

"That could've been Newt, Beansy, Earl or any of the other young ones around here. If we want to tell the truth about it, then we would say it's our fault—all the Christians, black and white, and teachers and office-holders and everybody who's supposed to have good in them."

"Yes—yes, you're right, Sarah. Guess you're right."

"Our young children's minds here are mixed up. This place with all its drinkin' and fightin' and murderin'—Jim Crow schools, picture shows and eatin' places is too much for these young ones to figure out. They've got bigger ideas about livin' than you and me had at their age, Maggie."

"We're in a rut for shore."

"We was born in a rut, and the reason we've been able to keep goin' is because we always thought someday we're goin' to git out of it. I ain't one to fool myself about my chances any more, but I'm goin' to do all I can to see that my children don't get bogged down here forever."

"It's a big problem, all right."

"Take that Savage boy—nobody's ever done anything big to help him. He should've been taken away from Booker when he was a little boy and put in a good home. There just ain't much good can come of him now."

"The only people tryin' to do anything a'tall is our church missionary society."

"That's true, Maggie, but it's mighty hard trying to push out misery and fill empty stomachs with the word of God. Booker Savage asked me one day if we had a Jim Crow heaven waitin' for our saints."

"That man's awful—just awful."

"Told me Chappie Logan was 'his god.' 'Least he's black like me,' he said."

"Awful—just awful," Maggie moaned. A moment later she got up to leave. "Well, I have to be moseyin' on. Tired after that long trip up there."

Passage 10

The crowd had grown ugly and boisterous. They were already making their bets. If he quit now no one would understand, and everyone would think he was a coward. If he didn't fight, he might take a worse beating from the crowd than he would from Marcus. He wanted to ask God to help him fight to win, but he suddenly remembered his mother's telling him on the river road, many nights back, that God couldn't favor one fighter against another. He thought next of Pete, wished he were there. The lesson began to come through (cock the right—jab with the left—feint him out of position—jab—throw the right—).

Passage 11

*   *   *

He wondered, as he had often done before, what the whites' real reasons were for denying them a part in the school's athletic and social affairs. "Why does our color make such a difference? . . . Didn't God know that we'd have a lot of trouble if he made us black? . . . Since he's white, maybe he don't care either." He smiled

wryly. "Never seen black angels . . . even the chariot horses are white."

Passage 12

"How'd you git over here so early?" Beansy asked.

"Got a new babe with a big new car," Skunk lied. "You ought to see her. She's got hair down to her ankles and a keester that would make old Rev'rend Broadnap throw his Bible in a privy hole."

Passage 13

*   *   *

Newt found himself repeating after the bailiff, "—to tell the truth and nothing but the truth, so help me God." He asked strength of something, be it God or whatever, to carry him, his family and the rest of the colored people safely through the trouble he now imagined his testimony would bring.

Passage 14

Newt sat on a barrel in the corner of the kitchen, listening to the downpour vibrate the tin roof above him and watching Lou and Clara ready the evening meal. Realizing that if his mother died he might have to live with one or the other sister, he observed them closely—trying to decide which one he would rather be with. He liked them both, so he sat mentally sifting their habits and dispositions, applying them to his own simple, yet important, personal plans and desires. "Clara's a little bossy," he thought. "She'd prob'ly want me to stay in all the time—want to pick all my friends, too, but she likes to dress fancy—prob'ly help me get some keen things to wear. Lou's easygoin' and easy to fool. I like the way she fries potatoes, but she'd prob'ly want me to go to church all the time. Sure had enough religion to last me a long time."

Passage 15

Dawn arrived painfully slow, and Newt, as if in a trance, lay gazing out the window through the dank lace curtains. He watched the sky pale as the sun climbed to the foggy horizon and brightened the upper reaches. His mind, with unaccountable calm, explored the reality of this hour over the deep, uneven snoring of Roy and Pete, sleeping beside him.

Their mother was dead, he knew, but it was hard to believe. Suddenly he wondered if, somewhere up there in the pale blue nothingness, her soul—free of tortured body and earthly things—was already floating silently about, knowing at last the real purpose of its sojourn on a complex and troubled earth. What if she found that all the praying and religious rites were just a lot of folly; that her soul floated with no more righteousness or dignity than that of Doc Chency, Big Mabel, or even Captain Tuck? What a shock it would be to her!

He now thought uneasily of such a possibility, and he couldn't help but feel that this was more than likely the case—and the feeling shamed him. Then he softened his shame with the reasoning that if such were true, she would never begrudge anyone such equality. Whatever judgment settled upon her, he thought, would surely be the best that eternity could possibly extend.

As Newt dressed quietly, the sun burned through the fog, warming the wet rooftops, drying the leaves and grass. And the moist cool earth took in the heat and in return gave forth little curlings of cloud that quickly disappeared in the clean morning air.

He entered the dining room and looked around. Everything was just about the same, except the door which the shot had blasted. Stepping to it, he ran his fingers over the splintered surface. Daylight leaked through it now, and a sudden fright gripped him, for he realized that this destruction was actually meant for Rende. Remembering the gun against his father's head, he shivered and stepped back involuntarily (this could've been Poppa's skull), then he moved warily across to his mother's room. They had already taken her to the undertaker's.

The odor of camphor and medicine still hung in the air, and a bouquet of withered posies lay on the rocking chair in the corner of the room. The sheets had been removed, and the mattress was doubled upon the sagging springs. Above the antique dresser hung an oval-shaped photograph of his father and mother, framed in a polished, worn wood. It had been taken their wedding day, and both stared straight ahead—unmindful of this faraway moment when their last child would stand silent, alone and uncertain in this room of death.

Almost in every sense, Newt had come to link death with violence. Even his mother's passing, he thought, couldn't escape a brush with it. Nearly everyone he had known intimately, and who had ceased to live, met their demise in bloodshed. And it was probably for this reason that he feared death so much—and this fear, he reasoned, was childish. His mother's easy, tranquil and unflinching acceptance of death enhanced his respect for her. Now, this morning, it was creating within him a near-fanatical desire to rid himself of this stigma that had dogged his soul since the day of Doc Cheney's death.

Turning from the room, he channeled his thoughts into an imaginary rectangular hole that someday would be his grave. And his whole being reacted against the eternal blackness, the unending airlessness, the unchangeable recumbent position of his body—never to eat, taste, feel, speak or hear again. He shuddered.

Now he envisaged the others reposing about him, acre after acre; worm-bored coffin sides, everlasting decay, dust piling forever upon eternal dust—entombed in the still, suffocating blackness.

Why, then, was life given, and for no logically explained reason taken away again? He recalled the rolling, wearisome voice of Pastor Broadnap. "—From dust you came and to dust you must returneth!" Newt remembered his authoritatively hollering such things over Big Mabel's coffin. He remembered, too, his swing about the pulpit, frock coat flying, sweat dripping, screaming of immortality—"of the spirit, of the soul" —not the good, solid body.

NOTES

1. Neutrality is designed to protect religion as well as government. "[A] union of government and religion tends to destroy government and to degrade religion." *Engel v. Vitale*, 370 U.S. 421, 431, 82 S.Ct. 1261, 1267, 8 L.Ed.2d 601 (1962).

2. Plaintiffs' position that government should be prohibited from establishing non-theistic ideologies in the schools, just as it is prohibited from establishing traditional theistic practices, is not without support. *See Abington School Dist. v. Schempp*, 374 U.S. 203, 313, 83 S.Ct. 1560, 1619, 10 L.Ed.2d 844 (1963) (Stewart, J., dissenting) (viewing refusal to permit religious exercises as arguably the establishment of a "religion of secularism"); *Abington*, 374 U.S. at 306, 83 S.Ct. at 1615 (Goldberg, J., concurring) (warning that "untutored devotion to the concept of . . . noninvolvement with the religious" can become "a brooding and pervasive devotion to the secular"); *see, e.g.,* Whitehead & Conlan, "The Establishment of the Religion of Secular Humanism and its First Amendment Implications," 10 Tex. Tech.L.Rev. 1(1978); *but cf.* Davidow, "Secular Humanism as an Established Religion: A Response to Whitehead & Conlan," 11 Tex.Tech.L.Rev. 51 (1979).

3. "[T]he use of this book constitutes the advancement of a religious doctrine called secularism, Secular Humanism, or humanism. . . . We believe that the terms 'secularism,' 'humanism,' and 'secular humanism' can be used interchangeably. . . . " Appellants' Brief 44 & 45.

4. "Secular Humanism . . . is a religion dedicated to affirmatively opposing or showing hostility toward Christianity. It has declared its pulpit to be the public school classroom and its 'bible' is adolescent literature like *The Learning Tree.*" Appellants' Brief 49.

5. Originally, "humanism" signified the recrudescence of interest in classical art and letters; a critical, liberal, and individualistic spirit; and the shift of emphasis from religious to secular concerns which blossomed during the Italian Renaissance. More generally, the term has come to signify any doctrine or set of values which rejects supernaturalism, asserts the essential dignity and worth of each human being, and commits itself to the achievement of individual self-realization and aggregate human welfare through reason and the scientific method. *See* 4 *Ency. of Philosophy* 69-72 (1967).

6. Historically, "[f]or all its antipathy toward asceticism and theology, humanism did not have an antireligious or anti-Christian character. Its interest in defending the value and freedom of man drew it into discussing the traditional problems of God and providence . . . —discussions that were frequently concluded in much the same form as that accepted by the medieval tradition." *Ency. of Philosophy, supra* n. 5, at 71. More recently, a number of celebrated theologians have viewed humanism not as the antithesis, but rather as the apotheosis of religion. Karl Barth, for example, declared that "there is no humanism without the Gospel" (*cited in 5 Ency. Brittanica* 199 (Micropaedia) (1982)); *see also* K. Barth, *The Humanity of God* (1960); H. Kung, *On Being a Christian* 530-602 (1974). Others are united in their general rejection of the God of traditional theism as a God " 'up there,' " *United States v. Seeger*, 380 U.S. 163, 181, 85 S.Ct. 850, 861, 13 L.Ed.2d 733 (1965), and adoption of a more personal, humanistic vision of religion. *See, e.g.,* P. Tillich, *Systematic Theology* (1957) (*cited in Seeger*, 380 U.S. at 180, 85 S.Ct. at 861); *The Shaking of the Foundations* (1948) (*cited id.,* 380 U.S. at 187, 85 S.Ct. at 865); J. Robinson, *Honest to God* (1963) (*cited id.,* 380 U.S. at 181, 85 S.Ct. at 861); D. Muzzey, *Ethics as a Religion* (1951) (*cited id.,* 380 U.S. at 182-83, 85 S.Ct. at 862-63).

7. Theism—exemplified by traditional Judaism, Christianity, and Islam—is the "belief in the existence of one God who is viewed as the creative source of man, the world, and value. . . ." *Webster's Third New International Dictionary* 2370 (1976).

8. The majority similarly suggests that "[s]ecular humanism may be a religion," citing *Rhode Island Federation of Teachers v. Norberg*, 630 F.2d 850, 854 (1st Cir.1980). Norberg, however, does not so hold. Instead, the First Circuit simply noted that even if secular humanism were to be so regarded, as plaintiffs urged, their suit to intervene nevertheless failed for failure to state a defense relevant to the challenged statute. *Id.* at 853.

9. *See generally* J. Choper, "Defining 'Religion' in the First Amendment," 1982 U.Ill.L.Rev. 579, 581 & 604.

10. *See United States v. Seeger*, 380 U.S. 163, 187, 85 S.Ct. 850, 864, 13 L.Ed.2d 733 (1965); *Welsh v. United States*, 398 U.S. 333, 340, 90 S.Ct. 1792, 1796, 26 L.Ed.2d 308 (1970) (plurality opin.) (both adopting functional definition, derived largely from Tillich, which treats as "religion" any set of beliefs addressing matters of "ultimate concern" occupying " 'a place parallel to that filled by . . . God' in traditionally religious persons." 398 U.S. at 340, 90 S.Ct. at 1796).

11. *But cf.* Justice Rutledge dissenting in *Everson v. Bd. of Educ.,* 330 U.S. 1, 32, 67 S.Ct. 504, 519, 91 L.Ed. 711 (1947): " 'Religion' appears only once in the [First] Amendment. But the word governs two prohibitions and governs them alike. It does not have two meanings, one narrow to forbid 'an establishment' and another, much broader, for securing 'the free exercise thereof.' 'Thereof' brings down 'religion' with its entire and exact content, no more and no less. . . ." *See also Malnak v. Yogi,* 592 F.2d at 210-13 (Adams, J., concurring).

12. Plaintiffs' brief, however, leaves the distinct impression that their objection is less to Parks' novel *per se,* than to the public school curriculum itself—a curriculum which, as a result of Supreme Court rulings removing inculcation in religious doctrine and dogma from the classroom, they perceive as "establishing" secularism. *See, e.g.,* Toscano, "A Dubious Neutrality: The Establishment of Secularism in the Public Schools," 1979 Brig.Young U.L.Rev. 177, 198.

Plaintiffs, however, fail to distinguish the process of secularization from the promotion of secularism. *See* H. Cox, *The Secular City* 18 (1966). While the promotion of secularism as a body of anti-religious doctrine is prohibited by the establishment clause, *see Zorach v. Clauson,* 343 U.S. 306, 314, 72 S.Ct. 679, 684, 96 L.Ed. 954 (1952), the process of secularization has been the means of achieving compliance with the establishment clause: "It is generally said that the secularization of public education was brought about in order to prevent domination of the system by a prevailing religious sect." Comment, "Humanistic Values in the Public School Curriculum: Problems in Defining an Appropriate Wall of Separation," 61 Nw.U.L.Rev. 795, 803 (1966). *See also* Gianella, "Religious Liberty, Nonestablishment, & Doctrinal Development (Part I)," 80 Yale L.J. 1381, 1386 (1967) ("original constitutional consensus concerning religious liberty was an outgrowth of Protestant dissent and humanistic rationalism, the viewpoints that dominated the thinking of the authors of the Constitution.").

13. After *Lynch,* the opinion in *Lemon* is best understood as reflecting factors which may be central to any establishment clause analysis, rather than as articulating a single invariable test. "[W]e have repeatedly emphasized our unwillingness to be confined to any single test or criterion in this sensitive area." *Lynch,*—U.S. at—, 104 S.Ct. at 1362.

14. This is not to suggest that the formal imprimatur of a particular church or religious body is necessarily fatal under the establishment clause. Even the Bible, if appropriately presented, may be included within public school curricula. *See Abington,* 374 U.S. at 225, 83 S.Ct. at 1573. Similarly, the works of self-described humanists published in *The Humanist,* official organ of the American Humanist Association, and appended to appellants' brief may themselves be studied in the schools, subject to the same constraints.

15. The district court found that *"The Learning Tree* is a novel with autobiographical overtones used in the English literature class of the school for the purposes of exposing students to expectations and orientations of Black Americans. It is also categorized as 'adolescent hero' literature. The book clearly serves a secular educational function."

16. *Engel v. Vitale,* 370 U.S. 421, 82 S.Ct. 1261, 8 L.Ed.2d 601 (1962) (mandatory reading of state-composed prayer); *Abington School Dist. v. Schempp,* 374 U.S. 203, 83 S.Ct. 1560, 10 L.Ed.2d 844 (1963) (mandatory Bible reading at beginning of school day); *Stone v. Graham,* 449 U.S. 39, 101 S.Ct. 192, 66 L.Ed.2d 199

(1980) (posting of Ten Commandments in classroom); *Epperson v. Arkansas*, 393 U.S. 97, 89 S.Ct. 266, 21 L.Ed.2d 228 (1968) (prohibition against teaching principles of Darwinian evolution); *McLean v. Arkansas Bd. of Educ.*, 529 F.Supp. 1255 (E.D.Ark.1982) (teaching of "creation-science").

17. "[T]he effect prong of the *Lemon* test is properly interpreted not to require invalidation of a government practice merely because it in fact causes, even as a primary effect, advancement or inhibition of religion. The laws upheld in [*Walz, McGowan and Zorach*] had such effects, but they did not violate the Establishment Clause. What is crucial is that a government practice not have the effect of communicating a message of government endorsement or disapproval of religion." *Lynch*, 104 S.Ct. at 1368 (O'Connor, concurring).

18. *Cf. West Virginia Bd. of Educ. v. Barnette*, 319 U.S. 624, 642, 63 S.Ct. 1178, 1187, 87 L.Ed. 1628 (1943) (Jackson, J.): "If there is one fixed star in our constitutional constellation, it is that no official, high or petty, can prescribe what shall be orthodox in politics, nationalism, religion, or other matters of opinion or force citizens to confess by word or act their faith therein."

19. *Cf. Lynch*, 104 S.Ct. at 1369 (O'Connor, J., concurring): "[T]he overall holiday setting changes what viewers may fairly understand to be the purpose of the display— as a typical museum setting, *though not neutralizing the religious content* of a religious painting, negates any message of endorsement of that content (emphasis added)."

20. The divine right of kings is "[t]he doctrine that a monarch in the hereditary line of succession has a divine and indefeasible right to his kingship and authority. . . . The origin of the doctrine is closely linked with the contest between the Holy Roman Emperor and the medieval papacy. In England . . . [u]nder the Stuarts, . . . the doctrine was professed by most leading Anglican divines." *Oxford Dictionary of the Christian Church* 412 (F.L. Cross ed. 1974); *see also* J. Locke, *First Treatise of Civil Government* (1689); A.P. d'Entrevas, *Natural Law* (2d ed. 1970).

21. *See Lynch*, 104 S.Ct. at 1379 (Brennan, J., dissenting) (referring to inclusion of the Bible or Milton's *Paradise Lost* in a course on English literature): "The purpose is plainly not to single out the particular religious beliefs that may have inspired the authors, but to see in these writings the outlines of a larger imaginative universe shared with other forms of literary expression (*citing* N. Frye, *The Secular Scripture* (1976));" *see also id.*, 104 S.Ct. at 1364 (no establishment despite "literally hundreds of religious paintings in governmentally supported museums").

22. The converse of the call to repentance and righteousness, the condemnation of oppression, injustice, and hypocrisy dominates the prophetic canon. *See, e.g.,* Isaiah 1:10-23; 9:17, 29:13; Micah 3:1-12; Jeremiah 6:13-15, 9:8-9; *see generally* J. Bright, *A History of Israel* (2d ed. 1972); A. Heschel, *The Prophets* (1962). Squarely in this tradition are numerous remarks attributed to Jesus. *See, e.g.,* Matthew 6:2-16; 7:1-5; 15:7; 22:18; 23:13-36; Mark 7-6, 12:15; Luke 6:42, 11:42-44, 12:1, 12:56, 13:15-17.

23. *See, e.g.,* G. Chaucer, *The Canterbury Tales* (A.C. Cawley ed. 1958); "Voltaire," *Ency. of Philosophy, supra* n. 5, at 1536; R. Pomeau, "Voltaire's Religion," in *Voltaire: A Collection of Critical Essays 140* (Bottiglia ed. 1968); N. Torrey, "Voltaire and the English Deists," *id.* at 69; T. Paine, *The Age of Reason: Part I* (Castell ed. 1957); *Mark Twain: Selected Writings of an American Skeptic* (V. Doyno ed. 1983); M. Twain, *Letters from the Earth* (B. De Voto ed. 1962); S. Lewis, *Elmer Gantry* (1927); *see also Classics in Free Thought* (P. Blanshard ed. 1977) (excerpts from these and other authors).

24. *See, e.g.,* Job 21:7-13, 24:1-25, 29031:40.

25. Honest, even agonizing doubt is not incompatible with Christian theism. *See, e.g.,* P. Tillich, *Dynamics of Faith* 18 (1957) ("[D]oubt is a necessary element in [faith]. It is a consequence of the risk of faith."); S.H. Miller, *The Great Realities* (1955); S. Kierkegaard, *Fear and Trembling* (W. Lowrie trans. 1941); *Concluding Unscientific Postscript* (Swenson & Lowrie trans. 1941); G. MacGregor, *Christian Doubt* (1951).

26. The allegation was not contested by defendants, and must be accepted here as true. No opinion is expressed as to whether Cassie Grove could meet the requisite burdens, and survive the necessary balancing tests, to establish a free exercise right to be exempt from the state's neutral school assignment. *See Wisconsin v. Yoder*, 406 U.S. 205, 214-216, 92 S.Ct. 1526, 1532-1534, 32 L.Ed.2d 15 (1972); *Sherbert v. Verner*, 374 U.S. 398, 406, 83 S.Ct. 1790, 1795, 10 L.Ed.2d 965 (1963); *Callahan v. Woods*, 736 F.2d 1269, 1273 (9th Cir.1984).

27. Cassie Grove was given a substitute assignment. She was also excused from class discussion of *The Learning Tree*, but chose to remain.

28. "[T]he very concept of ordered liberty precludes allowing every person to make his own standards on matters of conduct in which society as a whole has important interests. Thus, if the Amish asserted their claims because of their subjective evaluation and rejection of the contemporary secular values accepted by the majority, . . . their claims would not . . . rise to the demands of the Religion Clauses." *Wisconsin v. Yoder*, 406 U.S. at 215-16, 92 S.Ct. at 1533-34.

29. *See e.g., United States v. Albertini*, 710 F.2d 1410 (9th Cir.1983), *cert. granted,*—U.S.—, 105 S.Ct. 562, 83 L.Ed.2d 504 (1984) (religiously motivated opposition to arms race); *United States v. Lowe*, 654 F.2d 562 (9th Cir.1981) (opposition to nuclear submarines).

30. While plaintiffs contend that Cassie Grove was subjected to some ridicule from her classmates and at least one arguably negative aside from her teacher because she objected to the book, there is no showing that this ridicule was sufficiently forseeable, orchestrated, or sustained for it to be attributable to defendants, or sufficiently coercive to violate plaintiffs' free exercise rights. Nor was such ridicule made a subject of the complaint.

A United States District Court in Kentucky decides against a school board which had voted unanimously to terminate the employment of a high school teacher because she had shown the videotape "Pink Floyd—The Wall" to two of her classes. In deciding for the teacher, who had taught in the school system for fourteen years and had been selected "teacher of the year" several times, the Court declared: "The board of education's contention that they could discharge the plaintiff because such material as "Pink Floyd—The Wall" should not be shown in the Lincoln County schools fails to establish a substantial and legitimate governmental interest to override the plaintiff's protected speech. . . . The federal court in *Chelsea* held that the assumption that offensive language and themes might be harmful to high school students was not enough to establish some substantial and legitimate governmental interest to override the protected speech in question. In the present case, the defendants have failed to do more than state their opinion that the language and themes of "Pink Floyd—The Wall" were harmful to high school students. Thus, defendants have failed to establish any substantial and legitimate governmental interest as to override the plaintiff's right to protected speech." The Court concluded that the teacher's "contract was improperly terminated because it was done in response to the plaintiff's exercising her rights protected under the First Amendment to the Constitution, and but for the exercise of these rights, plaintiff's employment with the board would not have been so terminated."

Fowler v. *Board of Education of Lincoln County, Kentucky,* No. 84-244, Slip op. (D.Ky. July 25, 1985)

REED, District Judge.

Upon trial to this Court, and the Court having considered the evidence offered herein and arguments of fact and law made by counsel, the Court hereby does make the following findings of fact and conclusions of law:

FINDINGS OF FACT

1. The plaintiff, Jacqueline Fowler, is, and was at all times relevant to this case, a duly certified teacher in the Lincoln County school system, Lincoln County, Kentucky.

2. At the end of the 1983-84 school year, plaintiff had been a teacher in the Lincoln County schools for the preceding fourteen school years and had achieved continuing contract status, or tenure, in that school system.

3. For the 1983-84 school year, plaintiff had been assigned the duties of a classroom teacher of civics and Latin at the Lincoln County High School in Lincoln County, a position she had held for several years prior to the 1983-84 school year. In May, 1984, the age of plaintiff's students in her civics class was 15 to 16 years of age. The age of a majority of the plaintiff's students in her Latin I class was 15-18, although two class members were 14 years of age.

4. Defendant Joseph G. Blair is, and was at all times material to this case, the duly appointed and acting superintendent of the Lincoln County school system, and as such is and was the executive agent for the

board with the authority to exercise the general, supervisory control over the public schools of Lincoln County. His duties included the making of recommendations to the board relative to the employment and discharge of teachers and all other school employees of the Lincoln County Schools.

5. Defendants Lloyd McGuffey, Jimmy Cooper, Ivan Singleton, Tom Blankenship and Paul Playforth were the five members who made up the Board of Education of Lincoln County in May, 1984. As the board, they had the authority generally to control and manage the public schools of Lincoln County under the laws of Kentucky, including the acceptance or rejection of recommendations of the superintendent relative to the employment and discharge of teachers of that school system.

6. Prior to May 31, 1984, plaintiff's performance record as a teacher in the Lincoln County schools was good. She had been selected "Teacher of the Year" in several prior school years.

7. May 31, 1984, was the last day of school for the students at Lincoln County High School. According to a practice accepted by those administering the high school, this day was not an instructional day for the students, but rather was a day planned as "report card day" in which teachers were to enter grades on report cards to be given the students. The teachers were further advised that they were to keep the students out of the halls on that day.

8. Since May 31, 1984, was a non-instructional day, plaintiff planned, as she and other teachers of the high school had done in past years, to show video films to the students that day. Her lesson plan for that day indicated she would show a TV film and prepare report cards. Those in charge of the school were aware of this practice, and it was an accepted activity for the last day of school.

9. The Lincoln County High School maintained televisions and video equipment for use by the teachers in showing taped movies. A library of video tapes was kept at the high school for showing to students.

10. There was no policy, regulation, or directive which required any teacher at the high school to show only films from the school video library.

11. There was no policy, regulation, or directive from anyone in a supervisory capacity requiring teachers to obtain prior approval before showing to students a film not in the school library and brought in from an outside source.

12. There was no policy, regulation, or directive requiring a teacher to preview material prior to showing it to students.

13. A few days prior to May 31, 1984, several of plaintiff's students requested to see "Pink Floyd—The Wall" during the last day of school. Mrs. Fowler was not familiar with this film and did not at first agree to show it.

14. On May 30, 1984, Mrs. Fowler did obtain a videotape of this movie from a rental store in Danville. There was no rating printed on the container of the film. She was advised by the person renting the film that while the film contained social issues of importance to teenagers, there was also some nudity in the film.

15. The movie, "Pink Floyd—The Wall," involves the life of rock star Pink Floyd, who has become insane and, in retrospect, attempts to understand the reasons for his problems. The film depicts Pink's fatherless childhood, failed marriage, drug abuse, and ruined career.

16. The movie, "Pink Floyd—The Wall," was given an "R" rating by the Motion Picture Association of America's Code and Rating Administration. An "R" rating requires that a film is not to be shown in a commercial motion picture theater to persons under 17 years of age unaccompanied by a parent or adult guardian.

17. Mrs. Fowler did not preview the film before taking it to school the following day, as the tape was suited for a VHS recorder, and the video equipment which she owned was in Beta format and could not be used to preview the film. She was advised that the rental store no longer handled Beta tapes; therefore, she could not be provided with a Beta tape to preview. Because of the film's length, she could not preview the film on May 31 prior to showing it to her students.

18. On May 31, 1984, Mrs. Fowler took the tape, "The Wall," to school and showed it to her students twice during the course of the day. The first showing was during her first-period civics class. One of the students, Charles Bailey, who had earlier seen the film at a theater, sat next to the television screen with a file folder in order to cover any scene involving nudity or any scene that might be sexually suggestive to avoid possible offense to some of the students. The film was shown in this manner, with either Charles Bailey, or at times plaintiff, blocking the screen when any material of a suggestive nature appeared during the first showing. The film is approximately ninety-five minutes in length.

19. During the first viewing of the film, plaintiff decided it contained sufficient value for her students to warrant showing it the second time to her Latin I class. The film was substantially edited the second time as it was the first, except a portion of the film, the "Young Lust" scene, was deleted altogether by "fast forwarding" the video machine on which the tape was played at the selected time.

20. The film itself, as shown in its entirety without any editing, contains a very limited amount of material

which is sexually suggestive. The film contains no "simulated" sexual acts. There are scenes in the movie in which there is an implication that a sexual act between a man and a woman has occurred, may be occurring out of sight of the viewer, or could occur in the future, but there is no depiction of any sexual act, nor any "simulation" of a sexual act. There are animated scenes which may have sexual overtones, depending on the perception of the viewer. The lyrics to the rock music which provides the background to the movie do contain a few four-letter words which are generally considered obscene. In addition, certain statements of the main character, Pink, contain a few four-letter words which are generally considered obscene. No particular emphasis is placed on these words in the movie, and one must listen quite intently to hear the words as they are spoken or sung.

21.   A substantial majority of the evidence establishes that any scenes involving nudity or suggestive conduct were edited from the view of students in the previously-discussed manner during the two times the film was shown at the Lincoln County High School. (Plaintiff's Exhibit No. 1).

22.   During the second showing of the film, an assistant principal of the high school, Michael Candler, visited plaintiff's classroom and viewed the movie for some forty-five minutes to an hour. Candler stated that he observed nudity in the film, but he left the room without complaining of the film to Mrs. Fowler and without any attempt to stop the showing of the film.

23.   Later on May 31, 1984, the film was seized by the principal, and after having been viewed by the superintendent and board members on May 31 and the following day, the charge to terminate the contract of Mrs. Fowler was brought by the superintendent and board pursuant to Kentucky Revised Statute 161. 790.

24.   The complaints regarding the film did not originate from the students seeing the film, or from their parents, but originated with the school administrators themselves.

25.   The notice to terminate plaintiff's contract was served on her on or about June 19, 1984. This notice advised that a hearing would be held before the board on July 10, 1984. Within ten days of receipt of this notice, plaintiff made a written response to the board, advising of her intention to appear at the hearing to contest the charges made against her.

26.   On July 10, 1984, plaintiff appeared with counsel at the hearing set by the board. At the beginning of the hearing, in the voir dire of the board members, facts emerged that showed that the board had previously viewed parts of the film. Furthermore, the board admitted that they had been approached by members of the community who felt Mrs. Fowler should be fired for showing the film.

27.   Three members of the school board were to stand for re-election in the fall of 1984. One of those members was not re-elected.

28.   The transcripts of the hearing before the Board of Education have been introduced as evidence and considered in full by the Court. The transcript establishes that counsel for Jacqueline Fowler conducted a detailed voir dire examination of the members of the school board, vigorously cross-examined all witnesses who testified concerning the circumstances surrounding the showing of the film, and offered testimony of the plaintiff and others in her defense.

29.   After reviewing the film once in its entirety and once as the plaintiff had shown it, the board retired into executive session. The five members of the board were accompanied in executive session by defendant Superintendent Blair, who had made the charge and had testified against plaintiff; Bruce Johnson, the assistant superintendent, who had testified against Mrs. Fowler; and Mr. James Williams, the school board attorney, who had served as prosecutor in the termination hearing.

30.   During part of the executive session held by the board, the plaintiff and her attorneys were invited to speak with the board. This discussion was recorded by the court reporter and made a part of the transcript of the board hearing introduced as plaintiff's exhibit #1.

31.   At that session, the board members questioned plaintiff as to whether she would show the film again if they had not brought the charges against her. Plaintiff stated that yes, she would show the film again; however, if it were to be shown again, she would have edited the film onto another tape rather than editing in the manner used on May 31, 1984.

32.   At no time did the board pass any regulation or policy or ever orally or in writing order the plaintiff not to show the film again or not to show "R"-rated films again. At no time did plaintiff ever refuse to follow such an order by the board.

33.   Following the executive session, the board returned to an open session and, acting upon the recommendation of the superintendent, voted unanimously to terminate the employment of Mrs. Fowler for "conduct unbecoming a teacher" and "insubordination" in the showing of the film.

34.   The action of the defendants in terminating the contract of the plaintiff was based on their disagreement and dislike of ideas and views expressed in the film, "The Wall." They disagreed with the fact that the film, in their view, reflected badly on motherhood, family, police, school authority, the judiciary, and other highly-held social values.

35.   The film, "Pink Floyd—The Wall," does have artistic, literary, social and political value. The film deals with numerous issues of public concern, espe-

cially to a teenage audience. Values which this film reflects include the consequences of war, the difficulty of establishing meaningful relationships, the dangerous appeal of totalitarianism, the ill effects of drug abuse and alienation, and importance of the nuclear family.

36. Within thirty days of the vote to terminate Mrs. Fowler's contract, plaintiff filed this lawsuit challenging her termination.

37. As a result of plaintiff's termination, she has suffered loss of wages in the amount of $19,640.00.

38. Due to the acts of the defendants set forth above, plaintiff has suffered damage to her professional reputation and will in the future suffer damage to her professional reputation in the amount of $10,000.00.

39. As a result of the acts of the defendants set forth above, plaintiff has suffered mental anguish and emotional distress as a result of said acts, to her loss in the amount of $10,000.00.

40. The plaintiff has suffered out-of-pocket expenses due to her termination, all to her loss, of: $77.60 in travel expenses in seeking other employment; $1.50 in telephone expenses in seeking employment; $91.25 in telephone expenses for contact with her attorneys and witnesses; $169.00 in travel expenses for meetings with her attorneys and for court appearances; $14.13 in prescription costs and medical bills.

41. The plaintiff has also suffered loss due to the necessity to remove her retirement contributions from the Kentucky Teachers' Retirement System.

CONCLUSIONS OF LAW

1. The plaintiff, Jacqueline Fowler, was a duly certified "teacher" as that term is used and defined in K.R.S. 161.720(1), and had, at the time of the termination of her contract, achieved "continuing status" as that term is defined in K.R.S. 161.720(5). As a result of plaintiff's continuing contract status, plaintiff had a right to continued employment under her contract which is protected by the fourteenth amendment right to no taking of property without due process of law. *Board of Regents* v. *Roth,* 408 U.S. 564 (1972).

2. The defendant Board of Education of Lincoln County, Kentucky, is a body politic and corporate and may sue and be sued as such. K.R.S. 160.160. The defendants are officials whose action to terminate the plaintiff was taken under color of state law. 42 U.S.C. §1983.

3. The defendant board is subject to suit and liability under 42 U.S.C. §1983 and enjoys no eleventh amendment or sovereign immunity as a result of same. *Mt. Healthy City School District* v. *Doyle,* 429 U.S. 274, 280 (1977); K.R.S. 160.160.

4. The federal and state claims asserted by plaintiff arise out of a common nucleus of operative facts, those being the defendants' action in terminating plaintiff's tenured teaching contract under K.R.S. 161.790 for showing "The Wall." Therefore, this Court has the authority to invoke, and does so invoke, pendent jurisdiction to hear the state claims raised by plaintiff. *United Mine Workers* v. *Gibbs,* 383 U.S. 715 (1966); *Culp* v. *Devlin,* 437 F.Supp. 20 (E.D. Pa. 1977).

5. Under the three-part test established by the United States Supreme Court in *Mt. Healthy City Board of Education* v. *Doyle,* 429 U.S. 274, 287 (1977), in order for the plaintiff to prevail, she must establish that she participated in a constitutionally protected activity and that the activity was a substantial or motivating factor in the decision to discharge her. As a defense, the defendants must prove by a preponderance of evidence that they would have reached the same decision to terminate her employment even in the absence of the protected activity.

6. Yet, teachers' exercise of first amendment rights in the schools is subject to reasonable regulation, just as it is in the community at large. *Pickering* v. *Board of Education,* 391 U.S 563, 568 (1968). The problem for the Court becomes one of arriving at the appropriate balance between the interest of the teachers in exercising their first amendment rights and that of the school board as an employer in promoting the efficiency of the services it provides through its teachers.

7. The defendants have admitted that the substantial and motivating factor in plaintiff's termination was her showing "Pink Floyd—The Wall" at Lincoln County High School on May 31, 1984. In addition, defendants have admitted that absent the showing of that film, they would not have terminated her tenured teaching contract. Thus, the issue to be decided is whether the plaintiff's showing of "Pink Floyd—The Wall" was protected speech under the first amendment.

8. While school boards have broad discretion in the management of school affairs, the discretion of the local school board in matters of education must be exercised in a manner that comports with the transcendent imperatives of the first amendment. *Board of Education, Island Trees Union Free School District No. 26* v. *Pico,* 457 U.S 853, 864 (plurality opinion) (1982).

Boards of Education . . . have, of course, important, delicate, and highly discretionary functions, but none that they may not perform within the limits of the Bill of Rights. That they are educating the young for citizenship is reason for scrupulous protection of Constitutional freedoms of the individual, if we are not to strangle the free mind at its source and teach youth to discount principles of government as mere platitudes.

West Virginia Board of Education v. *Barnette*, 319 U.S. 624 at 637 (1943).

9. It is well established that public school teachers do not lose their constitutional rights simply because of their occupation. As the United States Supreme Court stated in *Tinker* v. *Des Moines Community School District*, 393 U.S. 503, 506 (1969):

First Amendment rights, applied in light of the special characteristics of the school environment, are available to teachers and students. It can hardly be argued that either students or teachers shed their constitutional rights to freedom of speech or expression at the schoolhouse gate. This has been the unmistakable holding of this court for almost 50 years.

10. Another important aspect to the application of the first amendment and the schools is the idea that the classroom should be a "marketplace of ideas." *Keyishian* v. *Board of Regents of the University of New York*, 385 U.S. 589, 603 (1967).

The fundamental notion underlying the First Amendment is that citizens, free to speak and hear, will be able to form judgments concerning matters affecting their lives, independent of any governmental suasion or propaganda. Consistent with that noble purpose, a school should be a readily accessible warehouse of ideas.

Right to Read Defense Committee of Chelsea v. *School Committee of the City of Chelsea*, 454 F.Supp. 703, 710 (D.C. Mass. 1978). These cases make it quite clear that Mrs. Fowler was entitled to complete protection of the first amendment while she was acting as a teacher for the Lincoln County Board of Education.

11. The United States Supreme Court has held, "Motion pictures are, of course, protected by the First Amendment." *Interstate Circuit* v. *City of Dallas*, 390 U.S. 676, 682 (1968). "Films convey ideas, and the right to receive the thoughts of others is a right protected by the first amendment. *Swope* v. *Lubbers*, 560 F.Supp. 1328, 1331 (D.C. Mich. 1983). The United States Court of Appeals for the Seventh Circuit, in examining the issue of the constitutional suppression of rock music held that suppression of the playing of rock music is a violation of free speech. *Reed* v. *Village of Shorewood*, 704 F.2d 943, 950 (7th Cir. 1983); *Fact Concerts, Inc.* v. *City of Newport*, 626 F.2d 1060, 1063 (1st Cir. 1980) *rev'd. on other grounds*, 453 U.S. 247 (1981).

12. The film shown by plaintiff to her high school students was a form of expression engaged in by her in relation to her students. The form of expression included the ideas portrayed in the movie, as well as the music. The film had significant artistic, social, literary, and political value and was expression which was entitled to protection under the first amendment to the U.S. Constitution.

13. The movie, "Pink Floyd—The Wall," contained important social and political messages and values relevant to young people. Included in the messages the film conveyed were the horrors of war and the personal disasters war leaves on individuals; the value of a child being raised in a two-parent household; the alienation of generations, spouses and persons in general; the horrors of drug abuse; and the terror and repression that results from a fascist government.

14. The members of the board of education objected to the film not only because of the language, suggested sex and fleeting nudity of the film in its *unedited* version, but also because they strongly disagreed with the message conveyed by the film *as they perceived it*. The board members believed that the movie reflected poorly on schools, motherhood, marriage, family, government, the judiciary, the police, and other valued institutions.

15. Yet, the board of education cannot discharge a teacher engaging in expression which is constitutionally protected simply because they do not agree with the content or the themes of that expression. *Minarcini* v. *Strongsville City School District*, 541 F.2d 577 (6th Cir. 1976). In *Minarcini*, the Court of Appeals for the Sixth Circuit stated that library books could not be removed by school boards who wanted to "winnow" the library for books with which they disagreed or disapproved due to content. The Sixth Circuit further stated that one could not "place conditions on the use of the library which were related solely to the social or political tastes of the school board members." *Id.* at 582. By analogy, this rationale is equally applicable to the showing of video films to students.

16. Numerous courts have examined the issue of censorship of controversial ideas in the school environment and have found that such ideas are protected by the first amendment. In *Right to Read Defense Committee of Chelsea* v. *School Committee of the City of Chelsea*, *supra*, an anthology of poetry was removed from the library due to its containing the poem, "The City to a Young Girl." Said poem contained various "street slang" obscenities. In holding the removal of the book unconstitutional, the Court stated that what was at stake was "the right to read and be exposed to controversial thoughts and language—a valuable right subject to first amendment protection." *Id.* at 714. In addition, the court stated that keeping the controversial work available was import, as "[t]he most effective antidote to the poison of mindless orthodoxy is ready access to a broad sweep of ideas and philosophies. There is no danger in such exposure. The danger is in mind control." *Id.* at 715.

17. The United States Supreme Court has held

that constitutional protection is provided to all ideas with even remote redeeming social importance, including unorthodox ideas, controversial ideas, and ideas hateful to the prevailing climate of opinion, unless excludable because they encroach upon the limited area of more important issues. *Roth* v. *U.S.*, 354 U.S. 476, 484 (1957). The Supreme Court also spoke on these same principles in *Hannegan* v. *Esquire, Inc.*, 327 U.S. 146, 157-158, when it held:

Under our system of government there is an accommodation for the widest varieties of tastes and ideas. What is good literature, what has educational value, what is refined public information, what is good art, varies with individuals as it does from one generation to another. There doubtless would be a contrariety of views concerning Cervantes' *Don Quixote,* Shakespeare's *Venus and Adonis,* or Zola's *Nana.* But a requirement that literature or art conform to some norm prescribed by an official smacks of an ideology foreign to our system.

18. The fundamental purpose of the first amendment is to protect free expression of controversial and unpopular ideas from state infringement. *Aumiller* v. *University of Delaware,* 434 F.Supp. 1273 (D.C. Del. 1977). Above all else, the first amendment means that government has no power to restrict expression because of its message, ideas, subject matter or content. *Police Department of Chicago* v. *Mosely,* 408 U.S. 92, 95 (1972); *Solid Rock Foundation* v. *Ohio State University,* 478 F.Supp. 96 (D.C. Ohio 1979).

19. Any portions of "The Wall" which include fleeting nudity or implied sexual activity constitute only minute segments of the one-hour-and-a-half film. In the edited version which the Court viewed, one had to listen very carefully to discern any of the four-letter words stated during the course of the film. In addition, one had to use great creative imagination to perceive any of the alleged sexual connotations, and had to watch the screen very intently to see a glimpse of nudity, if any. In the Court's viewing at trial on April 1, 1985, it did not observe any nudity in the version as edited by the plaintiff and student Charles Bailey.

20. The defendants do not contend that the film, "Pink Floyd—The Wall," was obscene as proscribed by *Miller* v. *California,* 413 U.S. 15 (1973), and *Ginzsburg* v. *New York,* 390 U.S. 629 (1968). The Supreme Court, in *Erznoznik* v. *City of Jacksonville,* 422 U.S. 205, 213-214 (1975), stated,

Speech that is neither obscene as to youths nor subject to some other legitimate proscription cannot be suppressed solely to protect the young from ideas or images that a legislative body thinks unsuitable for them. In most circumstances, the values protected by the first amendment are no less applicable when government seeks to control the flow of information to minors.

21. This Court is of the opinion that any fleeting nudity or vulgar language which might have been seen or heard in the showing of "Pink Floyd—The Wall" in the plaintiff's classroom on May 31, 1984, does not remove the expression from first amendment protection. The Supreme Court in *Erznoznik* held that all nudity could not be deemed obscene even to minors, *Id.* at 213; and in *Roth* the Court held that, in fact, "the portrayal of sex . . . in art, literature and scientific works is not itself sufficient reason to deny material the Constitutional protection of freedom of speech." *Id.* at 487.

22. Judged in its entirety, "Pink Floyd—The Wall" is not profane, vulgar, or obscene. The movie is protected by the Constitution, both as it was shown in the plaintiff's classroom on May 31, 1984, and in its edited form as viewed by the Court on April 1, 1985.

23. The fact that "Pink Floyd—The Wall" was rated "R" may not be used as a "standard for determination of constitutional status." *Swope* v. *Lubbers,* 560 F.Supp. 1328, 1334 (D.C. Mich. 1983), *citing Engdahl* v. *City of Kenosha, Wisconsin,* 317 F.Supp. 1133 (E.D. Wis. 1970), and *Motion Picture Assoc. of America* v. *Spector,* 315 F.Supp. 824 (E.D. Pa. 1970).

24. The board of education's contention that they could discharge the plaintiff because such material as "Pink Floyd—The Wall" should not be shown in the Lincoln County schools fails to establish a substantial and legitimate governmental interest to override the plaintiff's protected speech. *Chelsea* at 713. The federal court in *Chelsea* held that the assumption that offensive language and themes might be harmful to high school students was not enough to establish some substantial and legitimate governmental interest to override the protected speech in question. In the present case, the defendants have failed to do more than state their opinion that the language and themes of "Pink Floyd—The Wall" were harmful to high school students. Thus, defendants have failed to establish any substantial and legitimate governmental interest as to override the plaintiff's right to protected speech.

25. In light of the fact that May 31, 1984, was a "non-instructional day," the plaintiff does not have to meet the "relevancy" requirement found in pure academic freedom cases. The question of "relevancy" in the first amendment context usually arises in those cases which involve a teacher who has used some method or material or language in the classroom during a regular school day—a day in which the teacher was required to teach his/her assigned subject. The "relevancy" requirement is a determination of whether

the teacher has performed the duties assigned. It is undisputed in the case at bar that May 31, 1984, was "grades day," and that no teacher was required or even expected to teach a substantive class. Therefore, the plaintiff is not required to show the relevancy between the showing of the movie, "Pink Floyd—The Wall," and the substantive classes, civics and Latin, which she usually taught during those class hours.

26. The board of education does not have greater power to control a teacher's speech due to the fact that it involved school-age children in the classroom, where the word of the teacher carries great authority and where students were a "captive audience." *James* v. *Board of Education of Central District No. 1 of the Towns of Addison,* 461 F.2d 566, 573 (2d Cir. 1972), *cert. denied,* 409 U.S. 1042, *rehrg. denied,* 410 U.S. 947, *on remand,* 385 F.Supp. 209. In *James,* the court determined, "More than a decade of Supreme Court precedent leaves no doubt that we cannot countenance school authorities arbitrarily censoring a teacher's speech merely because they do not agree with the teacher's political philosophy or leanings." *Id.* at 573.

27. K.R.S. 161.790(1)(b), which provides for termination of a teacher for "conduct unbecoming a teacher," is not unconstitutionally vague or overbroad. In addition, the board of education's textbook regulation which the plaintiff allegedly violated and the Kentucky statute from which it was taken, K.R.S. 158.190, are not unconstitutional for being vague and overbroad as well.

28. The plaintiff was provided adequate procedural due process at the July 14, 1984, school board hearing. She has failed to establish any improper procedures or that the board was biased in making their decision. The transcript of that hearing establishes that the plaintiff was represented by able counsel, who conducted an extensive voir dire of the board, vigorously cross-examined witnesses presented to support the charges, introduced lengthy testimony on behalf of the plaintiff, and made a vigorous closing argument, though no closing argument was made in support of the charges. The contention that the board of education had prejudged the facts and was biased against the plaintiff before the hearing began was not supported by the evidence. Inevitably, all the board members had heard about the showing of the movie in the plaintiff's classroom, which necessarily created some stir in the community. However, the Supreme Court, in *Hortonville Joint School District No. 1* v. *Hortonville Education Assn.,* 426 U.S. 482, 493 (1976), held that knowledge of the facts giving rise to the controversy and even expression of an opinion about it before the hearing does not disqualify a member of the board of education from considering or arriving at a decision.

29. The presence of the superintendent, the assistant superintendent, and the board attorney in the school board's executive session following the conclusion of the hearing did not taint the proceedings so as to establish a failure of procedural due process. The testimony established that there was no discussion or debate of any substance after the hearing except negotiations with plaintiff and her counsel in a vain attempt to try to arrive at a compromise.

30. This Court hereby finds that the plaintiff was terminated in violation of K.R.S. 161.790 in that her conduct as a matter of fact and law did not constitute conduct unbecoming a teacher or insubordination. As discussed previously, the showing of the film by the plaintiff was protected speech under the first amendment and, therefore, its showing did not constitute conduct unbecoming a teacher.

31. Plaintiff was terminated in violation of K.R.S. 161.790 because her conduct as a matter of fact and law did not constitute insubordination. K.R.S. 161.790(1)(a) defines insubordination as a violation of lawful rules and regulations established by the local board of education for the operation of schools and refusal to recognize or obey the authority of the superintendent, principal, or any other personnel of the board in the performance of their duties. The evidence clearly established that there was no rule, regulation, or order forbidding outside materials to be shown with or without previewing or prior approval. It is undisputed that on May 31, 1984, there was no requirement that the plaintiff teach civics or Latin; she was only to find some means to keep her students out of the hallways. Therefore, she could not be legally insubordinate for failing to teach her classes when the day was not an instructional day. As has been discussed previously, the film was not in itself, as a matter of fact or law, immoral so as to violate the school's textbook regulation or the statute from which it was derived, K.R.S. 158.190. Therefore, the plaintiff was not insubordinate to any textbook regulation as to what instructional materials she may use in the classroom. In addition, at no time was the plaintiff ever instructed not to show the film again; at no time did the board of education ever pass a regulation or policy that would prohibit the same. Thus, plaintiff did not refuse to obey the board's authority thereby constituting insubordination. Clearly, plaintiff's termination under K.R.S. 161.790 is totally without basis in law or fact, and it is therefore declared void, thus returning her to her position.

31. In light of the above, the Court concludes that the plaintiff's contract was improperly terminated because it was done in response to the plaintiff's exercising her rights protected under the first amendment to the Constitution, and but for the exercise of these

rights, plaintiff's employment with the board would not have been so terminated. *Mt. Healthy City School District* v. *Doyle,* 429 U.S. 274 (1977).

32. Due to the actions taken by the defendants, the plaintiff is entitled to reinstatement to her former position as teacher at the Lincoln County High School, and is further entitled to receive back pay from the date of discharge until her reinstatement. *Mt. Healthy City Board of Education* v. *Doyle, supra,* at 283–284. In addition, plaintiff is entitled to interest on her back wages, an undisputed sum taken directly from the salary schedule. *Bituminous Casualty Corp.* v. *Lynn,* 503 F.2d 636 (6th Cir. 1974). If such a claim is liquidated, as is the claim in this action, interest flows as a matter of right. *McNutt* v. *State Farm Mutual Auto Insurance Co.,* 369 F.Supp. 381 (W.D. Ky. 1973), *aff'd.* 494 F.2d 1282 (6th Cir. 1973). The plaintiff is further entitled to reimbursement for any and all interest which she must pay to the Kentucky Teachers Retirement System to have her retirement account reinstated with said system.

33. Due to the above-described actions by the defendants, the plaintiff has suffered emotional distress, and is therefore entitled to recover the sum of $10,000.00; she has suffered out-of-pocket expenses for travel and telephone in her job search and contact with her attorneys, and is therefore entitled to recover the sum of $353.48; she has suffered damage to her professional reputation, and is entitled to recover the sum of $10,000.00. *Carey* v. *Piphus,* 435 U.S. 247 (1978).

34. The plaintiff is entitled to recover the set-forth amounts from the defendant board of education as a corporate entity, and the school board members and superintendent in their official capacities only. The defendant board is subject to suit and liability under 42 U.S.C. §1983 and enjoys no eleventh amendment or sovereign immunity. *Mt. Healthy City School District* v. *Doyle, supra;* K.R.S. 160.160. The individual school board members and the school superintendent are entitled to a qualified immunity from individual liability for damages under §1983 as established in the Supreme Court case of *Wood* v. *Strickland,* 420 U.S. 308 (1975). In *Wood,* the Court held that members of the school board were immune from personal liability in performing their duties, unless they acted maliciously or knew or should have known that the actions taken within the sphere of their official responsibility would violate the constitutional rights of the student affected. The Supreme Court more recently in *Harlow* v. *Fitzgerald,* 457 U.S. 800 (1982), has held that government officials performing discretionary functions generally are shielded from liability, as their conduct does not violate clearly-established statutory or con-

stitutional rights of which a reasonable person would have known. *Id.* at 818.

35. It is clear to this Court that no reasonable person would or should have known that the discharge of the plaintiff for showing the movie, "Pink Floyd—The Wall," would be a violation of her constitutional right of freedom of expression. This entire body of constitutional law is very cloudy and confusing, and it cannot be expected that lay school board members would know whether their actions were in violation of plaintiff's constitutional rights. The plaintiff's right to freedom of expression was not clearly established so as to expect the defendant board members and superintendent to know they were violating plaintiff's rights. Board members are not charged with predicting the future course of constitutional law. *Sapp* v. *Renfroe,* 511 F.2d 1972 (11th Cir. 1975). Therefore, under *Wood* v. *Strickland,* and *Harlow* v. *Fitzgerald,* the school board members and superintendent are entitled to qualified good-faith immunity and are not liable in their individual capacities.

36. The monetary award of the salary unlawfully withheld from plaintiff represents equitable restitution and constitutes liability of the members of the board in their official capacity which is payable by the school district. *Brown* v. *Bathke,* 566 F.2d 588 (8th Cir. 1977); *Owen* v. *City of Independence,* 560 F.2d 925 (8th Cir. 1977). The good-faith immunity which the school board members and superintendent enjoy applies only to the compensatory damages, and not equitable relief. *Brown* at 593.

37. The defendant school board shall reimburse the plaintiff for her costs expended in this action and reasonable attorneys' fees incident to the prosecution of this action.

38. The acts of the defendants were not intentional, willful, nor performed with malice, and therefore the plaintiff is not entitled to punitive damages.

* * *

FINAL JUDGMENT AND ORDER

In accordance with the Findings of Fact and Conclusions of Law entered on the same date herewith, IT IS HEREBY ORDERED AND ADJUDGED as follows:

1. The plaintiff has met her burden of proof that the defendants violated 42 U.S.C. § 1983 when they terminated her employment because she showed the film "Pink Floyd—The Wall" to Lincoln County High School students on May 31, 1984.

2. The defendant school board, as a corporate entity, and the school board members and superintendent, in their official capacity, are liable to the plaintiff for the following damages:

a. The plaintiff shall be reinstated to her former position as teacher at the Lincoln County High School.

b. The plaintiff shall receive back pay from the date of discharge until her reinstatement.

c. The plaintiff shall receive interest, at the legal rate, on her back wages.

d. The plaintiff shall receive reimbursement for any and all interest which she must pay to the Kentucky Teachers Retirement System to have her retirement account reinstated with said system.

e. The plaintiff shall receive the sum of $10,000.00 for the emotional distress the plaintiff has suffered due to the defendants' improper actions.

f. The plaintiff shall receive the sum of $10,000.00 for the damage to her professional reputation she has suffered due to the defendants' improper actions.

g. The plaintiff shall receive the sum of $353.48 for out-of-pocket expenses for travel and telephone calls in her job search and contact with her attorneys, all due to the defendants' improper actions.

h. The plaintiff shall be reimbursed for the costs expended in this action and the reasonable attorneys' fees incident to the prosecution of this action.

3. This action is now DISMISSED and STRICKEN from the docket.

4. This is a FINAL and APPEALABLE Order.

Index

EDUCATION LIBRARY

DATE DUE

DUE	RETURNED	DUE	RETURNED